# In Defense of the Textus Receptus

## God's Preserved Word to Every Generation

*Are all Bibles Created Equal?*

*Does it matter which Bible I use?*

*If it does matter, then Why??*

Dr. Jim Taylor, D.R.E.

**IN DEFENSE OF THE TEXTUS RECEPTUS**

In Defense of the Textus Receptus, Second Edition

© Copyright 2016 ● Dr. Jim Taylor

Publisher's info:

The Old Paths Publications, Inc
142 Gold Flume Way
Cleveland, GA 30528
Email: TOP@theoldpathspublications.com
Web Address: www.theoldpathspublications.com

ISBN 978-0-9968079-2-0

Second Edition

All Rights Reserved. No part of this work may be reproduced without the expressed consent of the publisher, except for brief quotes, whether by electronic, photocopying, recording, or information storage and retrieval systems.

All Scripture quotes are from the King James Bible except those verses compared and then the source is identified.

Although a number of other authors have been quoted or mentioned in this book, this author does not share or endorse the various theological positions of everyone who is mentioned. Additionally, it can be reasonably assumed that those mentioned would not necessarily agree with every position or viewpoint mentioned herein. The mere citing or mention of others is NOT to be considered an endorsement of their beliefs.

2.0

*God's Preserved Word to Every Generation*

## DEDICATION

This book is dedicated to the LORD first of all. If He had not saved me in 1984, I would never have developed such a love for His Word, not to mention that fact that He has made me a child of the King and I am no longer on my way to an eternal hell. I have to say that since the day I was born again, nothing has ever thrilled my soul like the precious scriptures.

Secondly, I want to dedicate this work to my wonderful wife. She has quietly sacrificed many hours that would have been spent with her in order that I could do the proper research for this project. She has always been a great source of encouragement to me.

Thirdly, I want to also dedicate this book to Earl Hodges. He was perhaps the most knowledgeable and humble man I have ever known. He not only taught the scriptures, but he exemplified the Christian life like none I have ever seen. Aside from his extensive knowledge in the scriptures, he gave me a great deal of his own personal time, teaching me so much about the great doctrines of the faith. But the greatest thing that he ever taught me was how to think for myself. And this is the reason for this book.

There have been many others who were great encouragers as well – Bill Stewart, Steve Zeinner, S.E. Hyde – to name a few. I owe you all a great debt of gratitude for making this work possible. These men have all been greatly used of God to challenge me in my walk and personal growth in the knowledge of our Lord and Saviour, Jesus Christ. To all of these men I owe a heart-felt thanks - But to God be the glory!

# IN DEFENSE OF THE TEXTUS RECEPTUS

## TABLE OF CONTENTS

**DEDICATION** ........................................................................................ 3
**PREFACE** ............................................................................................. 7
**INTRODUCTION** ................................................................................. 11
   A Simple Explanation of the Various Positions ............................................ 16
      *The Position of Unbelief* ................................................................. 17
      *All Inclusivism* ............................................................................... 17
      *Eclecticism* ..................................................................................... 18
      *Selectivism (Sentimentalism)* ........................................................ 21
      *Inspired Translation Position* ........................................................ 21
      *The Preserved Translation Position* ............................................. 24
      *The Textus Receptus Position* ..................................................... 26
   Does It Matter? ............................................................................................ 27
   Answer based Upon Belief in Inspiration and Preservation ....................... 29

**INSPIRATION** ..................................................................................... 32
   False Views of Inspiration ............................................................................ 32
   The Biblical View of Inspiration .................................................................... 36
   Important Passages on inspiration ............................................................. 41
   The Application of Inspiration ..................................................................... 45

**PRESERVATION** ................................................................................ 51
   Four Views Concerning Preservation .......................................................... 53
   Important Facts Concerning Preservation .................................................. 56
   Implications of Preservation ........................................................................ 67
      *Are The Original Autographs necessary?* .................................... 71
      *Can Originals be Validated or Verified?* ....................................... 74
      *Proof the TR (Byzantine Text) Was Used in Every Generation* .... 75

**CANONIZATION** ................................................................................ 88
   The Canon Recognized ............................................................................... 91
   False Views of Canonization ....................................................................... 97
   Correct View of Canonization ...................................................................... 98

**TRANSMISSION** .............................................................................. 102
   False Assumptions Concerning Transmission ......................................... 102
   Materials Used in Recording the Scriptures ............................................. 104
   Scribal Errors ............................................................................................. 107
   Six important Features in the Transmission of the New Testament ......... 111

## IN DEFENSE OF THE TEXTUS RECEPTUS

**TRANSLATION** .................................................................................. 119
- ENGLISH TRANSLATIONS FROM THE TEXTUS RECEPTUS ............................. 119
- COMPARISON OF TEXTUS RECEPTUS-BASED TRANSLATIONS ..................... 122
- METHODS OF TRANSLATING ................................................................... 124
- LEGITIMACY OF A TRANSLATION ............................................................ 126
- COMPARISON OF ONE TRANSLATION TO ANOTHER .................................. 129
- MODERN TRANSLATIONS AND MODERN LINGO ...................................... 131
- ITALICIZED WORDS IN THE KJV .............................................................. 133

**GREEK MANUSCRIPTS** .................................................................... 137
- MANUSCRIPT TYPES ............................................................................. 139
- CATALOGING THE MANUSCRIPTS ............................................................ 142
- HOW MANUSCRIPTS ARE NUMBERED ..................................................... 144
- COLLATING OF THE TEXTS ..................................................................... 145
- MANUSCRIPT "FAMILIES" ..................................................................... 146
  - *Alexandrian Family* ...................................................................... 148
  - *Major Manuscripts of the Critical Text* ........................................ 167
  - *The Byzantine family* ................................................................... 172
- MANUSCRIPT SUPPORT FOR THE TEXTUS RECEPTUS ............................... 181
  - *Greek Manuscript Support* ........................................................... 183
  - *Lectionaries* ................................................................................. 184
  - *Early Translations* ....................................................................... 185
  - *Early Christian Writings* .............................................................. 189
  - *Support in Unexpected Places* ..................................................... 191
- CONFLICT IN THE FAMILY ..................................................................... 194
- THE ROLE OF GEOGRAPHY IN TEXTUAL ANALYSIS .................................. 195

**HISTORY OF TEXT-TYPE CRITICISM** ............................................ 200

**CONSIDERATION OF PREVAILING TEXTUAL CRITICISM** ........... 203

**DEAN BURGON'S SEVEN TESTS OF TRUTH** .................................. 207
- AGE OF THE MANUSCRIPT ..................................................................... 207
- NUMBER OF EXISTING MANUSCRIPTS .................................................... 210
- VARIETY OF WITNESSES FROM DIFFERENT LOCATIONS ........................... 211
- RESPECTABILITY OR WEIGHT AS A TEST OF TRUTH ................................ 212
- CONTINUITY AS A TEST OF TRUTH ......................................................... 214
- CONTEXT AS A TEST OF TRUTH .............................................................. 226
- INTERNAL EVIDENCE AS A TEST OF TRUTH ............................................ 226

**EARLY CORRUPTIONS OF THE NEW TESTAMENT** ..................... 228
- EARLY TRANSLATIONS BASED ON INFERIOR TEXTS ................................. 230
  - *The Septuagint (LXX)* .................................................................. 230

*God's Preserved Word to Every Generation*

*Origen's Hexapla* .................................................................. *233*
*Constantine's 50 Bibles* ........................................................ *234*
*Jerome's Latin Vulgate* ......................................................... *236*

**THE REAL ISSUE** ............................................................................. **238**

**APPENDIX A – TABLE OF MANUSCRIPTS** ...................................... **241**
    PAPYRI ................................................................................................. 241
    UNCIALS .............................................................................................. 250

**APPENDIX B - THE MEANING OF "WORD OF GOD"** ................... **275**

**APPENDIX C – THE MAJORITY TEXT** ............................................. **280**

**APPENDIX D – OFTEN DISPUTED READINGS** ............................... **285**
    MARK 16:9-20 .................................................................................... 286
    I JOHN 5:7-8 - COMMA JOHANNEUM ............................................... 290
    REV 22:14 – BOOK OF LIFE ................................................................ 293
    ACTS 8:37 ........................................................................................... 294
    HEBREWS 8:9 ..................................................................................... 297
    1 PETER 2:2 ........................................................................................ 300
    JOHN 7:53 - JOHN 8:11 - PERICOPE ADULTERAE .............................. 308

**APPENDIX E – THE SEPTUAGINT** .................................................. **312**

**APPENDIX F - KJV RULES FOR TRANSLATION** ............................. **321**

**APPENDIX G – TERMS AND DEFINITIONS** .................................... **324**

**BIBLIOGRAPHY** ............................................................................. **336**

# IN DEFENSE OF THE TEXTUS RECEPTUS

## PREFACE

As I began to write this book, I have to tell you that I honestly thought that I had a good grasp on the subject at hand. But the more I read, researched, wrote, and re-wrote, I found out that there is so much information concerning the issue that it is almost impossible to treat it fully.

Admittedly, I began doing the very things that I was charging some of my brethren of doing – the academic error of repeating information that I had not thoroughly researched for myself.[1] As I began to read literature from other viewpoints on the issue, I found that some of the charges by both sides against their opponents were accurate. I also found out that many of those who would hold to the same position as myself were not presenting the full truth on some points. I believe it is because they were guilty of regurgitating information that they had learned from others without validating it. And in some cases, I think that it is entirely possible that information was withheld simply because a particular piece of information challenged their position.

I found this to be especially true when it came to the number of manuscripts, what families each manuscript belonged to, and the age of each manuscript. It seemed to me that the age of some of the manuscripts is disputed simply because of personal bias. I have also found that some of the charts concerning the numbers of existing manuscripts have just been repeated over and over without any real attempt at updating. In as much as it was possible, I have researched each manuscript. Obviously, I don't have the manuscripts at my fingertips but much of what has been discovered has been photocopied and put online for all to see. I have been able to examine photos and other resources that were available to me, making it possible to validate the claims made by others.

I have read many books on the issue. I think I have probably read an equal amount of books on all sides of the issue. I can honestly tell you that some of the books were absolutely ludicrous in their approach and allegations. Others contained helpful and balanced information. And still others were down-right inflammatory! I have seen good men called heretics. And I have seen bad men exalted beyond measure. And it is shameful.

As a result, I have tried as much as possible to state positions without mentioning names. I know that some people would disagree with that approach.

---

[1] I have honestly tried not to commit the same critical mistake in this book. However, I already know from the proofing process that this is extremely difficult. It is very difficult to spot bias in yourself!

## IN DEFENSE OF THE TEXTUS RECEPTUS

Some people would say that my sources need to be cited so that proper research can be done in order to validate the claims. But I would simply say this. It is possible to research the factual information presented in this book without my citing the source. And I highly recommend that the reader do so. That would be honest and academically wise.

In some cases I do cite my sources. And at first glance it would appear that I am inconsistent with this. But the main reason I am careful with this is because I am not "on the attack" against anyone in particular. The reason why I am not "naming names" is because I have absolutely no desire to get into a rock-throwing contest with others who do not agree with me. In a few cases, I have named sources for various reasons, but when I found the need to do so, I tried to be as respectful to that source's character and reputation as possible.

I have found in the past that citing a source does nothing more than shift the responsibility from the writer to the source anyway. It does not validate the truthfulness of the statement made unless the source is the Word of God Himself. On one occasion, when I cited the source, I was bluntly informed that just because my source made a statement to the fact, it was not necessarily true. I was then asked to reference my source's source! So in the words of a statement made famous by President Harry S. Truman, "The buck stops here."

In the course of writing this book, I have shared a few quotes and information gleaned from many various sources. I would like to offer a carte blanche statement that just because I quote from a particular source, I don't necessarily agree with all that the source believes. However, the information provided has been researched and validated insofar as I was able.

Throughout this book, I use the term "King James Version" as versus "King James Bible". I do not mean any offense and I certainly do believe that the King James Version is the Word of God. However, "King James Version" is the correct name and it seems to me that so many writers and preachers have taken to using the term "King James Bible" as a means of declaring that any other translation is not the Bible.

To this I would have to say that any translation, in any language, must be able to stand on its own merits before the original Greek and Hebrew texts. It really doesn't matter to me what the name of a translation is, if it does not pass the test of formal-equivalency to the Textus Receptus, then it will inevitably fall short.

Keep in mind that I am limiting this book to a discussion of the New Testament Manuscripts. Thus, I don't address the translation of the Old Testament very often throughout this book. But for the curious reader, I also would state the same thing concerning the Old Testament. It needs to be a formal equivalent translation of the Masoretic text.

Throughout the book I have tried to keep things at a level that all saved believers in Jesus Christ, regardless of position (pastor or laymen) could understand. I will use the following five terms when referring to scriptural manuscripts - Byzantine, Textus Receptus, Alexandrian, Critical text, and mixed.

Throughout the book I tried to be fairly consistent in the way I used the terms "Textus Receptus" and "Byzantine text". I have sought to use the phrase "Textus Receptus" when the context of the discussion concerns the Greek text after the time of Erasmus' first Greek text in AD 1516 while trying to use the name "Byzantine" when discussing the Greek texts before the time of Erasmus. My reason for this is because so many people make an unrealistic fuss over the names. For instance, if I were to say that early translations from the 3$^{rd}$ century match the Textus Receptus, someone would reply that in the 3$^{rd}$ century, there was no Textus Receptus. And technically, he would be right, though he would be missing the whole point of the original statement. So, to avoid unnecessary conflict, I have tried to use the terms in their historical contexts.

I have also tried to be consistent with the use of "Alexandrian" and "Critical" Text for the same basic reasons. I would admit that there may be places where I may not be totally consistent but for the most part, the reader should not have any problems understanding the way the terms are used.

The fifth term used throughout the book is the term "mixed text". This is used to refer to Greek manuscripts that do not really fit in either category of Byzantine or Alexandrian texts.

In summary, although I am aware there are five differing categories of manuscripts used by Aland's method of grouping, I have purposely decided to use a more simplified set of five terms that I think bring greater understanding and clarity to the subject.

Admittedly, there are places where certain facts, figures, quotations, and general information are repeated, but only when I feel it necessary to allow the information in those sections to stand on its own and be fully understood. In other words, sometimes I felt it necessary in order to provide clarity of the information and thoughts being discussed at the time, and also because it is my desire that this book be as much a reference work as it is a treatise on the topic.

Initially, I had given some thought to including discussion of Old Testament texts, but decided against it since most Hebrew scholars consider both Old Testament manuscripts, available to us today, to be nearly identical making such discussion fruitless and not germane to the scope of the book.

*God's Preserved Word to Every Generation*

## IN DEFENSE OF THE TEXTUS RECEPTUS

One last note. This book is not scripture and therefore is fallible. If my readers look long enough, I am sure that they can, and most likely, will find mistakes. I am not presenting this as the definitive work on the subject but I am seeking to put forth the subject as a fresh look from a biblical perspective. It is my hope that it will increase your knowledge of the issue as well as deepen your trust in the biblical texts that we have available to us today.

## IN DEFENSE OF THE TEXTUS RECEPTUS

## INTRODUCTION

The discussion of the relevancy of the King James and it superiority to other written translations of the Bible continues to be an issue in many of our churches today.[2] It takes its name from the King James Version of the Bible upon which the bulk of the controversy rests. If there were any questions as to whether this is a "hot issue" or not, a simple search of the Internet or visit to a local Christian bookstore would certainly clear up any misconceptions.

The mass of articles, books, blog, and web sites, is simply overwhelming. It seems that new books and other related material on the issue are being produced weekly if not daily. If you want to see a good example of the magnitude of the issue, simply peruse a bookstore or search the Internet (a simple search on Google revealed over 655,000 web pages) and you will see volumes of new material at each visit. It has gotten to the point that in order to sell the new products, writers and advertisers are promising "new and important information" or "information never before written".

The allegations made by people on both sides of the issue are simply astounding. One writer states that the King James Version has ALWAYS been the Bible of choice among conservative believers. Another writer states that the issue of translations has never been considered a fundamental doctrine until recent years. To both viewpoints, I would simply like to point out that the King James Version did not exist until 1611. From the mid-1600s until 1881, it was virtually the only English Bible translation in use.[3] So on the one hand, it WAS the Bible of choice because there simply was no other Bible to choose. And on the other hand, the purity of the scriptures is the natural outcome of a holy God inspiring and preserving his holy Word. Inspiration and preservation are DEFINITELY fundamental doctrines of our faith!

Many of the books on the issue today are either mean-spirited or blatantly biased. Some books range from the sentimental (That's the Bible my momma used.) to the ludicrous. Other authors seek to be a bit more balanced and intellectual in their approach. Sadly, very little material is available which addresses the issue from a biblical viewpoint. However, it does not seem to matter

---

[2] Interestingly enough, outside of the independent Baptist realm, very few people are concerned about the issue at all. In fact, as one dear brother put it, "I listen to other brothers and that debate to them is [crazy]..." Thus, it may or may not be the biggest controversy in churches today, but it most likely is the biggest in fundamental Baptist churches.

[3] Technically, there were other English translations in print before the King James Version. But historically, by the mid-1600s, the only English translation in major use was the KJV.

which position you hold, you can rest assured that there is plenty of material to shore up your point of view. There is no shortage of friends to help you and certainly you can find a circle of churches which will receive you with open arms. Conversely, there are also a number others who will treat you as if you were the greatest heretic that ever lived. And sometimes, even those whom you thought should at least understand your position will vilify you!

This controversy has even stretched across denominational lines and is causing quite a stir in both fundamental and more moderate Bible colleges. My observation, however, is that the Independent Baptists [4] seem to be more concerned about this issue than any other group. It has become a point of separation between otherwise like-minded churches and pastors. I personally know men who were in close fellowship with each other years ago but who have now parted fellowship because they cannot agree on the issue. Sometimes, this separation is deliberate. At other times, it is simply a matter of preference. Yet, the fact remains that this issue itself is charged with emotion along with doctrinal positions.

The question remains as to whether a church's position on this issue should be an issue of separation. Some would say, "Yes, there is no greater subject than the Bible itself." Others say, "No, as long as all the major doctrines are held and supported, then it does not matter which version a church or believer chooses to use."

But let us think this through for a moment. No one would deny that there are some very good books written on the subject of Theology. And yet, we would never claim those books as "the Word of God" simply because the doctrine is straight. Biblically, God did not merely inspire the doctrines or thoughts expressed in the scriptures. No, he inspired every word. Note the wording of Proverbs 30:5.

> **Psalms 30:5** *For his anger endureth but a moment; in his favour is life: weeping may endure for a night, but joy cometh in the morning.*

Opinions vary. The opinions seemed to be based upon several factors. First, there is the subject of the translations themselves. Is the King James Version the best? Are all other translations corrupted? Are any of the translations good? Does inspiration extend to the translation? Can a translation be "double-

---

[4] For the sake of clarity, I do not consider true Baptists as a denomination since one of our Baptist distinctives is "local church autonomy". Denominational churches do not have exclusive local church autonomy. I point this out for those who may misunderstand my statement concerning denominations.

inspired"? Did God, in some way, guide the translation of any of the current translations? Is God preserving his Word through translations? Are the modern versions some kind of Satanic plot to discredit the gospel?

And then there is the subject of the Greek and Hebrew texts themselves from which the translations are accomplished. And again, questions abound. Which text is the trust worthiest? Which text is preserved? Can we trust copies? Do we know what the original autographs looked like? Do God's promises of preservation extend to copies or translations? And what about textual revisions? It is common knowledge that the Greek texts have all been revised. Which revision is the best?

Thirdly, there is the issue of the men who prepared, collated, or otherwise "edited" the texts. Should we consider their doctrinal beliefs? Or, should we simply focus on the work they accomplished? Are we to concern ourselves with the men or their manuscripts? Or should we concern ourselves with both?

So, as you can see, this is not a simple issue. As we discuss this issue, we should seek to keep an appropriate balance. It does not help our position to attack the character of others. This has been done far too often. Nor can we support our views with intellectualism or sentimentalism. Every doctrine, conviction, and standard that a believer takes must be based upon the scriptures themselves. The Bible is the foundation of all that we believe. Thus, whatever position we hold, we must be able to show the truthfulness and the application of that position from the Bible. In fact, according to $2^{nd}$ Timothy 2:15-26 is a direct challenge to study the scriptures, rightly divide (proper exegesis) and then teach the truth without getting caught up in doctrines which are unbiblical, extra-biblical, and unprofitable. I hope that I will be able to adequately satisfy all the questions we have just asked in a way that is faithful to the Bible itself.

The purpose of this book is not so much to show the superiority of the King James Version. Not that there is anything wrong with the King James Version, but the real crux of the matter is not so much on the level of translation but more on the level of transmission and preservation of the Greek text.

I am well aware that there are words and phrases hard to be understood today. Words such as churl, collops, hoised, wimples, sackbut, habergeon may require the modern reader to consult a dictionary. Phrases such as "pisseth against the wall" may be difficult to preach from. But I am referring to the KJV's formal equivalent style. Sure, today, we could have used synonyms for those words. But we cannot say that the word choices made by the KJV translators were inaccurate. And obviously, phrases such as the aforementioned one may be hard to read in a public format, but discomfort does not make a phrase inaccurate.

## IN DEFENSE OF THE TEXTUS RECEPTUS

In other words, before we can evaluate which translation we should be using, we must first be settled on which Greek text we should be using! This leads us to the subject of "textual criticism".

Textual criticism concerns itself with the study of texts or manuscripts in order to determine the most authoritative form of a text. It is a branch of literary criticism and is not exclusive to the area of biblical manuscripts. A critic seeks to reconstruct the original text as closely as possible. Naturally this presupposes that the existing manuscripts are: 1) not the original manuscripts; and 2) contain differences from the original manuscripts.

As applied to biblical texts, we must keep two facts in mind. First, God promised that we would always have exactly what he gave by the process of inspiration. This is called preservation. Secondly, it is not up to the intellect of modern textual critics to "discover" God's Word. Because of the history of the manuscripts, the historical evidence concerning the manuscripts, and how we must apply the principles of preservation as expressed in the scriptures, the choice is very clear.

There are basically three approaches made in application of textual criticism, the first of which is eclecticism. This is the practice of considering a wide diversity of manuscripts with the idea that the manuscripts with independent[5] readings were less likely to have been transmitted. This method allows for the opportunity to draw conclusions based, not on the similarities, but the differences in manuscripts. The resulting text therefore contains readings from a variety of sources. In reality, this has been the dominant approach to textual criticism since the late 1800s and was widely popularized by the theories of Westcott and Hort.

A second approach to textual criticism is called "stemmatology". This is a three-step process where manuscripts are first grouped according to common errors. The logic behind this is that common errors would point to a common source. Once this grouping has been made, then the manuscripts of that group are examined and decisions are made concerning the variants as to which are preferred. Usually one variant reading will be found more frequently. In this case, the most frequent reading is selected. Sometimes, the variants occur with equal frequency. When this is the case, then the critic chooses based upon his own judgment. Those who employ this method then conclude that there may be

---

[5] By independent, it is meant that there are readings which are not in agreement with any other manuscripts.

passages where no correct reading exists.[6] At this point a process called "emendation" is applied where choices are made but these choices are usually very "conjectural". Because of this, some of the choices are even called "conjectural emendations."[7]

The third approach is called copy-text editing. In this method, a base text is selected and the critic makes changes based upon the witness of other manuscripts. Sometimes, in using this method, choices between variant readings can pose difficulties. In these cases, decisions are usually made in favor of the base-text reading. This is the method that Erasmus used when producing his Greek text. The base text was the readings found in the Byzantine family.

Someone could conceivably claim that the Critical Text was also formed using the copy-text editing method, and in a sense that is true. However, the wrong base text (Codex Vaticanus) was utilized which guaranteed that the outcome would be wrong. But to be totally honest, the method that Westcott and Hort employed was more eclectic than copy-text editing.

Another aspect of textual criticism that we should be familiar with is the difference between "higher criticism" and "lower criticism". Lower criticism concerns itself more so with the text itself. It focuses on the individual readings and seeks to determine which readings are correct. Thus, it begins with the hypothesis that there IS a correct reading which can be determined. The natural outcome to this approach is belief in the finished product.

Higher criticism seeks to discover the source of a manuscript or reading. It is also called "source criticism" and begins from the hypothesis that the biblical texts already existed in some other form but was brought together at a later date. Since the Bible teaches that all scripture came from God himself, saints through the ages have typically held to certain beliefs concerning the origin of the books of the Bible. But higher criticism often contradicts the traditional views concerning the source of various books in the Bible.

Many proponents of higher criticism treat the scriptures as the work of man in contrast to the biblical principles of inspiration and preservation. The natural outcome to this approach is a lack of faith in the reliability of the

---

[6] Obviously, this would completely rule out any faith-based approach with the principles of preservation applied. For if God preserved his word, and He did, then obviously a true reading must exist!

[7] Conjectural should not be taken to mean "on a whim" or without any rhyme or reason whatsoever. Scholars typically have sound reasons why they prefer one reading or text over another. We may not always agree on their conclusions but their choices are not typically made "on a whim".

scriptures. We should also note that there are good men who hold to the Critical Text who would readily reject the methods of higher criticism, though we may differ with them on how to apply the principles of lower criticism. in fact, there is such a strong reaction to the word "criticism" that some are beginning to use the term "textual analysis" to better distinguish between "criticizing the Bible" and analyzing the text.

This book is not so much a rebuttal of higher criticism as it is a discussion of how to apply the principles of lower criticism. It is not a discussion of "if" God inspired the Bible, but, "how" God inspired the Bible. It is a critical analysis of the different viewpoints concerning "lower criticism". As such, we will seek to be both technically accurate, and yet not so technical that it cannot be clearly understood by both layman and scholar. Thus, we begin with a very simple explanation of the various positions.

## A SIMPLE EXPLANATION OF THE VARIOUS POSITIONS

Defining the various positions can be a bit difficult. First of all, if we seek to define them based on the Greek texts, then we will not have a category for those who believe that the scriptures are now preserved in another language other than Greek. If we seek to limit ourselves to the various positions concerning translations, then we will invariably become distracted from the heart of the issue, which is the Greek text itself. Thus, the following positions are an attempt to adequately cover both aspects.

I realize that there are many different positions on the Bible issue. I am also aware that in seeking to explain the basic positions, I will invariably miss something and most likely, there are some who hold positions that may not even fit these categories. But for the sake of clarity, we should attempt to classify the various basic viewpoints on this crucial issue.

In seeking to do research, I have found a variety of explanations ranging from two views (right and wrong) to seven views. Each writer had his own definition for the positions and some of the things that have been said are logical and sound. On the other hand, some writers have approached this with an almost belligerent attitude. I have sought to represent the mainstream positions while at the same time, I tried not to misrepresent anyone's particular beliefs.

With that being said, here are some very basic positions on this issue. The names of each position are not completely my creations but at the same time, they are not altogether derived from other sources either.

## IN DEFENSE OF THE TEXTUS RECEPTUS

### *The Position of Unbelief*

This position is held by those who do not believe we have a trustworthy text in ANY form. These people don't believe the promises of preservation, and therefore, nothing we say will ever convince them. They tend to treat the Bible as if it were a secular book, without any respect to the doctrine of inspiration or preservation.

This is a position of doubt. Those who hold this position do not believe we have the exact words of God that were originally penned by the prophets and apostles. And if they are consistent, they must admit that they do not believe that the Bible is given by inspiration at all! This is a thoroughly modernistic approach to textual criticism.

I strongly disagree with this position since I believe that God inspired and preserved His words to every generation. I will explain a lot more about this later in this book on the section dealing with the doctrine of preservation.

It is possible to approach textual criticism from this aspect and still hold to a nominal belief in the doctrine of inspiration and preservation although it tends to lead to disbelief in any supernatural occurrence. Often those who take this position hold any account of miracles, angels, etc. as possibly folklore, legend, or embellishment. Basically, this would be the Sadducee approach – a denial of the supernatural!

### *All Inclusivism*

Simply defined, this position holds that although God promised to preserve His word, He didn't necessarily mean He would do it in any single text or in any particular textual family for that matter. In other words, both the Critical Text and the Textus Receptus can both be received as valid copies of the scriptures. Often, the statement is made that since it is possible to teach every Bible doctrine from either text, then either text can be called "scripture".

This particular view is held by a significant group of believers and is surprisingly popular among many of our fundamentalist churches.[8] This view

---

[8] I am aware that some people don't consider them fundamentalists but at the same time, others do. I am not seeking to pass judgment one way or another. I am simply saying that I have noticed an increasing popularity of this position among a number of those who would consider themselves fundamentalists.

seems to be more of an academic approach (as versus a faith-based approach) to the text issue.

Those who hold this view do not deny that the Textus Receptus is scripture, but would argue that the Critical Text is just as valid. Often they would make the argument that all of the doctrines of God can be taught from either Greek text. But, while it is true that we can teach any Bible doctrine from either the Textus Receptus or the Critical Text, we need to keep in mind that we could do the same thing with any well-written and thorough book on Bible doctrines, theology, or commentary.

But commentaries are not the Word of God. They may contain good doctrinal teaching but they are not what God gave. There is more to being a Bible than simply containing good teaching. Sound doctrine is obviously important but it is not the only criteria in our obligation to identify the correct text.

In all fairness, those who hold this view are smart enough to know there are contradictory readings between the Greek texts and they would readily admit that both readings cannot be the correct reading. Instead they would say that God did not choose to preserve them all in one place, and that because of the redundant nature of languages, the minor variants are not that big of a deal and certainly not worth fighting over. They are content with the minor amount of uncertainty. Also, I think they would argue that there is a big difference between textual variants and commentaries.

Based upon what the Bible says about itself, and we will discuss this more in depth later, we must make a choice. We cannot believe that these two manuscripts are equally valid.

## Eclecticism

Just as those who believe that the Textus Receptus is the inspired and preserved text, there are also those who believe that the Critical Text (as constructed by Westcott and Hort) is the superior text. If asked to give an explanation of inspiration and preservation, this group would say basically the same thing as the Textus Receptus Only group. The big difference is that those who hold this position generally believe that the Greek text CAN be improved. In fact, the majority of those who hold to this view would readily agree that the current Critical Text (NA28 or UBS4) is better than the Westcott-Hort text of 1881.

This viewpoint is usually based upon the age of manuscripts. The argument is that since the Critical Text is an eclectic text constructed from the

## IN DEFENSE OF THE TEXTUS RECEPTUS

"oldest and best" manuscripts, then the Critical Text must be closest to the original autographs. This particular position appears to be most prevalent in New Evangelical and a few Fundamentalist colleges and seminaries.

This was the basic belief of Brooke Foss Westcott and Fenton John Anthony Hort. In constructing their eclectic text, which is now known as the Critical Text, they approached the scriptures as if it were just another ancient book. Both men were known for their dislike of the traditional Greek text, which we call the Textus Receptus, even calling it "vile".

We would strongly disagree with the position of Eclecticism since we believe that God inspired and preserved his words to every generation. I will explain a lot more about this later in the section on inspiration.

But there are other problems with this position. First of all, older is not necessarily better. I have in my office a very old copy of the New World Translation (a corrupted translation done by the Jehovah's Witnesses - a cult). I have in my hand, a brand new King James Version. I have only been using it for six months. Clearly, older is not necessarily better.

Someone may say that this is a bad illustration because my example deals with printed editions and not hand written manuscripts. Their point is that older manuscripts are nearer the originals because there are fewer generations in which errors could be introduced, unless of course, there is some other overriding consideration.[9]

But that is not the point of the illustration at all. The point is simply to illustrate that the age of the manuscript, though helpful, does not in and of itself determine the purity of the text. It can only prove that the text existed. In the same respect, scientists who find dinosaur bones cannot use the bones to prove evolution. They can only use the bones to prove that a certain kind or species of animal existed during a particular period of time. So the existence of a certain family of texts or certain Greek reading cannot prove the superiority of that reading. It can only show us that the particular family or reading existed.

So I don't think I am comparing apples to oranges. Copies made by a machine or copies made by hand are both still copies. I understand the argument concerning being closer to the original but that is just the point. If the original is corrupt, then even the best copy would still be corrupt.

Usually, when you read "the older and more reliable manuscripts" in a footnote or commentary, it is usually referring to the Codex Vaticanus or Codex

---

[9] And, of course, we would say that the over-riding influence would be the preservation of God.

## IN DEFENSE OF THE TEXTUS RECEPTUS

Sinaiticus. These two manuscripts date from the 4th century. But we have to remember that we have also found an ancient papyri (P90) which is dated to the 2nd century which is as much in agreement with the Byzantine family as it is with the Alexandrian family.[10]

But even if the scholars could show that P90 is Alexandrian and not Byzantine, we can still prove that the Byzantine existed in the 2nd century based upon translations that were done at that time.[11] So the "older is better" argument may appear to make sense on the surface, but upon closer examination, it is not as strong as we may initially be led to believe.

The second problem I have with the Eclectic position, the position that believes the Critical Text is God's inspired word, is that of agreement. The Textus Receptus comes from the Byzantine family. There are 5369 Greek manuscripts in support of the Byzantine family, either in full or in part. The readings of those manuscripts are in nearly perfect agreement (over 98%)[12] with each other. The Critical Text is derived from the Alexandrian family of manuscripts. There are 207 manuscripts in support of the Alexandrian family, either in full or in part. The readings of these manuscripts disagree with each other in literally thousands of places. With this number of disagreement between copies, it is very difficult to understand why anyone could view the Alexandrian family of manuscripts as trust-worthy on any level.

---

[10] It is not conclusive that P90 is Byzantine. It is also not clear if it is Alexandrian either. The reason for this is because what remains of the manuscript could very well be placed in either family. In all, I could find only 3 independent readings where P90 did not agree with either the Alexandrian or the Byzantine manuscripts. I found only one place where it agreed with the Alexandrian manuscript against the Byzantine manuscripts, and one place where it agreed with Byzantine manuscript against the Alexandrian manuscript. P90 is also the second oldest manuscript to date - some dating it as early as 165 AD. Anyone interested in making their own comparison can go to http://en.wikipedia.org/wiki/Papyrus_90#Greek_text where the text is laid out very nicely. I strongly recommend comparing it personally rather than take the words of the "scholars"!

[11] The Greek Orthodox Bible (2nd century); Old Syriac (150-160 AD); Diatessaron (150-160 AD); Peshitta (150 to 170) - all translations from Byzantine manuscripts, from where we get the Textus Receptus. With that being said, in all honesty, none of these were really great translations anyway. They come with their own set of problems. But they do at least show us that the Byzantine manuscripts existed as far back as 150 AD.

[12] I have not personally compared every Byzantine manuscript with every other Byzantine manuscript but this figure seems to be the basic consensus among the textual scholars no matter what their position on the textual issue is.

# IN DEFENSE OF THE TEXTUS RECEPTUS

## Selectivism (Sentimentalism)

This position is really not a position of the Greek and Hebrew texts but more of a sentimental viewpoint. It may be true that there are those who hold to one of the above positions because, "That is what I was taught" or, "That is what my parents believed". But usually, this position is more focused on the translation rather than the text from which it is taken.

Since this is not really a position on the text at all, I will not really be dealing with this at length. I believe if we are truly aware of what the scriptures say, and truly aware of the problems with the Critical Text, we will not choose a translation based upon sentimental feelings.

It is interesting that this view doesn't really have anything to do with the text or even the accuracy of the translation. It is more about the sentimental attachment that someone has to their particular translation. Typically, this is the position that we hear from those who use the King James Version. (Well, this is the Bible that I have always used. . .) But as a missionary, I have met others who were raised on a translation that is not only from the wrong Greek text, but also inferior in translation. Yet they said the same things that some of our sentimentalist King James supporters do!

On the other hand, I have met men who defended their favorite translation with the statement, "This translation is good enough to build a church on, to grow as a believer with, and to evangelize the lost with." And that is true. As a missionary, I have seen men do that very thing! And in many cases, missionaries are not left with any other option. Often, mission work has to be performed with tools that are sometimes less than optimal and missionaries do a great job with what they have to work with. In some languages, there may not even be a completed New Testament translation, and yet the missionary wins souls and starts a church. But "good enough" is not good enough.

Years ago, there did not exist a good translation in our field of labor. And I can assure you that, though we missionaries used what we had, many of us greatly desired something more trustworthy. It is difficult to instill a level of confidence in the scriptures in young believers when we are constantly having to "correct" a bad word choice in an inferior translation. The fact that God can use something inferior (and He often does. He uses man!) does not signify that we should not try to use the best available.

## Inspired Translation Position

## IN DEFENSE OF THE TEXTUS RECEPTUS

This position is usually held concerning the King James Version. The idea is that God somehow supernaturally inspired the translators as they did their work. Those who are purists in this position believe that if there were any differences between the King James Version and the Textus Receptus, then the King James Version takes precedence since it is an "advanced revelation". This is often called "double-inspiration" because according to this teaching, the King James Version translators were "double-inspired" as they translated from Greek and Hebrew to English.

But there are several problems with this view. First, the translators took 3 years to complete the work. If it were inspired, then it should have only taken a few days since there were at least 43 (and probably more) working on it simultaneously. Second, why did they need to proofread the King James Version to ensure accuracy? If it were inspired, there would have been no need for proofreading because it would have been perfectly translated the first time! Thirdly, why did the translators place alternate possible translations in their notes?[13] Shouldn't they have known with certainty which word God wanted? Fourthly, why are there differences between the King James Version and the Textus Receptus?

And, yes, there are differences between the King James Version and the Textus Receptus. Nothing of any real doctrinal consequence, but nonetheless, things that are different are not the same. For example, in Acts 19:20 the King James Version says, "God" but the Textus Receptus has "Kurios" or "Lord". "Kurios" is translated "Lord" 761 times in the King James Version but only one time as "God". There is no denial. They are different. We may not be comfortable with that fact but facts are very unmovable things, aren't they?

One "Critical Text" supporter, after having read some of my articles on the Textus Receptus made this charge:

*"TR advocates, frankly, do not practice textual criticism. Rather, to be a TR advocate, you have to take the work of two or three dead textual critics (Erasmus, Stephanus, and Beza), and insist that they were right in all of their decisions, or at least all of the decisions that were finally put into Scrivener's*

---

[13] Some of their column notes are really quite contradictory to what was put in the main text. For example, in Judges 19:2, the translators put "four months" in the main text but in the column notes they put "a year and four months". In Hebrews 11:35, the translators cross-referenced to a book that is not even a part of the canon – 2 Macc. 7:7!

Actually, the very fact that they USED column notes shows that the translators knew they were not inspired.

*edition. Rather than working from evidence to edition, a TR advocate works from the edition that they've already decided is true and then backtracks to the evidence and selectively chooses those evidences that confirm their premade conclusions. I don't mean to sound overly critical, but this is just what I see in your book and Edward F. Hills' book, and other TR advocates. Any evidence is sufficient as long as it supports the desired conclusion."*

And that is true to a point. But facts are very obstinate things."Any evidence" that is true is still evidence. If it can be used to support both texts, it should be disregarded. But if not, it must be properly explained, but CANNOT be disregarded simply because it disagrees with one's position. That's why some of my KJV friends take just about as many shots at me as my Critical Text friends. I am not afraid to discuss differences between the Textus Receptus and the King James Version and they don't like those facts. But no matter. They are still facts.

But what we "TR advocates" don't appreciate is when someone says there is no reason for reading "x" to be in the Bible and then they try to discredit any reason given. For the record, I don't like some of the approaches taken by some TR defenders myself. But if a point of evidence is valid, it has to be dealt with. It cannot be ignored or explained away.

There is a little Greek conjunction "kai" that is often used in the Bible. Sometimes, it is left totally untranslated in the King James Version simply for readability sake. Examples would include John 17:25 where it says, "O righteous Father the world hath not known me." If the translators had translated "kai", it should say, "O righteous Father (also/moreover/indeed) the world hath not known me." Rev 8:7 begins with "kai" but it is left completely untranslated.

Sometimes verb tenses are different. Matt 21:13 has "And said unto them" when in the Greek the verb "said" is in present tense. So, the phrase should read "and saith unto them". Does it matter? Not so much, really. I mean, when you think about it, the whole story is in past tense from our perspective anyway.

Now, before anyone gets too upset, and begins to accuse me of being a Bible hater, let me clarify. Every preacher I have set under has said, "The Bible is inspired." and I totally agree. I have said the same thing many times myself! But the King James is not "double inspired".[14] The King James Version is a trustworthy, faithful and accurate translation of what God gave us in the original languages of Greek and Hebrew. It is the Word of God. It is completely trustworthy. Yet every language has its own specific nuances and limitations so

---

[14] Some people prefer the phrase "advanced revelation" over "double inspiration" but they both mean basically the same thing.

we should not expect a perfect match. On the other hand, we should not think that differences between the two texts totally invalidate the King James Version. But we cannot have our cake and eat it too. Whatever allowances that we make for ourselves concerning the King James Version must also be afforded to other translations.

One writer blatantly stated that if a person is not "King James Only" then he must be "Critical Text" only. But in reality, this issue is not that simple. In fact, I know quite a number of people who are not "King James Only" and yet they do not agree with the eclectic position or the inclusive position as I mentioned earlier. Let's consider two other positions which are also very popular, and which are not necessarily "KJV Only".

## The Preserved Translation Position

There is a rather sizable group which believes that a translation can be called "God's preserved Word for the English speaking people". You may have read that same statement in a church constitution or on a website somewhere. And it is quite possible it is even in the doctrinal statement of your church.

But this position misses the point, theologically speaking. In fact, this position not only misses the point, but actually clouds the issue. And again, I don't mean to cause unnecessary controversy over terms, but I don't think we fundamentalists have given enough thought to what we are saying when we make this statement. According to God's Word, the LORD preserves several things – His people, his church, and His Word. But when we say He preserves His Word, what is it exactly that He preserves? Again, God <u>preserves</u> what He <u>inspired</u>. So if we say that God did not <u>inspire</u> a translation, then we cannot say that God <u>preserved</u> a translation.

For the most part, those who make the statement are seeking to defend the King James Version from the onslaught of modern criticism. Because there is a sizable group of "scholars" who attack the King James Version, or at least attempt to cast doubt upon its accuracy, quite a number of conservative Bible believers have taken to defending the King James by referring to it as a "preserved" translation. I understand the desire to defend it. But I still think we would be better off if we thought through our defense, and then presented a defense that was more theologically accurate. Statements like "God's preserved word for the English speaking people" may have little to no impact to the effectiveness of ministry in the church pew. But it can have much a more serious impact on the mission field.

## IN DEFENSE OF THE TEXTUS RECEPTUS

This belief that a translation can be preserved is quite binding when we move into the area of translation. One man said to me, "Why even look at the Greek and Hebrew when the King James is perfect?" I answered, "I am sure that God would rather we translated from what was given by inspiration than from what was given by translation." And please understand, I am not seeking to cast doubt upon any translation. I just believe we need to be more careful with how we use biblical or theological terms. Their misuse can cause more problems than what is immediately apparent.

Another man said, "We cannot know the Greek and Hebrew because it is a dead language. Let's just translate from the King James Version." I answered, "Well, then, let's save a lot of time and just teach people English! It sure is easier than translation work!" Yes, biblical Greek and Hebrew are dead languages in the extent that we do not use them in their biblical forms today. But that very fact actually helps us tremendously because that very fact also means the definitions of the words and grammar usage are set and will not change.[15]

A third man said to me, "What if you find a difference between the King James Version and the Greek? You are still going to use the King James Version for translation, right?" I replied, "If the Textus Receptus is God's preserved word and the King James Version is a perfect translation, then what differences do you suppose we will find?" This man was the most disturbing to me because first of all, he thought it was a bad idea to look at the Greek in any case. He felt that if we found a significant difference between the Greek (that which was given by inspiration) and the King James Version (that which was given by translation), we must use what was given by translation. He would not even entertain the thought of looking into the Greek because he did not want to face the possibility of finding out he was wrong in his beliefs. How could he believe that the Greek was inspired and the English was perfect if he found a difference? So to ensure that he never found a difference, he would not even consider looking at the Greek! I call this willful academic dishonesty! If the King James Version is as good as we claim it to be, then it can stand on its own merits. Any examination would only further vindicate its accuracy and instill greater confidence.

---

[15] For the record, I am not against translating from the King James Version. There have been plenty of missionaries who did fine translations from the King James Version. But it is still my contention that it is safer to use what God gave by inspiration rather than use what has been translated. I do not think it is the only way to do a translation but I firmly believe it is the best way. It is a fact that any person who has ever taken a class in biblical Greek or Hebrew – the more you learn about the original languages, the better you understand the English!

# IN DEFENSE OF THE TEXTUS RECEPTUS

## The Textus Receptus Position

This is the correct position and the one which aligns with the doctrines of the scriptures. Those who hold this position believe that God inspired and preserves his words in the Textus Receptus. Although the Textus Receptus is not a "family" per se, yet it is constructed solely from manuscripts in the Byzantine family.

The first "Textus Receptus" was put together by Erasmus in the early 1500's (first edition was printed in 1516) with the last revision done by Scrivener in the 1890's. During that time there were scores of editions which are sometimes referred to as the "Textus Receptus" family.

There are several variations of the Textus Receptus position. Some believe it is superior based upon historical evidence and logical deduction. This group typically takes a look at the types of manuscripts that have been in use throughout history and based upon this, have come to the conclusion that the Byzantine manuscripts were considered superior by the majority of believers throughout history.

Others have come to a "Textus Receptus" position based upon theological teachings. By looking at the biblical doctrines of inspiration and preservation, coupled with the knowledge of which manuscripts have been available and in use throughout history, this group believes the Textus Receptus to be the manuscript that God preserved.

The interesting thing about all of this is that both groups have come to the same position from two different approaches. One approach is more of a faith-based approach while the other approach is more of an academic approach. Yet both witnesses agree to the same conclusion.

Among those who hold to a Textus Receptus position there are those who feel that the other families of manuscripts are simply inferior while some people believe that the other manuscripts are heretical or even Satanic deceptions. We may debate the accuracy of their individual opinions but one point should not be missed - whether a person believes the other Greek manuscripts or inferior, or whether he believes they are a Satanic attempt at sabotage, both would agree that it is best to use the Textus Receptus.

Normally, this group (at least those who use an English Bible) use the King James Version because it is an accurate and faithful translation of the Textus Receptus. Some would state that the King James Version is absolutely perfect while others simply believe it to be exemplary but not necessarily perfect.

## IN DEFENSE OF THE TEXTUS RECEPTUS

My position is that that the King James Version is a faithful, accurate, and trustworthy translation of the inspired and preserved Textus Receptus. When I set out to write this book, "In Defense of the Textus Receptus", I believed that the Textus Receptus was God's inspired word and that the King James Version is a faithful and accurate translation. I now have a deeper conviction based upon a greater understanding which has only strengthened my belief in the Word of God.

### DOES IT MATTER?

One could obviously ask the question as to whether it matters which position a person holds concerning the controversy. The answer is "yes" for the following reasons.

**It strikes at the core of our belief concerning the doctrine of inspiration.**

When talking about the variations between manuscripts, some people say, "the differences are minor", "the differences are, for the most part, not even translatable.", or "it doesn't affect any major doctrine". While many of these people are genuine brothers who love God and His word, we are driven back to the point of considering how literally we should take the doctrines of verbal/plenary inspiration and the extent of preservation.

Keep in mind that the purpose of this book is not to show which translation is the best. Although we will invariably discuss the accuracy of numerous translations, that is the secondary consideration. Our primary consideration is to discuss the superiority of one Greek text over the other. Thus, the issue is not really the translation so much as it is the text from which the translation is taken.

If we believe that God has given every word, and if we believe that God has preserved every word, then we are left with no option but to admit that no matter how minor the difference, no matter how "untranslatable" the change, no matter how much we can teach from one manuscript as versus the other – it certainly does matter!

**It gives us a framework for evaluating new translations.**

Aside from the new translations that are obvious corruptions designed to support heretical doctrines, there are also a number of other translations that are not motivated by heresy at all. Some people would argue that whether it is motivated by heresy or not, they contain heresy. Although nothing comes to mind, I know it is quite possible.

## IN DEFENSE OF THE TEXTUS RECEPTUS

Others would argue that any doctrine of the scriptures can be taught from any of the Greek manuscript families. And therefore, it is not worth fighting over. The first part of this statement may or may not be true. I have never personally tried to exhaustively validate the argument. I have, however, been able to support the major doctrines of the Bible from either manuscript (Textus Receptus, Critical Text) but I am well aware that there are literally thousands of other teachings – some very minor – and I certainly have not been able to validate them all! I do disagree, however, with the conclusion that it is not worth fighting over.

Some claim that not only doctrine, but even the very order of the words are important. For example, if a passage says "the fruit of the Spirit is love, joy, peace", it should not be changed to read, "the fruit of the Spirit is love, peace, joy". Logically, the change of order does not have an impact of the truth set forth in the context, but some would argue that the very order itself is set to teach some truth that we do not, at this point in our understanding, comprehend. Add to this the fact that God gave the word order and we do not have the right to change it, whether it matters or not!

Others state that the existence of each word, no matter how insignificant, is important. To give another example, "The Lord Jesus Christ" should never be changed to "the Lord Christ", "Jesus Christ", or any other variation of this holy title for the Savior.[16]

We agree that the content is obviously a key issue in this discussion. But we must also acknowledge that other issues such as authorship, degree of purity, correct understanding of verbal-plenary inspiration, and accurate application of the doctrine of preservation are also of equal vital importance in determining the correct text family.

***It gives us a framework for evaluating our relationships to fellow believers with different beliefs.***

Aside from the obvious doctrinal implications, we can also ask ourselves whether or not the issue should be a basis for separation. And if it is a basis for separation, to what extent should separate? Should we exercise separation in the same sense that we would toward Jehovah's Witnesses? Can we associate with,

---

[16] Interestingly enough, upon this point, there is a difference between the Textus Receptus and the King James Version. In Galatians 5:6 the Textus Receptus says Χριστῷ Ἰησοῦ (Christ Jesus) while the King James Version says "Jesus Christ". Understand that this is in no way an attack upon the King James Version. One would have to establish that there is some valid reason to say "Christ Jesus" versus saying "Jesus Christ" and I don't think that this can dogmatically be done! Call it minor, call it insignificant, but we cannot call it anything other than different!

## IN DEFENSE OF THE TEXTUS RECEPTUS

yet not yoke up with, those who hold a different position than ourselves? Or should we take the position that it is a personal matter and not a point for division?

The truth is, the issue has ALREADY caused division. What we must ascertain is whether this division is right, or even necessary. Then, we must ascertain, to what extent the division should be made, and in what context we ought to view those we have separated from!

Also, we must remember that people hold to their various positions from varying motives or beliefs. Some take a more lenient approach while others are very dogmatic. For example, some believe that the King James Version is the best translation while others believe it bears the mark of "double-inspiration". The point is, although two people may come to the same conclusion, they may not agree on how to get there. Some hold to the King James Version from an unbiblical position.[17] Do we really want to consider them our allies when their doctrine is severely flawed? Once again, we are driven back to evaluate, not only the conclusion, but why we have reached it, and whether it is a basis for separation.

### ANSWER BASED UPON BELIEF IN INSPIRATION AND PRESERVATION

Ultimately, your answer to the question, "Does it matter?" will stem from your personal beliefs concerning inspiration and preservation. At this point, it will be important to examine both doctrines in order to set the foundation for our discussion.

Unless we have a proper understanding of what the Bible teaches concerning itself, we do not possess the theological tools to draw the proper conclusions concerning the issue. Without a sound biblical foundation, our choices must ultimately rest on one or several faulty bases.

We may base our decision upon intellect. However, this is not only unwise but actually quite dangerous for several reasons. First, the intellect of man is finite, corrupted by sin, and often downright prideful. Since the Bible clearly illustrates the inclination of man to deceive his own self through pride, he can't even see that he is wrong! Note the following verses on self-deception:

---

[17] Peter Ruckman believed that the English of the King James Version 1611 is superior to the Greek manuscripts. If this were true, we would have to believe that we did not have the perfect Word of God until the 1600s. He arrived at his conclusions from an unbiblical and unbalanced perspective.

## IN DEFENSE OF THE TEXTUS RECEPTUS

*__Isaiah 40:20__ He that is so impoverished that he hath no oblation chooseth a tree that will not rot; he seeketh unto him a cunning workman to prepare a graven image, that shall not be moved.*

*__Obadiah 1:3__ The pride of thine heart hath deceived thee, thou that dwellest in the clefts of the rock, whose habitation is high; that saith in his heart, Who shall bring me down to the ground?*

*__Galatians 6:3__ For if a man think himself to be something, when he is nothing, he deceiveth himself.*

Obviously, if it is possible for a man to deceive himself, he must ensure that his choices are made upon a foundation surer than his own intellect. This does not mean that the world of academia should be avoided but a true biblical perspective requires that we first place our faith in the word of God by which we may judge all secular knowledge, including the world of academia!

Another faulty foundation that is often used in choosing a position is one that I like to call, "the parrot position". This is where a person is simply repeating what he has been taught by his pastor, seminary professor, mamma, etc. but has never really sought to validate the beliefs for himself.

Although we should be able to trust our leaders, the Bible does not mandate a blind faith in their teachings. Rather, it encourages each believer to seek the truth of a doctrine from the scriptures for himself. The "parrot position" is especially dangerous because it shows a tendency to trust in the wisdom of man without ensuring that it aligns with the Word of God. And by the way, there are plenty of people in every camp who are guilty of this!

A third faulty foundation often used in coming to a position is simply choosing a position to identify with a particular person, group, or organization. Let's face reality, a lot of people simply hold to a particular position for the reason of acceptance. Since they want to "fit in" with a particular group of preachers, they will espouse a position that is held in common by the group. The cause of this may be an idolization or a favorite preacher, a desire to be "promoted up the ranks" of a particular group, or a need for support from some organization. One dangerous aspect of this mentality is that if a person should decide that his position is wrong – the reason for his decision doesn't matter at this point – he will feel the pressure to say nothing, continue as he has always done, in order not to be ostracized by his peers.

So to answer the question, "Does it matter?" is not a simple "yes" or "no". The short answer is, 'Yes, it matters." But we must also take the time to explain why it matters, and how we should apply this understanding. As stated earlier, the

## IN DEFENSE OF THE TEXTUS RECEPTUS

answer to the question, "Does it matter?" will stem from one's personal belief concerning inspiration and preservation. So let's take a good look at these doctrines to ensure we have a solid foundation before we discuss our positions on the Greek texts.

## INSPIRATION

In order to avoid the problems we have already discussed, we need to come to a balanced understanding of biblical truth. Rather than approach the issue from a purely academic perspective, a believer must discern from the Bible whether a certain philosophy or method of textual analysis is biblically based and fundamentally sound. In other words, "What does the Bible say about itself?"

Immediately, an accusation is made by those who view this as circular reasoning. But is it really? Consider this illustration:

A man is taken to court for suspicion of some crime. The prosecutor will seek to discredit his witness by various means but you can be sure that he will always seek to place the man on the witness stand and examine his story.[18] He will dwell on every word the defendant says. He will question, probe, and reexamine every assertion. In short, he will do all that he can to discredit the defendant's story.

On the other hand, the defendant, if he is innocent, will desire to take the stand and testify on his behalf. He will be as clear and exact as he possibly can to ensure that the jury and judge are totally convinced of his innocence. He will state his case, clearly and concisely so that he can, not only support his claim, but also explain it as fully as he possibly can.

This is exactly why we must begin with an examination of the claims of the scriptures themselves. However, we do not approach the scriptures as a prosecuting attorney seeking to discredit the testimony. We approach as an objective jury, allowing the Bible to speak in its own defense. This places upon us the choice of simply believing its claims by faith, or rejecting it all together.

Hence, it is a simple matter of faith. It ultimately comes down to what we believe about the Bible's claim to inspiration. Since this is true, then we must be sure to have a correct understanding of what inspiration is, and how the process worked. The following is an examination of various views on the issue.

### *FALSE VIEWS OF INSPIRATION*

In one sense, the doctrine of inspiration is as much a mystery as the incarnation. And there are some rather striking similarities between the two doctrines. For example, in the person of Christ there is his human nature and his

---

[18] I understand that in America, a man does not have to testify against himself and that the prosecutor cannot force him to do so. However, that is not true in many other nations. In either case, a prosecutor wants the defendant to speak so he can try to discredit his testimony.

## IN DEFENSE OF THE TEXTUS RECEPTUS

God nature. Neither detracts from or adds anything to the other. He is at once, 100% God and 100% man.

In the same way the Bible has both a human nature and a God nature. It is completely given by God through men. And yet, the very words of God do not destroy the character or style of the man who wrote.

Also, consider the eternal nature of Christ as well. The scriptures are quite clear that Jesus Christ is the same yesterday, today, and forever (Hebrews 13:8). Yet at the same time, his person has been manifest in history in various ways. In the Old Testament He appears as the Angel of the LORD, In the New Testament, He took upon Him the form of a servant, and was made in the likeness of men. Today, He indwells the believer in the person of the Holy Spirit. Many of us who have gone to Bible college or seminary learned the age-old statement concerning the trinity, "The Father is God. The Son is God. The Holy Spirit is God. There is one God." Yet in his various manifestations, Jesus, the eternal Word, remains unchanged.

And so it is with the Bible itself. It has come to us in many forms – Greek, Hebrew, Aramaic, and a host of other languages through history. The truth of God has been carried in numerous "containers" over the years and yet the truth is unchanged. Try as man might, he cannot destroy or alter God's Word. It remains forever settled in heaven far above the reach of mortal men!

Josh McDowell[19], in his handbook on apologetics, outlines four basic perspectives on inspiration. He states that "one can view the Bible and its inspiration from several different perspectives."

***"1. The Bible is an inspiring book but no different from other great literary works of the past."*** *This view places the scriptures on the same level as other human productions[20]. It denies the possibility of God's providing a revelation of himself through the books of the Bible."*

---

[19] Although I think that Mr. McDowell has made certain well-constructed observations concerning these four perspectives on inspiration, I am by no means endorsing him or his views. I also think that regarding any theological view you may find those who can't be neatly fit into our categorizations. I do not know Mr. McDowell personally, and therefore I am not qualified to speak on his character and I do not wholly agree with all of his theological positions. However, many of his statements concerning inspiration are applicable to this discussion.

[20] This is one of the problems with the method that Westcott and Hort used as they approached the Greek manuscripts. Instead of using a set of guidelines that were based on a sound faith and respect of the scriptures, they formed their own guidelines based upon opinion and secular reasoning. As

***God's Preserved Word to Every Generation***

## IN DEFENSE OF THE TEXTUS RECEPTUS

This view holds that the Bible is a great literary work that "inspires" man to do great and charitable things. But as far as being a divine message? Not a chance! The Bible is viewed as a work of man and nothing more.

According to the Bible, mankind may have a certain degree of natural insight, but in matters of morality and religion, his nature is corrupt to the point that he requires supernatural guidance in order to understand truth. (2 Cor 2:14) Therefore, man could not produce, apart from the work of God, an inerrant work such as the Bible.

McDowell then states a second perspective:

***"2. The Bible is "in part" the Word of God."*** *This view limits the manner, quantity, and quality in which a revelation of God can be contained in the books of the Bible. Proponents of this view say, "The Bible contains the Word of God," or "The Bible becomes the Word of God."*

McDowell seems to be describing a Neo-orthodoxy / Christian existential view that accepts intellectually that the Bible is not errant, but that it becomes the Word of God as a believer receives it by faith.

Let's be realistic. How many people know enough Greek and Hebrew to be able to objectively examine the manuscripts? And given that there are many people who know Greek and Hebrew, how many of them will ever have the opportunity to actually see the manuscripts? And then again, how many have a biblically sound basis for deciding which parts are inspired scripture and which parts are not? The idea that "the Bible contains the Word of God" makes the individual reader the final determiner of inspiration.

This is the approach that many textual critics take when viewing the Greek manuscripts. Their belief is that the manuscripts contain the inspired message of God, but man, by academic wisdom, education and experience, must decide where it is! And truthfully, there is a sense in which this is the right thing to do. But, in order to decide what is God's inspired word, we must begin with a standard. I believe that standard to be the Byzantine manuscripts because for several centuries, that was all that was in use. If preservation is a true doctrine, and it is, then the Byzantine family is the only family of manuscripts that qualify.

Mr. McDowell outlines the third perspective in this way:

---

a result, they treated the scriptures as they would have treated any other ancient writing. The end result was that the scriptures were placed on the same level as other human productions. In essence, they denied the doctrines of inspiration and preservation.

## IN DEFENSE OF THE TEXTUS RECEPTUS

***"3. The Bible is the divine Word of God dictated by God to selected human authors."***

The third view is much closer to the biblical truth. In fact, it may simply be the result of an unintentional misunderstanding of terms. The term in question is the word "dictation". If by saying "dictation", we mean that the writers had no self-control at all, then we leave no room for the existence of the personal styles that are clearly evident in the writings. Mr. McDowell states:

*"Although it is popular among liberals and nonreligious persons to accuse all serious or conservative Christians (evangelicals) of holding this position, it is actually not a tenable position."*

Mr. McDowell goes on to clarify his point by quoting James I. Packer:

*"This "dictation theory" is a man of straw. It is safe to say that no Protestant theologian, from the Reformation till now[21], has ever held it; and certainly modern Evangelicals do not hold it....It is true that many sixteenth and seventeenth-century theologians spoke of Scripture as "dictated by the Holy Ghost." But all they meant was that the authors wrote word for word what God intended....The use of the term "dictation" was always figurative....The proof of this lies in the fact that, when these theologians addressed themselves to the question, What was the Spirit's mode of operating in the writers' minds? they all gave their answer in terms not of dictation, but of accommodation, and rightly maintained that God completely adapted his inspiring activity to the cast of mind, outlook, temperament, interests, literary habits, and stylistic idiosyncrasies of each writer."*

His point is simply that the writers of the scriptures were not mere robots. While it is true that they recorded exactly what God told them to write, it is also true that God used the literary styles, educational levels, and vocabulary limitations of the men who penned the Bibles.

On the other hand, something should be said concerning the greatness of God himself. Is it proper to think that God was somehow limited by man's ability, style, or linguistic limitations? Is it not more accurate to think that God, knowing how he would deliver the message, and knowing exactly what he wanted to say, prepared the men that He would ultimately use?

McDowell goes on to list the fourth perspective:

---

[21] Actually, statements concerning this position can be found in the writings of numerous men such as John Calvin, Louis Gaussen, Matthew Henry, Clarence Larkin, Frances Turretin and numerous others.

## IN DEFENSE OF THE TEXTUS RECEPTUS

***"4. The Bible is a book that is both divine and human.*** *In expanded form, this view reflects the biblical teaching that the Bible itself, in all that it states, is a product of divine revelation, channeled through, but not corrupted by, human agency, by which the unique talents, backgrounds, and perspectives of the authors complement rather than restrict what God intended to reveal."*[22]

Hayford's Bible Handbook states it this way:

*"Although the Bible does not tell exactly how God inspired its writers, it was certainly not in a mechanical way. The Holy Spirit's work in the Virgin Mary's conceiving of Jesus might be an example of how the Spirit worked with the biblical writers. A fully human woman of Adam's sinful race bore a sinless child who would be called the Holy One, the Son of God (Luke 1:35). How could that be? The power of the Highest "overshadowed" her so that she conceived Jesus. Likewise, the power of the Highest "overshadowed" the biblical writers so that what they wrote could be called the Holy Bible, the Word of God."*[23]

Again, many theologians have argued whether the correct view is "mechanical" or not. Yet when asked to define their views, they give the same biblical points concerning the absolutely control of God over the writings. It is my contention that in many cases, it is merely an argument of semantics. No one would argue that the styles of John's writings are different from the style Paul's writings.

And those who hold to the "dictation theory" as well as those who believe that God used the writers' style both acknowledge that we received exactly what God meant to say. And that is the main point. We know that we have exactly what God gave!

### THE BIBLICAL VIEW OF INSPIRATION

In order to grasp the doctrine of inspiration, we must first be reminded of some very basic principles concerning the revelation of God's truth to man. In a theological sense, revelation means the giving of truth by God to man. Simply put, there are two basic types of revelation.

---

[22] Josh McDowell, Josh McDowell's handbook on apologetics [computer file], electronic ed., Logos Library System, (Nashville: Thomas Nelson) 1997, c1991 by Josh McDowell.

[23] Jack W. Hayford, Hayford's Bible Handbook [computer file], electronic ed., Logos Library System, (Nashville: Thomas Nelson) 1997, c1995.

First of all, there is a natural or "general" revelation of divine (or, spiritual) truth concerning God to man. God has chosen to reveal himself in a limited way through creation itself.

> ***Psalms 19:1-4 To the chief Musician, A Psalm of David.*** *The heavens declare the glory of God; and the firmament sheweth his handywork.* ***2*** *Day unto day uttereth speech, and night unto night sheweth knowledge.* ***3*** *There is no speech nor language, where their voice is not heard.* ***4*** *Their line is gone out through all the earth, and their words to the end of the world. In them hath he set a tabernacle for the sun,*

> ***Romans 1:19-20*** *Because that which may be known of God is manifest in them; for God hath shewed it unto them.* ***20*** *For the invisible things of him from the creation of the world are clearly seen, being understood by the things that are made, even his eternal power and Godhead; so that they are without excuse:*

God's Word declares that the very creation around us speaks to us of God. Although God finished the work of creation on the sixth day of creation, the voice of creation continues to speak to man. In the same sense, the Bible was completed in the first century and yet, it continues to speak to man as well.

General revelation is enough to show mankind that there is a God, that he is eternal, powerful, and supreme. Yet, this revelation is not enough to lead him to salvation. It leads him to an understanding that he needs more information. General revelation is enough to point a person toward God, but not enough to reconcile a person to Him. God's creation is visible evidence that supports the second form of revelation, that is, special revelation.

Often, we think of special revelation as being the Bible itself but in actuality, there were numerous forms of special revelation before the completion of scripture -- angels (Genesis 18); dreams (Daniel 7:1); visions (Ezekiel 1:1); audible voices (1 Samuel 3:10); Urim and Thummim (Numbers 27:21); lots (Jonah 1:7); and Christ Himself (Hebrews 1:1-2).

But inspiration, properly understood, is not the <u>revealing</u> of truth but the <u>recording</u> of truth. Inspiration is not the "voice" of that truth because if it were, then we would have to conclude that the heavens and the earth, which speaks to us concerning God, were inspired. Yet we know that they are not.

There were times when God revealed things He did not inspire. For example, John the Apostle sought to write something that he heard but was specifically told not to write it (Revelation 10:3-4). God gave revelation through

Christ that is not recorded (John 21:25). Revelation may also be partial in the sense that John received a revelation of things that were a combination of things previously known as well as things not previously known. (Rev 1:1)

In addition, God inspired some things that cannot be considered truth. For example, the words of Satan to Eve in the Garden of Eden are recorded and revealed by God, but certainly not truth! (Genesis 3:4, etc.). For the most part, however, what is inspired and what is revealed is the same.

God's final and complete revelation is God's Word, the Bible. God has included everything man needs to know about God. We should understand that things may be written which are not new revelations. (ex: the many times where the phrase, "it is written"[24]) We should also understand that there were things revealed that were not recorded (Rev 10:3,4)

Thus, we must not confuse the idea of revelation with inspiration. Where revelation is the mere unveiling of a truth, inspiration is concerned with the accurate and guided recording of what God has given. Inspiration is, therefore, an extension of the doctrine of revelation. The doctrine of revelation is concerned with the disclosure, the origin and giving of truth (1 Cor 2:10). Revelation is not "new truth", for all truth preexisted with God. In relation to the scriptures, the truth that is being revealed may be a person (Gal 1:16; Rev 1:1) or a doctrinal truth. (Psalm 119:89)

Inspiration relates to the reception and recording of truth. It involves man in an active sense, while revelation (the actual "breathing out of the words) is solely the act of God himself.

As a theological definition, inspiration is a process. It is the process by which God, working through holy men, delivered his message, without destroying the style or personality of the writer, and yet, maintaining divine authority, control, and inerrancy in the writings.

As previously stated, inspiration is a process - a process which is now completed. That means - now get ready for this thought – it is not exactly theologically accurate to say that the scriptures ARE inspired. It is more accurate to say that the scriptures WERE inspired. Lest some would think that I am saying the Bible is any less than the Word of God, inerrant, infallible, and incorruptible, nothing could be farther from the truth. I am simply saying that God is no longer

---

[24] Mat. 2:5; 4:4, 6, 7, 10; 11:10; 21:13; 26:24, 31; Mark 1:2; 7:6; 9:12, 13; 14:21, 27; Luke 2:23; 3:4; 4:4, 8, 10; 7:27; 19:46; 24:46; John 6:31, 45; 12:14; Acts 1:20; 7:42; 15:15; 23:5; Rom. 1:17; 2:24; 3:4, 10; 4:17; 8:36; 9:13, 33; 10:15; 11:8, 26; 12:19; 14:11; 15:3, 9, 21; 1Co. 1:19, 31; 2:9; 3:19; 9:9; 10:7; 14:21; 15:45; 2Co. 4:13; 8:15; 9:9; Gal. 3:10, 13; 4:22, 27; Heb. 10:7; 1Pe. 1:16

"breathing out" his revelation to man. That process is complete. God is now preserving what He initially gave by inspiration.

One writer stated that inspiration "resides" in the autographs. But again, inspiration is a process and not an attribute. It doesn't "reside" in anything. Inspiration is a word which tells us how we got the Bible. It is not an attribute. Perfection is an attribute. Indestructibility is an attribute. Inerrancy is an attribute. The Bible is perfect, indestructible, and inerrant because it was inspired by God. Inspiration is the process through which God imparted to man his infallible, inerrant, incorruptible message. But inspiration doesn't "reside" anywhere. As a process, it is complete.

Some would seek to make a point of the present tense – "All scripture **is** [emphasis mine] given by inspiration of God. . .(2 Timothy 3:16). However, in the Greek text, "is" isn't there. The word has been placed in italics, which means the translators inserted it to clarify the meaning of the text. Think of it this way. If we make the bed, and then some time later someone says, "Hey, did you make the bed?" We may answer quite simply, "Yes, the bed is made." We are no longer in the process of making the bed but it IS made!

Also consider that King James Version English generally uses "be" + the past participle for a past or perfective idea. For example, 1 John 4:2 states, "Every spirit that confesseth that Jesus Christ **is** [emphasis mine] come in the flesh is of God". It is the rare person that would claim that this means something more than Jesus coming in the past with results that continue in the present. But I mention this because there are a few folks out there that do!

Notice that the translators did not say, "all scripture is being given by inspiration". Why didn't they do this? Since we don't have their notes we cannot say with any certainty, but I believe it is because of the context. Paul was merely seeking to emphasize the qualities of the scriptures, not give a definition of inspiration. The process of God breathing out his words so that holy men of God could record them is called "inspiration". The end result of inspiration, what has been recorded, is scripture.

Yet at the same time, since the Holy Spirit was in control of the pen, the writers did not write something that would contradict the truth – they wrote something that reveals it. The translators, understanding that the qualities to which Paul was referring are all presently true, used present tense "state-of-being" verbs to translate this point.

Others stretch the meaning of the verse to say that the King James Version must be inspired because if it isn't, then it can't be called scripture. Should we argue the point of whether a translation can legitimately be called scripture? Not yet. We still have much to say concerning inspiration first.

Faithful, accurate, formal-equivalent translation of God's preserved words into any language, English or otherwise, does not in any way diminish the purity, authority, or any other attribute found in the apographs[25] that come as the result of inspiration. Thus, any accurate translation, King James Version included, communicates the truths originally given by God through the process of inspiration.

Years ago I was teaching a young adult Sunday School class when one of my students accused me of believing that the King James Version was not the Word of God because I made the statement that a translation is not inspired. But when you really think about it, how can a translation be inspired if inspiration is a process by which God delivered his message? What we have today is a faithful and accurate translation of what God gave. But this is not inspiration. It isn't even preservation. In reality, we would have to refer to this as either transmission or translation. But it could never be called "inspiration" because inspiration is a process which was completed when the last New Testament writer wrote the last word.

So what does this mean? Does this mean that an accurate translation is not the Word of God? Absolutely not! Any accurate translation, whether it be the King James Version or any other[26] may rightly be referred to as "the Word of God"[27]. Notice that I said, "any accurate translation". Some folks would accuse me of being a bit broad in my statement. But if I am broad, then the King James translators were VERY broad. Notice what they wrote:

*"Now to the latter we answer; that we do not deny, nay we affirm and avow, that the **very meanest translation** [emphasis mine] of the Bible in English, set forth by men of our profession, (for we have seen none of theirs of the whole Bible as yet) containeth the word of God, nay, **is** the word of God. As the King's speech, which he uttereth in Parliament, being translated into French, Dutch, Italian, and Latin,*

---

[25] An "apograph" is a copy of the original "autograph". In the context of a discussion concerning Greek or Hebrew texts, any reference to the autographs is a reference to the very document penned by the writer whereas apographs are the copies made from the autograph.

[26] By this we mean that there may be translations in other languages that are just as much the Word of God as the King James Version as long as they are an accurate translation of the Textus Receptus. I do not believe that any other English translation is as good as the King James Version, and thus, I stand by the King James Version as the Word of God for English speaking people.

[27] See APPENDIX B for a discussion of the term, "Word of God".

## IN DEFENSE OF THE TEXTUS RECEPTUS

*is still the King's speech, though it be not interpreted by every Translator with the like grace, nor peradventure so fitly for phrase, nor so expressly for sense, everywhere. " (THE TRANSLATORS TO THE READER, Preface to the King James Version 1611)*

As these incredible scholars have so rightly stated, a translation may not be done "with like grace" or "fitly for phrase" or "expressly for sense", it is still the Word of God because it is a representation of God's message. So a translation might not be the best, but we don't necessarily need to refer to it as "heretical" until it can be shown to be such! But again, terms are very important and should not be confused.

### IMPORTANT PASSAGES ON INSPIRATION

#### 2 Timothy 3:16 - Four Chief terms

2 Timothy 3:16 contains four critical terms that must be considered as we seek to define inspiration. First of all is the word, "pasa" or "all". In the context by which Paul penned it, it refers to the Old Testament canon which Timothy had been familiar with from a young age (2 Tim 3:15).

Keep in mind that Timothy did not have the original manuscripts penned by the Old Testament writers. He had copies at best. Since Paul refers to what Timothy had as "scripture", and then goes on to explain that all scripture is given by inspiration, then we can firmly believe that even copies, because of God's preservation, are as good as the originals themselves. As far as the Old testament scriptures were concerned, the process of inspiration was complete but God did not allow any of his Word to grow weaker or perish away!

At the time that the book of 2$^{nd}$ Timothy was written, all of the New Testament books which were written by Paul had already been written. However, the statement made in 2 Tim 3:16, 17 is speaking of books that existed at the time that Timothy was a child, hence, the Old Testament scriptures. However, in principle, it also extends to the New Testament by virtue of the very fact that the New Testament is scripture as well. Note the following verses which validate the New Testament as scripture as well as the Old Testament:

**1 Timothy 5:18** *For the scripture saith, Thou shalt not muzzle the ox that treadeth out the corn. And, The labourer is worthy of his reward.*

How does this validate the New Testament as scripture? This particular passage is not found in any Old Testament passage. It is a quotation of Luke 10:7. Paul, in quoting from the Gospel of Luke, refers to it as "scripture". In other words, Paul called the Book of Luke scripture! And since Acts is a continuation of Luke, an argument could be made for considering it along side of Luke in the same regard.

Also consider 2 Pet 3:15,16.

> **2 Peter 3:15-16** *And account that the longsuffering of our Lord is salvation; even as our beloved brother Paul also according to the wisdom given unto him hath written unto you;* **16** *As also in all his epistles, speaking in them of these things; in which are some things hard to be understood, which they that are unlearned and unstable wrest, as they do also the other scriptures, unto their own destruction.*

According to this passage, Peter fully understood that some of the writings of Paul were to be considered on the same level as "the other scriptures". When Peter says, "the other scriptures", he is speaking of the Old Testament.

The point is simply this. By comparing scripture with scripture, we have a biblical basis for declaring the writings of the New Testament equal to the Old Testament in its claims as "scripture".

Another important word is "graphe" which is translated in 2 Tim 3:16 as "scripture". Based upon this word, we may confidently state that it was not the writers, but the writings which were inspired. This contradicts the false notion that God gave ideas to the writers and allowed them to express the ideas as they felt necessary. It also eliminates the notion that just because a particular epistle was penned by Peter, Paul, or any other writer, that it is on the same level as the scriptures themselves.

We know for a fact that Paul wrote other letters that are not included in the New Testament. For instance, Paul refers to an earlier letter that he had apparently sent to the Corinthian believers in 1 Cor 5:9:

> *"I wrote unto you **in an epistle** not to company with fornicators:"*

So even though it was penned by Paul, it was not considered "scripture" and was not included in the canon by first or second century believers.

Some would argue that although God promised to preserve his words, he did not promise to preserve them through any particular manuscript or language. In order to be consistent with this view, we must relegate preservation to general doctrinal teachings and not the very words themselves. If not, then we are left with the insurmountable task of trying to determine which readings are inspired and which teachings are spurious. Since there are thousands of differences between the thousands of extant manuscripts, the task would be near to impossible. This becomes even more obvious when we consider that some of the readings only occur in one manuscript or another. In other words, there are readings, which are often referred to as "independent" readings, which have no support in any other source. So how is one to know whether or not it should be included or not?

However, the truth of inspiration deals, not only with doctrine, but with the very writings themselves. Remember, not all that was inspired was necessarily true. (The words of Satan – Gen 3:4) The word, "graphe", which literally means, "writings" points to each word as God gave it and not merely the ideas or doctrinal teachings of the writers.

The third term of importance is the word "Theopneustos". This is a compound of two different words. "Theo", from "theos" means "God. "Pneustos" means "breathe or wind". The root of this word is "pnuo", which according to Strong's Concordance, means "to breathe hard, that is, breeze: - blow." Thus the idea of inspiration is that God literally breathed out the words that were recorded. As we have already noted, it does not mean that God breathed into the words. But rather, God breathed out the very words that were recorded. Note the wording of Matt 4:4.

> ***Matthew 4:4*** *But he answered and said, It is written, Man shall not live by bread alone, but by every word that proceedeth out of the mouth of God.*

Every word proceeded out of the mouth of God. This is in accordance with the teaching that inspiration means "God-breathed". This is the same idea that David expressed in 2 Sam 23:2, when he said,

> ***2 Samuel 23:2*** *The Spirit of the LORD spake by me, and his word was in my tongue.*

The word "inspiration" is derived from the Greek word "theopneustos" (2 Timothy 3:16), meaning literally "God-breathed". The English word, "inspiration" seems to imply that God breathed "in" something; whereas the true meaning of the Greek word is that God breathed "out" something. So what difference does that make?

If we say that God breathed into something, then that would mean men wrote the words and then God "breathed into" them. This would naturally lead to the idea that God merely approved of what men had written but did not literally dictate the exact words that He wanted us to have! But if we say that God "breathed out" the words, then man becomes merely a vehicle by which God records his exact words.

Of course, the translators could not use the word "exhale" because the word "exhalation" does not properly describe the concept either, even though it would be more etymologically correct! Inspiration is neither a spontaneous idea nor enthusiasm, as some would assert.[28]

This also does not imply a mindless or mechanical action or the suspension of the cognitive abilities of the writers. It is very clear from a basic examination of the various books of the Bible that the writings of Paul differ in style from the writings of John. The conclusion that we are led to is that God, knowing the background, education, and style of each person, used them so that his exact words could be conveyed to mankind.

There is one more passage in the Bible that uses the word "inspiration" and that is found in Job 32:8:

> ***Job 32:8*** *But there is a spirit in man: and the inspiration of the Almighty giveth them understanding.*

Here, the word "inspiration" is translated from the Hebrew word "neshamah". This word is translated "breath" or "breathe" in 14 passages. The interesting thing to note is that it is also translated as "blast", referring to the breathing out of air in several passages as well. So, just as we found in 2 Tim 3:16, we are dealing with the idea of something that is breathed out. Inspiration never describes something that is breathed into.

Again, as far as the exact mechanics are concerned, we are at a loss to explain exactly how the process of inspiration occurred. Nevertheless, this is the clear assertion of scripture and we believe it by faith!

The fourth word of importance is "ophelimos" or "profitable". We should note that the scriptures are profitable because they are inspired. Some have tried to reconstruct the verse to read "All scripture that is inspired. . ." or some facsimile thereof.[29] If we were to accept this translation, then we must assume that there are two classes of scripture – those that are inspired, which are profitable, and those scriptures which are not inspired and not profitable. But the

---

[28] That is certainly true, used in the Biblical sense. However, inspiration can have those connotations when used, for example, with secular literature.

[29] This type of interpretation can be found in: *1901 American Standard Version*, (Oak Harbor, WA: Logos Research Systems, Inc.) 1994.; Adam Clarke's Commentary on the Bible, Adam Clarke, LL.D., F.S.A., (1715-1832); The People's New Testament (1891) by B. W. Johnson as well as other sources.

construction of the Greek does not support this view. It literally says, "All scripture is God-breathed".

### 2 Pet 1:19-21 – The Operation of Inspiration

Another important passage to the teaching of inspiration is 2 Peter 1:19-21:

> **2 Peter 1:19-21** *We have also a more sure word of prophecy; whereunto ye do well that ye take heed, as unto a light that shineth in a dark place, until the day dawn, and the day star arise in your hearts:* **20** *Knowing this first, that no prophecy of the scripture is of any private interpretation.* **21** *For the prophecy came not in old time by the will of man: but holy men of God spake as they were moved by the Holy Ghost.*

The Apostle Peter not only indicates the origin of scripture, but also adds a description of how it was produced. God used holy men. Holy men would not claim to write the words of God unless it were true. Otherwise, they could not be called holy men. Neither would holy men include their own thoughts or message with God's message. Therefore, since God used holy men, we can rest assured that what they wrote was nothing more and nothing less than what God directed.

The question could always be raised as to whether we can consider the writers of the scriptures as truly holy. I think it can be shown that they were certainly men of great depth, deep experiences, and religious character. We understand that true holiness is a characteristic imparted by God and that no one is holy in and of himself. If we seek to hold these men up to this standard, then no one would be qualified to write the scriptures! The point that Peter seeks to make is that they were men of pure character, who, having been justified by faith, and guided by the Spirit of God, were counted holy in the sight of God, and thus, able to transmit his very words to paper.

The Holy Ghost moved these men. The Greek word for "moved" is "phero". According to Strong's Concordance, it has the idea of "to bear" or "carry". Thayer's Greek definitions state that the word means, "to carry, to bear, to bring forward". In light of these explanations, the word clearly means that the writers were "carried along, borne up by" the Holy Spirit. These men did not speak for or of themselves, but only as the Spirit gave them utterance. They could not proceed along the lines of their own personal thoughts or ideas. They were supernaturally guided by the Holy Spirit so that the things that they wrote were exactly what God wanted to say. Nothing more, nothing less!

### THE APPLICATION OF INSPIRATION

## IN DEFENSE OF THE TEXTUS RECEPTUS

A proper understanding of inspiration must also include a discussion of exactly how inspiration should be applied in our determination of the correct manuscripts. To what extent do we carry the doctrine of inspiration? Can we consider accurate copies of the original manuscripts as "inspired"?

Does inspiration extend to translations provided that those translations are faithful and accurate to the original texts? What about derivative inspiration? In other words, can a translation be inspired because it derives its inspiration from the Greek and Hebrew texts?

And how exactly does inspiration operate? What was the process that God used? How much were the writers aware of what was happening to them? Was it a mechanical process or a mere passing on of thoughts from the mind of God to the mind of man?

The extent of inspiration is simply understood as applying to the original autographs only. Why? Because Inspiration is a process by which God used holy men to record his words. When the last verse of the last book was finished, inspiration ceased.

Also, since the scriptures teach "verbal-plenary inspiration"[30], then it must certainly apply to each word written in the original autographs. Not even one word could have been inserted at the whim or desire of the writer. Neither could the writer be at liberty to leave any part of the message out. God did not give the writers a general thought or subject and then allow them to write as they pleased. God guided each and every word selection that the writers made so that the end result was exactly what God wanted.

But, inspiration cannot extend to copies because inspiration is a process which was completed when the original autograph was finished. So, does this mean that we can no longer trust the copies? No, it simply means that the technical application of inspiration applies to the originals while the process of preservation applies to the copies. We may trust the copies just as fully as we can the originals because God has preserved the very words exactly as he gave them! Therefore, we should not speak of the copies as inspired in the same sense that we speak of the originals.

And just as inspiration cannot extend to the copies, inspiration does not extend to a translation either[31]. Many Bible scholars teach that since the original

---

[30] In short, this means that God literally breathed out each individual word that was written. It also means that all parts of the scriptures were equally inspired and are equally preserved by God.

[31] A number of King James defenders use the term "derivative inspiration" in the sense that the King James Version derives its inspiration from the Textus Receptus. But again, inspiration is not an

text is inspired, a faithful translation derives its inspiration from the original texts. I know that these fine men have a high regard for the Bible and mean well. They want us to have a complete trust in our Bibles. But theologically, this cannot be so. First of all, as we so often must reiterate, inspiration is a completed process. As such, it cannot extend beyond the original autographs.

Secondly, and this is a very crucial point, we don't even have the original autographs penned by the hands of the writers. This means the copies from which we take our translations aren't inspired but merely a perfect preservation of the originals! The copies can stake no claim to inspiration since inspiration is a completed process. Thus we must conclude that the copies, provided that they are faithful and complete, are divinely preserved.

But keep in mind that preservation is also not an attribute. It also is a process by which God ensures that each word that he gave exists unchanged to every generation. So, if we say that a translation is not inspired because inspiration is not an attribute, then we must also conclude that translations are not preserved because preservation is not an attribute either. Add to this the fact that God preserves what he gave. God gave us his words in Greek and Hebrew and thus, he preserves his words in those languages.

But now let's be practical. Many pastors and teachers, myself included, speak of the scriptures as being inspired, or preserved, and rightly so. In the same way, I can refer to my cup of coffee in this way. "This cup of coffee is made." But I do not mean that it is in the process of being made. I mean that it is already made and I now have the blessing of drinking of its full qualities! I am in no way saying that we should no longer speak of the copies or even a faithful translation in that way. I am simply saying that there is a difference between general terms and technical terms and when we apply the doctrine of inspiration, we need to use the technical terms in order to avoid error.

As to the question of exactly how inspiration operated, we cannot be sure. It belongs to the realm of faith. Many have tried to explain how the writers were "moved" or in what measure they understood what was happening. As to how they were moved, we do not know. The scriptures merely state that they were moved but offer no explanation as to how this occurred.

---

attribute. It is a process. I understand their desire to defend the King James Version but the approach is not theologically correct.

## IN DEFENSE OF THE TEXTUS RECEPTUS

As to the subject of whether or not the writers understood what was occurring, there are three logical combinations[32]. Either they knew they were writing under the process of inspiration or they didn't. Either they understood what they wrote or they didn't. These are the factors, and when combined, we come up with three possible combinations. What's more, it appears from the words of the scriptures themselves that all three possibilities occurred.

The first possibility is that <u>the writers knew their writing was inspired and they understood the message</u>. There are 854 places in 815 verses in the scriptures where we find the statement "saith the LORD" showing quite clearly that the writer understood that he was recording a message from God himself. While we cannot say that the writer understood everything they wrote when they said, "Thus saith the Lord", it is quite obvious, that in many cases, they clearly understood the message. Additionally, it is obvious that the writer knew he was speaking under the control of the Holy Spirit as in 2 Samuel 23:2 where David very clearly states, "The Spirit of the LORD spake by me, and his word was in my tongue."

Logically, if a writer knew he was writing under inspiration, he would be very careful not to insert his own thoughts or words as if they were on par with God's words. Keep in mind that the writers of scripture were holy men. A holy man would not claim "thus saith the Lord" unless thus saith the Lord!

The second possibility is that <u>the writers knew their writing was inspired but they did not understand the message</u>. Obviously, the writers did not always have perfect knowledge of what they wrote, for we are told in 1 Pet 1:10, 11:

> *"the prophets have enquired and searched diligently, who prophesied of the grace that should come . . .Searching what, or what manner of time the Spirit of Christ which was in them did signify, when it testified beforehand the sufferings of Christ, and the glory that should follow."*

In other words, they wrote what God moved them to write but did not really understand what was written.

We should also consider the fact that if the writers were merely given an idea or subject to write upon, they would have written what they knew and therefore had full understanding of what they wrote. But in the case of verbal-plenary inspiration (every word inspired - all equally inspired) it is not only

---

[32] There is a fourth possibility that the writers did not know they were inspired and they did not understand the message but I could not find a biblical example. I have therefore concluded that this is not a biblical possibility.

possible, but quite probable that a finite man would be moved to write something from an infinite God which he simply could not comprehend!

The third possibility is that the writer <u>did not know the writing was inspired but understood the message</u>. For example, as Paul wrote upon the subject of marriage he clearly states in 1 Cor 7:25, "I have no commandment of the Lord: yet I give my judgment" but yet 15 verses later, as he wraps up the subject he ended by saying, "I think also that I have the Spirit of God" (1 Cor 7:40).

There are various interpretations on what exactly Paul meant when he wrote these two phrases, but I think the best interpretation is to take the statements literally. Paul began by saying, "Now, this is not God's command specifically, but here is my personal judgment on the matter". Then he ends by saying, "But I think I have been given this message by the Spirit of God". In this case, we would expect the writer to make the kind of statements mentioned above.

But we must remember that one's understanding of inspiration does not change the reality of God's operation. In 1 Cor 7:6 Paul wrote, "But I speak this by permission, and not of commandment." He is referring to the words of verse 1-10 where he gives out some very simple and clear directions concerning who or when one should be married. We find another similar statement a few verses later in 1 Cor 7:12, "But to the rest speak I, not the Lord". Apparently Paul, at this point, thinking he was speaking of his own accord, gives advice concerning marriage between believers and unbelievers. Yet we know now that it was given under the inspiration of God.

The inspiration of scripture touches on every truth expressed in the Bible -- whether this is a theological truth, a scientific truth, or a simple statement of fact - regardless of the subject. This naturally implies that every statement of fact in the scriptures must be true since it issues forth from a God that cannot lie. But what do we mean by "true"? We do not mean that everything the scripture says is true without context! For example, the lies of Satan in the Garden of Eden (Gen 3) are certainly not true. However, their occurrence certainly is! There are plenty of examples in which statements are made in scripture which certainly were not true. We should also keep in mind that the Bible is recorded in "laymen's terms". It is not meant to be a treatise on science or history. Thus, we should not be confused or concerned by statements such as, "the sun went down" (Gen 15:7, etc.), "So the sun stood still" (Josh 10:13), "four corners of the earth" (Rev 7:1), and so on. We need to keep in mind that in the time that the scriptures were being recorded, scientific language would not have been understood anyway! Can you imagine Paul's generation trying to understand "DNA strands", "relativity", or "quantum physics"? The thought is almost laughable!

There is also a difference between inspiration and importance. All scripture is equally inspired but all scripture is not equally important. For example, it is very obvious that it is far more important to know that Jesus came to save the sinner (Luke 19:10) than to know that there were five porches on the pool of Bethesda (John 5:2). Both statements are equally inspired but they are obviously not equally important. Critics would immediately cry, "If God said it, then it is important!" That is certainly true but again, we are not denying that it is important. We only point out that some things are more important than others. It is understood that God had a reason for telling us that the pool had five porches. We may not know why, but there is a reason. But the fact still remains that you cannot get to heaven through the knowledge that the pool had five porches. But knowing that Christ came to save sinners is infinitely more important for this has an eternal impact!

Thus, a proper understanding of inspiration is foundational to the issue at hand. Second to this, and in my estimation, equally important, is the doctrine of preservation. In order to grasp the complexity of the issues surrounding the Greek and Hebrew manuscripts, we must begin with the basic framework of the truths of inspiration followed by a clear understanding of the doctrine of preservation. It is upon these two great doctrines that our position in this debate will be based. So at this point, let's take a look at preservation and its application to the issue at hand.

## IN DEFENSE OF THE TEXTUS RECEPTUS
**PRESERVATION**

If all we had were the principles of inspiration, we would not have enough information to make a sound choice concerning the Greek (or Hebrew for that matter) texts. Thankfully, the doctrine of inspiration does not stand alone for it has as its companions several other important and relevant truths by which we can make logical, biblically based choices concerning which text is to be preferred above the others. Depending on your understanding and application of these two important doctrines, you will be led to definite conclusions concerning the Greek and Hebrew texts.

The whole issue concerning Bible texts, and by extension, translations, hinges on the doctrine of preservation. Either God preserved his word or he did not. If he did not, then it does not matter which textual family you prefer and we cannot be sure if we have the uncorrupted Word of God. If he did not, then God did not keep his promises to preserve his word. And we shall see later that God made ample promises concerning the doctrine of preservation.

But since we believe that God **most certainly did** preserve his word, then we must now define what exactly we mean by preservation. Did God preserve the exact words that he gave? Or did he merely preserve the ideas or main gist of what he gave? Since we have already clearly stated our belief in verbal-plenary inspiration, we can logically assume that God would preserve his exact words. Beyond this, there is ample Scriptural evidence pointing to this very fact!

So how we define "preservation" will determine, in a large part, how we will respond to the subject of textual criticism. This will in turn define our position, on the texts themselves which will then also greatly affect how we view translations.

The subject of textual criticism itself is really nothing more than a determination of "if" or "how" to apply the principles of preservation to the extant manuscripts. This is why it is so crucial to have a biblical understanding of this doctrine.

Many, if not most, modern textual critics have approached the issue of textual criticism from a purely historical or academic perspective. This makes the foundation of their decisions either personal education or logic. Therefore, many have come to conclusions which may appear to be rational or academically sound, but are not really balanced because, in order to correctly approach any issue concerning the word of God, we must begin with the foundation of faith – what we believe about what the Bible says concerning itself. From this position, we then examine all evidence in the light of biblical principles. If there is a contradiction between our belief and the scriptures, then we are to conclude that the biblical principles are right and all other opinions are wrong. Biblical principles always take precedence over human logic and understanding.

Why must this be our approach? This MUST be our approach because the Bible is not like any other book. It claims to be the message from God and therefore is a book to be approached from the aspect of faith. It saddens me to see how some Bible teachers ridicule others for taking a faith-based approach to the textual issue. In one case, a certain textual critic who even supports the Textus Receptus from a logical and academic standpoint somewhat ridicules another because his approach is faith-based. But in reality, a faith-based approach does not negate the other. Provided that the academic and logical approach does not violate scripture, it is a valid argument and should be used in stating our case. However, it cannot be the main argument!

Any approach that either rules out or contradicts a faith-based approach to the textual issue must be rejected on the grounds that it is humanistic and thus anti-God. Let's stop and think about this for a moment. Our faith is the whole reason why we discuss the manuscripts at all! If the Bible were simply an ancient book of stories and anecdotes, then word-for-word transmission would cease to be so important.

If the Bible is just another book, then who really cares whether there are differences? Who cares if something was added or something was mistakenly edited out as long as the general ideas or the writer is kept intact? Why should we care if the Bible is simply a book from the hands and hearts of men? What makes one man's opinions any better than another man's opinions? But if the Bible is truly from God, then it really matters! And we better make sure we have it right!

Much of the disagreement today, tends to be more semantic than concrete. Where two people can both agree in the end result, how they arrived at their conclusion could be, and in many cases, is very different. For example, some refer to the King James Version as "the Inspired Word of God" while others would rather say "The Preserved Word of God". Others would simply say that the King James is a faithful and accurate translation. Then there are yet others who would argue that all three statements are simultaneously true.

There are also many different arguments concerning the nature of preservation. Does God preserve his word? Does God preserve his Word in only one manuscript? Does God preserve every word or just the main ideas? Does preservation demand accessibility to what God has given? These questions, and many others, boggle our minds day-in and day-out! But these questions have been answered by God himself in his Word. Additionally, theologians and scholarly men have written abundantly (especially in recent years) upon this very issue.

But we do not follow Dr. So-and-So. We must base our beliefs concerning God's Word on the Word itself. This is a faith-based approach. In the course of this book, history and science will be used to support our conclusions. But ultimately, these are merely supporting evidences that what the Bible says about itself is true. So it all comes down to an issue of faith. Do we believe that God can do and did do what he promised? As we shall see, God has amply promised to preserve his Word and clearly did just that!

As we speak of preservation, what we are really speaking of is the divine safeguarding of the manuscripts, and manuscript evidence. As we study preservation, we are unavoidably drawn into a discussion of the thousands of extant documents, where they came from, who wrote them, how old they are, how readable or trustworthy they are, and so on.

And if you will think about it for a few minutes, the answers to many of these questions will ultimately fall upon the decisions of "textual critics". Most of us don't know enough about history, geography, or biblical languages to enter into a discussion of such magnitude. Does this mean my faith in God's Word must now rest in the hands of other men? No, because the promises of preservation are placed in the hands of all men to believe. God keeps his promises. All we need to determine is exactly what God promised, to what does his promise apply, and whether or not we are willing to believe Him!

Bible preservation refers to the biblical doctrine and historical process by which God has kept his word pure from corruption after he gave it by inspiration to man. Therefore, if we are to truly understand the extent of preservation, we must also consider doctrinal and historical principles.

## FOUR VIEWS CONCERNING PRESERVATION

As we discussed the different viewpoints concerning inspiration, we noted that it is almost impossible to place every person's position in a category. Some positions fit very well. But, due to the nature and ability of man to be inconsistent, and sometimes down-right contradictory in his beliefs, it is next to impossible to adequately state every position on preservation. However, for the sake of academic clarity, I present to the reader the following four positions as being a basic discussion concerning the doctrine of preservation.

***First there is complete unbelief.*** Those who hold this view doubt that God could divinely inspire his word to man at all. They may agree that a historical figure named Paul, James, or Peter could have written the documents but they

## IN DEFENSE OF THE TEXTUS RECEPTUS

certainly do not believe that those men received this information from God! In their minds, the Bible is simply a moral or religious treatise and nothing more.

They may also believe that somehow, even the original documents, written by the apostles themselves, are even further marred by imperfection. There may be a number of contributing factors which leads a person to this position:

A person may be an Atheist. If a person does not believe in God at all, he will never believe in a book that is said to have come from the heart of God! In an Atheist's mind, since there is no God, then the Bible is simply a collection of the writings of men and therefore of no special or divine significance.

Or a person may also be an Agnostic. An agnostic would take the position that it is impossible to know God, if he really does exist. So then how could such a God give his exact words to any man? And how can we know what God said at all?

***A second position is that the scriptures are perfect in the originals but not perfect in any other existing manuscript or text.*** The reasoning is that God certainly COULD preserve his word but chose to allow minor corruption. Or, they simply do not believe it is possible for God to keep his Word. The two angles of thought are different but the results are the same. In either case, they can never really be sure that what they have is in fact, exactly right. Usually, this group will acknowledge that the majority of the text is correct but they think that some of the "less important" passages or phrases are in some way different.[33]

***The third position is a belief in perfect preservation of the Greek text but not necessarily in a perfect translation.*** However, I would argue that if a translation is faithful and accurate in a formal-literal[34] sense that it is just as good as the Greek manuscripts from which it was translated. In essence, this is a true statement.

***The fourth position is a belief in a perfect translation.*** Usually, this position is stated in reference to the King James Version of 1611. This position is normally derived from one of three approaches. Either, they believe that the

---

[33] We acknowledge that since all scripture was given by inspiration, it is all important. If it were not important, then God would not have given it!

[34] Formal equivalence attempts to render the original document into the receptor language in a word-for-word manner. While we acknowledge that sometimes it may take two words to convey the meaning of one Greek word, or vice versa, the goal is to be as literal to the text as possible. A formal equivalent translation does not ignore the necessity of readability or idiomatic expression, but chooses to convey the duties of proper interpretation to the reader!

## IN DEFENSE OF THE TEXTUS RECEPTUS

King James Version was somehow "double-inspired" and therefore superior to the Greek manuscripts, or that God providentially guarded and guided the King James Version translators so that their work is just as perfect as the Greek manuscripts and thus meets the conditions necessary to be called "preserved." Thirdly, that the translation is a perfect copy of the Greek and Hebrew by virtue of the excellence of the translators. In any case, the end result is a belief in the absolute superiority of the King James Version.

Before anyone jumps to the false conclusion that I am somehow attacking the King James Version, let me state quite clearly that I believe whole-heartedly that the King James Version is God's Word in the English language. Some would seek to point out the few-and-far-in-between differences between the Greek Textus Receptus and the English of the King James Version and then seek to discredit the trustworthiness of the King James Version altogether. But this is quite rash and very illogical.

And yes, there are differences between the King James Version and the Textus Receptus. I don't deny that. In fact, any time that a translation from one language is made into another language, there will be minor differences. But those differences are not vital and have no doctrinal impact whatsoever.

In fact the majority of the differences are the result of verb tense changes or conjunctions that were not translated into the English language because they were simply not needed for proper understanding or flow of the text. Some people are uncomfortable with this thought but in actuality, it makes no difference since the <u>meaning</u> that is to be conveyed by the Greek word is clearly there. Thus, although a word may not have been carried over into English in a literal sense, its meaning is still conveyed by the context of the passage. Some of the other differences are not nearly as easy to dismiss but at the same time, do not change the sense of the passage.

For the record, I believe whole-heartedly that the King James Version is a faithful and accurate translation of God's Word to the English-speaking world. However, with a little study, you can find differences between the King James Version and the Textus Receptus. As someone has rightly said, "things that are different are not the same." Although we will discuss this issue later in greater detail, for the present, let's just consider one example:

> ***2 Corinthians 12:15*** *And I will very gladly spend and be spent for you; though the more abundantly I love you, the less I be loved.*

One interesting fact concerning this verse is the word "you". In the Greek Textus Receptus, we find the following:

## IN DEFENSE OF THE TEXTUS RECEPTUS

*εγω δε ηδιστα δαπανησω και εκδαπανηθησομαι υπερ των **ψυχων** υμων ει και περισσοτερως υμας αγαπων ηττον αγαπωμαι*

For most, it is "Greek to me"! And as the translators of the King James did a wonderful job of translating, what I am about to share means virtually nothing as far as doctrine or understanding are concerned. However, nestled in the middle of all those Greek words is the word "ψυχων" (psuchon). This word is normally translated as "life" (41 times) or "soul" (58 times). Yet, here, following Tyndale's translation[35], the word is rendered "you". In actuality, it could have also been rendered, "for your souls". Does it make a difference? Not really. There is absolutely no vital difference or doctrinal impact. But it should be sufficient to illustrate the fact that there can be differences.

I am told that in Washington DC there is a placed called the Bureau of Standards where the "perfect" yardstick is kept sealed away. I have never seen this yardstick but I know that every other yardstick being produced is in some way imperfect. But the consumer does not care, and in most cases, isn't even aware of the imperfections because they are for all intents and purposes, invisible to the average user. And so it is with the King James Version as compared to the Greek and Hebrew text. There may be some minor differences but for the average user, the differences are totally insignificant and if question ever arises, we can always appeal to the standard, the Greek and Hebrew text for absolute clarity.

### IMPORTANT FACTS CONCERNING PRESERVATION

There are two very important facts to remember as we study the doctrine of preservation. The first is the fact that God has promised to preserve His Word. But secondly, we should note that there have also been those who would seek to corrupt the scriptures as well. And both of these facts are operating at the same time. And seeing that these two forces are happening simultaneously, it is very important to have a good understanding of preservation so that we may come to the proper conclusions. So we should take a look at these two forces as they are explained in the scriptures.

---

[35] Actually, it should come as no surprise to find such similarities between Tyndale's work and the King James Version. Somewhere close to 90% of the two translations are the same. The King James Version translators felt no need to fix what was not broke!

## IN DEFENSE OF THE TEXTUS RECEPTUS

Let's first consider the fact that God promised to preserve his Word. This act of preservation does not extend merely to the doctrinal ideas of scripture, but to the very words themselves. Consider Psalm 12:6-7:[36]

> ***Psalms 12:6-7*** *The words of the LORD are pure words: as silver tried in a furnace of earth, purified seven times.* ⁷ *Thou shalt keep them, O LORD, thou shalt preserve them from this generation for ever.*

I realize that there is a long-running scholarly debate about whether or not this passage refers to God preserving his words or God preserving his people. But just for the sake of argument, let's say that this refers to God preserving his people. And if this is the correct understanding, then why did God tell us about his words being pure and tried?

The purpose would obviously be so that his people would know that God made some pure and tried promises about keeping them safe. And the obvious reason for bringing this up is so that his people would know that when God gives us his words, they are going to be fulfilled. So by extension, if these verses do not directly teach the doctrine of preservation, they at least demand it to be so in practice!

Most of those who deny these verses teach preservation appeal to the Hebrew in order to point out the differences between the masculine pronouns of verse 7 and the feminine nouns in verse 6. Their point is that in Hebrew, gender must always match. But this is simply not the case.

Here is a statement by Thomas Strouse, Dean of the Emmanuel Baptist Theological Seminary of Newington, Connecticut, which clearly explains this point:

*"... the rule of proximity requires 'words' to be the natural, contextual antecedent for 'them.' Second, it is not uncommon, especially in the Psalter, for feminine plural noun synonyms for the 'words' of the Lord to be the antecedent for masculine plural pronouns/pronominal suffixes, which seem to 'masculinize' the*

---

[36] There really are a lot of verses that impact the doctrine of preservation. And quite a number more that practically require preservation in order to be efficacious. (Dt 4:1-2; Proverbs 30:5-6, Mark 13:31, Revelation 22:18-19, Matthew 5:18, Matthew 24:35, Psalm 119:89, Psalm 119:152, Psalm 12:6-7, Psalm 100:5, Matthew 4:4, 1 Peter 1:24-25, Psalm 119:160, Job 42:2, Luke 16:17, Isaiah 40:8, etc.) Understand what I am saying here. Some of these verses have a direct bearing on preservation. Others cannot be possible without preservation. The three verses I used in my book are not possible without preservation. The strongest support is Psa 12:6-7 so I dealt more specifically with that passage.

verbal extension of the patriarchal God of the Old Testament. Several examples of this supposed gender difficulty occur in Psm. 119. In verse 111, the feminine plural 'testimonies' is the antecedent for the masculine plural pronoun 'they.' Again, in three passages the feminine plural synonyms for 'words' have masculine plural pronominal suffixes (vv. 129, 152, 167). These examples include Psm. 119:152 ('Concerning thy testimonies, I have known of old that thou has founded them for ever')..."(Dr. Thomas Strouse, "Article Review," April 2001)

In another article, Dr. Strouse explains further:

"...the psalmist deliberately masculinized the verbal extension of the patriarchal God of Scripture. As this phenomenon exists throughout the Tanak, the interpreter has been prepared for gender discordance in this psalm. Furthermore, the examples set forth in Ps. 119 preclude the exegete from moving prior to the closest antecedent for the sake of gender concordance. It would be ridiculous to seek gender concordance where this phenomenon occurs in Ps. 119:111, for then the gender concordance would teach that the psalmist rejoiced in his heart for the masculine plural "wicked" (v. 110). Again in v. 129, applying the exclusive "rule" of gender concordance, the psalmist promised to keep the Lord's masculine plural "precepts" (v. 128)--a synonym for "testimonies" which is the closest antecedent anyway. Observing v. 152, the psalmist recognized that the Lord had "founded" what "forever"--the feminine plural "testimonies" or masculine plural participle "they that follow after mischief"? Finally, what did the psalmist love "exceedingly" (v. 167)? Was it the feminine plural "testimonies" or the masculine plural participle "they which love" (v. 165)?

Throughout the Hebrew OT, pronouns usually correspond to their antecedent nouns in proximity and with gender/number concordance. However, a phenomenon exists, which fresh Hebrew exegesis observes,17 that feminine synonyms for Word of God are addressed by masculine pronouns for the apparent purpose of masculinzing the patriarchal Jehovah God." (The Permanent Preservation of God's Words:Psalm 12:6-7 Expanded)

And something else that we should consider is that if this verse is speaking of God preserving the poor and needy then why did they all die and why were so many martyred? Don't be so literal, you say? Well, we can't have our cake and eat it too. Either God did not preserve those individuals or else he did. And if he did, where are they? In heaven, you say? But wait a minute! Wasn't David speaking of God's protection in a very literal and personal sense?

No, it makes much more sense to simply refer to the closest antecedent. God will keep them (the words). God will preserve them (the words). I find it interesting that those who hold to the position that God was referring to keeping his people will refer to the Hebrew in order to prove their point. Typically, they don't believe this is a promise for preservation and yet they are, in effect, saying, "Look at the Hebrew because that is really where we can find the answer. The English is no good but God's standard in Hebrew will clear it all up for us." Aren't they really just admitting that there is a preserved standard whereby we are to measure things when they do this?

But let's stay on course here. What we are saying is that God said his words - plural - are pure and tried. It is not just the thoughts in general. It is not just the promise of protection in general. But each and every word is pure.

There are many aspects of preservation that are brought out in this verse. We could begin by making a case concerning the inerrancy of scripture (pure words). We could also make a case for inspiration (words of the LORD) but our purpose here is to make a case for preservation.

In these two verses we find that the very words of God are kept by God himself. Strong's Concordance states this about the Hebrew word for "keep":

*"A primitive root; properly to hedge about (as with thorns), that is, guard; generally to protect, attend to, etc.. . . ."*

The meaning is obvious. God has placed a hedge about his Word. He guards, protects, and attends to it so that what I am reading in this century is exactly what he gave 2000 years ago!

There are some who would take issue with the statement that the "very words" of God are protected. However, there is ample scriptural support for such a position:

> **Matthew 5:18** *For verily I say unto you, Till heaven and earth pass, one jot or one tittle shall in no wise pass from the law, till all be fulfilled.*

> **Luke 16:17** *And it is easier for heaven and earth to pass, than one tittle of the law to fail.*

> **John 10:35b. . . .** *and the scripture cannot be broken;*

Actually, the context of these verses is not primarily the teaching of preservation so much as they teach the sovereignty of God's plan, will, and truth. Yet, the principle of preservation is clearly stated and we can see that God has placed a protective limitation to his revelation to man. And nothing can change this!

The second truth that we must consider as we look at the doctrinal foundation of preservation is the fact that there have always been those who have sought to corrupt the truth. 2 Corinthians contains two different statements concerning the state of religion in Paul's day:

> ***2 Corinthians 2:17*** *For we are not as many, which corrupt the word of God: but as of sincerity, but as of God, in the sight of God speak we in Christ.*

It would appear that even in the first century, there were those who were bent on presenting a corrupted message. Presumably, this would be both verbally as well as in written form. At one point, Paul warned the church of Thessalonica that there existed those who apparently had sent a letter as if they were him. Note the following:

> ***2 Thessalonians 2:1-2*** *Now we beseech you, brethren, by the coming of our Lord Jesus Christ, and by our gathering together unto him, 2 That ye be not soon shaken in mind, or be troubled, neither by spirit, nor by word, nor by letter as from us, as that the day of Christ is at hand.*

Although we do not know exactly who wrote the false letter, it is very clear that it was filled with false teachings. In the very next verse Paul stated, "Let no man deceive you by any means," which makes it very clear he is referring to some communication they had received from a false teacher. Albert Barnes, in commenting on this verse, mentions that it was common for forgeries to be made in the first century. He then goes on to cite several passages where Paul apparently signed the epistles he wrote as a signet of authenticity. (2 Thess 3:17; Gal 6:11; Philem 1:19)

The second statement in 2 Corinthians is in Chapter four. It also alludes to first century corruption of the gospel message:

> ***2 Corinthians 4:2*** *But have renounced the hidden things of dishonesty, not walking in craftiness, nor handling the word of God deceitfully; but by manifestation of the truth commending ourselves to every man's conscience in the sight of God.*

Thus, there were those who corrupted the scriptures as well as others who mishandled the scriptures. This may have taken either the form of verbal false teaching of what had been written or it may have been in the form of physically changing what was written. No doubt, both conditions existed. Most commentators date the book of 2 Corinthians between A.D. 54 and A.D. 60. This means that the Devil was already busy seeking to corrupt the Word of God before the New Testament was even finished!

## IN DEFENSE OF THE TEXTUS RECEPTUS

The first corruption of God's message to mankind was actually begun long before the Bible was written. It was in the Garden of Eden where we find the serpent (Satan) intentionally bringing doubt and confusion to the mind of Eve by first questioning the commandments of God:

*Genesis 3:1b "Yea, hath God said, Ye shall not eat of every tree of the garden?"*

This was followed by the <u>un-intentional</u> corruption[37] of God's command on Eve's part when she responded with:

*Genesis 3:2-3 We may eat of the fruit of the trees of the garden: But of the fruit of the tree which is in the midst of the garden, God hath said, Ye shall not eat of it, neither shall ye touch it, lest ye die.*

Actually God never said not to touch the fruit. He simply said not to eat it. Why did Eve say this? Did Adam wrongly explain God's command to her? Did she read into God's command? Was she adding a stipulation in order to ensure obedience? We can never know for sure what Eve was thinking but the fact remains that she changed, i.e. corrupted, God's command! What were God's exact words?

*Genesis 2:16-17 And the LORD God commanded the man, saying, Of every tree of the garden thou mayest freely eat: But of the tree of the knowledge of good and evil, thou shalt not eat of it: for in the day that thou eatest thereof thou shalt surely die.*

So we find that Eve, however unknowingly, added to God's Word by saying, "neither shall ye touch it". Then she weakened the force of the command by saying "lest ye die" when God said, "thou shalt surely die"! I am sure that she was sincere. No doubt, she meant well. But in the end, God's command was corrupted nonetheless!

So, Eve was not intentionally changing God's words but yet there have been many more people throughout history who have intentionally changed God's Word. One example is Marcion.

Marcion lived in the early first century and was condemned by the church at Rome as a heretic. Irenaeus states that Polycarp, a personal disciple to the

---

[37] I realize that some of my fellow brethren believe that ALL corruptions of the scriptures are a Satanic attack upon the Word of God. And, although I agree, we have to at least be willing to acknowledge that some corruptions are unintentional, just as Eve's was. She may have been instigated by Satan, but her corruptions were not intentional.

Apostle John, called Marcion "the firstborn of Satan"![38] Marcion rejected all the books of the Bible except for 10 of Paul's epistles. He also included 'the Gospel of Marcion" which replaced the Biblical Gospels of Matthew, Mark, Luke and John!

There are many reasons why men would desire to change God's words. In many cases, the changes are effected as a result of a desire to adhere to some false teaching (as was the case with Marcion). Since the scriptures condemn their heresies, some go so far as to change the scriptures in order that their heresies can go undiscovered. Note the following quote for the 2nd Epistle to the Corinthians:

> *2 Corinthians 11:1-4 Would to God ye could bear with me a little in my folly: and indeed bear with me. For I am jealous over you with godly jealousy: for I have espoused you to one husband, that I may present you as a chaste virgin to Christ. But I fear, lest by any means, as the serpent beguiled Eve through his subtilty, so your minds should be corrupted from the simplicity that is in Christ. For if he that cometh preacheth another Jesus, whom we have not preached, or if ye receive another spirit, which ye have not received, or another gospel, which ye have not accepted, ye might well bear with him.*

In this passage we find that false teachers were presenting, and are still presenting a false Christ, by a false spirit, through a false gospel. A couple of examples of this would be the writings of Mormonism or the New World Translation done by the Jehovah's Witnesses.[39] The saddest part of this passage is that Paul seemed concerned that the Corinthians might follow after the false teachers!

Another reason for intentional corruption is religious tradition:

> *Mark 7:10-13 For Moses said, Honour thy father and thy mother; and, Whoso curseth father or mother, let him die the death: But ye say, If a man shall say to his father or mother, It is Corban, that is to say, a gift, by whatsoever thou mightest be profited by me; he shall be free. And ye suffer him no more to do ought for his father or his mother; Making the word of God of none effect through your tradition, which ye have delivered: and many such like things do ye.*

---

[38] Irenaeus, Adversus Haereses, III.3.4.

[39] According to the doctrines of Mormonism, Jesus is a created being, spirit brother of Satan, and had numerous wives! The Jehovah's Witnesses believe that Jesus is "a god" but certainly not Jehovah! In other words, they deny the doctrine of the trinity.

## IN DEFENSE OF THE TEXTUS RECEPTUS

In this case, it is not so much the written word that is corrupt but the interpretation or application of the scriptures. False philosophies or false science can very easily be added to this list! (Col.2:8; I Tim.6:20-21)

In modern times, the biggest corruptors of God's word seem to come from the world of scholarship. This has taken the form of higher criticism.[40] The scriptures warned of a day in which man would become academically adept yet never really grasping the truth because God is rejected. Ever learning, yet never able to come to the knowledge of the truth.

Sadly, those who claim to be correcting the word are actually corrupting it. In many cases, those who are guilty of corrupting the scriptures, sincerely think they are doing a good work! 2 Peter 3:15, 16 states:

> *2 Peter 3:15-16 And account that the longsuffering of our Lord is salvation; even as our beloved brother Paul also according to the wisdom given unto him hath written unto you; As also in all his epistles, speaking in them of these things; in which are some things hard to be understood, which they that are unlearned and unstable wrest, as they do also the other scriptures, unto their own destruction.*

The focus of textual criticism is centered on examining the many differences in the extant manuscripts. These differences take one of three forms – diminishing the text, adding to the text, and changes to the text.

In many cases, the text has been diminished (shortened). In fact, one of the main objections to the Critical Text, which was assembled by Brooke Foss Westcott and Fenton John Anthony Hort, are many missing verses, words, etc. Naturally, the counter argument is, "No, our text [Critical Text] does not have subtractions. Your text [Textus Receptus] has additions!"

And this is exactly the kind of logic that has been employed by both sides of the issue. In fact, one writer went so far as to cite the Western text of Luke

---

[40] Textual analysis, as a practice, is not wrong. In fact, no matter which Greek text you choose, you are in some way employing a form of textual analysis to come to your position. The problem arises when the biblical framework of inspiration, preservation, and canonization is either ignored or ridiculed. Some very good works have been written concerning textual criticism from a historical aspect, such as Wilbur Pickering's book entitled, "The Identity of the New Testament Text". He shows very clearly why the Textus Receptus is supreme from a historical and logical basis. He intentionally does not emphasize the supernatural aspects of inspiration and preservation until the very end of the book in order to show that even from a purely textual basis, the Textus Receptus is superior. Although we do not consider Pickering guilty of overlooking a faith-based approach, it is nevertheless true that any work that does not consider the supernatural act of God's preservation will ultimately be lacking in proper focus, foundation, and understanding.

24:53 as saying, "blessing God" while the Alexandrian text said, "praising God". So the scribes of the Byzantine text combined them into one reading "praising and blessing God". His point was that the Byzantine text had additions. But isn't it just as logical to assume that the others had subtractions?

But what about Matt 17:21, 18:11, 23:14, Mark 7:16, 9:44, 9:46, 11:26, 15:28, Luke 23:17, John 5:4, Acts 24:7, 28:29, and Romans 16:24? These verses are normally left out of the text of modern Critical Text editions but with a footnote or other indication that it is missing. These verses are found in the majority of manuscripts[41] and yet are left out. Why? The "scholars" believe that the verses in question were added for various reasons and so they felt the need to "purify" the text. And against all logic, they not only used a minority of manuscripts to make their supposed corrections, but also used inferior manuscripts!

Later, as we discuss the principles of preservation, we will show that historically, the Textus Receptus is God's preserved words and therefore the standard by which all other manuscripts are to be compared. In light of this truth, the Critical Text is riddled with "subtractions" from God's Word. According to one count, there are over 1900 omissions between the two texts. Note these warnings from the scriptures concerning the intentional shortening of God's Words:

> **Deuteronomy 4:2** *Ye shall not add unto the word which I command you, <u>neither shall ye diminish ought from it</u>, that ye may keep the commandments of the LORD your God which I command you.*
>
> **Deuteronomy 12:32** *What thing soever I command you, observe to do it: thou shalt not add thereto, <u>nor diminish from it.</u>*
>
> **Revelation 22:19** *And if any man shall take away from the words of the book of this prophecy, God shall take away his part out of the book of life, and out of the holy city, and from the things which are written in this book.*

Often defenders of the Textus Receptus mention that the Critical Text weakens a doctrine by not including references to deity, etc. One example that

---

[41] One person pointed out that these verses are not found in the majority of the over 5000 manuscripts. What he did not realize is that most of the manuscripts are nothing more than just a few lines of text or maybe a few pages. Very few manuscripts actually contain the sections that these passages come from anyway. And for the manuscripts that do contain these portions, I must reiterate, these verses are found in the majority of the manuscripts.

could be cited would be Luke 4:4. In the Textus Receptus, and the King James Version, it reads thus:

> και απεκριθη ιησους προς αυτον λεγων γεγραπται οτι ουκ επ αρτω μονω ζησεται ο ανθρωπος αλλ επι παντι ρηματι θεου *(And Jesus answered him, saying, It is written, That man shall not live by bread alone, but by every word of God.)*

But the Critical Text states:

> και απεκριθη προς αυτον ο ιησους γεγραπται οτι ουκ επ αρτω μονω ζησεται ο ανθρωπος *(it is written, man does not live by bread alone)*

The argument is that since the phrase "but by every word of God" is missing from the Critical Text, it may not deny inspiration, preservation, or whatever doctrine you seek to support by this passage, BUT it certainly limits the amount of support you could use this verse for!

Another example that is often pointed out is the doctrine of the ascension. Although it is very commonly believed and taught by fundamentalists, there are actually relatively few passages which teach it. (John 20:17; Heb 9:24; Mark 16:19; Luke 24:51; Acts 1:2-11) The first two mentioned references are fairly indirect and although they can be used to teach about the ascension, they are limited. The final three contain the full record of the ascension itself. Yet The Critical Text does not contain Mark 16:19. Luke 24:51, after years of being in brackets, or taken out altogether, has finally been added back to the NA28. So now we have left two clear passages teaching the ascension. From Mark we learn that immediately after the ascension Christ sat on the right hand of the Father. This is not mentioned in Acts 1. Luke 24:51 mentions that while He blessed them He was taken up out of their sight. This is also not mentioned in Acts 1. Thankfully, SOMEBODY involved with the NA28 realized that it should be in the Bible. It's too bad that it was held in suspicion for so long though.

Thus, to say that the textual variants do not affect doctrine is misleading, or at the very least, naive. It stands to reason that it is much easier to teach a certain Bible doctrine when there are numerous verses in support of it. Add to this the simple fact that when younger or less knowledgeable believers see these differences in the various translations, it may very well have a negative effect on their assurance in God's Word. And I understand that the issue is truth and not the assurance of younger believers. But this does not change the fact.[42]

---

[42] I am not advocating the practice of hiding difficult issues in the area of textual criticism simply for the sake of making believers feel secure. I believe that pastors, preachers, and Bible teachers

## IN DEFENSE OF THE TEXTUS RECEPTUS

A second type of corruption takes the form of textual additions. It is estimated that there are approximately 467 additions to the Critical Text. And again, we must take note that the Bible unequivocally warns against such actions:

> ***Deuteronomy 4:2*** *<u>Ye shall not add unto the word</u> which I command you, neither shall ye diminish ought from it, that ye may keep the commandments of the LORD your God which I command you.*

> ***Proverbs 30:6*** *<u>Add thou not unto his words</u>, lest he reprove thee, and thou be found a liar.*

> ***Revelation 22:18-19*** *For I testify unto every man that heareth the words of the prophecy of this book, <u>If any man shall add</u> unto these things, God shall add unto him the plagues that are written in this book: And if any man shall take away from the words of the book of this prophecy, God shall take away his part out of the book of life, and out of the holy city, and from the things which are written in this book.*

A third type of corruption is changes to the text. These changes are normally in the form of word substitutions. This is where one word is substituted for another word in the text itself. In some cases, at least initially, it does not appear as if doctrine is directly affected, yet in other cases, the changes can lead to heretical teachings.

A good example of this would be John 1:18. In the Critical Text, the Greek μονογενης θεος (only begotten God) whereas the Textus Receptus reading is μονογενης υιος (only begotten Son). Some would state the case that if the Critical Text reading is accepted as valid, then we must come to the conclusion that God had a parent. However, the Textus Receptus reading points out that the Son of God is the only begotten of the Father. Others argue that this is simply a play with semantics since Jesus is God. In either case, the point is, a substitution in the text has occurred which may very well affect doctrinal teachings.

The clear warning of scripture is that not only should the words, NOT be added to or subtracted from, they should also NOT be diminished. By one count, there have been upwards to at least 3,185 changes to the text of the New Testament alone.

---

need to help Christians understand the issues. There are plenty of heretics out there which will do their very best to make a shipwreck of a young believer's faith. But at the same time, there is a proper timing for the instruction. You simply can't teach multiplication until the student can grasp simple addition!

## IN DEFENSE OF THE TEXTUS RECEPTUS

Now, the crux of the matter is based upon the premise that God has divinely preserved every word that he gave. If we do not believe this, then any discussion concerning the two texts becomes a matter of personal preference based upon man's intellect or will. But since we firmly believe that God has preserved, not just the basic truths, not just the general ideas, not just the basic thoughts, but even the very words themselves, we must conclude that one text or the other has been corrupted.

Therefore we can simplify it by noting a basic "if/then" clause in our rationale. If we belief that God has preserved every word that he initially gave by the act of inspiration, then we are forced to come to the conclusion that one text or the other is corrupt. But both texts cannot be pure because they are certainly not the same in every word!

The only other option would be to conclude that our understanding of plenary-verbal inspiration is somehow flawed. And there are those who believe just that way. They contend that even though God promised to preserve each word, He never said that it would all be in the same text. But this is a very confusing and complex position because we are left with nothing to guide us into what is the pure reading and what is corrupt. How is a person to know? Again, rather than having concrete, scripturally based evidence, we are left to our own intellect, opinions, theories, and suppositions. Any variant in readings become subject to human reasoning and choices based upon everything but the promises of God.

As we have already pointed out, there can be numerous reasons why the text may become corrupted. But at this point, the reason why corruption exists is not the real issue. The fact that corruption exists is plain for all to see. The facts are simple. God has preserved his word. The two texts are different. Only one of them can qualify as God's preserved scriptures.

### IMPLICATIONS OF PRESERVATION

As with all Bible doctrines, there are necessary implications to each one. So after coming to a sound understanding of preservation, how should we apply this truth to the area of textual analysis? In what ways can this vital doctrine help us in understanding the textual issue? And how can this fundamental doctrine help us know whether or not the Textus Receptus should be considered God's preserved word to every generation?

The answers to these questions is not so difficult when we consider that we have almost 2000 years of history to observe which helps us see very clearly which family manuscripts bear the divine stamp of authority. All we need to do is determine which manuscripts were being transmitted and used by God's people in every generation.

Let's remember that the scriptures were given to God's people who being guided by God are instrumental in His preservation of the scriptures. So just as God used human instruments in the process of inspiration, He also used, and is using, human instruments in the act of preservation. Note the following passages:

> ***Acts 7:38*** *This is he, that was in the church in the wilderness with the angel which spake to him in the mount Sina, and with our fathers: who received the lively oracles to give unto us:*

According to this verse, God gave his "lively oracles" or "λογια ζωντα" to his "church" or "εκκλησια". We understand that the church did not come into existence until the New Testament time period but the Greek word simply means "assembly". Some seek to teach that the "church" existed in the Old Testament from this passage but that is not what Steven was speaking of. In actuality, his point was that the local assembly of the Jews had received the scriptures from God himself but yet disobeyed them. He goes on to point out that they had been greatly blessed to be given the message of God. This same thought is again expressed in Romans 3:2:

> ***Romans 3:1-2*** *What advantage then hath the Jew? or what profit is there of circumcision? Much every way: chiefly, because that unto them were committed the oracles of God.*

Again, it was a great blessing to be a part of the Jewish nation because they were given the Word of God.

We understand that both of these passages refer to the Old Testament scriptures but the same principle can be seen concerning the New Testament scriptures as well:

> ***1 Timothy 3:15*** *But if I tarry long, that thou mayest know how thou oughtest to behave thyself in the house of God, which is the church of the living God, the pillar and ground of the truth.*

According to this verse, the church is both the "pillar" or "στυλος" (a post of support) and the "ground" or "εδραιωμα" (support) for the truth. Truth does not come from the church; rather the church supports the truth. Thus, if you want the truth, you should be able to find it in the midst of God's people.

So, along with the doctrine of inspiration, the doctrine of preservation becomes an important key to choosing the right text. It is unfortunate that so many good people misunderstand the doctrine of preservation. And because of this, the term "preservation", "preserved", etc is often misapplied or simply misused. It is not uncommon to hear good men speak of translations as being "preserved". But in a strict biblical sense, preservation only applies to what God has given by inspiration, and not what has been accomplished by translation. The past 2000 years have seen many translations come and go – some of the translations were good, some not so good. But the fact is, none of them were preserved.

Some would argue that the King James Version is over 400 years old so it MUST be preserved. I would simply make two observations on this thought. First, the fact that the King James Version is over 400 years old is a testimony to its beauty, accuracy and influence. No one can take away from that. God's people would not have used it for so long if they felt it was not trustworthy. So its age becomes a great witness to its superiority as a translation.

But its age does not prove "preservation" because this is a Bible doctrine which only should be applied to what God gave by inspiration. What we have by translation is no doubt the best this world has ever seen, but we cannot use words like "inspiration" or "preservation" to describe a translation.

But let's not lose sight of the fact that languages are "containers" of that which has been eternally settled in heaven. It does not matter whether the "container" is in the form of a faithful translation, or the original languages themselves – the truth has not lost its identity or power in any way. Insofar as a translation is a faithful and accurate representation of the exact message God gave, it can be called God's inspired and preserved Word[43].

Yet we must understand that as we make this statement, we are not referring to the containers themselves but to the truth of God within the containers, as revealed to man. What we are discussing is <u>how we choose the container</u>. Or, to put it another way, we are discussing the condition of the container and whether or not it has effectively preserved its contents (the truth). Personally, I want to drink my spiritual drink from the container that has ALL the truth and ONLY the truth. Thus, I stand upon the Textus Receptus, and by extension of its faithfulness and accuracy to the Textus Receptus, the King James Version.

---

[43] Lest I be misunderstood, let me clarify. There are some very bad translations available in any bookstore. No one would deny that. Anyone who has done some studying in this area, regardless of whether they hold to the Textus Receptus or the Critical Text, would readily admit that there are some pretty bad translations out there. But even a bad translation, inasmuch as a phrase, verse, etc., is a faithful representation of what God gave, can contain portions of God's Word. Thus, we may make the statement, "This translation is not God's pure Word but contains God's Word."

## IN DEFENSE OF THE TEXTUS RECEPTUS

Some would argue that the King James Version has not "come and gone" like so many other translations, which proves it has been inspired or preserved. Although this is true, we should at least be honest enough to admit that if Jesus tarries his coming, English, like the Greek language spoken by the whole Roman empire in the first century, could become a dead language.

Remember that Koine Greek is very different from what is used in Greece today. Today, there are really two forms of Greek in use (and I use the term "in use" loosely) Katharevusa and Demotic. Katharevusa was an attempt to purify the Greek language from foreign influence, and so was based largely on Koine and Byzantine forms of Greek. But nowadays Greece and Cyprus favor Demotic Greek as their official language.

Demotic Greek, is related to Koine Greek but with a large number of grammar and vocabulary changes. The result of these changes has made it very difficult for a modern Greek person to read with understanding anything written in Koine Greek. They may be able to recognize certain words but since the grammar is so radically different, would not be able to relate the words to each other. The result would be that though they understand the words, they cannot understand the meaning. Let me furnish you with an example:

*"In opposition right and left of the iris and upper side white self-consolation becomes known at is low three hundred securities three hundred easy is bad far in the tubular school register the fact that as inside upper three hundred."*

Got that? Add to this the fact that modern words have crept in, foreign vocabulary has crept in, spelling has changed - a modern Greek reader would really have his hands full!

So again, modern English may be very popular and very well known today; just as Koine Greek was in the first century. But in time, languages evolve. English is no exception. If this ever happens, then the King James Version will become a historical glory to be cherished and studied by those who are schooled in ancient languages.

Let's be reminded of what the biblical definition of preservation is. We define preservation as the act of God whereby He protects His text from any possible corruption from its very inception forevermore. Therefore, in order for us to claim that a translation is preserved, we must first believe that it was inspired. If we cannot claim inspiration for a translation, then we cannot claim preservation for a translation. So when we speak of preservation, we are not referring to a translation but to the Greek and Hebrew texts.

## IN DEFENSE OF THE TEXTUS RECEPTUS

Biblically, we must limit preservation in the strictest sense to the Greek and Hebrew manuscripts because those were the languages and words that God chose to deliver his message to man. As we apply the doctrine of preservation to the Greek manuscripts, several questions must logically and biblically be answered. Namely, "If a text had fallen out of use, does it still meet the criteria of "preservation"?" "Can we reasonably claim to have the pure Word of God if we do not know what the originals looked like?" These questions and others should be answered.

As we seek to keep a balanced view, we should objectively examine both the Textus Receptus and the Critical Text with the same criteria. So let's begin with the most basic and logical question of all.

### *Are The Original Autographs necessary?*

It would surely be nice if the original autographs, from the very hands of the apostles and other New Testament writers, were somewhere resting protected in some vault, museum, or else, were discovered buried in some previously undiscovered cave. However, the original autographs have never been found. At least, if they have been found, there was no indication that it was an original autograph. And even if we had found an original autograph, how would we know it was an original? No one knows what the handwriting of any of the writers looked like anyway. Therefore, the whole issue concerning the necessity of original autographs is a moot point.

Most likely, the original autographs no longer exist. It is no longer even a question of whether or not they will ever be discovered. They probably do not exist at all. In all likelihood, because they came from the hands of the apostles, one of two things happened. They were either worn out from frequent use and then discarded or else copied and destroyed.

It was not uncommon among Jews to copy an Old Testament manuscript, and after having verified that the copies were accurate, to destroy the original manuscript. Since the Jews made up a large segment of the New Testament churches, it is possible that they followed already established practices and did the same thing with the original autographs.[44]

---

[44] www.biblegateway.com/resources/asbury-bible-commentary/Masoretic-Text; Another source stated that the Jews would bury or store the old manuscripts in a genizah which was basically a storage area or cemetery. Then, later, the manuscripts would be properly disposed of by burning. (http://claudemariottini.com/2008/06/06/on-bibles-and-manuscripts/)

## IN DEFENSE OF THE TEXTUS RECEPTUS

But it is more likely that the first century Christians used, circulated, and copied the original autographs so much that they simply wore out. Remember that the first century documents were written on papyri. It is not a very durable material and we should not expect to find an abundance of papyri 2000 years after it was written anyway. As you may note in Appendix A, there are less than 150 extant papyri manuscripts in existence. Quite a few of the ones that we have discovered are either in poor condition, fairly useless, or else found in areas which helped to preserve their physical condition.

But let's not lose sight of the original question. The original question is – Are the original autographs necessary? Is there a valid and essential need to locate them? Once again, how we answer these questions will depend largely on our belief and understanding of the doctrines of inspiration and preservation.

So to put it plainly, we believe that God delivered his message to man by a process that we call inspiration. This process insured that what God wanted the writer to record was indeed exactly what they wrote.

From the point where God's process of inspiration ceased, we know that God preserved those exact words so that they would be free of corruption, whether such corruption be intentional or unintentional. The result is a text that could be used by each proceeding generation exactly as God gave it! Consequently, if we were to find an original autograph from the very hands of Paul himself, it would look no different than what is in use today. So to answer the original question - no, we do not need the original autographs. If the scriptures were inspired and preserved, then we have exactly what God gave.

One Critical Text supporter, in his own smug way, supposed that those of us who hold to the Textus Receptus should then explain which copy of the Textus Receptus bears the stamps of God's approval. In other words, "Since there are differences between the various revisions of the Textus Receptus, which one is pure?" I wonder what this same person would say if I were to turn the question around and ask the same thing concerning the Critical Text? After all, it has been revised too. But then again, they have no problem with this because in their way of thinking, they are still trying to recover what they believe may have been lost.

Modern textual critics, especially those who are seriously lacking in a solid belief or understanding of the process of inspiration and principles of preservation, are constantly on the look-out for "older and better" manuscripts. The logic behind this is that the closer we come to the original writings, the more pure the manuscript will be. But this presupposes that all copies have been corrupted and that God did not honor his promises to preserve his word.

## IN DEFENSE OF THE TEXTUS RECEPTUS

However, as you can see from the following chart, this is not at all a logical approach to this issue. In fact, it can be shown that several of the textual families[45] date back to the 2nd century:

| Name | Date | Text Type |
|---|---|---|
| P[98] | 2nd | Unclassified |
| P38 | 2nd-3rd | Western |
| P64 | 2nd | Alexandrian - originally given a 3rd-century date by Charles Huleatt, the one who donated the Manuscript to Magdalen College, and then papyrologist A. S. Hunt studied the manuscript and dated it to the early 4th century. But in reaction to what he thought was far too late a dating for the manuscript, Colin Roberts published the manuscript and gave it a dating of ca. 200, which was confirmed by three other leading papyrologists: Harold Bell, T. C. Skeat and E. G. Turner, and this has been the general accepted date since then. |
| P90 | 2nd | Many scholars like to place P90 in the Alexandrian family but it is as much in agreement with the Byzantine family as it is with the Alexandrian family. |

Thus, we can show that there were several existing text types in the 2nd century within 100 years of the writing of the original autographs. The only thing that the age of a manuscript can prove is that it existed. It cannot prove superiority. From the above chart, we can see that numerous text-types were in existence from the 2nd century.

But honestly, are they really text types? Would it not be more realistic to simply speak of them as manuscripts with variants? None of them are very big pieces of papyrus anyway. If the scholars were to be totally honest, they would have to admit that, at least in the case of the manuscripts mentioned in the chart above, there isn't a very large "sample size" to make a concrete determination as to which text type the manuscript should be placed in.

So to answer the question, "are the original autographs necessary" we must give an emphatic, "no". To think anything else would be either to cast doubt or to misunderstand the application of the doctrine of preservation. If we believe that God has preserved his words to every generation, then we must believe that

---

[45] There are some very knowledgeable, and well-respected men who would argue that there really aren't any "families" of manuscripts. Rather, there is one true text and all others are corruptions of that text. Although I understand their point, and even agree. Fundamentally, this would have to be true since God gave the true text first. All of the other manuscripts have a very low percentage of agreement between themselves making it irrational to consider them a family. But throughout this book, I refer to the generally accepted references so that it is clear what point is being made.

*God's Preserved Word to Every Generation*

whatever we have today must be exactly as God gave it. In actuality, if we ever find an original autograph, it will look exactly like the Textus Receptus. If it does not, then God did not keep his promise to preserve his word

## Can Originals be Validated or Verified?

This question is similar to the previous question in that the answer lies in our belief of preservation and inspiration. Again, if God gave us his exact words, should he be rendered incapable to preserve his exact words by any action or beliefs of man? The question is obviously rhetorical. If we have an omniscient and omnipotent God, then he is fully capable of keeping his promises of preservation to the end of time.

From a purely earthly sense (as Paul would say, "I speak as a man"), it would be impossible to validate or verify the original autographs if they cannot be found. The principles of empirical science would require that the autographs be examined in order to verify their readings. Additionally, if the writings of the apostles were found, the chances are good that they would not be in a useable condition, portions unreadable or missing due to deterioration, and we still could not say with 100% certainty that what we use is exactly the same as what the apostles wrote! So from a purely empirical standpoint, it is an insurmountable dilemma!

Therefore, if we are to validate or verify the original autographs, it must be done by the proper application of sound doctrine and faith. Since the Bible is empathetic concerning the doctrines of inspiration and preservation, we are placed in the position of either believing or disbelieving the truth of God's Word. We cannot prove it. It is simply something that we either believe or disbelieve. So the answer to this question hinges on how we view the scriptures.

If we believe that the scriptures are true and accurate, then we would have to say that although we do not have the originals, by virtue of the promises of inspiration and preservation, we already know what they must have said. Therefore, the original autographs are not necessary to a Bible believer in order to validate what they say. The existence of the original autographs is not required.

But, if we do not believe in the inerrancy of the scriptures, any and all doctrines, thoughts, verses, and even individual words contained therein are subject to personal scrutiny and cannot be trusted without empirical evidence. This would be the approach of one who does not believe in pure inspiration or preservation. If we require empirical evidence, then salvation, heaven, hell, angels, devils, or any other unseen factor of our beliefs must be doubted. Since very few people are willing to go to such extremes, it is more logical to simply believe that God has given us exactly what he wanted us to have.

## Proof the TR (Byzantine Text) Was Used in Every Generation

The doctrine of preservation demands that each word and each phrase be, not only available, but also in use by each generation (Psalm 12:6,7). In all actuality, both the Alexandrian Text from which the Critical Text is constructed and the Byzantine Text from which the Textus Receptus was constructed were available but it is clear from history that they were **not** both in use by every generation.

Why do we make such a statement concerning the use of the documents? Well, there are really a couple of reasons. First of all, It is important to note that many religious and non-religious writings have survived through time. Take a look at this chart:

| Author | Date Written | Number of Copies |
| --- | --- | --- |
| Pliny | 61-113 A.D. | 7 |
| Plato | 427-347 B.C. | 7 |
| Herodotus | 480-425 B.C. | 8 |
| Aristotle | 384-322 B.C. | 49 |
| Sophocles | 496-406 B.C. | 193 |
| Homer (Iliad) | 900 B.C. | 643 |

So simple existence does not mean that a manuscript has been in use by every generation. Nor does it validate a manuscript as scripture. But secondly, we have a principle from the Bible itself that informs us of how God delivered his words to men. When God gave man the Old Testament, he gave it to the Jews to keep and propagate.

> *Act 7:38 This is he, that was in the church in the wilderness with the angel which spake to him in the mount Sina, and with our fathers: who received the lively oracles to give unto us:*
>
> *Romans 3:2 Much every way: chiefly, because that unto them were committed the oracles of God.*

In the same respect, we can find several passages denoting that the New Testament was committed to New Testament believers for the keeping and propagation. We are told quite clearly that the church (God's people) is the keeper of the truth:

> ***Jude 1:3*** *Beloved, when I gave all diligence to write unto you of the common salvation, it was needful for me to write unto you, and exhort you that ye should earnestly contend for the faith which was once delivered unto the saints.*

> ***1 Timothy 3:15*** *But if I tarry long, that thou mayest know how thou oughtest to behave thyself in the house of God, which is the church of the living God, the pillar and ground of the truth.*

Some would state that the Alexandrian Text (Critical Text) was obviously in use since the Latin Vulgate agrees most frequently with it. With that being the case, why then do we even bother to ask the question?

It is an important question because it is not a matter of whether or not a translation was in use but whether or not the Greek readings were preserved and in use. After all, God did not inspire a translation. He inspired the original Greek and Hebrew writings.

Historically speaking, the Alexandrian Text fell out of use in the 800s to 1000s. Even after the discovery of the Codex Vaticanus in the 1400s, it was still not used for any translation work until the late 1800s. And why did the Alexandrian text fall into disuse? We cannot state dogmatically because we were not there. But it may have something to do with all of the variant readings.

However, whatever the reason, what is obviously true is that the Codex Vaticanus, a manuscript greatly revered today, was not used by scholars from the 1400s to the late 1800s. Men like Erasmus, Beza, Stephanus, and Cardinal Francisco Jiménez de Cisneros, when constructing their Greek texts, knew about the Alexandrian manuscripts, but chose not to use them. Along with the men who constructed Greek texts, none of the translators during this time used the Alexandrian manuscripts either. And again, no one can say with any certainty why they did not use them but there are certain reasons that could be ruled out.

One supposed reason that has been mentioned is that the Catholic authorities would not allow the Codex Vatican's to be used. This however, is highly suspect for a couple of reasons. First of all, Cardinal Jimenez did his work with the blessings of the Pope himself. If he wanted to use it, no doubt, he could have gotten permission. Erasmus worked independently yet he commanded the respect of nearly everyone because he was considered to be one of the greatest

## IN DEFENSE OF THE TEXTUS RECEPTUS

minds of their time. If he would have asked, most likely he would have been given the codex. yet neither of these men wanted to use it.

A second supposition is that they simply did not know about the codex since it was kept secured in the Vatican archives. But that is precisely the point. If they knew about the codex, they rejected it. If they didn't know about the codex, it wasn't in use anyway. And according to our understanding of inspiration and preservation, in order to meet the criteria, it had to be in use by every generation. This means that the Alexandrian manuscripts, from which the Critical Text was constructed, does not meet the requirements of the above stated criteria. It may have existed, but it certainly was not in use!

On the other hand, the Byzantine text (Textus Receptus) was the only manuscript that was widely in use for hundreds of years.[46] The following information should suffice to illustrate this point:

| Number | Approx. Date | Type |
|---|---|---|
| 02 | 450 AD | Byzantine in the Gospels; Alexandrian Text in the rest books |
| 04 | 450 AD | Mixed text containing Byzantine and Alexandrian Text readings. |
| 016 | 450 AD | Alexandrian Text with one reading in agreement with the Byzantine. Numerous other spurious readings. |
| 026 | 450 AD | Byzantine but also contains Alexandrian Text readings. |
| 069 | 450 AD | Byzantine |
| Papyrus 084, P84 | 500-600 AD | Mostly Byzantine |
| 0253 | 550 AD | Byzantine |
| 0265 | 550 AD | Byzantine |

---

[46] I realize that some of my critics would quickly point out the Textus Receptus as a manuscript had its beginnings with Erasmus in AD 1516. But I am not speaking so much of a single document or codex. I am speaking of the family of manuscripts which we refer to today as being "Textus Receptus". Or as other scholars prefer to say, the "Byzantine" text. Through the course of this book, I will invariably make references to both. But I will try to stick to using "Textus Receptus" when referring to the single codex that has been constructed from the Byzantine family. I will try to use "Byzantine" when referring to other manuscripts in the family but not the Textus Receptus proper.

*God's Preserved Word to Every Generation*

## IN DEFENSE OF THE TEXTUS RECEPTUS

| | | |
|---|---|---|
| 074=064 =090 | 550 AD | Byzantine |
| Papyrus 073, P73 | 600-700 AD | Byzantine |
| 0303 | 600-700 AD | Byzantine |
| 097 | 650 AD | Byzantine |
| 0116 | 750 AD | Byzantine |
| 0134 | 750 AD | Byzantine |
| 07 | 750-800 AD | Byzantine |
| 011 | 800-1000 AD | Byzantine |
| 041 | 800-900 AD | Byzantine |
| 013 | 850 AD | Byzantine |
| 0257 | 850 AD | Byzantine |
| 0272 | 850 AD | Byzantine |
| 0273 | 850 AD | Byzantine |
| 041 | 900-1000 AD | Byzantine |
| 046 | 950 AD | Byzantine |
| 0142 | 950 AD | Byzantine |
| 055 | 1050 AD | Although it have never been categorized, the text is distinctively Byzantine. |

Keep in mind that this is not an exhaustive list. It is merely a sampling to show the availability and use of the Byzantine Text from which the Textus Receptus is derived. The Byzantine Text was clearly available and in use to every generation. If we were to try and construct a chart showing the same thing for the Alexandrian manuscripts, it would become abundantly clear that the Alexandrian manuscript fell out of use between the 800s and the 1000s.

Add to this the fact that the Codex Vaticanus and the Codex Sinaiticus were "lost" during this time period and were not discovered until the 1400s. So no matter how you want to view it, the Alexandrian manuscripts, by all intents and purposes, did not exist. Of course, they physically existed in their respective hiding places, but in practice, they might as well have not existed because nobody wanted to copy them. No one wanted to translate them. No one wanted to use them for anything!

Let me restate that. These two revered manuscripts were written in the 300s, then at some point, were lost. Then later, they were found - in the 1800s for the Codex Sinaiticus and in the 1400s for the Codex Vaticanus. It would appear that they fell into disuse and were forgotten about for at least 1000 years. Then, for the Codex Vaticanus at least, even though it was known to exist, none of the men who worked on the Greek text tried to use it. Why? The manuscripts were not considered to be of value enough to use. One might say that this is simply my opinion. But before my opinion is discredited, somebody needs to present another logical reason why nobody wanted to use these manuscripts.

One author stated that the Byzantine text originated in the middle of the $4^{th}$ century. His point was that it was a text that was somehow constructed around that time period since we don't have any Byzantine manuscripts before that time. His point is not really a fair criticism. Almost half of the extant manuscripts from before the fourth century are mixed texts anyway. So while it may be true we don't have any "Byzantine" manuscripts before the 4th century, we only have a handful of "Alexandrian" manuscripts anyway. We should keep a few other important facts in mind as well.

First, it is possible that Papyrus 90 (P90) dates to 100-200 AD. It is commonly dated to 400-550 AD but more than one independent examination concluded that it should be dated much earlier. Papyrus 90, though it is small and only contains a portion of the Gospel of John, may be one example of the existence of the Byzantine text from the very beginning! Yet the same folks who give it a later date also have concluded that it is Alexandrian.

However, the manuscript is on the internet and easy for anyone who can read Greek to examine for himself. It could just as well be classified as Byzantine as it was Alexandrian. Taking a look at the variants only, it agrees almost equally with the Byzantine Text as well as the Alexandrian Text. But it disagrees with both manuscripts an equal number of times. So Papyrus 90, though it may be ancient, is not conclusive proof of anything, really.

Secondly, we still have the quotations of church fathers from the Byzantine manuscripts which number into the thousands. This shows us that the Byzantine manuscripts were not only in existence, but also in use. So even if we don't have any manuscripts from that era, we still have evidence of their existence. It's kind of like the dinosaurs. We don't have any dinosaurs but we see lots of evidence that they did indeed exist!

## IN DEFENSE OF THE TEXTUS RECEPTUS

Then thirdly, we have a good number of translations which attest to the existence of the Byzantine manuscripts. One could argue over whether or not the translations are accurate but we cannot argue their existence. And again, their existence proves that the Byzantine text not only existed, but it was clearly in use.

The majority of manuscripts after the third century definitely point to a common use of the Byzantine type manuscripts. And again, I need to emphasize that we are not merely talking about availability but we are also talking about common use of the Greek manuscripts.

We mentioned the writing of the early church leaders and existing translations so it may be helpful to take a bit of a closer look before we move on.[47]

### The Writings of Early Church Leaders

There is a type of evidence considered in court cases upon which only a limited judgment can be made. This is called circumstantial evidence. It is called by this name because although it does not prove beyond a shadow of a doubt that a thing is true, it is a very good indicator.

When we speak of circumstantial evidence in relation to the Textus Receptus, we are referring to signs of the existence of the Byzantine manuscripts from which it is taken. In this category we should consider early church writings as well as early translations. These are not primary evidences because they are not Greek manuscripts but at the same time, they clearly illustrate the existence of the Greek Byzantine manuscripts.

Numerous authors cite the fact that quite a few early Christian writers used the Byzantine manuscripts in their writings - Irenaeus (A.D. 180); Clement (A.D. 200); Tertullian (A.D. 150-220); Origen (A.D. 182-251); Cyprian (A.D. 200-258); Chrysostom (A.D. 345 – 407).

In fact, one of the most controversial passages which show a difference between the Critical Text and the Textus Receptus is the last 12 verses of Mark[48]. The passage is included in the Textus Receptus but is not found in the Critical Text because it is not found in the manuscripts from which the Critical Text was taken. This is one major difference between the two texts. Therefore, it stands to reason that if an early church writer quoted from Mark 16:9-20, then they must have been using the Byzantine manuscripts. The following writers did just that!

---

[47] Much of this information will be expanded on later in a section on the History of the Textus Receptus.

[48] See Appendix D for more information on this controversial passage.

## IN DEFENSE OF THE TEXTUS RECEPTUS

From the 2nd century, Papius, Justin Martyr, Irenaeus, Tertullian. From the 3rd Century – Hippolytus, Vincentius at the seventh counsel of Carthage. From the 4th Century – Eusebius, Macarius Magnes, Aphraates, Didymus, Chrysostom, Jerome, Augustine. Although some of these men also quoted from sources other than the Byzantine Texts, the fact that they quoted from a passage found only in the Byzantine text shows that not only were the manuscripts in existence, they were also in frequent use.

By one count, Tertullian, Irenaeus, Hippolytus, Origen, and Clement quoted or paraphrased over 30,100 scripture citations with the majority agreeing with Textus Receptus readings. The resulting evidence from the early church writers alone would lead us to the conclusion that the Textus Receptus was not only in existence, but also was greatly used.

### Early Translations

In addition to the writings of the early Christians, we also have some very important support from early translations. Keep in mind that the Byzantine manuscripts and the Alexandrian manuscripts are significantly different in many places. Some of the differences are additions to the text, some are subtractions from the text, some are substitutions, and some are changes in order or spelling. So the Critical Text and the Textus Receptus are significantly different in thousands of places. Understanding that the Textus Receptus comes from the Byzantine manuscripts and the Critical Text comes from the Alexandrian manuscripts, we would expect that they would also be significantly different in many places.

When it comes to examining a translation to determine its source, those significant differences come in very handy. The translation is compared to the Critical Text and the Textus Receptus to see what matches and then what does not match. In some cases, a translation may simply be wrongly translated. But keep in mind that we have places where several verses are either missing or added, depending upon which text you hold to. But these significant differences in reading become great determining factors. And based upon those differences, it becomes fairly simple to determine which text the translation was taken from.

The Greek Orthodox Bible, is said to have been used from Apostolic times to the present day by the Greek Orthodox Church, The Waldensian Bible (around 120 A.D); the Old Syriac (AD 150-160); The Peshitta (AD 150-170); the Gallic Bible (AD 177); the Armenian Bible (AD 400); the Gothic Bible (AD 330-350); the Palestinian Syriac (AD 450); the Philoxenian Bible (AD 508) – these are all translations from Byzantine manuscripts thereby showing that the

## IN DEFENSE OF THE TEXTUS RECEPTUS

Byzantine manuscripts from which the Textus Receptus was taken, were clearly in existence and in use.

### Lectionaries

One of the most important sources of manuscript evidence comes to us in the form of lectionaries. Basically, a lectionary was a section of scripture that was selected and transcribed for public reading. Churches used lectionaries during worship services.

Now, if churches were to have the same practice today, we would find lectionaries that would be King James Version, others might be New American Standard, others would be New International Version, and so on. It would be very difficult today to determine which Bible is the Bible of choice because we have so many different translations to confuse the issue. But they didn't have that problem in the early church for a couple of reasons.

First of all, the lectionaries are all Greek, or else diglots[49] (Greek/Coptic) because that is what they used in the worship services. So there isn't any difficulty with regard to translations because all of the lectionaries are Greek. And secondly, not only are all the lectionaries Greek, but they are almost exclusively Byzantine[50]. To date, every lectionary that has been examined and classified has been placed into the Byzantine family with the possible exception of Lectionary 1575. So what does this tell us? Since there are over 2400 lectionaries, and so few have any Alexandrian influence at all, we can conclude that the churches preferred the Byzantine manuscripts.

Some would argue that there was influence from Catholicism. Others make the point that more likely, it tells us that the churches of the Byzantine empire preferred their own Byzantine manuscripts, or more likely still, the churches largely unaware of the differences in the manuscripts because the Byzantine manuscripts were all they knew.

But I would remind you that there have always been groups of believers who were not Catholic as well. And it is interesting to me that there is so much Byzantine influence in the lectionaries found in Egypt yet at the same time, so

---

[49] Except for Lectionaries 1993 and 1605, which are triglots.

[50] With that being said, although the lectionaries are all classified as being Byzantine, several of the lectionaries, lectionary 0269 and 1602 for example, contain spurious Alexandrian readings. And we should expect this to be the case with at least a few of the lectionaries since at least four of them were located in Egypt. Lectionary 1575 was said by the Alands to be in remarkably good quality, which, from their perspective may have meant that it is heavily Alexandrian. Since it was part of a codex with Uncial 0129 it is most likely Alexandrian although this has not yet been verified.

*God's Preserved Word to Every Generation*

## IN DEFENSE OF THE TEXTUS RECEPTUS

little Alexandrian influence in the lectionaries found elsewhere. Clearly, the Byzantine manuscripts were preferred and in use by God's people in all parts of the world.

The last official count of manuscripts was placed at 5,686 manuscripts in existence. This is the figure currently reported by the Institute for New Testament Textual Research (INTF) in Münster. However, our own private research has a total of 5,773. Of this number, 2,412 are Greek lectionaries. Almost all of these lectionaries are from the Byzantine family from which the Textus Receptus manuscript is derived.

It is also helpful to remember that the earliest lectionaries are dated as far back as the $6^{th}$ and $7^{th}$ centuries. So, from the 800s until the 1800s, absolutely no other type of manuscript was in use during public worship by God's people!

What does this mean in terms of textual analysis? It simply means that the churches, many which varied in doctrinal position and social influence, all recognized and used the same standard Bible. Some would point out that there are a few extant manuscripts from that time period which were Alexandrian. So logically, it would seem to indicate that at least a few churches may have used manuscripts other than the Byzantine manuscripts. I would have to say that if they did, then they were certainly much different than all the other churches and must have never used lectionaries because none of the lectionaries are Alexandrian. And if these churches didn't use lectionaries, I would have to ask why not?

The reason churches used lectionaries is because Bibles were expensive and few people could actually afford to have their own copy. And since the scriptures are so important to our faith and practice, churches would dedicate a portion of their worship services to public reading of the Word of God. I would just like to point out that any church that didn't have lectionaries probably had a high percentage of Biblically ignorant members simply because they had no scriptures. But given that this is a remote possibility, it is still absolutely impossible to say that this was the common practice!

These lectionaries span a period of over 1000 years of church history. Some would argue that the Catholic Church was in power during a majority of that time and so they seek to discredit the Byzantine family based upon this fact. However, the same crowd remains mysteriously silent when it is mentioned that the Codex Vaticanus and Codex Saniaticus both came from Catholic sources as well! And I would also like to point out that the Catholics were not the only ones using the Byzantine manuscripts. So were all the others! And if we were to be totally honest about it, the Catholics were using the Latin Vulgate which agrees

## IN DEFENSE OF THE TEXTUS RECEPTUS

with the Alexandrian manuscripts in very many places. So it is a bit dishonest from an academic standpoint to say that the Byzantine manuscripts became prominent because of Catholic influence! Historically, the Catholic Church oppressed the use of the Bible by the common man. They believed only the priests had the knowledge to properly interpret the scriptures. If anything, they would have hindered the spread of the Byzantine manuscripts and promoted the use of the Latin Vulgate which, again, agrees with the Alexandrian manuscripts. But the reality is that none of this can be proven to have happened. And in fact, it makes more sense that it did not!

Now, we have covered a lot of ground in our discussion of preservation. We have looked at it from a biblical and historical perspective and come to the determination that God has preserved his words and message to every generation. There are quite a few passages which have a bearing upon the doctrine of preservation, such as, 1 Chron 16:15; Psa 119:89; Isa 40:8; Matt 5:18; 1 Pet 1:23-25, and so forth. God has much to say about preserving his word. Yet he does not specify exactly how he would do it.

But a major point that I think should be reemphasized throughout this book is the fact that God promised to preserve his truth. He never promises to preserve the container that holds his truth. Thus, if we were to find inconsistency in a particular manuscript or translation, it would not shake my faith because I don't personally believe God promised to preserve the container.

There are those who would point to the King James Version and make allegations concerning the translator's word choices. But let's at least be honest enough to admit that *we don't always know why the translators made all the word choices that they made*. What is obvious to us is that they were incredibly brilliant men so before anyone begins to criticize their scholarship, they should ask themselves if they really believe they have found something that over 40 of the best scholars in the world missed. In other words, do we really believe we have more knowledge, for whatever reason, than all of them?

With that being said, the translators were still mere mortals and just as susceptible to making mistakes as anyone else. In fact, in comparing the King James Version to the Textus Receptus we can find some places where we simply do not know why they translated it the way they did. Here is one example:

*Act 19:20  So mightily grew the word of God and prevailed.*

Here, the word in question is the word "God" which is the King James Version's rendering for "kurios" in the Greek Textus Receptus. The problem with this is that kurios is always translated as "Lord", "sir", or "master". It is never translated as "God" (except here). The Greek word for God is "theos". Even a first-year student of Greek can see the difference. So it appears that the word choice made here is simply wrong.

Does it change the meaning? No. Does it impact theology? No. But things that are different are not the same and we would be academically dishonest to assert that the King James Version and the Textus Receptus were a perfect match when they really aren't.

Additionally, it is extremely rare to find perfect synonyms in any language. Words carry with them certain nuances which make even the best synonyms ever so slightly different. Some would argue that we use "God", "master", and "Lord" fairly interchangeably. I would agree but at the same time the words are still different. The real question at hand is whether or not it is acceptable to translate "kurios" as "God" in this context. In order to make the determination we must ask certain questions.

The first being the most obvious, "Is God an acceptable, literal translation of kurios?" By examining the use of kurios in the Bible as well as other 1st century Greek writings, we would have to conclude that it is RARELY done. (I say "rarely" only because of Acts 19:20 and the fact that I have not read every book translated into English from Greek). But given that it may be remotely possible, we would have to find SOMETHING that would lead us to believe it should be different in this one case.

As I look at the scriptures, I find for "word of the Lord":

- λογου του κυριου - Luke 22:61; Acts 8:25; Acts 13:48, 49; Acts 15:35, 36; Acts 16:32; Acts 19:10; 1 Thess 1:8; 1 Thess 4:15 (slightly different but still kurios); 2 Thess 3:1
- ρηματος κυριου - Acts 11:16; 1 Pet 1:25(again, slightly different but still kurios)

For word of God:

1. Mark 7:13; Luke 3:2; Luke 4:4; Luke 5:1; Luke 8:11, 21; Luke 11:28; John 10:35; Acts 4:31; Acts 6:2; Acts 6:7; Acts 8:14; Acts 11:1; Acts 12:24; Acts 13:5; Acts 13:7; Acts 13:44, 46; Acts 17:13; Acts 18:11; Acts 19:20; Rom 9:6; Rom 10:17; 1 Cor 14:36; 2 Cor 4:2; Eph 6:17; Col 1:25; 1 Thess 2:13; 1 Tim 4:5; 2 Tim 2:9; Tit 2:5; Heb 4:2; Heb 6:5; Heb 11:3; Heb 13:7; 1 Pet 1:23; 2 Pet 3:5; 1 John 2:14; Rev 1:2; Rev 1:9; Rev 6:9;Rev 19:13; Rev 20:4

All of these references use "theos" except for Acts 19:20, of course.

I discussed this same issue with a person a few years ago and his answer was that the translators chose this as a translation in order to make it clear that "the word of God" clearly defines that "all the words of God were growing and not just the words of Jesus that were being magnified". A very weak, in fact, fairly nonsensical defense.

How is it any different than the way "word of the Lord" is used in Acts 13:48-49 or any of the other references after that? And I am taking into account that one could make an argument that the other references may refer to some revelation by Jesus personally (although I don't personally believe that to be the case). In either case, I don't think you could get any other meaning out the verse other than the fact that the Word of God was taking root and changing lives.

Now, with all that being said, we have allowed for dynamic translation in other places of the King James (such as "God forbid"). But usually, there are factors that explain why the translators were more dynamic. In this case, there is no reason. At least none that I have been able to find.

To take it down to "sandbox level", we are trying to figure out if the translators should have used "Lord" because it very clearly looks as if they could have and yet did not. We stop just short of saying it was a wrong translation because we do not want to believe there could be an error so we choose to believe it is a dynamic translation instead. But my question is, are we being academically sound and honest when we do this?

So why do I think the translators used "God"? I think they were simply following an established translation which was technically acceptable and yet was already established. It was in the Tyndale, Wycliffe, Geneva, Matthews, and Bishops Bibles already. It had already been accepted. They simply followed suit.

I don't mean to be brutal or blunt here, but I think it is high time that we take a step back and take a good hard look at what we really believe. Are we afraid to say we think the word should be "Lord" simply because we don't want anyone to think we are criticizing the King James? Can we not simply say it is a faithful, accurate, and true translation without having to ascribe to it the quality of inspiration?

Another good example would be Acts 19:37 where the King James Version has "robbers of churches" whereas the Greek says "hierosulous". This is a Greek word made from two other Greek words, "hieron" and "sulaō". The latter means "rob" but the former is always translated as "temple".. If we read the context of Acts 19:37, "temple" would seem to make more sense, contextually. So we have to ask ourselves, why did the King James Version translators use the word "churches" when it is pretty clear that it could have been translated as "temples"? We simply do not know. Personally, I find it hard to believe that men of their caliber ALL missed this obvious difference. Yet, facts are such obstinate things! Again, we don't always know why the translators made the words choices that they made, but I would be hard-pressed to say they made such an obvious "mistake". I believe their word choice was intentional.

My contention is that they had other factors in mind which drove their decisions and since we don't have any of their notes, we will never really know why. Some would say that I am trying to criticize the King James Version which is not true at all. I emphatically believe it to be the best English translation ever done and do not think that a better one could be made.[51]

With that being said, what is it that God inspired? And what does he promise to preserve? He inspired his very words and promised to preserve each word, just as he gave it. So it is not the language of men which bears the marks of inspiration or preservation but the very truth itself. To put it in simple terms, God does not preserve the container (translations, individual Greek manuscripts) but God preserves the exact words of the truth which is contained therein.

---

[51] You may ask, "Since you have just pointed out some areas where the Greek and English don't match, why don't we just fix them and make the King James Version better?" I would say that this was the very thing that brought to us the Critical text and a whole stream of other translations to start with. It all began with someone thinking that it would be okay to "tweak" the King James Version and make it better. I would not want to be responsible for reopening that can of worms. So I will repeat myself. I do not think a better translation can be made.

## CANONIZATION

What exactly is "canonization" and how does it relate to the New Testament text? Canonization is a word used to describe the process of determining which books ought to be included in the Bible and which books should not be included. The word "canon" comes from the Greek word "kanon" and the Greek word is a derivative of the Hebrew word "qaneh".

The Hebrew word "qaneh" means "reed". The word itself is found in Ezekiel 40:3:

> ***Ezekiel 40:3*** *And he brought me thither, and, behold, there was a man, whose appearance was like the appearance of brass, with a line of flax in his hand, and a measuring <u>reed</u>; and he stood in the gate.*

In this passage it is combined with another Hebrew word which is translated "measuring". In biblical times, a reed was often used as a measuring stick as we see in Eze 41:5-8 and Eze 42:16-19:

> ***Ezekiel 41:5-8*** *After he measured the wall of the house, six cubits; and the breadth of every side chamber, four cubits, round about the house on every side. (6) And the side chambers were three, one over another, and thirty in order; and they entered into the wall which was of the house for the side chambers round about, that they might have hold, but they had not hold in the wall of the house. (7) And there was an enlarging, and a winding about still upward to the side chambers: for the winding about of the house went still upward round about the house: therefore the breadth of the house was still upward, and so increased from the lowest chamber to the highest by the midst. (8) I saw also the height of the house round about: the foundations of the side chambers were a full <u>reed</u> of six great cubits.*

> ***Ezekiel 42:16-19*** *He measured the east side with the measuring <u>reed</u>, five hundred <u>reeds</u>, with the measuring <u>reed</u> round about. (17) He measured the north side, five hundred <u>reeds</u>, with the measuring reed round about. (18) He measured the south side, five hundred <u>reeds</u>, with the measuring <u>reed</u>. (19) He turned about to the west side, and measured five hundred <u>reeds</u> with the measuring <u>reed</u>.*

The literal concept of a measuring reed provided the basis for the word's later usage which came to be a "rule", or, standard as in 2 Cor 10:13-16:

> ***2 Corinthians 10:13-15*** *But we will not boast of things without our measure, but according to the measure of the rule which God hath*

*distributed to us, a measure to reach even unto you. (14) For we stretch not ourselves beyond our measure, as though we reached not unto you: for we are come as far as to you also in preaching the gospel of Christ: (15) Not boasting of things without our measure, that is, of other men's labours; but having hope, when your faith is increased, that we shall be enlarged by you according to our rule abundantly,*

As far as the current usage of the word "canon", Gal 6:16 and Phil 3:16 probably come closest to the modern idea of canon:

**Galatians 6:16** *And as many as walk according to this rule, peace be on them, and mercy, and upon the Israel of God.*

**Philippians 3:16** *Nevertheless, whereto we have already attained, let us walk by the same rule, let us mind the same thing.*

The early Christians used the word "canon" to describe their rule of faith or the authoritative nature of the scriptures. But the first concrete application of the word as it refers to the Bible was made by Athanasius in 350 AD. He wrote in his *39th Festal Epistle of Athanasius* concerning the 27 books of the New Testament while at the same time, he referred to the Apocrypha as being heretical. He also mentioned that it was acceptable to read the Didache and the Shepherd of Hermas but that even these should not be considered a part of the canon of scripture.

The Jews did not use the word "qaneh" or "kanon" to describe the scriptures, preferring rather to use three other terms. The first term was "Sacred Writings" This title was ascribed to those books which were kept by the ark of the covenant, and later, kept in the temple.

They also spoke of the scriptures as being "authoritative writings" because everyone, including the king himself, was to submit to the rule of the scriptures.

Sometimes, in Jewish literature (and especially the Talmud), the scriptures were referred to as "books that defile the hands". And that sounds a bit odd! But the phrase actually meant the opposite of how it sounds. If it were possible for the Bible to do anything of this nature, we would think that it would make the hands "clean" rather than defile them! But the Jews drew this term from the principles of Lev 16:24:

**Leviticus 16:24** *And he shall wash his flesh with water in the holy place, and put on his garments, and come forth, and offer his burnt* *offering, and the burnt offering of the people, and make an atonement for himself, and for the people.*

The idea is that if anyone were to touch the scriptures, he had to wash his hands before he could touch something else. From this we understand what they really meant. Their thinking was that "books that defile the hands" were synonymous as saying "sacred writings".

The subject of canonicity is important to us because it explains how the various writings of the Bible received their relevance. In other words, how did the 66 books now contained in the Bible get there? And why aren't there other books included?

Keep in mind that inspiration describes the process by which God recorded His words for man. But preservation describes the act of God in keeping every word that He inspired to every generation from the time that He gave them until now. Because of this, an understanding of the process of canonization is crucial.

Every book of the Bible was written by either an apostle, a prophet, or someone who knew an apostle. These people were God's spokesmen and their writings were foundational. This was especially true at the beginning of the church.[52]

The apostles were endowed with certain gifts of the Holy Spirit by which they confirmed the writings and messages they were delivering to God's people.

*2 Corinthians 12:12 Truly the signs of an apostle were wrought among you in all patience, in signs, and wonders, and mighty deeds.*

*Hebrews 2:3-4 How shall we escape, if we neglect so great salvation; which at the first began to be spoken by the Lord, and was confirmed unto us by them that heard him; (4) God also bearing them witness, both with signs and wonders, and with divers miracles, and gifts of the Holy Ghost, according to his own will?*

Keep in mind that not all of the apostles' writings were necessarily considered scripture. For example, Paul mentioned another epistle that he had written to the church of Corinth but it is not a part of the canon (see 1 Cor 5:9). There are also other writings referred to in the New Testament that were not

---

[52] In this case, the word "church" is used in a generic sense to describe the first churches in the New Testament.

included in the canon either. (such as the Book of Enoch referred to in the Book of Jude). In each case, the books in question no longer exist.

So what does that mean? Have we lost a part of God's inspired words? No, for if the books of Jasher and Enoch have been lost, then we must conclude that God did not preserve them. And since we know that God has promised to preserve his words, we must come to the conclusion, based upon our faith in God's promises, that those books were never received as a part of God's Holy Word!

## THE CANON RECOGNIZED

So is it possible that God could inspire another book to be added to his Word today? Or, is it possible for someone nowadays to stake the claim of inspiration for one of his writings? Could a modern believer write a book which should be included into the canon of scripture?

We must answer "no" for several reasons. The first reason is the most obvious. Since a writer had to be a prophet, apostle, or someone who knew an apostle, no one living today is qualified. Secondly, even with the fact that there are those who would claim apostolic authority, historically, they have been rejected as false apostles, who again, would not be qualified to write a word of inspiration. God used holy men. A false apostle is certainly not a holy man!

Thirdly, since God has preserved his Word, it is not possible that a true writing of the apostles could ever be "found" and consequently included in the scriptures since no part of the scriptures could ever be lost. So even if we were to find manuscripts signed by Peter or Paul, we would have to conclude, based upon the doctrine of preservation, that they were not inspired!

So how was the canon selected? Who decided what should be included and what should be excluded? What was the basis of their choice? How do we know that they didn't include something that should have been excluded? And how do we know that they didn't exclude something that should have been included?

The first thing we should know is that no man or counsel ever sat down and decided on the canon. Canonization is not really the idea of selection of the books anyway. It is more the idea of recognition. No one ever selected the books. Rather, the first century believers recognized what God had inspired.

In fact, it is my opinion that the canon was pretty close to completion by the end of the first century (and certainly by the end of the second century) based upon various New Testament passages which we will examine in a short while. A close examination of the New Testament and history reveal to us that the

## IN DEFENSE OF THE TEXTUS RECEPTUS

process of recognition, and therefore reception, was being applied to the writings of the apostles, even during the 1st century.

One of our first evidences of this is found in Luke 1:1 where Luke mentioned many other accounts of the life of Christ:

> **Luke 1:1** *Forasmuch as many have taken in hand to set forth in order a declaration of those things which are most surely believed among us,*

Obviously, we don't have "many" gospels. We must therefore conclude that there was a selectivity happening among God's people. In fact, Luke seems to imply that he wrote the Gospel of Luke because others were writing accounts of the life of Christ and since he had "perfect understanding", it seemed only proper that he should write an account also.

We also find in the New Testament references to certain books that were to be read in the churches, such as in:

> **Colossians 4:16** *And when this epistle is read among you, cause that it be read also in the church of the Laodiceans; and that ye likewise read the epistle from Laodicea.*

> **1 Thessalonians 5:27** *I charge you by the Lord that this epistle be read unto all the holy brethren.*

The interesting thing about this is that not everything which was recommended to be read was automatically accepted. For example, the Epistle to the Laodiceans was never received as scripture. It may have been very instructive, but it obviously did not bear the qualities of scripture and was never received by the New Testament churches. Clearly, God's people were practicing an extremely selective reception of the writings, even from the apostles!

The New Testament also indicates that the letters were being circulated through the churches. Most likely, this is where the first copies of the original manuscripts began to be created. Again, Paul directed that the Colossian epistle be read in Laodicea. Jesus commanded that the Book of Revelation be circulated among the churches as well.

> **Revelation 1:11** *Saying, I am Alpha and Omega, the first and the last: and, What thou seest, write in a book, and send it unto the seven churches which are in Asia; unto Ephesus, and unto Smyrna, and unto Pergamos, and unto Thyatira, and unto Sardis, and unto Philadelphia, and unto Laodicea.*

## IN DEFENSE OF THE TEXTUS RECEPTUS

The natural outcome of circulation would be that the churches would begin to collect the writings which were considered inspired. According to 2 Peter 3:15, 16, Peter had a collection of Paul's writings. And Jude seems to refer to the writings of Peter.

> ***2 Peter 3:15-16*** *And account that the longsuffering of our Lord is salvation; even as our beloved brother Paul also according to the wisdom given unto him hath written unto you; (16) As also in all his epistles, speaking in them of these things; in which are some things hard to be understood, which they that are unlearned and unstable wrest, as they do also the other scriptures, unto their own destruction.*

> ***Jude 1:17-18*** *But, beloved, remember ye the words which were spoken before of the apostles of our Lord Jesus Christ; (18) How that they told you there should be mockers in the last time, who should walk after their own ungodly lusts.*

Also note the wording of 1 Tim 5:18:

> ***1 Timothy 5:18*** *For the scripture saith, Thou shalt not muzzle the ox that treadeth out the corn. And, The labourer is worthy of his reward.*

In this case, Paul is quoting from the Gospel of Luke:

> ***Luke 10:7*** *And in the same house remain, eating and drinking such things as they give: for the labourer is worthy of his hire. Go not from house to house.*

He is not quoting from Matt 10:10. We know this because Paul uses the word "reward" which is the same Greek word as "hire" in Luke 10:7. Matthew used the word "meat", which means basically the same idea but is a different Greek word. With all that being said, what do we have here? Paul gives internal and apostolic authority to the Gospel of Luke. And naturally, that means Paul had a copy of Luke's gospel. But the simple point we are seeking to establish is that even the first century believers were already collecting the writings they knew to have divine authority.

According to Eusebius' Ecclesiastical History, Book 3, chapter 24, the apostle John also had a hand in guiding which gospels should be accepted as scripture. Since John the apostle died around 100 AD, we have yet another indication that the canon was well on its way by the end of the first century.

Another strong indication that the canon had been basically formed and recognized by the end of the 2nd century comes from the existing canonical list and from the early translations.[53]

The Old Latin translation was in circulation prior to the 3rd century and it included all but Hebrews, James, 1st and 2nd Peter. The Muratorian Canon, more correctly, Muratorian Fragment is the oldest known list of canonical books of the New Testament dating to around 170 AD. It was discovered by Ludovico Antonio Muratori in a library in Milan and published in 1740. It agrees with the Old Latin translation.

The Syriac translation was in circulation around 400 AD the choice of books clearly indicates an accepted canon. It included the entire New Testament except for 2nd Peter, 2nd and 3rd John, Jude, and Revelation.

You may wonder why some of the books were not found in the above mentioned writings but the answer may be simply that they were not in wide distribution yet. But by 367 AD, Athanasius had listed all 27 of the New Testament books as canonical.

It can also be shown that every one of the New Testament books was used by the early church writers as illustrated by the chart below:[54]

|  |  |
| --- | --- |
| Matthew | Quoted in the Epistles of Pseudo-Barnabas (70-A.D. 79) |
| Mark | Quoted by Papias (A.D. 70-162) |
| Luke | Quoted in the Muratorian Fragment (A.D. 170-180) |
| John | Quoted by Papias (A.D. 70-162); Also quoted by Ignatius (A.D. 110-117) |
| Acts | Quoted by Polycarp in the Epistle to the Philippians (A.D. 69-155) |
| Romans | Quoted by Polycarp in the Epistle to the Philippians (A.D. 69-155) |
| 1 Corinthians | Cited in the Didache (A.D. 70-130) |
| 2 Corinthians | Quoted by Polycarp in the Epistle to the Philippians (A.D. 69-155) |
| Galatians | Quoted by Polycarp in the Epistle to the Philippians (A.D. 69-155) |
| Ephesians | Quoted by Polycarp in the Epistle to the Philippians (A.D. 69-155) as well as Clement of Rome (A.D. 95-97) |
| Philippians | Quoted by Polycarp in the Epistle to the Philippians (A.D. 69-155) |
| Colossians | Quoted by Polycarp in the Epistle to the Philippians (A.D. 69-155); Also quoted by Ignatius (A.D. 110-117) |

---

[53] Geisler and Nix, General Introduction to the Bible, pg 288

[54] Ibid, pg 291- 294

## IN DEFENSE OF THE TEXTUS RECEPTUS

| 1 Thess | Quoted by Ignatius (A.D. 110-117) |
|---|---|
| 2 Thess | Quoted by Polycarp in the Epistle to the Philippians (A.D. 69-155); Also quoted by Ignatius (A.D. 110-117) |
| 1 Timothy | Clement of Rome (A.D. 95-97) quoted from this book on many occasions. |
| 2 Timothy | Quoted in the Epistles of Pseudo-Barnabas (A.D. 70-79) |
| Titus | Clement of Rome (A.D. 95-97) quoted from this book on many occasions. |
| Philemon | Alluded to by Ignatius (A.D. 110-117) |
| Hebrews | Clement of Rome (A.D. 95-97) frequently quoted from this book |
| James | Clement of Rome (A.D. 95-97) frequently quoted from this book |
| 1 Peter | Quoted in the Epistles of Pseudo-Barnabas (A.D. 70-79) |
| 2 Peter | Quoted in the Epistles of Pseudo-Barnabas (A.D. 70-79) as well as Clement of Rome (A.D. 95-97) |
| 1 John | Quoted by Polycarp in The Shepherd (A.D. 69-155) |
| 2 John | Quoted by Polycarp in the Epistle to the Philippians (A.D. 69-155) |
| 3 John | Quoted by Irenaeus (130-202 AD) |
| Jude | Quoted by Polycarp in the Epistle to the Philippians (A.D. 69-155) |
| Revelation | Accepted as authoritative by Papias (A.D. 70-162) |

As you can see from the above chart, every one of the New Testament books had been recognized as scripture by the end of the second century.

The New Testament books were quoted or alluded to by quite a number of writers in the first and second century. For instance, Polycarp, a personal disciple of John the Apostle, lived from 69 to 155 AD. Polycarp's writings refer to passages from Matthew, John, Romans, 1st Timothy, 1 Peter, 1 John, 2 John, and Jude.

Justin Martyr, who lived from 100 to 165 AD quoted or alluded to all the gospels, most of the Pauline epistles. 1st Peter and Revelation. And there were probably more except that only two of his works now exist to be examined.

Irenaeus, who lived from 130 to 202 AD quoted from every book in the New Testament except for Philemon, James, 2nd Peter, and 3rd John. One story from his life demonstrates the great care and love he had for the Word of God. According to his writings on Rev 13:18, he defended the traditional reading "666" against those who thought that the reading ought to say "616". Interestingly enough, in Greek, there is only one letter's difference. Yet the translation is radically different.

Clement of Alexandria, who lived from 150 to 215 AD was a theologian in the catechetical school of Alexandria, Egypt. He quotes from 25 of the 27 New Testament books omitting only 2 Timothy and 2 John. And this is really quite amazing because that shows us that the majority, if not all of the New Testament books, had, not only been received, but had already made their way to Egypt.

Someone could legitimately ask the question, "If these men did not quote from certain books but quoted from others, does this mean they did not think the others were not authoritative?" Not in the least. First of all, we haven't found copies of everything these men wrote. They may have quoted from the other books but we just haven't found the evidence yet. Second, it may be that they just didn't quote from those books and that's all. It's just that simple. After having preached for over 30 years, there may be one or two of the minor prophets I haven't quoted from but I certainly believe them to be inspired!

But again, let's stay on track. What we are seeking to establish is how fast the existing canon was actually recognized. The fact that they quoted from so many of the books is a clear evidence that the canon was pretty well established by the end of the second century. And it appears that it happened naturally and fairly immediately after the book was written.

Several well-known church councils also recognized the canon. And we say that they recognized the canon because it is important to remember that the canon was never selected in the sense that it was voted upon by any group of people. The council meetings did not select the canon. Nor did they approve of the canon. More exactly, the canon that was currently in use was officially confirmed and acknowledged.

The First Council of Nicaea, which met in AD 325, was called together to discuss the false teachings of Arianism. In doing so, they also discussed another false teacher, Marcion, who had produced his own heretical canon by replacing Matthew, Mark, and John with a gospel bearing his name. He also had mutilated the Gospel of Luke in order to remove any reference to Jesus being of Jewish stock. Marcion also rejected all but 10 of the New Testament epistles. By the time the discussion of the Council of Nicaea had come to a close, they had listed the books of the New Testament as those which they recognized as God's Word. This came as an attempt to combat the heresy of Marcion, not as a stamp of approval on one epistle versus another. The issue was recognition, not ratification.

## IN DEFENSE OF THE TEXTUS RECEPTUS

The Council of Laodicea of 364 AD met to discuss the conduct of church members and church practices. In doing so, they listed the books which they believed should be the only books read in church services. The canon was clearly defined and all New Testament books recognized as canonical.

Two more important councils were the Council of Hippo in 393 AD and the Synod of Carthage in 397 AD. In both cases the entire New Testament was recognized. Unfortunately, they also recognized a few of the apocryphal books as well but what could we expect seeing the world of Christendom was fast falling under the control of Catholicism.

## FALSE VIEWS OF CANONIZATION

Again, we want to emphasize that the canon was never voted upon. Rather, it was recognized and generally accepted by the people of God over a period of time during the 1$^{st}$ to the 2$^{nd}$ centuries. But it has not always been quite as cut and dried as that! In fact, there were certain influential writers who argued quite strongly against the inclusion of some of the books in our Bible. But why did this happen?

For the most part, disagreements in the canon arose from inadequate views in how the canon is determined. In some cases, believers failed to make a distinction between what was known among believers and what was considered as scripture. In some cases, even today, questions arise over the canon among Bible students and scholars alike simply because of a failure to recognize the differing views of various groups in church history. For the most part, these types of problems are easily solved.

It is both amazing and unfortunate that still today, so many inadequate views concerning the selection of the canon still prevail. One such view is the idea that age determines canonicity.

But it can be easily shown that this is certainly not the case. Consider the following verses:

> **Numbers 21:14** *Wherefore it is said in the <u>book of the wars of the LORD</u>, What he did in the Red sea, and in the brooks of Arnon,*

> **Joshua 10:13** *And the sun stood still, and the moon stayed, until the people had avenged themselves upon their enemies. Is not this written in the <u>book of Jasher</u>? So the sun stood still in the midst of heaven, and hasted not to go down about a whole day.*

These two verses mention "the book of the wars of the LORD" and the "book of Jasher". Both of these books are very ancient. And they have both been lost in antiquity.[55] As such, though they are spoken of in the Bible itself. They are not a part of the canon. God never prompted His people to take care to preserve these books. On the other hand, many "young" books were received practically immediately and placed in the canon. We have already mentioned that Peter had a collection of Paul's writings which he considered to be scripture (2 Pet 3:15-16). Another example is Daniel, a contemporary of Jeremiah, who wrote:

> ***Daniel 9:2*** *In the first year of his reign I Daniel understood by books the number of the years, whereof the word of the LORD came to Jeremiah the prophet, that he would accomplish seventy years in the desolations of Jerusalem.*

Daniel not only received the writings of Jeremiah as scripture, but had been diligently studying them!

Another inadequate idea of canonization is the notion that in some way, language is a determinant in canonicity. The thought is that a book should be Hebrew or Greek if it is to be canonized. But there are places in the scriptures which were not written in Hebrew or Greek, such as Dan 2:4 – 7:28, Ezra 4:8 – 6:18 and Ezra 7:12-26. These sections were written in Chaldee.

Perhaps one of the most common false views is that religious value of a book helps to determine its qualifications for canonization. But the false logic in this is easily disputed. Any casual reading of the Apocrypha would reveal some religious value, but it was not accepted as canon. Any decent Bible dictionary, commentary, or atlas has religious value, but value does not indicate inspiration.

Before we move on to the correct view of canonicity, we should also add that the church, or to put it another way, the society of believers, have never "determined" canonicity. A book of the Bible does not become the Word of God because it is approved or accepted by the church. No, it is accepted because it is the Word of God. God's sheep hear his voice. They know when He speaks.

Consequently, the authority of the scriptures does not require the approval of men. If it did, many of the Minor Prophets would not have been canonized because the majority of the Jews rejected their counsel. No, the people of God merely recognize and receive God's Word. We have never sat in judgment over it!

### CORRECT VIEW OF CANONIZATION

---

[55] It is possible to buy a copy of the Book of Jasher today but it is highly doubtful that it is authentic.

## IN DEFENSE OF THE TEXTUS RECEPTUS

Ultimately, God determined what would be canonized. While it is true that men acknowledged Scriptural authority, God was the divine causality of inspiration, and therefore the only authority in canonical selection. Man merely recognized what God had already predetermined. A book was found to be valuable because it had the stamp of inspiration upon it. The people of God canonized the scripture immediately upon reception. We saw this as we studied 1 Tim 5:18 and 2 Pet 3:15, 16. Councils did not create the canon; they merely recorded it.

The saints of the 1st and 2nd century saw the marks of inspiration upon the writings – accuracy, power, and life-changing truth in the books that they received. Knowing that these books bore the marks of divine origin, they received them as scripture.

It is very evident that a large quantity of literature was written during the first century. This is what Luke was referring to:

> ***Luke 1:1*** *Forasmuch as many have taken in hand to set forth in order a declaration of those things which are most surely believed among us,*

But we should not jump to conclusions concerning the words of Luke. Many things were being written. And according to Luke 1:2, at least some of the writers were even eyewitnesses of the ministry of Christ. But Luke felt the need to write one more account because, as he says in verse 3, he had "perfect knowledge of all things from the very first". That is why he states that he wanted to also write an epistle to Theophilus so that his friend could have the exact truth. Note Luke 1:3:

> ***Luke 1:3*** *It seemed good to me also, having had perfect understanding of all things from the very first, to write unto thee in order, most excellent Theophilus,*

Luke did not condemn the other writings as heretical or devilish. But he simply implied that there was a need for something better. But the New Testament also makes it abundantly clear that false epistles were in circulation as well.

This implies that the people of God had to exercise the process of selection in order to discern what was scripture, what was acceptable religious literature, and what was heresy. This process did not happen overnight. In fact, it took around 200 years before all the books now considered canon were widely received as the Word of God.

So what took so long for the majority of the believers to finally receive what we now recognize as scripture? There were several factors involved but at least three factors should help remove any doubt of the canon's authenticity.

First of all, communication was extremely slow in the early centuries. Augustus Caesar (62 BC–AD 14) had organized a mail service but it was mainly used for government correspondence. Later, a service for private mail was added but it was still slow and not nearly as trustworthy as one would hope! There doesn't seem to be any indication in the New Testament that the believers ever tried to use the mail service, even if it was available to them. No, they would pass letters along by sending them in the hands of another trusted believer. The result of this was that believers in the West were not even aware of some of the books until quite a few years after their initial circulation in the East.

Another reason why it took so long for the process of canonization was because the first three centuries were times of great persecution. Whereas you and I are afforded the opportunity, time, and resources to study the scriptures, the 1st century believers did not have that blessing! There was very little time for research, reflection, or recognition of anything new – much less scripture! So rather than taking the risk of receiving something that was not inspired, there would have been a tendency to rely on what they already had until they were given something else that they could fully trust.

And then, let us also remember that much of what was written throughout church history came as a result of conflict over various Bible doctrines. It was not until the teachings of Marcion in the early 2nd century that it became necessary to list what books were considered authoritative.

With that being said, let's restate the facts. Canonization was not a council but an informal process of recognition by the saints of the first two centuries. However, in considering any writing that they would have received, they would have had to employ certain principles to make a determination. I don't mean to suggest that anyone had a formal checklist but whether purposeful or not, they would have had to answer certain basic questions. As we look at the various discussions and counsel meetings, we can define six basic principles:

- **Is the writing authoritative?** Does the writing claim any special authority with phrases such as, "thus saith the LORD" or "It is written". Phrases like this were significant because a Christian would never write such a thing unless it was true.

- **Did the writing come from a recognized prophet, apostle, or someone endorsed by the apostles?** Naturally, writings of this nature would have been more highly considered. This was the line of argument that Paul used for his own ministry in Galatians chapter 1. Understandably, the writing still had to pass the litmus test of the other principles, but this one was a pretty important point!

- **Was the writing theologically sound?** The early believers knew the principles of the Old Testament which stated that a prophet's words must be 100% accurate (Dt 13:1-3) and if not, he was a false prophet.

- **Were the claims of the writing true?** For example, if a book claimed to be written by Peter or Paul, it had to truly be written by Peter or Paul. The idea is that God does not lie and so a penman of the scriptures would not be able to record a lie under the influence of the Holy Spirit. This point also touches on the area of historical accuracy as well. This was the biggest reason for the rejection of the falsely attributed books known as the Pseudopigrapha.

- **Has the writing shown itself to have a dynamic character?** In other words, if a writing had shown the propensity to change lives because it spoke with spiritual power and authority, it was highly considered. This principle led to the rejection of a vast amount of $1^{st}$ century literature. Though many writings may have been spiritual in content, they were devotional at best.

- **Was it received, used, and preserved by the people of God?** Early believers straightway acknowledged much of what is now considered canon. But this does not mean there was total acceptance because even a prophet or an apostle could be rejected on occasion (2 Chron 36:11-16; 2 Tim 1:15) Nowadays, the question is not so much canonicity but authenticity. We no longer have access to the writers or those who received the letters and therefore, it becomes very easy to call the writings into question. However, it doesn't pass the "common sense" test to reject that which has been traditionally received by untold millions down through history. This is especially true since those who are living today have less evidence than those who initially received the books as scripture.

Many years ago, a group of scholars posed an interesting question. Supposing that the entire New Testament were destroyed, could it be reassembled from the writing of the early Christians? David Dalrymple (1726 – 1792) took up the challenge and in less than three months, he was able to reconstruct the entire New Testament (except for 11 verses) from the writings of the $2^{nd}$ and $3^{rd}$ century saints. This fact is especially important to the discussion concerning the validity of Greek texts. Thus by the end of the $2^{nd}$ century, almost all of the New Testament books had been accepted as canon though an official list was never made.

## IN DEFENSE OF THE TEXTUS RECEPTUS

## TRANSMISSION

In a sense, we are about to rehash some information that we have already been exposed to but at the same time, it is helpful to see it in a more systematic approach. As we speak of transmission, we are talking about how the scriptures were passed from one generation to another. So in this section, we will be taking a closer look at how the original autographs were copied and distributed.

You may remember that we have already pointed out how we no longer have the original manuscripts penned by Peter, Paul, and so on. Today, we have over 6600 copies of what they wrote. The originals no longer exist. And even if they did, how would we even know that they were originals? A lot of Bible scholars believe that the reason they don't exist is because God knew that if they did exist, man would make idols of them. We do have a problem worshiping things like that!

But for whatever reason, we do not have the original autographs. It would be nice if we did because then we could very easily compare other manuscripts to the originals to see if they "measure up" or not. But since we don't have the originals anymore, we have nothing to compare the existing manuscripts to. Therefore it is absolutely impossible to say what the originals looked like. All we have to go on is the promises of God's preservation. And for most of us, faith in God's promises would be enough. But with others, whose approach is not one of faith, it is disturbing to say the least!

But what do we have? We have over 6600 manuscripts in Greek alone. Then we can add to this another 19,000 manuscripts translated from the Greek. The internal consistency of these documents is an amazing 99% accuracy!

### FALSE ASSUMPTIONS CONCERNING TRANSMISSION

It is fairly common to hear someone today make the comment, "It is impossible to know what the originals looked like since the Bible has been copied thousands of times by so many different people". And initially it does sound like a pretty monumental task and a fairly reasonable argument! How can we know, some 6600 copies later, that the scriptures have not been altered? Never mind the discussion as to whether the alterations were intentional or not, what type of assurance do we have that the scriptures have not been corrupted? Again, we are left with nothing concrete but our faith in the promises of preservation.

But the reason why the task seems so difficult to us is because we often think of the transmission of the text as being somewhat like the telephone game. Many of us played the game as kids where one child would whisper something into the ear of another child. The message would get passed from child to child

## IN DEFENSE OF THE TEXTUS RECEPTUS

until the last child finally repeated out loud the message that he or she received. The game rarely ever ended with the same message that it started with.

Many people view the transmission of the scriptures in the same manner. Unfortunately this view is mistaken for several reasons. First of all, the telephone game was strictly linear, meaning it is a "one-to-one" system. Whereas the scriptures were mass copied.

Let me try to illustrate this. Imagine for a moment that the apostle Paul has just sent a letter to your church in Ephesus. The messenger would arrive with this letter and it would be read to the church. The church, realizing that this letter was God's message, and knowing that it must be passed on to other churches, would desire to have a copy of their own. So someone would be given the task of making an exact copy of Paul's inspired letter. Then, either the copy or the original would be sent on to the next church. And in the next church, the process would be repeated.

In the meantime, back in the first church, other copies would be made for distribution to anyone who wanted one. So one copy of a manuscript would become the source document for numerous others. So we don't just get a copy of a copy of a copy. We get numerous copies from a single manuscript. And then, we also get numerous copies from a copy. So, unlike the telephone game, we are afforded much more than one witness to the original message.

Another problem with the telephone game was that the message was passed from child to child verbally. Not so with the scriptures! In fact, as the letters were copied, the copyists took great care to ensure that the copies were accurate. Did they make mistakes? Yes, sometimes they did. Is it possible that a copyist or two decided to change the text? Yes, and we have evidence that this sort of thing happen from time to time. As a result, modern textual analysts have sought to classify the copies into families where each family is identified by the same characteristics based upon the variants found in the manuscripts. While it is true that there are many variants in the existing manuscripts, it is also true that the sheer volume of manuscripts make it easy to determine where the copyists' mistakes were made.

Along with this is the very obvious fact that just as errors can be propagated from one text to another, we can also safely assume that corrections could have been made as well. Poor readings could have been eliminated. Corruptions could have been set aside. Deletions could have been added back to the text. Additions could have been removed. It is just as much an assumption that errors HAD to be propagated as it is to say errors HAD to be eliminated. Any time we start using phrases like "could have", we should be careful how dogmatic we become.

A third mistake, and I believe to be the most crucial error of all, is the assumption that God could not, or, did not actually preserve his words.[56] Usually, a person will not vocally admit to doubting God's promises. And in some cases, if we were to ask them if they believe the Bible is completely true, they would agree. But then, as they approach the subject of manuscript evidence, they begin to move from a faith approach to an approach based on human reasoning. Typically it is simply an approach that does not consider the supernatural ability of God to providentially protect and guide the transmission of his exact message.

I have noticed that recently there seems to be a growing number of people who state that the Bible does not specifically promise preservation. They will proceed to take each passage that is typically used to support preservation and explain that the purpose of the verse was not to teach preservation but something else. In other words, those of us who use those verses to teach the doctrine of preservation are in effect, mis-using the verses. While I would agree that, in many cases, the primary interpretation is that God upholds his covenant and His laws. Yet we cannot miss the fact that these same verses also teach us about preservation as well. If we were to read these verses without any knowledge of the controversy, I don't think we would be pitting one truth against the other. I think we would naturally understand that a necessary part of God upholding his promises is that the promises would also be preserved. So I don't think we need to choose one truth over the other. I believe we must have both truths in order for either one to be true!

With that being said, it is helpful to be reminded of how the scriptures were transmitted down through the centuries until they finally arrive in our hands.

## MATERIALS USED IN RECORDING THE SCRIPTURES

You might be wondering why we need to take a look at the materials used in recording the scriptures. It is because this knowledge will help us understand why we have so many of one type of manuscript and so few of another. It will also help to explain why it is easy to read some manuscripts and more difficult to read others.

---

[56] We have already dealt with the scriptural promises of God concerning the preservation of his word in the section on preservation. It may do the reader some good to go back and review these promises!

## IN DEFENSE OF THE TEXTUS RECEPTUS

Let's say that you found an old notebook that you used to use when you were a child. On one page you might have an ink doodle of a bird. On another page you might have written next week's homework assignment in pencil. A few pages later, you draw an old church building using various colors of ink. And of course, let's not forget the page of school notes that your little brother colored all over.

But time has passed and you can see that the pages have deteriorated with age. You can read the ink but it has long since begun to bleed into the next page making it difficult to read either page. The pencil notes have faded too and are almost unreadable at this point. And the colorful ink drawing? Well, some of the colors have faded away altogether and the others have bled together making the red more of a purple color and the yellow more of a green. . .

Maybe this little illustration has begun to help you understand the impact that the materials have on whether a manuscript is even useful today. Add to this the fact that not only did they use various kinds of ink, various styles of writing, and various forms of the letters, they also used various types of paper. And all of these factors have a direct impact on whether or not a manuscript can stand the wear or time. So let's take a look at the materials used in writing the scriptures.

In the first century, paper was made from the pith of the papyrus plant. It was first manufactured in Egypt and Sudan as far back as 4000 BC.[57] Although other forms of paper were used during the first century, papyrus was the standard and almost everything was written on papyrus.

Initially, papyrus books were not actually books at all. They were scrolls. And this presented some real durability problems because papyrus also wears out fairly quickly and easily. So it wasn't too long before people began to fold the papyri in order to form "books". But the problem with this was that the pages were a bit brittle and did not fold easily. And of course, quality played a big factor in this as well. Soon, people were cutting the folds and forming what we refer to as a "codex". A codex is basically a book form.

After the use of papyri, next came the use of vellum. This is basically animal skin. Vellum was the material of choice and used very extensively from the 300s through the 1700s. Vellum also had a much longer life span than papyri.

---

[57] Most conservative Bible scholars date the earth at around 6000 years old. This date is usually arrived at by using the ages and dates given in the scriptures. When we take all of this into account, we come to the conclusion that man has been writing since almost the very beginning!

## IN DEFENSE OF THE TEXTUS RECEPTUS

That's one reason why we have so few papyri manuscripts and so many uncials and minuscules.[58] They were written on vellum.

When we speak of "uncials", we are speaking of the type of writing and not the material upon which it is written. Uncials are completely written in capital Greek letters. This particular style was popular until the 900s. Uncial, as a style certainly had its problems.

One problem is with punctuation. In fact, one of the earlier manuscripts with punctuation is Uncial 087 which has been dated around 550 AD. Keep in mind that punctuation in the Greek did not occur in the first century. This means that punctuation was added later by scholars and is not inspired by God. In fact, we are not really sure when the punctuation came in – but it can and does make a difference on how something will be translated, Consider the following examples:

*Woman, without her man, is incomplete.*

*Woman, without her, man is incomplete.*

It is pretty easy to see the difference that punctuation can make! One place in the scriptures where this becomes a translational challenge is in Romans 8:20, 21 where, based upon the punctuation, the Greek word "hoti" could be translated as "that" or "because".

Another drawback to the uncial script was the lack of spaces between words. Obviously, if a person were familiar with the readings of the scriptures, this problem was not as pronounced. But then again, who could possibly know every exact word and its order? Here is a good example of how word spacing can make a difference:

*ISAWABUNDANCEONTHETABLE*

Is that, "I saw abundance on the table" or is it "I saw a bun dance on the table." Normally, a sentence would be easy to read. But this example serves to prove that there can be times when it is not so obvious. Again, it is pretty simple to see how this could cause a problem!

The final form of script used in the Greek manuscripts was called the minuscule. It was basically Greek writing as we know it today. It had all of the

---

[58] Another reason is that there were fewer copies of the scriptures during the time period when the use of papyri was popular. The originals had just been penned and copies were just beginning to be multiplied. Add to this the very real possibility that copies of the papyri would have been destroyed by persecutors before Constantine made Christianity legal in the early 300s.

## IN DEFENSE OF THE TEXTUS RECEPTUS

proper spaces, breathing marks, etc. However, this style of Greek writing did not come into the textual realm until the 800s.

### SCRIBAL ERRORS

We should not assume that those who copied manuscripts in the first three centuries were any less concerned about accuracy than we are. In reality, they would have been just as aware of the possibility of copyist errors as we are. So what does this mean? It means they would have done whatever they could to ensure their copy was as accurate as they could make it. And this is fairly apparent as we proceed through history from the first century until now. In fact, by the time we come to the 9th century, about the only family of manuscripts that was in use was the Byzantine family from which the Textus Receptus is constructed.[59]

We find written in history that different groups devised their own rules for how the Bible was to be transcribed from one manuscript to another. One example would be a monastery at Constantinople in the early 800s. According to their rules, if a scribe was found to be careless in transcription, he was to be punished by given only bread and water to eat. If their manuscripts were not kept clean and neat, then they would have to pay 130 penances.[60]

Those who copied the manuscripts throughout the years had to sort through many different types of scribal errors that, thanks to the printing press, we no longer have to deal with. Some of those copying errors were accidental and some were intentional.

Some errors were caused by faulty eyesight. If a scribe had bad eyesight, he might mistake certain letters that looked similar. This may have been the reason for the well-known variant in 1 Timothy 3:16 where the Critical Text, constructed from the Alexandrian manuscripts, reads "'ὅς- "he who") whereas the Byzantine Text reads "θεός - "God". It is well known that common words were often abbreviated and a special mark was placed over the word to show that it is an abbreviation. So the theory is that θεός was abbreviated with θς. It is easy to see how the middle bar of the theta (θ) could have faded out and then assumed to be ὅς. According to some scholars, the abbreviation mark exists in the Alexandrian manuscripts but was faded and therefore was not copied.

---

[59] This becomes self-evident when we look at the dates and classification of manuscripts that are extant from before the 900s and after the 900s. Refer to the Appendixes.

[60] Bruce M. Metzger, The Text of the New Testament, 2d ed. (New York: Oxford Univ. Press, 1968), pp. 15, 16, 19.)

## IN DEFENSE OF THE TEXTUS RECEPTUS

Sometimes two lines of text would end in the same way and the scribe would unintentionally omit a line while copying from one manuscript to the other. This is called a homoeoteluton. One example could be found in the Codex Sinaiticus at Matt. 5:19-20 where the first sentence of verse 19 ends with ἐν τῇ βασιλείᾳ τῶν οὐρανῶν and the end of the verse also ends with ἐν τῇ βασιλείᾳ τῶν οὐρανῶν. Apparently, the scribe had accidentally omitted everything from the first occurrence to the end of the verse.

Another error that was made in copying the manuscripts arose from impaired hearing. It was common practice in medieval European monasteries to have a "scriptorium" where one scribe read a passage and several other scribes would write what the first scribe read. Sometimes the reader was not as clear in speaking as he should have been. And sometimes the listener did not hear as well as he used to!

There are a group of vowels and diphthongs that sound virtually the same. When the writer heard what the reader spoke, he understood him to say something different and therefore wrote the wrong word. One good example of this can be found in the Codex Sinaiticus and Codex Alexandrinus at Rev 4:3 where the Greek reads "και ιερετς" (and priests) when it should have said "και ιρις" (and a rainbow).

Add to this the fact that sometimes the scribe thought he knew what a passage was supposed to say and so wrote from memory without adequately checking the source manuscript. If the scribe's memory was not exactly accurate, he could very easily write something that was different. He might write a synonym or maybe inadvertently change the sequence of words. He might also inadvertently assimilate the wording of a similar passage into what he was writing. All of these mistakes can, and were, made because the scribe wrote from memory without carefully checking the source manuscript.

Obviously, some scribes introduced intentional changes into the text as well. And before anyone jumps to the wrong conclusion, I do not mean that a scribe intentionally sought to destroy or diminish any of the doctrinal teachings of the scriptures. I am aware that there were those evil men who tried to slice the scriptures as Jehudi did in Jer 36:23. Their disdain for some particular doctrine (or their love for some particular heresy) drove them to pervert the Word of God. But for the most part, this was simply not the case. For the most part, the scribes made honest mistakes. Yes, the changes were intentional but typically meant to be helpful. Sometimes, a scribe thought he was fixing a mistake while he was actually introducing an errant reading into the text!

## IN DEFENSE OF THE TEXTUS RECEPTUS

On the other hand, we know from history that there were also intentional corrupts as well. Dr. Wilbur Pickering, in his book, *The Identity of the New Testament Text II* states this:

*"Gaius, an orthodox father who wrote between A.D 175 and 200, names Asclepiades, Theodotus, Hermophilus, and Appollonides as heretics who prepared corrupted copies of the scriptures and who multiplied copies of their fabrications" (pg 16)*

One area where intentional changes were made was in the area of spelling and grammar. Remember that the biblical texts are written in a form of Greek that is called "Koine". But this form of Greek was slowly replaced by what is referred to as Medieval Greek which was pretty much the standard by 500 AD. Thus, there are places in the manuscripts where a scribe sought to "update" the grammatical structure or spelling to conform to what he believed to be a more correct form.

Another type of change is called a "harmonistic" change. This is where a scribe would assimilate portions from one passage into another in order to harmonize the two passages. For example, the Lord's Prayer as given in Luke 11:2-4 is noticeably different than the more familiar passage in Matt 6:9-13. In some cases, the scribes borrowed from Mathew in order to better harmonize Luke.

In some cases, a scribe would desire to "fix" what he believed to be a historical or geographical error in the copy. One example of this may very well be the famous passage of John 1:28 where it is said that "These things were done in Bethabara beyond Jordan" where many manuscripts say "These things were done in Bethany beyond Jordan". The argument is that it is well known that there existed a place called Bethany on the east side of the river Jordan about 12 miles above Jericho. To Bethabara's defense, Both John Chrysostom and Origen[61] believed that the text should say "Bethabara". There is also a place called "Bethabara" on the Madaba Map which dates to around 600 AD. According to Hasting's Dictionary of the New Testament,

*"The form 'Bethabara,' on the other hand, is found in a few extant manuscripts of the Greek text, both uncial and cursive, and in the Curetonian and Sinaitic Syriac."*

---

[61] It seems to me that if Origen felt the need to research this issue for himself then there must have been a reason for it. In my opinion, it is probably because of conflicting manuscript readings. Since he could not find a place beyond Jordan called "Bethany" but could find a place called "Bethabara" he concluded that "Bethabara" must be the correct reading.

## IN DEFENSE OF THE TEXTUS RECEPTUS

Keep in mind that the Curetonian Syriac dates to around 200 AD. Also keep in mind that "Bethabara" is found in uncials 083 and 0113 dating to the 500s as well.

The International Standard Bible Encyclopedia has this to say:

*"Bethabara has also been identified with Bethbarah, which, however, was probably not on the Jordan but among the streams flowing into it (Jud 7:24). It is interesting to note that LXXB reads Baithabara for Massoretic Text Beth-`arabhah, one of the cities of Benjamin (Jos 18:22). If this be correct, the site is in Judea."*

But the Bible <u>never</u> said that Bethabara was on the Jordan. It says Bethabara is "beyond" Jordan. And according to the Madaba Map, it was <u>beyond</u> Jordan. Recent archeological work in and around Wadi Kharrar, Jordan has discovered some ancient baptismal ruins going back to at least the 300s so it appears that the early believers identified this location with John's baptism as well.

So along comes a scribe who thinks he knows the truth about the baptismal site. He reads the passage, assumes the scribe who copied the passage was in error, and seeks to correct what he believed to be a geographic mistake.

And then there is the intentional introduction of errant readings that are referred to as a "conflation". Sometimes a scribe would be faced with having to choose between two existing readings. But what if he chose wrongly? Then the true reading would be lost! So rather than doing this, some scribes would use both readings and thereby preserve both variants. In this way, both readings would be preserved.

I almost hesitate to even bring up the subject of conflation because this is one of the main charges that Critical Text Supporters make concerning the Textus Receptus. Time and again we read books and magazine articles pointing to the "conflation" of the Byzantine family but could we not just as easily say that the Alexandrian family is incomplete? Could we not look at the shorter readings of the Alexandrian manuscript and make the claim that it is riddled with omissions?

I suppose our discussion of intentional changes would not be complete if we did not also address those scribes, who, for doctrinal reasons, corrupted the text. We often see this in action in the area of translations but we should not be ignorant of the fact that it also occurred in the sense of transmission of the text as well. One good example would be a heretic named Marcion from the 1st century. He not only rejected all the books of the Bible except for ten of Paul's epistles but also expunged his copies of the Gospel of Luke of all references to the Jewish background of Jesus.

## SIX IMPORTANT FEATURES IN THE TRANSMISSION OF THE NEW TESTAMENT[62]

As we look at the area of the transmission of the text from the originals of the 1st century to what we currently use, we should also take a step back and consider that there are five very crucial features that ensures that the text we have today is exactly what God gave.

As we consider these features, they will invariably appear to be simple logic and somewhat man-centered. But at the same time, we must never lose sight of God's providential hand in the preservation of his text. Although we can see these five important features, we need to remember that the providence of God was operating behind the scenes to ensure that his word was never lost or corrupted.

The **first important feature** in the transmission of the true text of scripture actually happened in the 1st and 2nd centuries as God used his people to protect and propagate his Word in the face of heretical attacks and persecution. By all rights the scriptures and those who carried them should have been snuffed out but instead Christianity grew. And not because the first century believers were so strong or so diligent, no, we must credit the promises of God to not only preserve his word but also his people.

A **second important feature** in the transmission of the text occurred in the 4th and 5th centuries at the end of the great persecutions. First of all, Constantine virtually created a state-church in 314 AD when he not only allowed for the recognition of Christianity as an acceptable religion but also promoted it above all other religions. He did not mandate Christianity but in practice, paganism was so discouraged that he might as well have. He promoted certain men to a place of great authority while at the same time punished or persecuted others who would not submit to a state religion.

But at the same time, Christian churches enjoyed a renewed freedom to evangelize. In relation to the biblical text, during the earlier persecutions, many of the manuscripts were destroyed. But during the 4th and 5th centuries, many

---

[62] I readily admit that this section is an adaption from another author. However, I cannot remember the source. The steps were written in an old college notebook of mine and I do not know the source. However, the features are far too important to skip. My apologies to the source.

copies of the texts were being made and distributed practically world-wide. Consider this statement by Kurt and Barbara Aland:

*"Innumerable manuscripts were destroyed during the persecutions and had to be replaced. The result was a widespread scarcity of NT manuscripts, which became all the more acute when the persecution ceased. For when Christianity could again engage freely in missionary activity there was a tremendous growth in both the size of the existing churches and the number of new churches. There also followed a sudden demand for large numbers of N.T. manuscripts in all provinces of the empire" (Aland, The Text of the New Testament, p. 65).*

Kurt and Barbara Aland are certainly no defenders of the Textus Receptus but even they could see why there was a sudden explosion of the numbers of existing manuscripts after the time of Constantine. I am not quite sure that I could agree with their statement "a widespread scarcity". I do not think the scriptures were scarce, but propagation was most definitely limited.

At that same time there were a number of Bible translations also in circulation such as the Gothic Bible which was a Germanic translation around 330 to 350 AD. This translation is very much in agreement with the Byzantine manuscripts. It is generally considered to have been the common language translation for a large part of Europe. Other Bible translations included the Armenian Bible, the Palestinian Syriac and the Philoxenian Bible. These were all very clearly taken from the Byzantine family. All of these translations are understandable in that they were done by missionaries from Antioch or Constantinople where the Byzantine family was predominant.

During this time, the Byzantine Text was reproduced in substantial numbers. At the same time the Alexandrian text was still very much in use by the Christians in Egypt. But due to the great persecutions in the Byzantine area, we would have expected that the Alexandrian text would have far outnumbered the Byzantine text during this time. But this is not what happened. In addition, when it comes to making copies of the Greek texts, we would expect that the Roman Catholic Church would have naturally wanted to use their own manuscripts, hence the Codex Vaticanus. After all, they certainly were using the Latin Vulgate. But again, the scriptures were not placed into the hands of religion but in the hands of God's people. So God again used his own people to preserve, protect, and propagate his Word.

Dr. Wilbur Pickering, ThM, PhD. notes in his book,

*"...if, as reported, the Diocletian campaign was most fierce and effective in the Byzantine area, the numerical advantage of the 'Byzantine Text-type over the 'Western' and 'Alexandrian' would have been reduced, giving the latter a chance*

*to forge ahead. But it did not happen. The church, in the main, refused to propagate those forms of the Greek text." (The Identity of the New Testament Text, ch. 5).*

Now, I would also like to address this line of reasoning from another angle because it is also true that Christianity was more popular around Greece and Asia Minor. This popularity was only magnified when Constantine moved his capital to Constantinople in AD 324. Naturally, this would have also been a propelling reason why the Byzantine manuscripts "forged ahead". A few supporters of the Critical Text point this out as if to say the Byzantine Text only became favored because of this fact. But let's keep in mind that we are talking about a period of history that predates the famed Codex Vatican's and Codex Siniaticus by over 100 years. Point being, during this period of history, the Byzantine family and the Alexandrian family were running neck and neck, numerically speaking. If Constantinople really did have an effect, it was a very slow one.

Quite a number of uncials date from this period, and it is obvious that the Byzantine Text had become the dominating text from the 5th to the 9th centuries. That is not to say that the Alexandrian text had totally faded from the scene, for there is ample manuscript evidence to show that there were still those who used the inferior texts.

The sad thing is that so many modern scholars have viewed a handful of uncials as the authentic text. And it seems that the basis of their decision is more on the age of manuscripts than on the weight of the manuscripts even though it can be clearly illustrated that the Alexandrian texts that they favor is neither oldest nor authoritative. And as I have already shown, the codices that they choose to favor are in major disagreement even with each other![63]

But as Edward Hills has already noted in his book, there was a deliberate move away from the Alexandrian manuscripts in favor of the Byzantine Text:

*"Thus during the 4th and 5th centuries among the Syriac-speaking Christians of the East, the Greek-speaking Christians of the Byzantine empire, and the Latin-speaking Christians of the West the same tendency was at work, namely, a God-guided trend away from the false Western and Alexandrian texts and toward the*

---

[63] Some would be quick to point out that there are also disagreements within the Byzantine manuscripts as well. But the sheer numerical differences, coupled with the types of differences are almost astounding.

## IN DEFENSE OF THE TEXTUS RECEPTUS

*True Traditional Text" (Edward F. Hills, The King James Version Defended, 4th edition, p. 188).*

The **third important feature** in the preservation of the true text type occurred in the 9th and 10th centuries as the copies were converted from uncial to minuscule forms. As I said, before this time, the Byzantine text and the Alexandrian text were running neck and neck, numerically speaking. Yet it was not the Alexandrian text which was copied over into minuscules. The Byzantine text is very obviously favored.

As of this writing over 2911 minuscules have been discovered. Of this astounding number of manuscripts, 2840 are purely Byzantine, 13 more are primarily Byzantine with mixed or Critical Text readings, 31 are Critical Text manuscripts, 3 are Mixed texts which cannot be classified as either Critical Text or Byzantine, and 1 manuscript which has not been classified. I think it is pretty clear which family of manuscripts was favored and intentionally transmitted.

Obviously, the change from uncials to minuscules would have required a critical analysis of the texts in order to ensure that the correct, and may I say, accepted, readings were propagated. The scribes involved had to deal with changes which included punctuation, word spacing, breathing marks, and so on. For the sheer volume of statistics stated above, in some cases inferior texts were copied. But it was very visibly not the norm.

In the main, those who made copies from the uncials to the minuscules chose the most important Byzantine uncials for use in the transliteration process. Modern textual critics should consider this matter with great care because many of the manuscripts that they would have used are no longer extant today. If the Alexandrian manuscripts truly are superior to the Byzantine manuscripts, then why did the 8th and 9th century scribes reject their use?

Supporters of the Critical Text maintain that the wrong manuscripts were copied and handed down, and this is supposedly proven with the statement that "the older minuscules have a different text". But the oldest known minuscule is minuscule 461 dated at 835 AD and it is purely Byzantine. Until the discovery of Minuscule 461, minuscule 14 was the oldest known minuscule, and it has been dated at 964 AD. It is also Byzantine. So the statement that "the older minuscules have a different text" is absolutely false. Those who make such a claim are too educated to be called ignorant. The only other conclusion I can come to is that they are not being academically honest.

A **fourth important feature** comes in the form of the Byzantine Empire itself from 330 AD to 1453 AD. The Byzantine Empire was principally Greek speaking and was essentially a continuance of the Roman Empire. This was

*God's Preserved Word to Every Generation*

crucial because the Koine form of the Greek language had begun to die out as a living language in areas outside of Asia Minor and Greece starting in the late 2nd century and 3rd century.

The areas that spoke Latin, Syriac, or Coptic were moving away from Greek in favor of the local languages. However, Bible believers in the Byzantine Empire guarded the Greek biblical manuscripts through the Dark Ages. Then, in 1453 AD, at the end of the Byzantine Empire, Byzantine manuscripts were taken to Europe after the fall of Constantinople, the capital of the Byzantine Empire. It is interesting, and I believe providential, that this was also around the time when Johannes Gutenburg invented the now famous "Gutenburg Printing Press" which was the first printing press with movable type. In 1455 AD, Gutenburg printed the "Gutenburg Bible" and the world moved into a new era of manuscript preservation.

We would be amiss if we did not consider the many translations of the Bible which were in circulation before and during the Dark Ages as a **fifth important feature** in the preservation of the true text. With that being said, we recognize that a translation is just that – a translation. And understanding that God did not promise to preserve a translation, but what he gave by way of inspiration, the translations give us a good indication of which text type was preferred.

It is believed that there were hundreds of translation works available in the first 500 years of Christianity. But by 600 AD things had radically changed. The Catholic Church was in full gear and the only Bible allowable was the Latin Vulgate. The only recognized church during the Dark Ages was the Catholic Church and they kept a pretty tight reign on who could read and who could translate the scriptures. With that being said, there still existed a number of translations that give us solid evidence of the textual family, whether Byzantine or Alexandrian, that the translators were using.

Many of the translations were incomplete for one reason or another and some were simply not that good. But they give us some idea of which text type the translators preferred. And this is important because that also indicates to us which text type the people of God in general were using.

There was of course the Gothic Bible translated between 330 and 350 AD which was translated from the Byzantine family of manuscripts. Thus, those of the Germanic language groups must have been using the Byzantine manuscripts.

Then there is the Armenian Bible of 411 AD and the Philoxenian Bible of 508 AD which also agreed with the Byzantine manuscripts.

## IN DEFENSE OF THE TEXTUS RECEPTUS

The Venerable Bede wrote a few commentaries that are fairly well known but he also worked on a translation of the Gospel of John, which was said to have been completed in 735 AD very shortly before his death. It is believed that Bede used uncial 08 which is classified as Western Text but is primarily a Byzantine manuscript.[64] Keep in mind that Bede was a Catholic monk and I suppose he could have used the Codex Vaticanus had he known about it, yet he did not. He had access to an elaborate library which included the works of Eusebius. No doubt, copies of Eusebius' Greek Bibles were in the library. Yet Bede chose to use a manuscript which was primarily Byzantine instead.

Another Byzantine translation was the Romaunt Version which was in use by the Waldenses as far back as the 12th century. The Bibles are described by William S. Gilly in his book, "The Romaunt Version of the Gospel according to St. John". It is said that the Bibles were, small, plain, and probably designed with missionary work in mind. It is apparent that the Byzantine Text was used in its translation.

Another important translation was the Tepl Bible, which was an old German translation also used by the Waldenses in the 14th and 15th centuries. This was one of Martin Luther's sources when he translated his "Luther Bible" in the early 16th century. Emilio Comba, a Waldensian pastor and historian, who lived from 1839 to 1904, recorded in his book, "History of the Waldenses of Italy: from their origin to the Reformation" that the basis would have been a translation of the Byzantine manuscripts since the Old Latin version (or Italic Version) is a translation of the Byzantine manuscripts.[65] However, we are not to assume that it is a perfect work as there are places where it does not match the Textus Receptus. For example, the Tepl has "Jesus" at Acts 9:20 which agrees with the Critical Text in contrast to the Textus Receptus reading of "Christ". In Acts 22:16 the Tepl says "his name" in agreement with the Critical Text in contrast to the Textus Receptus which says "name of the Lord". And in Rev 1:8, the Tepl has "Lord God" in agreement with the Critical Text where the Textus Receptus has "Lord".

The fact that the Waldensian Bibles are based on the Byzantine manuscripts is significant because the Waldensians, as a movement, started in Lyons, France and spread through the Cotton Alps which borders both Italy and France. We would expect that the churches in this area would have used a different text than the Byzantine text since they were not really a part of the Greek

---

[64] http://www.skypoint.com/members/waltzmn/ManuscriptsUncials.html

[65] History of the Waldenses of Italy: from their origin to the Reformation" [1889] (pp. 190-192)

speaking world. But contrary to our expectations, they used the Byzantine texts. This is an exceptional stamp of approval for the Byzantine text.

Of course, we cannot forget Wycliffe's translation of the New Testament from the Latin Vulgate into English in 1380 AD. It was not from the Byzantine manuscripts because John Wycliffe did not know Greek. However, his translation was later revised by John Purvey who was a Lollard and a disciple of Wycliffe. Purvey's completed work was actually a better translation yet still inferior as it was a translation of a translation which was inferior as well.

Personally, I find it a bit of a mystery why some King James Version defenders vilify the Latin Vulgate on the one hand and then make the statement that God providentially guided the first Greek New Testament printers by the use of the Latin Vulgate. This was a position that Edward Hills took in his book, "The King James Version Defended" as he discusses how God used the first printed text of the New Testament in His providential preservation. It is almost as if, since Hills wrote it, it becomes gospel truth! Thus, it has been repeated by other writers since! But we can't have our cake and eat it too. We cannot vilify the Latin Vulgate as a "heretical translation" or "Catholic corruption", and then state that God used it simply because we cannot fill in the gaps of historical transmission in any other way. In my opinion, this is yet another perfect example of academic dishonesty.

For the most part, these Bibles were the forerunners of the reformation Bibles of the 16th through the 19th century. And whenever the Greek text was the basis, the Byzantine Text was the text of choice. And it is a well-known fact that every Bible translation of the reformation period was taken from the Byzantine manuscripts.

A **sixth important feature** in the preservation of the Byzantine Text came in the 16th century when the Greek manuscripts were converted to print. Prior to this time, manuscripts were hand-written which practically guaranteed that there would be errors that would have to be dealt with.

But printing set the text into a standardized, repeatable form that led to an increasingly smaller and smaller margin of error. Edward F. Hills records in his book:

*"A further step in the providential preservation of the New Testament was the printing of it in 1516 and the dissemination of it through the whole of Western Europe during the Protestant Reformation. ... In all essentials, the New Testament text first printed by Erasmus and later by Stephanus (1550) and Elzevir (1633) is in full agreement with the Traditional Text providentially preserved in the vast majority of the Greek New Testament manuscripts. ... In it the few errors of any*

*consequence occurring in the Traditional Greek Text were corrected by the providence of God operating through the usage of the Latin-speaking Church of Western Europe"* (Hills, *The King James Version Defended, pp. 106, 107).*

# IN DEFENSE OF THE TEXTUS RECEPTUS

## TRANSLATION

So what is the purpose of this book anyway? We have looked at a lot of information in an effort to clearly show why the Textus Receptus is superior to the Critical Text. But why? It is because there is a great battle going on today in many churches around the world concerning translations. But before we can ever choose a correct translation, we must first begin with the right text. The basic issue should not be about superior translations but about the superiority of the Greek text. Once this is settled in our minds, then we can begin to approach the issue of translations.

### ENGLISH TRANSLATIONS FROM THE TEXTUS RECEPTUS

In America we have hundreds of Bible translations and the number grows every year! However, almost all of these translations come from the Critical Text, which is the inferior Greek text. So, no matter how accurate the translation is, it will not be as good as a faithful and accurate translation of the Textus Receptus.

With that being said, how many translations of the Textus Receptus are there in English? That all depends on how you want to count them. If you want to count only those that were translated directly from the Greek and Hebrew, then the answer is five – The Modern King James, Young's Literal Translation, Jesus' Disciples Bible, the Modern English Version, and the King James Version. If we want to count revisions of the King James Version (American King James Version, Children's King James Version, King James 2000 Version, King James Easy Reading Version, New King James Version (NKJV) , KJ3, Updated King James Version) then there are a total of 10.

So how does a person decide which translation is the best? The first thing that should be done is to compare the translation to the Greek and Hebrew text for accuracy. If more than one translation is deemed to be a faithful and accurate translation, then readability should also be considered. Readability does not mean, "does it have small words" or "can it be understood by an 8th grader". By readability we mean, "Is it easy to read, and does it flow well?"

A third question that we could ask is whether or not a translation is free to use. Some translations are copyrighted in such a way that the "owner" of the translation must give permission before it can be reproduced for distribution. Copyrights are not necessarily a bad thing unless the copyright limits the free use and distribution of the translation. We must remember that God gave the scriptures freely and they are not ours to own or control.

Some people are of the opinion that a copyright only exists on these translations in order to make a profit for someone. I am sure this is true in some cases but may not be true in every case.[66]

But to me, it seems a bit odd that someone would try to limit the use of the scriptures. Any truly evangelistic person would want the Bible to be produced and distributed to as many as possible irrespective of money or ownership.

So these are some things that a person should consider when choosing a translation.[67] Also, it may be helpful to know a little about the translation as a whole:

**The Modern King James** – Transliterates the Greek word "tartarus" rather than translating it as "hell". This is actually a good thing seeing that, doctrinally speaking, hell, the bottomless pit, the lake of fire, and hades are not really synonymous terms anyway. But it also has "Passover" rather than "Easter" in Acts 12:4 even though it can be clearly shown that "Easter" is the correct translation.[68] In John 3:8 it reads, "The Spirit breathes where He desires" which may be an acceptable word-for-word translation but it ignores the obvious context and is therefore wrong.

---

[66] Sometimes an organization or person has to pay people to translate the scriptures, and they want to recoup their investment. If it wasn't for the copyright, no one would pay the translators. If people want to do this work as a labor of love, that is their choice, but it does not mean that all Bible translators have to forgo an income, especially those that do so full-time.

[67] Some of my TR or KJV brothers might wonder why I would even care to discuss this since we already have a faithful and accurate translation in the King James Version. And since I have already said I believe it to be the best, why even discuss it? To answer the question, it is simply because English is not the only language in the world.

[68] First of all, neither the word "Passover" or "Easter" existed in the English language until William Tyndale coined it in his translation in 1535. Before this time, the Greek word was simply transliterated as "paske". In fact, Tyndale was fairly consistent in translating the Greek word "pascha" as Easter in the New Testament because in 1526, that is what English Christians called the time around Passover. Why did they call this time period Easter? Most likely it goes back to a pagan festival celebrating the arrival of spring. However, when Tyndale translated the Old Testament, he knew that Easter would not be an appropriate translation so he coined another phrase, "Passover". Later English translations such as the Coverdale, the Matthew-Tyndale, Great Bible, Geneva Bible and Bishops Bible, changed practically all of the passages to "Passover" except for Acts 12:4. The King James Version translators intentionally left this as "Easter" because of the context. If you will note the context, you will see that those were the days of unleavened bread which actually comes after Passover. Thus, Luke must have been referring to the pagan festival of Easter.

## IN DEFENSE OF THE TEXTUS RECEPTUS

**Young's Literal Translation** – In reality, this translation used both the Textus Receptus and the Critical Text so it cannot rightly be considered a Textus Receptus translation. In 1887, Young produced a revision taking into consideration the Critical Text. In fact, I don't get past Gen 1:1 before I already have problems with the way it was translated.

**Jesus' Disciples Bible** – Although I have found this listed in a few places as a translation of the Textus Receptus, I was not able to actually find a copy to evaluate. So based upon its unavailability, I would have to say it would not be a good choice for a Bible!

**King James Version** – As translations go, the King James Version has been considered one of the most beloved translations ever produced. It has been the second most purchased translation since 2006 behind the New International Version. It is known for its formal equivalency to the Textus Receptus and is very poetic due to its style and prose. It is considered by many to be the most trustworthy, faithful and accurate translation ever accomplished in any language.

**Modern English Version** – This translation has already earned a reputation for being "the newest effort to replace the KJV". Its translation committee was an ecumenical mix of Orthodox, Catholic, and Protestant members. It is said to be a formal translation of the Textus Receptus and Masoretic Text. There are numerous translational issues which have a direct impact on doctrine. One of the most notable is the change from "baptism" to "washing". It also has a footnote casting doubt on the validity of 1 John 5:7.

Here is some very basic information on the revisions:

**American King James Version** – The greatest obvious difference is that all of the "thee's [69]" and "thou's" have been updated to "you". But many of the more "archaic" terms, such as "let" in 2 Thess 2:7 remain untouched so what is the difference, really?

**Children's King James Version** – Basically a reading tool more than a Bible. It is designed specifically for children and even in their promotional ads they mention that it is geared toward helping children transition into the King James Version.

---

[69] It is not wrong to replace "thee", "thou", and "ye" with you because that is exactly what these terms mean. However, in some cases, the old English terms are actually helpful, such as in Exo 16:28 where the New King James Version says, "And the LORD said to Moses, "How long do you refuse to keep My commandments and My laws?" which makes it sound like God is talking to Moses. The King James Version says, "And the LORD said unto Moses, How long refuse ye to keep my commandments and my laws?" making it clear that God is speaking to the Jews.

*God's Preserved Word to Every Generation*

## IN DEFENSE OF THE TEXTUS RECEPTUS

**King James 2000 Version** – This is another update of the King James Version in order to "eliminate obsolete words by reference to the most complete and definitive modern American dictionary, the Webster's New International Dictionary, Second Edition, unabridged. Spelling, punctuation, and capitalization have also been updated." One problem is its copyright limitation of 200 words unless you obtain written permission from the publisher.

**Updated King James Version** – It is just that - an update! Unfortunately, I think it loses some of the poetic beauty of the King James Version by making some of the updates such as the one found in Genesis:4:1 where "Adam knew" is changed to "Adam had sexual contact with" (try reading that to your children during family devotions!). It might be dynamically correct but it is certainly not the formal equivalent to the Hebrew word "know". Unlike the other revisions, this one has absolutely no copywrite limitations.

**KJ3** – Basically the latest (and last) revision done by Jay Green using the original languages. Some readers have stated that its grammatical structure is a big awkward due to its extremely literal style. Thus, readability suffers a bit. But it also has "Passover" rather than "Easter" in Acts 12:4 even though it can be clearly shown that "Easter" is the correct translation.

**New King James Version** – According to the Flesch-Kincaid Grade level indicator, the NKJV is slightly more difficult to read than the King James Version. It also has strict copy write limitations. In changing the "thee's" and "thou's", the translation actually becomes less precise.

### COMPARISON OF TEXTUS RECEPTUS-BASED TRANSLATIONS

|  | Accuracy | Readability | Availability | Free to Use | Total Rating |
|---|---|---|---|---|---|
| **MKJV** | 8 | 10 | 10 | 7 | 10.5 |
| **LITV** | 8 | 7 | 10 | 10 | 10.75 |
| **YLT** | 8 | 7 | 10 | 10 | 10.75 |
| **KJV** | 10 | 9 | 10 | 10 | 12.25 |
| **AKJV** | 10 | 9 | 6 | 10 | 11.25 |
| **KJV21** | 10 | 9 | 8 | 5 | 10.5 |
| **UKJV** | 9 | 8 | 6 | 10 | 10.5 |
| **KJ3** | 9 | 8 | 6 | 7 | 9.75 |
| **NKJV** | 7 | 9 | 10 | 5 | 9.5 |

*God's Preserved Word to Every Generation*

| MEV | 5 | 9 | 10 | 5 | 7.25 |

The chart above shows all the Textus Receptus translations (including revisions) and their rating in the four basic areas mentioned earlier. The ratings are from 1 to 10 with 10 being the highest (best) possible in that area. It should be observed that these ratings are subjective (except for whether or not the translation is free to use) and are my opinion[70] based upon personal research and observation in each Bible.[71]

As you can see, none of the translations score as high as the King James Version. So even if there are other translations from the Textus Receptus, the King James Version still shows itself to be the best translation. The only translation that even comes close to the quality of the King James Version is the American King James Version, however, a Bible that requires an internet connection to read is certainly not worth recommending!

I realize that readability is a subjective requirement based upon my own personal abilities and preferences. However, accuracy to the Greek text, availability, and freedom of use are fairly concrete. You may notice in the chart that the only translations that did not fair well in the readability category were the LITV and the YLT. And the fact that they do not flow as smoothly as many other translations is a fairly popular opinion among Bible readers. However, you should note that even if these two translations rated higher, they would still not outscore the King James Version.

There are also a few translations of a new text which is called the "Majority text". However, since we have already determined that the Textus

---

[70] Evaluation was performed by a 5-step process: (1) Reading Genesis chapters 1-12; Job chapters 1-5; Isaiah chapters 6 and 53; Matthew chapters 1-4, 24, 25; Mark chapters 1-4; John chapters 14-19; Acts chapters 1-4; Romans chapters 6-8; Hebrews chapters 1, 9, and 12; 1st John; Revelation chapters 1-5. (2) Researching known variations between the translations and examining the Greek or Hebrew for accuracy. (3) Evaluating comments or opinions of other writers for accuracy. (4) Checking for ease of availability was simply trying to order a copy from the internet. If I could not find it on the first five pages of any search engine, I considered it not available. (5) Checking the copy write information to see what could or could not be done with each translation keeping in mind that missionaries all over the world would need freedom of use. Final analysis was done by doubling the "accuracy" score since it is by and far the most important category and then adding then total from every area together. This number was then averaged by "4" for the final score.

[71] The translation known as the "Jesus' Disciple Bible" is not rated because all attempts at obtaining a copy were fruitless. The Children's King James Version is also not rated due to the fact that it is not meant as a "church" Bible per se. It is a children's Bible.

## IN DEFENSE OF THE TEXTUS RECEPTUS

Receptus is the superior text, the only thing necessary is to determine which translation from that text is the best to use.

### METHODS OF TRANSLATING

When it comes to Bible translation we are often told that there are two basic approaches to the actual work of translation itself. These two approaches are commonly referred to as formal equivalency and dynamic equivalency. The average believer does not know a great deal about these terms and I suppose it is not necessary to have an in-depth knowledge. But when it comes to the translator himself, he must have a very good understanding of the work of translation and thus, he will need to know what these two approaches are, when to apply each approach, and why.

You see, translation is not as simple as making a message in one language to appear in another language. Sometimes, in order to make a message clear, we have to work around language limitations and therefore, there will be times when one approach is needed over the other. You will find that almost all translators agree that the message must be a faithful reflection of the source language but there is wide disagreement concerning how to best do this.

Thus, translations typically use both approaches to one extent or another. On one hand, we have formal equivalency which is a more rigid, word-for-word approach. It is a method of approach that seeks to preserve the form as well as the content of the source language. It is an approach that seeks to preserve the exact language, syntax, and grammatical structure in as much as the target language limitations will allow.

But on the other end of the spectrum we have dynamic equivalency which is not so much focused on similar word order or syntax but more concerned with communicating the idea of the source language in such a way that it produces a similar result to the reader today as it did to the reader in the first century. In short, dynamic equivalency seeks to capture the meaning without overmuch concern for the exact language used to communicate that meaning.

We often hear about formal equivalency and dynamic equivalency and are told that one is "bad" for whatever reason while the other is "good" for whatever reason. But the world of translation is just not that simple. A translator will begin his work with one of the approaches above but at the same time, he will be faced with translational issues that will challenge his approach. He may see word plays or idioms that will force him to make decisions on how to handle a passage. He may come across words that simply do not exist in the target language and he will have to decide how to handle this.

## IN DEFENSE OF THE TEXTUS RECEPTUS

But on a basic level, our approach to the methods of translation is guided by our understanding of inspiration. If a translator believes in verbal-plenary inspiration, and understands that God gave each individual word, he will most likely seek a more formal equivalent approach to translation. However, if a translator limits inspiration of preservation to the concept of "doctrine" or 'truth" he will most likely lean more toward a dynamic approach to translation.

So a translator begins with a certain philosophy in practice. But at the same time, no translation has ever been purely formal-equivalent and no translation has ever been purely dynamic either. Why? Because languages are different. Each language has its own set of limitations and peculiarities which make translation a challenge.

A good translator knows that if he seeks to be too formal his translation will be too rigid and readability will suffer. This is one reason why we can find the same Greek word translated in several ways in the King James Version. A good example would be the Greek word "aperchomai" which is translated as "went" 54 times, "go" 25 times, "depart" or "departed" 28 times, and even "come" in 4 places! Now, take note that we would consider "go" and "come" to be opposites and we would naturally think that this would be the case in other languages as well. But it is simply not the case. In this case, a translator may take into consideration the location of the speaker, the location of the hearer, normal usage of the expression in the target language[72], or the implication of the text.

Translators must also face the challenge of alliteration, such as in Psalm 119 where the psalm is broken into sections. The first section is called "aleph" and every verse in that section begins with the letter "aleph". So how can a translator be true to the text and yet preserve this? Well, it is practically impossible. There are times where a translator will notice a word-play in the Greek text and desire to bring it our in the target language. In some cases, it is possible, but in many cases it simply cannot be done. In cases like this, more than one translator has sought to resolve the difficulties by going to a more "dynamic" approach in passages like this.

Sometimes a translator will be faced with the knowledge that no matter how he tries to capture the meaning of a particular passage, it will not be readily understood anyway. In these situations, he may be tempted to add a bit of "interpretation" to his translation. This is especially true when faced with idioms

---

[72] For example, we would not say, "come not into the way of evil doers" because it would sound as if we were already in the way of evil doers and do not want others to join us there. So, even though it may be "formally acceptable", we just don't say it that way!

that simply do not make sense in the target language.[73] So what is a translator to do? Should he try to find a similar idiom in the target language and be "dynamic"? Or should he leave the understanding in the hands of preachers and teachers? These are tough choices but these are the types of situations that translators face!

To summarize quickly - since we believe that God inspired each and every word in the original documents, and since we are clearly concerned that the copies that we place our trust in are a word-for-word rendering of the original documents, it stands to reason that we would want a translation that is as much of a formal equivalent as possible.

Someone might ask, "But isn't there a place for other styles?" Let me be clear. I am not saying it is wrong to have other Bibles as reference works in order to get the "feel" of a passage, or to take a deeper look at certain words or phrases. I don't think there is anything wrong with this at all as long as we recognize what we are using and why. It is my opinion that it would be easier to stick with translations that come from the Texts Receipts just for consistency sake. As I have already mentioned, we use commentaries and other helps which are not considered scripture and that is okay. Then why would we want to limit the use of other Texts Receipts based translations as long as we are clear on their place? For example, the LITV may be helpful in taking a deeper look at a certain phrase. The MKJV may help a person get a feel for a certain passage. But these would be helps, not the main thing.

### LEGITIMACY OF A TRANSLATION

When we say the "legitimacy" of a translation, what are we really talking about? What makes a translation legitimate? Does this mean that there are some translations that we could not be considered "legitimate"? Let's look at these questions one at a time.

First of all, when we speak of the legitimacy of a translation, what we are really asking is if the translation is of such a quality that it can be called "scripture". Therefore, to answer the question concerning what makes a translation legitimate, the answer is whether or not the translation is a faithful and accurate reflection of the preserved Greek and Hebrew manuscripts.

But on this point, we must tread carefully. Should we conclude that a translation must be perfect to be called "scripture"? Should we conclude that

---

[73] One good example of this could be, "... I am escaped with the skin of my teeth."(Job 19:20) Since teeth do not have skin, it would require teaching to make the verse understandable.

only a perfect translation could be called the Word of God?[74] Again, insofar as a translation is a faithful and accurate reflection of what God gave in the preserved Greek and Hebrew manuscripts, it can be called the Word of God. But what if the translation is accurate in some places but not in others? For example, what if a translation contains a few errors here or there? Does that invalidate the whole translation? Again, the answer is not as simple as that.

When a person considers which translation he will use, he should want to choose a translation that is as faithful and accurate as possible. This should be his first consideration. But his choice of one translation over another does not invalidate the other translations. Again, insofar as a translation is a faithful and accurate reflection of the preserved Greek and Hebrew manuscripts, it may be called the Word of God.

There are many bad translations available. Many of them are so bad that we could not say anything positive concerning the translation or its influence. With that being said, there are others that contain portions of the Word of God but are not as good a translation as others.

I realize that some of my more strict King James supporters would balk at the idea that the New International Version or the New American Standard Bible could ever be called the "Word of God" but many of them would readily agree that a good gospel tract must contain scripture. Yet a gospel tract is certainly not the complete Bible and much of what we read in the average tract is not scripture at all. Yet, because a tract uses the King James Version, some of my more militant King James Version brethren would say it contains the Word of God. But they would never say that the NIV or NASB contain the Word of God. Yet, it can be shown in both of those translations that there are places where it is identical to the King James Version. For example:

- *Gen 1:3 (NIV) And God said, "Let there be light," and there was light.*

- *Gen 1:3 (ESV) And God said, "Let there be light," and there was light.*

- *Gen 1:3 (NASB) Then God said, "Let there be light," and there was light.*

- *Gen 1:3 (KJV) And God said, "Let there be light," and there was light.*

So, are we to say that these passages are NOT the Word of God because they are in translations that we do not believe are as good as the King James

---

[74] See Appendix B for a fuller Discussion on the meaning of the phrase "Word of God" and how it is used in the Bible.

Version? No, if we were to be academically honest, based upon our understanding of Bible doctrine, we would have to conclude that these other translations may contain portions of the Word of God and yet, at the same time, are not what we endorse for use based upon either the source text or the accuracy of translation.

By the way, this reasonable approach to how we view other translations is not a new or controversial approach. The translators of the King James Version made similar statements in their preface. In fact, some of my more insistent KJV Only friends would not agree with them. Notice this quote from their preface:

*"Now to the later we answere; that wee doe not deny, nay wee affirme and avow, that **the very meanest translation** of the Bible in English, set foorth by men of our profession (for wee have seene none of theirs of the whole Bible as yet) **containeth the word of God, nay, is the word of God**. As the Kings Speech which hee uttered in Parliament, being translated into French, Dutch, Italian and Latine, is still the Kings Speech, though it be not interpreted by every Translator with the like grace, nor peradventure so fitly for phrase, nor so expresly for sence, every where."*

Another very interesting passage is in 2 Timothy chapter 3 where Paul is exhorting Timothy to continue in the doctrines that he had been taught since he was a young child. There are several aspects to this passage that are very revealing.

First of all, Timothy's father was not a Jew and so he was taught the things of God by his mother and Grandmother who are both mentioned in 2 Timothy 1:5. Since they lived in Lystra, it is probable that Timothy was far more fluent in Greek than he would have been in Hebrew and we can safely assume that any instruction he received around the house would have been in Greek as well.

Add to this the fact that scrolls in those days would have been expensive and it is highly unlikely that the synagogue would have allowed young Timothy or his mother to borrow the Hebrew scrolls from the synagogue. Since the Bible tells us that Timothy was uncircumcised, we can also be sure he would not have been allowed into the synagogue to hear the Jewish rabbis read from the Hebrew scrolls. He would have had either a copy of the Hebrew scriptures, or a Greek translation of the Hebrew scriptures at home. It is possible that Timothy's mother and grandmother had memorized portions of the scriptures in their younger years and then taught them to Timothy. But even if they did, they would have still had to use either copies at the very least. But in any case, they did not have the originals. But knowing all that we know about the life of young Timothy, was can be relatively sure that whatever he had was a translation. But notice what Paul says in 2 Timothy 3:15:

## IN DEFENSE OF THE TEXTUS RECEPTUS

***2 Timothy 3:15*** *And that from a child thou hast known the holy scriptures, which are able to make thee wise unto salvation through faith which is in Christ Jesus.*

The conclusion that we come to is that it is perfectly acceptable to refer to a translation as scripture. Some people get a bit nervous at this because they think that calling a translation "scripture" is concluding that a translation is inspired. The reality is, the word "scripture" merely denotes a message of divine origin and the word does not have any bearing on the process of inspiration or preservation. The word "scripture" merely describes the source of a writing as being divine without any intended comment on inspiration, preservation, or translation.

### COMPARISON OF ONE TRANSLATION TO ANOTHER

In regards to the subject of what is called the "King James Controversy" or "King James Onlyism" I suppose I have read somewhere in the neighborhood of 35 books, countless articles, and even more web pages. One of the more glaring errors that I see is the natural tendency of the writers to compare one translation to another in order to bolster their argument.

But the plain fact is that the foundation of the argument should not begin with the translations. The argument must begin with the Greek texts. What does it matter if I show that the English Standard Version and the King James Version are different? We should expect them to be different since they are translated from different Greek texts. Showing that they are different does not validate one translation over the other. It only shows that they are different.

Some of the writers who support the King James Version as a superior translation are the guiltiest of this error. They begin with the presupposition that the King James Version is perfect and then criticize anything that does not exactly match the readings of the King James Version. But how are we to know if the King James Version is an accurate translation unless it is first compared to the Greek and Hebrew texts from which it was translated?

You might say, "I believe that the King James Version is the Word of God and is perfect. So why shouldn't I compare other translations to it?" The problem is that you cannot know that the King James Version is an accurate translation unless you know that it came from an accurate source!

I have seen charts that tried to prove that the other translations purposefully subtracted, added, or changed the words of God. In some cases, the translators did purposefully try to change the text. But in most cases, the translators simply used a different Greek text and that is why the readings are

## IN DEFENSE OF THE TEXTUS RECEPTUS

different. The reason why the English is different is because the Greek texts from which they are translated are different.

And contrary to some people's opinion, neither Greek text (the Textus Receptus or the Critical text) is heretical or full of gnostic influence. No doubt one is inferior and corrupted, but not heretical. It has been said, and pretty well proven, that any doctrine can be taught from either text. But again, I want to restate what was previously said. It is possible to teach doctrine from a theology book too. But that doesn't mean we should use it as our Bible. Thus, the majority of the translations are not a purposeful attack upon any doctrine. They are simply translated from an inferior text.

In making comparisons between translations, it is not uncommon to see some poorly thought out allegations. One common allegation is that some translation or another was purposefully attacking the deity of Christ and this is usually "proven" by showing all the places where the non-KJV translation "removed" the word "Lord" in reference to Jesus. Yet, at the same time, these same people neglect to see other passages in the non-KJV translations where "Lord" has been "inserted". For example:

- ***Jude 1:25*** *(Bible in Basic English) To the only God our Saviour, through Jesus Christ our Lord, let us give glory and honour and authority and power, before all time and now and for ever. So be it.*

- ***Jude 1:25*** *(Darby) to the only God our Saviour, through Jesus Christ our Lord, be glory, majesty, might, and authority, from before the whole age, and now, and to all the ages. Amen.*

- ***Jude 1:25*** *(English Revised Version) He is the only God, the one who saves us. To him be glory, greatness, power, and authority through Jesus Christ our Lord for all time past, now, and forever. Amen.*

- ***Jude 1:25*** *(ESV) to the only God, our Savior, through Jesus Christ our Lord, be glory, majesty, dominion, and authority, before all time and now and forever. Amen.*

- ***Jude 1:25*** *(GNB) to the only God our Savior, through Jesus Christ our Lord, be glory, majesty, might, and authority, from all ages past, and now, and forever and ever! Amen.*

- ***Jude 1:25*** *(NASB) to the only God our Savior, through Jesus Christ our Lord, be glory, majesty, dominion and authority, before all time and now and forever. Amen.*

## IN DEFENSE OF THE TEXTUS RECEPTUS

- ***Jude 1:25*** *(NIV) to the only God our Savior be glory, majesty, power and authority, through Jesus Christ our Lord, before all ages, now and forevermore! Amen.*

- ***Jude 1:25*** *(KJV) To the only wise God our Saviour, be glory and majesty, dominion and power, both now and ever. Amen.*

You may have noticed that the King James Version does not have "through Jesus Christ our Lord". Why? It is the difference between the Textus Receptus and the Critical Text. So, if the other translations are a purposeful attempt to corrupt the doctrine of the deity of Christ, they did a pretty lousy job! In fact, the scribe should have been fired for his utter failure!

Another allegation that has been often repeated is that some of the modern translations weaken the deity of Christ by the way Acts 3:13, 26; Acts 4:27, 30 where they use the word "servant" instead of "son" or "child" in reference to Jesus. But a simple look at the Greek explains the difference. The Greek word is "pais" which even the King James translators themselves translated as "servant" in eight places. One of these places referred to Christ himself:

> ***Matthew 12:18*** *Behold my servant, whom I have chosen; my beloved, in whom my soul is well pleased: I will put my spirit upon him, and he shall shew judgment to the Gentiles.*

So this was not an attempt to weaken the doctrine of the deity of Christ. It was merely a translational choice based upon possible ways the word could be translated.

That is not to say that I agree with the other translations. On the contrary! I do not endorse any translation other than the King James Version. Yet, I believe that we need to be sure we support our position with credible evidence based on a solid premise and not on a presupposition. So I hold to the King James Version because it is a faithful and accurate translation of the preserved Greek text.

### MODERN TRANSLATIONS AND MODERN LINGO

Another common allegation is that the modern translations are written in modern lingo which is not worthy of the Word of God. And I would readily admit that this is true in many cases. Here is a passage of Luke 24:1-9 from a translation called "The Street Bible" by Rob Lacy:

> *"Crack of dawn, Sunday, the women get to the tomb-cave. Their bags are packed with the burial spices – they've not had time Friday night, and Saturday was Flyby Day. This is the first chance they've had.*

## IN DEFENSE OF THE TEXTUS RECEPTUS

> *They get there and the boulder's been shoved to one side. They go in, but Jesus' body's not there. They're stunned: 'What could've happened to it?' Next thing, two angels are lighting up the whole cave with their dazzling bright clothes. The women hit the deck, petrified. The angels ask, 'Why you looking in a grave for someone who's alive and well? D'you think he'd hang around in a tomb? He's out of here. He's back from the dead! Remember what he said up in Galilee? He'd be handed over, executed and then he'd come back after two days. Don't you remember?' Suddenly they do! It all comes back. He told them and they missed it!"*

And who could forget the Ebonics Bible? It definitely rates in the top ten of the most irreverent translations ever:

> *[1] In da beginnin' Big Daddy created da heaven an' da earth. [2] And da earth wuz widdout form, an' void; an' darkness wuz upon da face o' da deep. And da Spirit o' Big Daddy groved upon da face o' da waters. [3] And Big Daddy enunciated, Let dere be light y'all: an' dere wuz light. [4] And Big Daddy seen da light, dat it wuz fine a\*\*: an' Big Daddy divided da light from da darkness. (Genesis 1:1-4)*

So, yes, there are definitely some translations with modern lingo and although some would try to defend them, I personally believe that they are substandard Bibles using substandard forms of English.[75] And the words of God to man ought to be expressed in the most respectful way.

But this is not always the case. In fact there are translations, though different from the King James Version, which are actually fairly respectful in style. Note the following example from the American Standard Version which retains some of the Old English prose:

> *1 Jehovah is my shepherd; I shall not want. 2 He maketh me to lie down in green pastures; He leadeth me beside still waters. 3 He restoreth my soul: He guideth me in the paths of righteousness for his name's sake. (Psalm 23:1-3)*

While I agree that the language used should be reverent, we should also be mindful of the fact that languages evolve and it is entirely possible that 200

---

[75] Before anyone begins to scream "racism", let me say that I am speaking of a language and not a people group. We may speak any way we desire but if we want a formal-equivalent translation, then we must use reverent language. The High and Holy God of the universe is not "Big Daddy" but GOD!

## IN DEFENSE OF THE TEXTUS RECEPTUS

years from now English will be so different from what was done in 1611 that an update will need to be accomplished.

### ITALICIZED WORDS IN THE KJV

With this subject, it is hard to know where to begin. But probably the best way is to see why the translators of the King James Version used italicized words. Realizing that languages are different in structure and limitations, they came to the conclusion that there would need to be word insertions in order to complete the meaning. Knowing this, they decided that the word insertions should be clearly shown by using small roman type. However, later, when the King James Version was printed in Roman type, the small Roman type was changed to italics. So the purpose of the italicized words was to indicate word insertions that are necessary to understanding yet not reflected in the Greek or Hebrew texts.

When translating from one language to another, it is impossible to give a word-for-word rendering. Inserted words become necessary in order to keep the sense of the passage. Why is this necessary? There are many reasons but consider this as one of the most obvious examples: The Greek language sometimes omits the verb and is perfectly correct, according to rules of Greek grammar. However, in English, this would make a very awkward sentence to say the least, and in some cases, this would greatly hinder one's understanding of it. An example: in 2 Timothy 3:16 "IS" is in italics. It is obviously necessary. Without the insertion of "is" in italics the sentence is grammatically incorrect in English.

Again, languages are different from each other. Sometimes, they are radically different. What would you think if you had to read a Bible that was a word-for-word, literal rendering of the Greek text? Sounds wonderful right? Well, not really. If we translated John 3:16 in a word- for-word literal rendering, it would read, "So for loved the God the world that the Son of him the only-begotten he gave, that all the ones believing into him not may perish, but may have life eternal."

According to some, the italicized words are not needed and yet there are passages that would be very difficult to comprehend if the italicized words are removed. Can you imagine the confusion that could come if Psalm 3:8 did not have an italicized word? It says, "Salvation *belongeth* unto the LORD: thy blessing *is* upon thy people. Selah." Without the italicized word, it would look as if the LORD needed or received salvation.

Here is another good example would be in Psalm 12:5 where the Bible says, "For the oppression of the poor, for the sighing of the needy, now will I arise, saith the LORD; I will set *him* in safety *from him that* puffeth at him." Without the italicized words it would say, "I will set in safety puffeth at him."

One of the most used passages to illustrate the importance of the italicized words is 2 Sam 21:19 which says, "And there was again a battle in Gob with the Philistines, where Elhanan the son of Jaareoregim, a Bethlehemite, slew *the brother of* Goliath the Gittite, the staff of whose spear *was* like a weaver's beam.". Notice what happens when the italicized words are removed:

> *"And there was again a battle in Gob with the Philistines, where Elhanan the son of Jaareoregim, a Bethlehemite, slew Goliath the Gittite, the staff of whose spear was like a weaver's beam."*

Without the italicized words, it appears as if Goliath was killed by Elhanan when in fact we know from 1 Samuel chapter 17 that David did it. And just in case you may be thinking that possibly Elhanan did it, here is another passage concerning Elhanan and Goliath:

> **1Chronicles 20:5** *And there was war again with the Philistines; and Elhanan the son of Jair slew Lahmi the brother of Goliath the Gittite, whose spear staff was like a weaver's beam.*

So the point is, without the italicized words, the passage in 2 Samuel 21:19 would actually be in contradiction to the rest of the Bible. It may be easy to talk about removing the italicized words, but in practice, it is just not reasonable.

I was once asked, "How can we know that the italicized words are accurate?" His point was pretty simple and actually fairly logical. If the italicized words were inserted by the translators in order to help clarify the meaning of a message, how do we know that they always chose the right words?

Obviously, we would have to examine every italicized word in order to prove that they chose the correct word and I have a feeling even then, there would still be a few people who would find fault with the results. So I will offer up a few examples of where italicized words in the Old Testament actually "disappear" in the New Testament.

Notice first of all this passage from Deuteronomy chapter 8:

> **Deuteronomy 8:3** And he humbled thee, and suffered thee to hunger, and fed thee with manna, which thou knewest not, neither did thy fathers know; that he might make thee know that man doth not live by bread only, but by every *word* that proceedeth out of the mouth of the LORD doth man live.

## IN DEFENSE OF THE TEXTUS RECEPTUS

Notice that the word "word" is in italics. The idea is pretty clear in the passage and beside that, you will notice that "every" precedes "word". If the translators did not insert "word" then we would have an adjective with nothing to modify. So how did the translators know to choose "word" as versus "doctrine" or " idea" How did they come to the conclusion that this was the correct rendering? Probably because they were familiar with the words of Matthew 4:4 where the word is reflected in the Greek.

A few authors that I have read after sought to establish a point over the fact that a word was italicized in the English Old Testament but yet is represented in the Greek New Testament. They imply that since this is the case, the italicized words are obviously "inspired" or "advanced revelation" or "divine providence". But I think that a good deal of what we find in the King James Version is simply basic grammar or else cases where the translators knew which word to insert into italics because they knew the same passage was represented in the New Testament.

But honestly, the whole issue about italicized words is usually nothing more than a smokescreen or straw man argument to try and bring discredit on the King James Version. It is normally brought up as a point of contention to somehow say that the King James Version translators added their own words to the work they were doing. Or else, it is used to show where the translators were somehow "dynamic" in their approach to translation.

If the truth were to be known, it would have to be acknowledged that many other translations "add" words too. But the other translations do not indicate this by italics or often, any other indication! Notice these examples or Deut 25:4

*(ASV) Thou shalt not muzzle the ox when he treadeth out [the grain].*

The American Standard Version adds "the grain" and reflects it with brackets. But when was the last time you heard anyone talk about the added words of the ASV?

- *(ESV) You shall not muzzle an ox when it is treading out the grain.*

- *(NIV) Do not muzzle an ox while it is treading out the grain.*

- *(NKJV) You shall not muzzle an ox while it treads out the grain.*

- *(RSV) You shall not muzzle an ox when it treads out the grain.*

## IN DEFENSE OF THE TEXTUS RECEPTUS

Notice that the above mentioned translations added "the grain" but made no indication of it with italics or brackets or anything else! Yet no one ever questions the additions of these translations. The same sort of thing could be illustrated with 1 Sam 2:3, Proverbs 24:28, John 1:18, John 4:26, and many other passages. It is only the King James Version which is so heavily scrutinized. To me, this shows a clear bias against the King James Version.

By the way, there are translations other than the King James Version which use italics and guess what? No version is consistent in italicizing words. For instance, in 2 Timothy 3:16, the King James Version italicizes "IS", since there is no Greek equivalent for it; but there is no Greek equivalent for "GIVEN BY", either! The New American Standard Version italicizes "DOOM" it 1 Peter 2:8, but not "BECAUSE". So any argument concerning the consistency of the italicized words would invalidate every translation.

## IN DEFENSE OF THE TEXTUS RECEPTUS

## GREEK MANUSCRIPTS

At last count, there are 5,773 existing (extant) manuscripts of the New Testament. These manuscripts have been sorted and placed into various "families" by textual critics so that they may be classified and examined.

Some say that there are only two families of manuscripts – the right ones, and the wrong ones. While I agree with the basic premise that there is only one "right" family, this approach is incredibly simplistic. In actuality, a family is defined by similarity in variant readings. Those manuscripts with the same variant readings are placed in the same family. But let's consider a couple of basic facts. First, the Byzantine manuscripts have a 99 percent agreement within the family. However, the Alexandrian family has thousands of disagreements within the family. So if each family is to be defined by similar variant readings, then what we really have are thousands of families! More will be said on "families" later.

Emerging from these various "families" are two main texts that have been the main focus of the disagreement concerning Greek texts. One family of the manuscripts is commonly referred to as the Alexandrian family from which we get the Critical Text while the other is the Byzantine family from which we get the Textus Receptus.[76]

It is a well-known fact that there are over 6000 differences between the two Greek texts. No one disputes this. The differences are a collection of spelling, juxtaposition, and depending on how you look at it, additions or subtractions in the readings of the text itself. There are also many form changes (person, number, case, etc.) and changes to vocabulary (changes in vocabulary are often synonyms, but not always).

It has been said that the number of changes is equal to the whole book of First John. 1st John actually has over 2100 words in Greek. So if there are over 6000 differences, then it would be more along the lines of 1st Peter, 2nd Peter, 1 John, 2nd John, 3rd John, and Jude. These books contain around 5900 words. So where does this leave us today?

Since inspiration is "verbal", in that every word is in the text because God wanted that word to be there, and since the scriptures are clear that God promises to preserve his Word, then we must conclude that there is corruption in either the Critical Text or the Textus Receptus. Much information has been written on

---

[76] The reader should know that depending on the author, both the Critical Text and the Textus Receptus can be addressed by different names.

*God's Preserved Word to Every Generation*

whether the corruptions were purposeful or accidental. At this point in our discussion it is irrelevant. The fact remains that there are thousands of differences between the Critical Text and the Textus Receptus. Right now, it is enough to know that the two texts are significantly different. We will discuss why they are different later.

Many people assume that when a scholar uses the word, "manuscript" that he is in fact talking about a whole Bible. In reality, the opposite is more generally true. The extant Greek manuscripts actually range in size from just a few words to nearly complete Bibles. Some of the manuscripts are so small in size that scholars have very little evidence to determine to which "family" of texts the manuscript actually belongs.

Some manuscripts contain extra writings that are obviously not part of the scriptural text at all. For example, the Codex Vaticanus contains the non-canonical books of Ecclesiasticus, Judith, Tobit, and Baruch while the Codex Siniaticus contains the Wisdom of Sirach, Tobit, Judith, and the Maccabees. Codex Alexandrinus contains $3^{rd}$ and $4^{th}$ Maccabees, the 14 Odes, the Epistle to Marcellinus, the Eusebian summary of the Psalms, $1^{st}$ Clement, $2^{nd}$ Clement, the Maccabees, Sirach, and an appendix listing the Psalms of Solomon. Most likely, there were other non-canonical books as well but a number of pages have been torn off or lost so we can't prove it.

Many of the manuscripts are in very poor condition due to a variety of reasons. Some were destroyed by climate conditions as they waited to be discovered. Frequency of use would also wreak havoc on manuscripts, especially the older papyri which were much more fragile to start with. With this thought in mind, we should not be surprised to find papyrus manuscripts that are simply worn out. And indeed, that is exactly what we find in many cases.

Add to this the normal deterioration of the natural aging process. Again, the farther back in history we go, the fewer practical or useful manuscripts will be found. Several factors will increase or decrease the effects of age upon a manuscript but generally speaking, we should not expect to find large numbers of older manuscripts.

Humidity plays a very large role in the preservation of any item whether it is a manuscript, or a clay pot. This is one reason why the Dead Sea scrolls were preserved for so long. They were stored in a very dry climate. Thus, we should expect to find manuscripts which are in better condition in areas where the humidity is typically lower.

Another factor in the aging process is the type of material the manuscript is made from. Two examples will suffice. Imagine that you store a bear rug and a dictionary in a damp basement. Which would outlast the other? Provided that there was no outside intervention, we could come to the conclusion that bugs, bacteria, and small creatures would find the flavor of the bear rug much more enticing than the book! On the other hand, if the same two items were stored in a dryer environment, the bear rug may very well outlast the book.

Frequency of use may also take its toll on the quality of a manuscript. A brief visit to the public library is all that is required to understand this thought. Those books that are most frequently used are in the poorest condition. Some of the books have been handling roughly. Others were handled with soiled hands. Some may have been inadvertently exposed to sun or rain. As you can see, the more a book is used, the higher the probability that it will wear out at a faster rate. Adversely, it stands to reason that those manuscripts that are the least used would have a better chance of being in good condition. And although I am quite sure that the scriptures were handled with much more care, still, the facts are obvious.

And yet, this in itself is not an indicator whether a manuscript is a quality copy or not. Keep in mind that a substantial number of the uncial manuscripts are Alexandrian while an almost equal number of uncials are Byzantine. It is anybody's call as to which ones are in the best condition and which ones were the most used. So based simply upon the uncials, we could not make a factual determination concerning what is the original, and hence, true reading. That is not to say we don't have any idea which text is the true text. I am simply saying that wear and tear by reason of use is not a good indicator.

The end result of these processes have taken their toll on the extant manuscripts leaving only a fraction of the original 5773 manuscripts in any reasonable condition even nominally practical for translation purposes.

## *MANUSCRIPT TYPES*

Since much of the discussion concerning manuscripts is often cluttered with terminology not generally known by the average believer, it is probably beneficial to take a brief look at various types of manuscripts. As we do this, we should also include some information which helps to paint a more accurate picture of the difficulties in classifying and cataloging manuscripts. Let's first consider the papyrus manuscripts.

Papyrus manuscripts are just that. They are basically paper made from papyrus plants. As of the time of this writing, there are 127 extant papyri manuscripts. When compared to the number of uncials, minuscules, and lectionaries, that is a pretty small number. But all things considered, we should not expect to find a large number of papyri for several reasons.

## IN DEFENSE OF THE TEXTUS RECEPTUS

First of all, unless conditions of handling, storing, and humidity are kept ideal, this type of paper would have a rather short life. Keep in mind that papyrus was the standard paper of the first two centuries and was even in common use into the third century. Both time and weather have taken a toll on the discovery of papyrus manuscripts. This is one reason why papyri are generally found in Egypt. It is not very humid in Egypt's desert-like environment.

Another reason why we have so few papyri is because there simply were not as many copies of the scriptures in the first two centuries. Common sense - the closer we get to the originals, the fewer copies we will find. Bear in mind that the Word of God was still in the process of being spread abroad. And, although the canon was completed when John wrote the final "amen" of Revelation, that didn't mean everyone else in the world knew about it yet!

A third reason why we find so few papyri is because the time period when papyri was popular was also the greatest period of persecution of the church. This is also another contributing factor to why the existing papyrus manuscripts come from Egypt. Persecution, though it existed, was not as intense as in Palestine.

So we have three very logical reasons why the number of papyri is so small. And these three reasons are also just as valid in determining why the majority of the papyri are Alexandrian. It is because the Alexandrian text was the text most in use in Egypt at that time.

Considering the conditions for better protecting the manuscripts were more favorable in Egypt, and considering that this would naturally lead to a greater number of papyri in Egypt, and considering that persecution was not as great in Egypt, we would expect to see the Alexandrian text to flourish more than the Byzantine texts. So as we approach the third century, the Alexandrian text should have been the one to flourish, eventually choking out the Byzantine Text. Yet the opposite is true. In spite of the odds, the Byzantine text flourished.

Even so, the majority of papyri manuscripts are small fragments. Initially, it was believed that the papyrus manuscripts unanimously support the Alexandrian Text. However, as more copies have been found, more and more Textus Receptus readings have been discovered. Some of these Textus Receptus readings were thought by some scholars to have been "invented" in the fourth or fifth centuries. But Papyrus 90, which attests to Byzantine[77] readings roughly as often as Alexandrian readings, dates to the 200s clearly showing that these claims are false.

---

[77] Many scholars like to place P90 in the Alexandrian family but anyone who can read Greek can clearly see it is as much in agreement with the Byzantine family as it is with the Alexandrian family.

## IN DEFENSE OF THE TEXTUS RECEPTUS

The second type of manuscript that should be considered is called an uncial (also known as a majuscule). These manuscripts are made from vellum (an expensive and durable parchment made from animal skins) and written in capital letters. This was the style used between 300 to 900 A.D. These were normally bound in a book form that is commonly called a "codex". Around 323 uncials are in existence and 74 are purely Byzantine, meaning they agree with the Textus Receptus. Five uncials are a mixture of Byzantine and Alexandrian readings. Another 81 agree with the Alexandrian text. In fact, the two most famous uncials, Codex Vaticanus and Codex Sinaiticus, were used as the basis for the Critical Text of Westcott and Hort. Ninety-seven of the uncial manuscripts are mixed texts, meaning it is so mixed that it is not possible to place it in one family of manuscripts or the other. The remaining manuscripts have either not been classified or cannot be classified for whatever reason.

The third type of manuscript is referred to as a minuscule because it is written in lower case, cursive style letters. This style began to be used in the 700's AD and was written on vellum or paper.[78] 2911 minuscule manuscripts have been discovered with the majority in agreement with the Byzantine text from where we get the Textus Receptus. In fact, 1864 of the minuscules are either purely Byzantine or else contain Byzantine readings. Only 31 are in agreement with the Alexandrian manuscripts from which we get the Critical text.

One of the major points of support for the Textus Receptus has to do with the transition from uncial to minuscule. The argument is that if the manuscripts that agree with the Critical Text were considered to be pure, then the copyists would have used them to make the newer manuscripts. However, the overwhelming majority of minuscules were copied from Byzantine manuscripts. What does this mean? It means that the Critical Text manuscripts were not considered to be respectable and were not in common usage. Thus, the Critical Text does not meet the criteria of being available and in use by every generation.

As you can see from what we have just discussed, the majority of all the existing manuscript evidence is in agreement with the Textus Receptus. Only a very small fraction of manuscripts disagree. It is often said that the remaining manuscripts fall into another "family" or grouping, but in actuality, the disagreements between them are so radical that each manuscript would have to be in a family of its own!

So let's try to summarize this a bit. If we include the lectionaries, we have a total of 5773 extant manuscripts. 5369 support the Textus Receptus in full or in

---

[78] Paper began to be imported from China and was in use around 1000 A.D.

part. 227 manuscripts support the Critical text in full or in part. Another 226 manuscripts are either mixed texts which have been thrown in to other so called "families" or else unclassified for one reason or another.

5369 Byzantine manuscripts versus 207 Alexandrian manuscripts. It's pretty clear which one was favored.

## CATALOGING THE MANUSCRIPTS

Textual analysis is not really a modern phenomenon. We like to think that we are the educated ones who have excelled in the area of textual research and examination but the truth is that textual analysis is nothing new. In fact, if we take a good look at the writings of the early Christians we find evidence that they were concerned about the quality of the text just as we are today.

Irenaeus, who lived in the 2nd century, lamented the corruptions that were being brought into the biblical text by such men as Marcion and Valentinus.

Origen, who lived from 182 to 251 AD, making him contemporary to Irenaeus, frequently discussed the variants contained in the manuscripts that he possessed.

*"...the differences among the manuscripts [of the Gospels] have become great, either through the negligence of some copyists or through the perverse audacity of others; they either neglect to check over what they have transcribed, or, in the process of checking, they lengthen or shorten, as they please." (Bruce Metzger, The Text of the New Testament: Its Transmission, Corruption, and Restoration, 3rd ed. (1991), pp. 151-152).*

And this is pretty ironic considering that Origen was ministering in Alexandria, Egypt and would have been speaking of the Alexandrian manuscripts!

Augustine, who lived from 354 to 430 AD, said concerning Matthew 27:9, 10.

> **Matthew 27:9-10** *Then was fulfilled that which was spoken by Jeremy the prophet, saying, And they took the thirty pieces of silver, the price of him that was valued, whom they of the children of Israel did value; (10) And gave them for the potter's field, as the Lord appointed me.*

He, realizing that this particular quote is not found in Jeremiah, appealed to the various codices for his explanation.[79], [80]

Jerome, in commenting on Matthew 5:22 also made mention of other codices in his explanation of the passage itself.

So the point is, textual analysis has been around for almost as long as the texts themselves. There came a point however, when certain guidelines were put forth that are now almost universally followed.

As early as 1550 Stephanus, also known as Robert I Estienne, began cataloging the Greek manuscripts. He also began listing variants in the column of his 3rd printed edition. In fact, his 3rd edition was the first Greek testament that had a critical apparatus. In 1657, almost 50 years after the translation of the King James Version, an English scholar by the name of Brian Walton listed the variant readings from Stephanus as well as 15 other manuscripts. He also listed where those manuscripts were being stored.

In 1707, John Mill published his Greek New Testament using Stephanus 3rd Edition, and produced an apparatus referencing at least 100 manuscripts including references to early church writers. In 30 years time he listed over 30,000 variants. His work caused an outcry among Catholics and Protestants alike because they felt that his work was an attack upon the scriptures. However, after closer examination, Swabian scholar, Johann Albrecht Bengel concluded that no doctrine was affected by the variants no matter which reading a person may prefer. Again, this was all happening long before there was such a thing as a critical text!

The modern system of cataloging manuscripts was first introduced by Johann Jakob Wettstein who published an edition of the New Testament in Greek in 1751. He designated the uncials with capital letters and minuscules by using a system of Numbers. Wettstein cataloged around 125 Greek manuscripts in his edition of the Greek New Testament.

---

[79] Nicene and Post-Nicene Fathers, ser. 1, ed. Philip Schaff; vol. 6, St. Augustine (Grand Rapids: Eerdmans reprint, 1974), p. 191.

[80] In case the reader is curious, there are a couple of fairly well thought out explanations to this seeming problem. The first is simply that the passage does not say Jeremiah "wrote" it, it merely states that he "spoke" it. Another variation is that the passage is actually found in the writings of Zechariah (11:12, 13) who recorded what Jeremiah had earlier taught. A third strong possibility comes from the way the Jews listed their prophetic books. Jeremiah was first and his name came to stand for all of the prophetic books. But the point is, this is no contradiction in scripture because various plausible explanations can be put forth.

## IN DEFENSE OF THE TEXTUS RECEPTUS

Between 1820 and 1836, he added another 616 additional new manuscripts to the list. But from 1861 to 1894, F.H.A. Scrivener cataloged over 3,000 Greek manuscripts. 1,000 more manuscripts were cataloged by C.R. Gregory from 1894 to 1912 bring the total to just over 4,000 total manuscripts.

Kurt and Barbara Aland produced a total of cataloged manuscripts in 1967 as being 5,255 manuscripts. Since that time the number has been increased to 5,814 catalogued although not all of them have been sufficiently examined yet. This book reflects a number of 5,773 based upon numerous sources. The difference, however, is not very critical since the disparity is in the number of lectionaries and all are said to be of the same family of texts anyway.

### HOW MANUSCRIPTS ARE NUMBERED

Papyrus manuscripts are numbered by the letter *p* followed by the number. For example, the Chester Beatty papyri: *p45, p46,* and *p47*. So as soon as a person sees the designation, he knows already that the manuscript is papyrus, and usually from the first three centuries. He also knows that it is most likely written in all capital Greek letters with no spaces or punctuation between words. All this from a basic knowledge of the manuscripts and a number! Not bad, eh?

Parchment manuscripts fall into two different categories – uncial and minuscule. Uncials are numbered beginning with the digit "0", such as "01", "02", etc. So again, simply by looking at the number a person can already assume within a reasonable parameter of accuracy, the style of writing, the type of material it was recorded on, and even a ballpark idea of the age.

There are four uncials that were considered to be very important and so these were given special designations. Uncial 01 is also known as ℵ (Aleph – Codex Sinaiticus). Codex Alexandrinus, which has been given the number 02, is also called "A". Codex Vaticanus, or, 03, is also called "B". Codex Ephraemi Rescriptus, given the designation 04, is also known as "C". These four are often referred to in scholarly circles as "the four great codices" or "the four great uncials". Codex Bezae, named after the Calvinist Reformer Theodor Beza, not one of the "four greats" is also called Codex D.

The minuscules are numbered very simply as "1", "2", and so on. And again, by looking at the chart below, it is easy to see that the more manuscripts we find, the more support that is lent toward the Textus Receptus:

| | Total | Byz. | Byz. with Alex. reading | Byz. with Mixed Readings | Mixed | Alex. With Mixed Readings | Alex. with Byz. Readings | Alex. | Unclass. |
|---|---|---|---|---|---|---|---|---|---|
| | | | | | | | | | |

## IN DEFENSE OF THE TEXTUS RECEPTUS

| | | | | | | | | | |
|---|---|---|---|---|---|---|---|---|---|
| Papyri | 127 | 2 | 0 | 0 | 11 | 1 | 2 | 86 | 25 |
| Uncial | 323 | 53 | 17 | 8 | 97 | 6 | 19 | 56 | 67 |
| Minuscule | 2911 | 2840 | 3 | 10 | 25 | 0 | 3 | 29 | 1 |
| Lectionary | 2412 | 2407 | 0 | 0 | 0 | 0 | 5 (?) * | 0 | 0 |
| Totals | 5773 | 5302 | 20 | 18 | 133 | 7 | 29 | 171 | 93 |

* Although the lectionaries are all classified as being Byzantine, several of the lectionaries, lectionary 0269 and 1602 for example, contain spurious Alexandrian readings. And we should expect this to be the case with at least a few of the lectionaries since at least four of them were located in Egypt. Lectionary 1575 was said by the Alands to be in remarkably good quality, which, from their perspective may have meant that it is heavily Alexandrian. Since it was part of a codex with Uncial 0129 it is most likely Alexandrian although this has not yet been verified.
* Admittedly, I was not able to verify the classifications of many of the minuscules and thus, the information related to the minuscules is reliant upon many different sources. But as much as possible, I have tried to verify the accuracy of the information reflected.

## COLLATING OF THE TEXTS

What exactly is collating? It is a close examination of the manuscript in order to compare and record variant readings. The work of collation is time-consuming and difficult. It requires a keen eye as well as knowledge of many other manuscripts and variants.

To add to the difficulty, it is a known fact that a number of early collators were not nearly as meticulous as some of our modern critics. The biggest reason for this is that, for the most part, they favored the Byzantine manuscripts over anything else. As a result, existing manuscripts which were obviously different, were largely ignored. Thus, there are existing variants which have not been properly examined or recorded. And in my opinion, a good deal of them will be found in the Alexandrian family since those were the manuscripts that the early collators ignored.

It was actually Constantine Tischendorf who first began to produce an accurate collation in his Greek editions taking careful note of the variants. Another well-known 19th century scholar was Samuel Prideaux Tregelles. Far from being a friend of the Textus Receptus, he actually believed that the Textus Receptus did not rest on ancient authority. This drove him to travel around the world in an effort to collate various manuscripts. It is said that he even traveled to Rome in order to collate the Codex Vaticanus but was not allowed to do anything more than take note of certain important readings.

F.H.A. Scrivener is probably one of the most well known 19th century textual critics. Scrivener did a lot of work on the Textus Receptus by making comparison to the editions of Stephanus, Beza, and Elzever making note of the variants within the Byzantine family. He also compared the Textus Receptus to the King James Version taking special care to note variations, examining manuscripts in the Byzantine family, and making further corrections to the Textus Receptus. He did this believing that the translators not only translated, but also made textual choices based upon manuscripts they had at their disposal as well.

According to Kurt Aland, while speaking to the Congress of New Testament Scholars in Oxford in 1957, around 77% of all existing manuscripts remain unused. Initially, this sounds like a lot. But we must remember that quite a number of these manuscripts are not in any condition to use:

Others are known to be "mixed" texts and therefore it serves no real purpose to collate them because they do not present any type of evidence to what would be the true reading. It would be like trying to discern which part of a testimony in court is true when the witness is known to say things that no one else agrees with.

So as you can see, there are some very good reasons why a good number of the manuscripts have not been collated. Suffice it to say that all of the manuscripts have been examined. But quite a number of them, though they are valuable and noteworthy, would serve no purpose in the process of collation.

## MANUSCRIPT "FAMILIES"

All extant Greek manuscripts are copies of other manuscripts. May I repeat that? All manuscripts are copies of other manuscripts. I know that sounds pretty simple and rather obvious but it is rather crucial. We now have around 6000 manuscripts and the numbers are increasing all the time. But let's not forget that there are only 66 original autographs for the Old and New Testament. And we don't have these any more. That means everything that we have now is a descendant from something else. We have copies of copies and copies of copies of copies!

Textual scholars have tried to establish relationships between all these manuscripts and placed them in to various "families". These "families" are based mainly on the amount of agreement between the manuscripts. The manuscripts are examined, cataloged, dated, and characterized. And since the "families" or "text-types" typically originate in the same geographic location, the families are

## IN DEFENSE OF THE TEXTUS RECEPTUS

named after the geographic locations themselves. Some manuscripts are "Alexandrian", and for the most part, originate from Egypt. Most manuscripts are "Byzantine" (sometimes referred to as "Syrian" or "Antiochan"). The Byzantine manuscripts, for the most part, are said to originate in the Byzantine Empire. An even smaller number are from Western Europe and therefore fall into the "Western" family with some coming from around Caesarea and therefore called, "Caesarean".

Again, this book is more of an examination of the Textus Receptus, which is taken from the Byzantine family, and the Critical text, which is taken from the Alexandrian family. The Byzantine text is the source of most of the later Greek cursive manuscripts and is the text underlying the earlier printed editions of the Greek New Testament - the *Textus Receptus*. Most Greek manuscripts in our possession today are of Byzantine origin. And actually, more than a few scholars are of the opinion that the Western and Caesarean families are really just mixed or divergent manuscripts which can't be placed anywhere else.

Before we begin to take a look at the Alexandrian or Byzantine families, we should clarify exactly what that means. When we speak of a "family" of manuscripts, what we are really saying is that there are enough similarities between the manuscripts to consider them closely related. We should also remember that this relationship may indicate a single source or single geographic location where the manuscripts originated. Yet in either case, this may not always be the case. It may simply be that a manuscript matches the types of readings found in a certain family and yet it does not come from the same source document and is not found in the same geographical location. One example would be the Codex Alexandrinus. The gospels are clearly Byzantine and yet it originates in Egypt.

In the world of textual criticism, there is some disagreement as to what exactly constitutes a "family" of text types. As a result, depending upon who is speaking, there are anywhere from four to seven text types, or "families". [81] However, there are only two "families" which are of any real debate today. It is upon these two text types that every translation into English, and it reality, every language, is based. These two text types are the Alexandrian manuscripts and the Byzantine family. The following is a list of the two major families and some of the major manuscripts in that particular family:

---

[81] See Appendix A for a fuller discussion of the text types.

## Alexandrian Family

### History of the Critical Text

It may come as a bit of a surprise but the Critical Text is actually newer than the Textus Receptus. Whereas most scholars and textual critics mark the beginning of the Textus Receptus with Erasmus in the 1500s[82], it was in 1881 that Brook Foss Westcott and Fenton John Anthony Hort published *The New Testament in the Original Greek,* which has come to be called the Westcott and Hort text or, as in this volume, the Critical Text[83].

But to be completely fair, in reality, Westcott and Hort no more constructed the Critical Text that is in use today than Erasmus construct the current Textus Receptus. They laid the foundation, collated a proto-Critical Text, and greatly influenced the area of textual criticism. But in actuality, the Nestle-Aland text of today is quite different from the Westcott-Hort text of 1881.

Obviously, it is the position of this book that the Alexandrian manuscripts, and therefore, the Critical Text is inferior to the Byzantine manuscripts. Thus, we believe that the Critical Text is inferior to the Textus Receptus. But why? In order to grasp the extent of the impact and problems with this text, we must also learn something of the methods, religious bias, and purpose of the men who were behind the text.

### Brooke Foss Westcott

Brooke Foss Westcott was born in Birmingham, England where he was influenced in his early years by James Prince Lee who was at that time the Bishop of Manchester and Head of King Edward VI School in Birmingham. Bishop Lee was said to be an exceptional classical scholar and manuscript critic in the area of the classics. It is quite probable that his approach to the uninspired classics was also influential in Westcott's thinking concerning the inspired and preserved texts of the New Testament.

---

[82] In seeking to be more accurate, we would state that it was the Byzantine family of manuscripts which were in use from the first century until now. But as far as a single collated manuscript, the Textus Receptus is usually accredited to Erasmus in AD 1516 just as the Critical Text is usually accredited to Westcott and Hort in 1881.

[83] Bear in mind that the modern Critical Text is comparatively quite different from the text of Westcott and Hort. In fact, their original text is almost as different from the modern Critical text as it is from the Textus Receptus. So if we were to be honest and accurate, we can't really call it a Westcott/Hort text any more.

## IN DEFENSE OF THE TEXTUS RECEPTUS

In 1844, Westcott entered Trinity College at Cambridge where he was invited to join the Cambridge Apostles. This was a secret society consisting of those who were considered to be the twelve brightest students at Cambridge. It was essentially a debate club where issues were discussed among its members on a weekly basis. Through this medium, Westcott would have been greatly exposed to many forms of political, philosophical, and religious thought.

Westcott was not simply a member of this society either. In fact, he is credited with writing the oath of secrecy and a related curse, both of which have been taken by every new member of the society since 1851. As one of the society's own members, Henry Sedwick, has openly stated, "the tie of attachment to this society is much the strongest corporate bond which I have known in my life."[84] Basically, he was stating that the influences of the society were greater than the influences of any other persons in his life – greater than his parents, greater than his church, greater than anyone!

As a debate club, many of its members would have been confronted with ideas and philosophies that are definitely unbiblical. In fact, a simple examination of some of its past members will serve to illustrate the influence this society must have had on Westcott's thinking:

- J.F.D. "Frederick" Maurice - Christian socialist writer (1823)
- Erasmus Alvey Darwin, brother of Charles Darwin (1823) – though there is no evidence that he followed Charlie's views on geology, he was a self-professed supporter of the view that "heterodoxy is the norm". On the other hand, he was an intimate friend of Charles Lyell, who popularized uniformitarianism. There is also much to be said about his laziness (retired at the age of 26) and adulterous relationship with a married woman, as well as his "medicinal use" of opium. Kind of makes a person wonder how he ever got a reputation as being one of Cambridge's brightest students.
- Richard Chenevix Trench, Christian writer, Archbishop of Dublin (1827) – believed that if you spoke of the devil then the devil would appear.[85] Occultists would say the same thing.
- Sir William Harcourt, Chancellor of the Exchequer (1847) - British lawyer, journalist and liberal statesman.
- Henry Sidgwick, philosopher (1857) - one of the founders and first president of the Society for Psychical Research, a member of the Metaphysical Society.

---

[84] http://en.wikipedia.org/wiki/Cambridge_Apostles

[85] www.phrases.org.uk/meanings/speak-of-the-devil.html

## IN DEFENSE OF THE TEXTUS RECEPTUS

- Henry Jackson, classicist (1863) - Prelector in Ancient Philosophy; Regius professor of Greek at Cambridge University; one of the founding members of the Cambridge University Liberal Club
- Oscar Browning, educator – dismissed from Eton College for his unbalanced and anarchic views.
- N. Whitehead, mathematician, logician and philosopher (1884) - believed that "there are no whole truths; all truths are half-truths. It is trying to treat them as whole truths that plays the devil."[86]
- Bertrand Russell, philosopher, mathematician, social activist and logician, member of the Royal Society, Nobel prize winner, member of the House of Lords (1892)

Westcott himself held to some pretty radical views[87]. No one could argue the fact that he wrote some pretty radical things in his days. But in all fairness, the King James translators were not all fine outstanding bastions of the Baptist faith either! However, one of the main things that make the difference is how these men felt about the Bible itself. The one position that we most concern ourselves with is Westcott's position on the scriptures. No doubt, many of Westcott's other beliefs are unbiblical but his beliefs concerning the scriptures would be the guide of his thinking and philosophy, or at the very least, influence his work in the area of textual analysis.

Usually, this is a point where those who support the Critical Text come to the defense of Westcott and Hort by claiming that they had written good commentaries in which they wrote many good things. Along with this, it is often pointed out that the King James Version translators were not Baptists either. I have even read that the King James Version translators were "baby baptizing Anglicans".

I have read portions of Westcott's writings and Hort's writings and they are typical as commentaries go. And I also understand that the King James Version translators were definitely not Baptists. And yet, they held to a high view of the scriptures, which kept them from intentionally altering its literal meaning even when that literal meaning grated against their own personal beliefs. On the other hand, Westcott and Hort set out to intentionally alter the only text that had been received and used by God's people for hundreds of years.

---

[86] Dialogues of Alfred North Whitehead, recorded by Lucien Price, p. 13, 2001

[87] He did not believe that Hell is a place of punishment for the lost (Westcott, Historic Faith, pp.77-78); did not believe in a literal and physical second coming of Christ (Westcott, Arthur, Life and Letters of Brooke Foss Westcott. (New York, 1903), Volume II, p. 308)

## IN DEFENSE OF THE TEXTUS RECEPTUS

Again, I must emphasize that what we are most concerned with is how these two men viewed the scriptures because their belief in inspiration and preservation would be the guide in their approach to the text. So what did Westcott believe concerning the scriptures?

First of all, he did not believe in the infallibility of the scriptures and stated such. (Westcott, The Life and Letters of Brooke Foss Westcott, Vol. I, p.207). One danger of this belief, among many others, is that it causes one to become a judge of the scriptures to determine what was from the hand of God and what was not. Naturally, a person who doubts infallibility must also deny preservation. Once the doctrine of preservation is thrown to the wind, anything goes!

So in the mind of Westcott, the scriptures, as preserved in the Textus Receptus, were suspect and needed to be evaluated to determine whether or not they were worthy of acceptance.

Secondly, Westcott also held to an allegorical view of biblical interpretation.[88] One thing that can be said about those who hold to an allegorical view of the scriptures is that they tend not to see each individual word as important to God's complete message. In fact, the literal meaning of the text itself is not so important to an allegorist because, in his mind, the truth is beneath the surface waiting to be discovered. But one who is a literalist MUST be concerned about the exact wording of the text!

Logically, Westcott would have been concerned that the meaning of a particular passage was maintained but he would not have been as concerned that each word was preserved.

And just as Amnon had a friend, so did Westcott. And his friend was Fenton John Anthony Hort.

### Fenton John Anthony Hort

Fenton John Anthony Hort's history is not much different from that of Westcott's. And again, the reason we even speak of their history at all is because it helps us to understand the philosophy behind their thinking. Hort was also a student of Trinity College in Cambridge and was contemporary with Westcott. Although he began his college years being somewhat conservative, in time he succumbed to the more liberal theological thinking of his peers.

---

[88] He did not believe creation, and even doubted the literal existence of Moses and David.( Westcott, Arthur. Life and Letters of Brooke Foss Westcott, (New York, 1903). Vol. 2, p.69)

## IN DEFENSE OF THE TEXTUS RECEPTUS

In 1870, he was appointed to a committee whose purpose was to revise a translation of the New Testament. According to Mark D. Chapman's <u>New Testament Revision Company</u> the committee was commissioned by the convocation of Canterbury to "adapt the King James Version to the present state of the English language" and to adapt it to the "present state of Biblical scholarship". On the first point, there is nothing legitimately wrong with wanting to update the spelling of certain words (such as draught to draft; or publick to public) and there is no harm in changing archaic words to perfect synonyms when it makes the meaning more clear (such as changing "let" to "hinder". "Let" no longer means hinder today). But the committee committed a grievous error in thinking that we need the input of "the present state of Biblical scholarship". I mean, think about this for a moment! That is where they went wrong because the majority of the men working on this revision did not have a very conservative "state of biblical scholarship."

So what do we make of this? Two thoughts come to mind. First, the original intention was to do some type of update to the King James Version but not necessarily to produce a completely new Greek text or to even produce a radically different translation. But unfortunately, the seeds of destruction are often sown in the beginning of a project. And in this case, the "seed of destruction" was their faulty premise of adapting the King James Version to the standards of the "present state biblical scholarship". So by the time the committee had finished their work, they had produced a new Greek text as well as a new translation.

Hort's beliefs were not much different from Westcott's[89] either. But again, in staying with the subject at hand, we should concern ourselves with his personal beliefs concerning the Bible itself:

Hort claimed that he had issues with the historical view of the authority of the scriptures (Hort, The Life and Letters of Fenton John Anthony Hort, Vol. I, p.400). But if the scriptures are not the authority, then what is? Later, Hort would become the authority as he and a few others made decisions concerning the text of the Bible itself.

---

[89] Was not sure if there was a literal hell. (Hort, <u>Life and Letters</u>, Vol. I, p.149); Believed that Catholicism was closer to the truth than any other (Hort, <u>Life and Letters</u>, Vol. I, p. 77); held to the doctrine of baptismal regeneration (Hort, Arthur Fenton, <u>Life and Letters of Fenton John Anthony Hort</u>, (New York, 1896), Volume I, p. 76, 81); Was a racist believing that "[n*gg*rs] . . . have surely shown themselves only as an immeasurably inferior race, just human and no more, their religion frothy and sensuous, their highest virtues, those of a good Newfoundland dog." ( Hort, Arthur Fenton, <u>Life and Letters of Fenton John Anthony Hort</u>. (New York, 1896), Vol. 1, p.459)

## IN DEFENSE OF THE TEXTUS RECEPTUS

Hort had a personal bias against the Textus Receptus, calling it "villainous" (Life, Vol. I, p. 211). In other words, he entered into the task of constructing a new Greek text after having already concluded that the Textus Receptus could not be trusted.

Hort believed that the Bible should be treated as any other book when it comes to applying the principles of textual criticism.[90] Therefore his approach to the textual issue was purely a secular approach, which did not consider the implications of the doctrine of inspiration and preservation at all!

In a letter he wrote to Rev. Rowland Williams in 1858, he stated that "if you make a decided conviction of the absolute infallibility of the N.T. practically a sine qua non for co-operation, I fear I could not join you."[91] Thus, in order for Hort to work with someone, they could not require him to subscribe to the infallibility of the scriptures.

### The Stated Purpose of Westcott and Hort

Some would find it hard to believe but the stated purpose of Westcott and Hort was to replace the Textus Receptus with a new text. They knew that their personal views would be called into question at some point so they worked as quickly and as fervently as possible to "cast [their] text upon the world" before they had to face the charges of heresy.[92]

The fact that they wanted to produce an entirely new Greek Testament is clear from the very words of Hort himself, "Our object is to supply clergymen generally, schools, etc., with a portable Greek Text which shall not be disfigured with Byzantine corruptions.".[93] Understand that when he referred to the Byzantine Text he was referring to the family of manuscripts upon which the Textus Receptus is based. He believed that the Textus Receptus was "disfigured" with corruptions. In essence, he was stating that God did not preserve the scriptures and that their committee would restore what had been lost!

---

[90] Hills, Edward, *Believing Bible Study*, (The Christian Research Press, Des Moines, 1967), p. 122

[91] Hort, The Life and letters of Fenton John Anthony Hort, Vol I, pg 420

[92] Hort, Arthur Fenton, <u>Life and Letters of Fenton John Anthony Hort</u>, (New York, 1896), Volume I, p. 400

[93] Hort, Vol. I, op. cit., p. 250.

## IN DEFENSE OF THE TEXTUS RECEPTUS

At one point, Westcott relayed to Hort, "I feel most keenly the disgrace of circulating what I feel to be falsified copies of Holy Scripture, and am most anxious to provide something to replace them."[94]

So regardless of what one may say about the character of the men, their purpose was clear – replace the Textus Receptus because they believed it to be inferior. This is what they thought and this is what they did.

I have read more than a few modern writers who vehemently defend what they refer to as the "biblical orthodoxy" of Westcott and Hort. By going through their writings, they have shown where these men made biblical statements concerning the deity of Christ and other fundamental doctrines which were true and faithful to the Bible. But what they believe on these things is not the issue here. What did they believe concerning the Bible itself? I think we have shown that regardless of what some may say about their "fundamental beliefs", they certainly were not fundamental or orthodox in their beliefs concerning the Bible itself. And that is what made the difference!

### The Philosophical Methods of Westcott and Hort

It is often said that the choice concerning which Greek text is superior should not be made based upon the men themselves because no man is perfect. We would agree with this to a point. However, the theological bias that a person has toward the Word of God itself will ultimately guide his thinking concerning the methods that he uses. Thus, a simple examination of the methods of Westcott and Hort in comparison to the truth of the scriptures themselves becomes very revealing.

In my opinion, the philosophy of Westcott and Hort was pure academic arrogance. They believed that only scholars who were properly trained and equipped with a thorough knowledge of Greek, as well as knowledgeable of the manuscript evidence, are able to discern the true readings of scripture. In their minds, a modern scholar, if thoroughly trained, may actually be better able to decide upon the truth than the ancient copyists. In fact, by their philosophy, modern textual criticism alone is all that is necessary and the guidance of the Holy Spirit is not needed at all.

Obviously, in the area of textual criticism, one would need to have a good understanding of Greek. Yet the scriptures clearly teach that without the Holy Spirit, man cannot know spiritual truth in any extent. (1 Cor 2:14)

---

[94] Life, Vol.I, pp.228,229

## IN DEFENSE OF THE TEXTUS RECEPTUS

*$^{14}$ But the natural man receiveth not the things of the Spirit of God: for they are foolishness unto him: neither can he know them, because they are spiritually discerned. **1 Corinthians 2:14***

I am not saying that person who knows absolutely nothing about Greek, but is filled with the Spirit, would be able to make good textual decisions. One requirement does not negate the other. But the Bible is not just another book. We cannot approach it from the secular aspect alone. It is a supernatural book, a spiritual book. And it requires the enablement of the Holy Spirit in order to understand its truths.

Another assumption that Westcott and Hort make is that in the process of time, the true readings of scripture have been either lost or corrupted and need to be recovered. They believed that some time during the 2$^{nd}$ or 3$^{rd}$ century a move to standardize the Greek text caused the original readings to be lost. They referred to this act as the "Lucian Recension" and yet there is not one shred of evidence to show that any such standardization ever happened. In fact, there is not one piece of evidence that a person named "Lucian" was ever involved with copying or altering the scriptures in any time period.[95]

But again, we need to reiterate that in order for the "Lucian Recension" to be true we would have to assume that God made promises concerning preservation that he could not keep. Yet the Bible states very clearly:

**John 10:35** *the scripture cannot be broken;*

**Matt 24:35** *Heaven and earth shall pass away, but my words shall not pass away.*

The methods of Wescott and Hort are the ultimate outcome of their philosophy. These two men developed and promoted some major points in their theory which, to put it kindly, are dangerous and very inaccurate. And yet, many modern scholars still believe we should follow their propositions. Note the following Westcott/Hort propositions:

---

[95] Now, here is an interesting thought. We know from church history that the "Bible-belt" of the ancient world was in and around Antioch. Even if the Lucian recension were true, wouldn't it make more sense that a manuscript prepared by a Christian leader in the "Bible-belt" of Antioch would be more trustworthy than a manuscript that came to fruition in Egypt?

*God's Preserved Word to Every Generation*

## IN DEFENSE OF THE TEXTUS RECEPTUS

> 1. In matters of textual criticism the Bible is to be treated like any other ancient book. No special considerations are to be made concerning its claims of inspiration and preservation.

The problem with this idea is that the Bible is not just "any other historical book". It stakes the claim of divine origin which gives it heavenly authority. Add to this God's promises of supernatural preservation and you have a book which is unlike any other book ever written. This must be taken into account because it forms the very foundation of faith by which correct textual evaluations can be performed.

If the Bible is all that it claims to be, then the special claims of inspiration and preservation must be taken into account. If God has indeed preserved his words, then nothing could be lost. Thus, any thought of "recovering", "discovering" or "uncovering" the true text is simply unbiblical. Those who say that modern scholarship can in any way recover the original texts are in effect saying that God could not keep his promises of preservation.

Suffice it to say that with the sheer volume of copies that have been discovered, we would be foolish to assume that we could consider the Bible like any other book. How could we miss the evident fact that this book has always been treated with greater care, and thus so many more copies have remained until the present? No other historical writing even comes close.

> 2. Because of their age (mid-fourth century), the primary basis of the Greek text is to be found in the Vaticanus and Sinaiticus manuscripts.

As we have already seen, it can be clearly shown that representative readings of both the Textus Receptus and the Critical Text have been dated as far back as the 2nd century.[96] So, age becomes a moot point. The age of a manuscript may make it more valuable but age does not make one manuscript superior over another. The only thing that the age of a manuscript proves is that it existed during a particular time period. The age of a manuscript cannot vouch for its accuracy.

Another thing that we should keep in mind is that the age of a manuscript does not show whether it was even being used. In order to determine if a

---

[96] Again, I would state the case that P90 is as much Byzantine as it is Alexandrian. I could find only 3 independent readings where P90 did not agree with either the Alexandrian or the Byzantine manuscripts. I found only one place where it agreed with the Alexandrian manuscript against the Byzantine manuscripts, and one place where it agreed with Byzantine manuscript against the Alexandrian manuscript. P90 is also the second oldest manuscript to date. Some date it as early as 165 AD.

particular text was in use, we would have to find multiple copies of the same manuscript in separate geographical locations over a span of time. This cannot be said for the Critical Text but it is very clear when considering the Textus Receptus!

Some would argue that the Alexandrian manuscripts must have been in use because they were copied. But again, it should be obvious that if they were, the copies themselves were very poor since these manuscripts disagree even within their own family in thousands of places. If scribes copied these, one would think that there would be greater agreement between at least a few of the Alexandrian manuscripts but the fact is, no such agreement exists! Additionally, based upon the dates assigned to the extant manuscripts, the Alexandrian text wasn't used in any sense from the 1400s until the late 1800s when Westcott and Hort literally revived them in the form of the Critical Text. By my estimation, that is at least 4 1/2 generations no matter how you count it![97] At this point, I should remind the reader that God has promised to preserve his truth to every generation.

> ***Psa 100:5*** *For the LORD is good; his mercy is everlasting; and his truth endureth to all generations.*

Looking at it from another angle, age of the manuscript actually works in favor of the Byzantine family because it stands to reason that the older a manuscript is, the more copies that can be made from it. The farther back in time we go, the more descendants a manuscript may have.

However, we must tread very lightly here because this is not a hard and fast rule by any means. The numerical superiority may indicate that the Byzantine text is older because that would allow for more time to make more copies. But, it may not mean that at all. We do not know that the rate of copying is constant. In fact, we know that the rate of copying was NOT constant. That would be like saying we think America is older than England because we have more people.

---

*3. Despite its numerical advantage, the Received or Byzantine Text (as it is called) is merely one of three or four competing text types.*

---

[97] There are several ways to count a generation. Some count 20 years, some count 70 years, some count 100 years. Everyone has their own reasons why they count a generation the way that they do. Since this book is not about generations, I have chosen to use the longest time period for a generation which is 100 years. So, I say "at least" 4 and a half generations based upon a 100-year generation. If the reader believes that a generation is shorter than 100 years, then you can add even more generations!

## IN DEFENSE OF THE TEXTUS RECEPTUS

Some people believe that the reason Westcott and Hort came up with this rule is so that they could make the strength of the Critical Text equal to that of the Textus Receptus. It stands to reason that sheer numbers would clearly indicate that the Byzantine manuscripts were preferred. Each manuscript should be allowed to testify on its own but in Westcott and Hort's way of thinking, each family testifies as one voice.

But even if we were to accept Westcott and Hort's methods, we still have some very major issues to deal with. For many years, there were four proposed text types – Byzantine (from which we derive the Textus Receptus), Alexandrian (also called Neutral or Egyptian and is the source of the Critical Text), Western, and Caesarean. However, in recent years a few scholars have concluded that the Western and Caesarian text types lack uniformity and therefore, cannot be considered true text types. Generally speaking, they can either be lumped in with the Alexandrian text or else considered to be so mixed that they can fit into no other grouping at all! But even if we were to add the Western Text and the Caesarian text to the Alexandrian family, the Alexandrian family would still be very small.

Consider this. There are only 127 papyri fragments. 25 are too small or too fragmentary to classify. Another 13 texts are not in agreement with the Critical Text because they are either mixed texts or Byzantine. This leaves 89 manuscripts that we would classify as Critical Text. That is exactly the type of data we should expect to find seeing that they come from Egypt. So the low number of Byzantine papyri manuscripts do not mean the Byzantine family was not in use. It simply means they were not favored in Egypt. But we already knew that! Alexandria, being the home of allegorical thought, would have favored the Critical Text readings. Or to put it more accurately, are RESPONSIBLE for the Alexandrian texts.

But what is good for the goose is also good for the gander, isn't it? If we apply the same logic to the smaller number of later Alexandrian manuscripts, wouldn't mean that one reason why there are fewer Alexandrian manuscripts in the later centuries is because they were not favored in the Byzantine Empire? Yes. In fact, this is exactly what some scholars teach. But again, we already knew this. The Byzantine Empire, being the home of literal interpretation, would have favored the Byzantine readings. Or to put it more accurately, it is responsible for the Byzantine texts.

There are 323 uncials (manuscripts written in capital letters) with 81 in agreement with the Critical Text. 74 of the uncials are purely Byzantine with the remainder being either mixed or unclassified. As you can see, the numbers are fairly even for the uncials. And this is where things are not as they should be.

## IN DEFENSE OF THE TEXTUS RECEPTUS

For if the Alexandrian text were the original text, and the numbers of papyri were indicative of all existing manuscripts of the first two centuries, then we would have to ascertain why the Byzantine manuscripts suddenly burst on the scene in such significant numbers. Since no plausible explanation exists,[98] we would have to, at least from an empirical scientific approach, allow for the possibility that the Alexandrian text was NOT the original text. And indeed, it wasn't.

But again, let's be fair about this. If we apply the same standard to the Alexandrian text, what can we deduce? If the Byzantine text were the original text, and the numbers of papyri were not indicative of all existing manuscripts of the first two centuries, then we would have to ascertain why the Alexandrian manuscripts were not copied in significant numbers. But we have no plausible explanation. The only thing that we can safely assume is that the Byzantine believers did not want to use the Alexandrian manuscripts.

However, if the absence of Byzantine manuscripts in the papyri CAN be explained, and they can,[99] then we would expect to find copies of both Alexandrian and Byzantine manuscripts until one family was finally suppressed by the overall acceptance of the other by God's people. And sure enough, that is exactly what we find.

There are 2911 minuscules (manuscripts written in smaller Greek letters). 31 of these can be said to agree with the Alexandrian texts and hence, the Critical text. Scholars are somewhat divided on whether or not any of the minuscules support the Critical Text but just for the sake of argument, we will concede that 31 are most likely Alexandrian. 2840 of these minuscules are Byzantine. This works out to about 4.0571 Byzantine manuscripts per year. On the other hand, with only 31 Alexandrian minuscules, this works out to 0.04428 manuscripts per year.

And again, I know there are numerous factors involved which make this simple mathematical illustration a bit simplistic. I am aware that the scribes were

---

[98] Westcott and Hort came up with the unfounded and unsupportable "Lucian Recension" theory in an attempt to explain what was obviously a big problem in their approach. More will be said about this as we look at Westcott and Hort's last proposition.

[99] Three basic reasons why the Byzantine papyri would be in such low number - 1) The area where the Byzantine manuscripts were most used did not have the type of weather conducive to preservation; 2) Persecution was stronger in the area where the Byzantine manuscripts were most used. Many Christian writings would have been destroyed. Fewer opportunities existed to make ample copies; 3) frequency of use because they were preferred.

not spacing out the manuscripts in order to meet our average. But it does go to show very clearly which family of texts were in use.

All in all, there are 207 manuscripts out of over 5,773 (if we include the lectionaries) which can be considered solely in support of the Critical Text. Westcott and Hort, knowing that these figures were greatly damaging, had to find a way to level the playing field. So they came up with this rule!

> 4. *The numerical prevalence of the Received Text can be explained by a study of the genealogical descent of its manuscripts. If, for example, nine out of ten manuscripts contain the same readings, nine agree against one, but the nine have a common origin, the numerical value is still one to one.*

To state the agreement simply, since the Byzantine manuscripts are copies of other Byzantine manuscripts, then the reading is merely one voice. True. The Byzantine manuscripts are copies of copies of copies which go back into history. It has been said that any "parent-to-child" relationship between manuscripts is hard to prove. Some even go so far as to state that "the great mass of Received Text manuscripts are not "mimeographed" copies; very few have a parent-child relationship. Instead they are individual representatives of lines of transmission which go deep into the past."[100]

The major problem with this rule is that it flies directly in the face of preservation. You see, the reason why a particular manuscript would have been copied and distributed to others is because the users believed it was God's Word. We should expect to find multiple copies of the manuscripts that they favored. And this is a key point in the method by which God preserved his Word. If nothing else, multiple copies prove the Byzantine text was the favored text. It was obviously the text that God's people copied and used. And that, as we have asserted all along, is how God preserves his Word.

But let's be realistic. Westcott and Hort are right about one thing. The Byzantine manuscripts are copies of copies of copies. They must be because we do not have the originals and yet we believe that the Textus Receptus is exactly the same as the original autographs. In order for this to be true, the Byzantine manuscripts must be copies of copies of copies.

---

[100] http://www.kingswaybaptist.co.za/MissingInModernBibles/VIIITheTheoryBehindtheShorterAlt eredTe xt/tabid/327/Default

## IN DEFENSE OF THE TEXTUS RECEPTUS

However, this is not an argument against the Textus Receptus. In actuality, it is a strong argument FOR the Textus Receptus because it shows that the Byzantine manuscripts were in use by God's people!

One could conceivably say that the Byzantine scribes merely copied what they knew until the 1400s while the Alexandrian scribes copied what they knew until the end of Greek-speaking Christianity in Egypt. Thus, we see the numerical superiority of the Byzantine manuscripts. And this may be historically accurate but we still have to ascertain why it would be the case. The crux of the issue concerning preservation rises and falls on the facts of God's providence. No doubt, God's providence is an unseen hand guiding the affairs of history. Then why is it so difficult to see where God would have done the same thing in this case by allowing the Byzantine to be much more greatly propagated than the Alexandrian texts?

> 5. *"The distinctive Received Text readings are not generally seen before 350 AD. For the most part they are absent from the Greek manuscripts, Versions, and Scripture quotations of the Church Fathers."*

This was either great ignorance in men who should have known better or a flat out lie. Of the 5,814 manuscripts in existence, only 111 can be said to have been written before 350 AD. While it is true that the majority of those manuscripts are Critical Text, it is because the majority are papyri which come from Egypt where the Alexandrian texts were favored. Yet even among those manuscripts there still exists Papyrus 90 (P90) though not yet conclusively identified, agrees with the Byzantine family is some places and with the Alexandrian family in other places.

As for the "church fathers" (I prefer to call them "early Christian writers"), one research showed that the early church writers (Tertullian, Irenaeus, Hippolytus, Origen, Cyprian, and Clement) quoted Byzantine readings countless times! The Byzantine manuscripts were not merely in existence. They were also very much in use! These writers were not limited to one geographical location either. This indicates that the Byzantine manuscripts were in WORLDWIDE use.

This was another one of Westcott and Hort's smokescreens[101] devised to discredit the Textus Receptus, which would obviously be different from their

---

[101] I am aware that the word "smokescreen" carries with it a negative connotation but I know that they made statements about getting their work done before folks found out what they were really up to. With this in mind, I have a hard time believing that they were drawing conclusions in good faith based upon their presuppositions and the information that they had.

**God's Preserved Word to Every Generation**

work. In order to accommodate this "guideline" Westcott and Hort invented a theory that is called "the Lucian Recension".

In their opinion, a man in Antioch, around 250-350 AD, held a church council meeting during which the Byzantine readings were standardized. The council then sanctioned this new text. And according to their theory, this explains why the Byzantine Text was so prevalent.

Westcott and Hort also gave a fancy, educated-sounding word to this action - "Conflation". What does that mean? Basically, it means that sometimes, when two or more things share some common characteristics, they sometimes take on the dissimilar characteristics until the dissimilarities are lost. And according to Westcott and Hort, this was intentionally done at a council meeting in Antioch.

Conflation does not necessarily refer to the recension of the text, but the combining of two readings into one reading which contains elements of the two separate readings. A recension may involve conflations, but it may just as easily involve choosing the entirety of one reading over the other.

The biggest problem with their theory is that we have manuscripts and translations which agree with Byzantine readings predating their supposed "recension". This conclusively shows us that those readings clearly existed before the time of the supposed "Lucian Recension".

However, this is not really a problem with the idea of a standardization of the text. As far as I know, Westcott and Hort never proposed that Lucian invented new readings but that Lucian chose from pre-existing readings. Logically, that is what Westcott and Hort was doing. And that is what we are doing right now! We are choosing one text over and against all others. So what is wrong with that? Nothing. But in Westcott and Hort's case, there is not one shred of evidence that indicates such a council ever existed.

Admittedly, there was a well-known church leader named Lucian who died around AD 311. But other than a name similarity, there is nothing else to indicate a recension ever occurred. And if such a council meeting ever occurred, it is almost unfathomable that somebody wouldn't have mentioned it since it had to do with altering the words of scripture! Surely, SOMEBODY would have mentioned it! But no, there is absolutely nothing. It is almost as if it never really happened!

Ira Maurice Price, author of "The Ancestry of Our English Bible" states:

*"Their theory is keyed to the fact that Lucian, a Christian of Samosata in Asia Minor, tried to produce a unified text, including all the Old Testament and New*

## IN DEFENSE OF THE TEXTUS RECEPTUS

*Testament. He gathered this from a variety of sources. Lucian had earlier studied in a Christian school at Edessa in Mesopotamia and, by the time he arrived in Antioch, had gained a reputation for scholarship. He worked with a Hebrew scholar in a revision of the Septuagint (the Greek translation of the Old Testament, prepared over a span of 150 years and completed about 100 B.C.) that was more thorough than that done by Eusebius of Caesarea.*

*Lucian, who only had a friend or two to help him, worked faithfully on his little project. Later, he was martyred under the persecution of Emperor Maximus in 312.*

*Westcott and Hort expanded that historical fact into a fabulous tale, that the emperor commanded that Lucian do his work and that it must be made the standard New Testament text of the Roman Empire!" (pg. 222)*

But time and reality sometimes have a way of revealing those unbending little problems that we like to call, "facts". When the theory was first put forth, it was commonly rejected. But it was later resurrected by Kurt Aland.[102] Currently, the majority of textual critics and scholars have also rejected this theory. Unfortunately, the damage has already been done!

The basic reason behind this whole premise is to establish the "older is better" argument, which we have already shown to be a false assumption. According to Westcott and Hort, the earliest manuscripts are to be considered more reliable than later manuscripts. And we would partly agree because the earlier the manuscript, the closer to the original writings, historically speaking. But common sense would tell us that the age of the manuscript in and of itself does not guarantee the purity of a manuscript. We may have a New World Translation (the Bible of the Jehovah Witnesses who are definitely a cult) that could be dated 1955 and a King James Version dated 2011. Obviously, the NWT is not better simply because it is older!

> 6. The shorter readings are to be preferred. Corruption from addition is much more likely than corruption by omission.

First of all, it can be clearly shown that when it comes to copying and recopying a work, there are greater dangers of missing something (i.e. shortening the text) than there is in adding something. Therefore, if we must suspect one

---

[102] New Testament Textual Criticism, Exegesis and Church History (Contributions to Biblical Exegesis & Theology) by aJ. Delobel and B. Aland (Jan 1994) pg. 17

reading over and against another, the shorter reading should be suspect, not preferred!

But what if the scribes understood this just as well as we do? What if they already knew that a shorter reading should be suspect? Would they not then be more prone to insert a marginal note written too close to the text, fearing that if they omitted them, they may be omitting part of the authentic text?

Again, we would have to assume that a scribe would be familiar enough with the scriptures to know what was text and what was not. And if not, that would be the exception and not the rule. In other words, we would end up with variant readings but it certainly wouldn't be the majority reading.

And secondly, before we can accept the idea that a reading was lost until Westcott and Hort blessed us with their scholarly recovery, we must first cast doubt upon our sovereign God's ability to keep his promises of preservation. And if we believe that God preserved His word, then we must also conclude that Westcott and Hort had nothing to recover!

## Westcott and Hort's Text-Types

According to Westcott and Hort, all the manuscript evidence can be sorted into four basic text types (families). The largest text type is the Byzantine family which they referred to as "Syrian". They considered it to be unreliable. A second text type was the "Western" text type. They considered it to be older but lacked dependability because of its numerous independent readings. Then a third text-type was called the "Alexandrian" text type. They believed that this family exemplified a polished style of Greek.

But according to Westcott and Hort, the best text-type was what they called the "Neutral" text. Now, why they thought the Western text was unreliable was because of its many independent readings. But why they considered the Alexandrian texts to be reliable IN SPITE OF their 1000s of disagreements within its own family is beyond my comprehension! The Critical Text is supposedly derived from the "neutral" text-type although the line between "neutral" and "Alexandrian" are almost non-existant.

Another fact which is not generally considered is that the original plan was not so much to construct a new Greek edition. Initially, the idea was to update the English style of the King James Version.

## IN DEFENSE OF THE TEXTUS RECEPTUS

In 1870 the English parliament authorized a revision of the King James Version[103]. Two teams were put together. One team was working in England and the other team was working in the United States. The two teams were supposed to work independently and then proof the other team's work.

But at some point, Westcott, Hort, and Bishop Lightfoot began to pressure the committee to go beyond the work of revision to actually making changes to the Greek text. Dr. Frederick Scrivener strongly opposed any changes to the Textus Receptus but in the end Westcott and Hort got their desires and a new Greek text was produced instead of a revision to the King James Version.

At that point, the original chairman, Samuel Wilberforce, resigned. Both Dean John William Burgon, who was a conservative Anglican and Dean of Chichester Cathedral, and Fredrick Scrivener, a teacher of the classics and incredible Greek scholar, stood strongly against the revision of the Greek text. But unfortunately, the damage had been done and their advice was disregarded.

One of the points of discussion among the members of the committee dealt with the availability of newer scholarship. And even today, we can hear some critics' claims that the translators of 1611 did not have as an extensive knowledge of the ancient Greek language as scholars of today. But it might prove interesting to compare the education and qualifications of the King James Version translators to the translators of today.

Consider that 54 men were chosen based upon their piety, scholarship, and linguistic abilities. Seven of these men were not able to serve because of death or other causes leaving 47 men to do the translation work. These men were chosen for their various expertise but every one of them were scholars in Greek and Hebrew.

Take for example Lancelot Andrews, who, besides possessing an intimate knowledge of Hebrew, Greek, Chaldee, and Syriac, was so familiar with 16 other languages that it was said of him, "had he been present at the confusion of tongues at Babel, he might have served as the Interpreter-General!" His brother, Roger Andrews, who was also a famous linguist of their day, served with him in the translation. Do we really believe we have a greater knowledge of the original languages? What intellectual arrogance!

---

[103] A common misconception is that the King James Version is not under a copywrite. But Actually, it is under United Kingdom Crown Copyright. Although this copywrite is not enforced outside of the United Kingdom, the rights are nonetheless held by the British Crown under perpetual Crown copyright. Why? Because King James commissioned it.

## IN DEFENSE OF THE TEXTUS RECEPTUS

Edward Lively, another King James Version translator, was considered to be one of the best linguists in the world. In fact, he was so good that his particular committee relied greatly upon his skills.

Francis Dillingham was so skilled that he would often hold public debates in Greek. Thomas Harrison was Vice-Master of Trinity College and was so skilled in Greek and Hebrew that it became his responsibility to examine any would-be professors of the languages. Do we really believe we have a greater knowledge of the original languages? What intellectual arrogance!

John Harding was the Royal Professor of Hebrew at Oxford University for 13 years. Another translator, John Spencer, had been elected as Greek lecturer in Oxford University at the ripe old age of 19! Dr. George Abbot, B.D., D.D. was regarded as the "head of the Puritans within the Church of England". He was known for his godliness and excellent leadership abilities. In fact, in 1611, the same year the King James Version went to print, Abbot was appointed Archbishop of Canterbury. Do we really believe we have a greater knowledge of the original languages? What intellectual arrogance!

John Rainolds, who is accredited for putting the idea of a new translation in the king's mind, was a lover of knowledge. He was known to study a subject until he could learn no more. He read the scriptures in their original languages. He also read the ancient writings of early Christians in Greek and Latin.

Dr. Henry Saville was so well known for his abilities in language and knowledge of the scriptures that he was appointed the Greek tutor to Queen Elizabeth during the reign of King Henry VIII. Dr. Miles Smith, the man who wrote the preface of the King James Version was expert in Greek, Hebrew, Latin, Chaldee, Syriac, and Arabic.

There is the thought that scholars today have the benefit of 400 years of accumulated knowledge that helps them in translation as well as textual criticism. This is true. But something is to be said about a group of men who did their work without the use of all the technological assistance that is available today. Do we really believe we have a greater knowledge of the original languages? What intellectual arrogance!

No, I think it is unfair to assume that modern scholars are more skilled. It could be said that the King James Version translation team had at its disposal a greater combined linguistic knowledge than has ever been seen in any other translation work in the history of the world. Yet these men, with all of their combined knowledge and learning, saw no need to produce a new Greek text!

But certainly, they didn't have the textual evidence nor the tools that we have today. It can only be speculation what those men would have done if they lived today. But again, the premise of this book is not so much a defense of the translation as it is a defense of the Textus Receptus. The King James Version is only as good as the text from which was taken, provided that it is accurate to the text.

The point we are making here is not about the translation but about the educational qualifications of the two translating committees. I am not saying that the committee of Westcott and Hort were ignorant because they most certainly were not. But I contend that any discussion of who had "more textual evidence" is a subject to consider in a discussion of translation - not in judging one groups educational qualities over another.

## Major Manuscripts of the Critical Text

The Alexandrian family consists of quite a few manuscripts[104] of which the following six are considered to be of the most importance:

**Chester Beatty** – This is actually a group of papyri which includes portions of the Old Testament, New Testament ($P^{45}$, $P^{46}$, $P^{47}$) portions of the non-canonical book of Enoch as well as a Christian homily. All of but two of the papyri are dated before the fourth century with the oldest being around A.D. 250. It was originally thought to be of the Caesarean family but it is now generally considered to be an eclectic text. The ones most crucial to New Testament textual analysis are $P^{45}$ and $P^{46}$. Interestingly, when the Chester Beatty Papyri were finally published, it was discovered that they agreed quite often with the Byzantine text. A number of readings often regarded as "late" were found in the Chester Beatty Papyri. In fact, Bruce Metzger, who is definitely not a Textus Receptus supporter, listed 23 places where Papyri 45, 46, and 66 agree with the Byzantine text <u>against all other text-types</u>.

**Bodmer Papyri** – This was a group of 22 papyri found in Egypt in 1952. They are named after Martin Bodmer, who bought them from an Egyptian man that smuggled them out of Egypt and into Switzerland. They contain portions of the Old and New Testament, as well as segments of other early literature (Homer, Menander). The oldest of the manuscripts is dated at approximately A.D. 200. It is said to be is agreement with the Codex Vaticanus, however it should be noted that there are signs of editing in a few places[105]. Even in the texts itself, (P75,

---

[104] See Appendix A for a complete list.

[105] http://www.earlham.edu/~seidti/iam/tc_pap75.html

P66) there are significant differences.[106] This has resulted in some scholars coming to the conclusion that this papyri should be counted as two witnesses. The Chester Beatty and Bodmer Papyri only share about 78 verses in common but differ in over 70 places within those 78 verses![107]

**Codex Vaticanus** – Said to have been written in the 4th century but not discovered until 1475. Interestingly, it contains a system of mysterious double-dots (umlauts) in the column which seem to indicate places of textual uncertainty. These dots were discovered in 1995 by Philip Payne who concluded that they indicated a place where a textual variant was known to the one who made the dots. Almost all scholars agree with this conclusion.[108] An interesting marginal note is found next to Hebrews 1:3, where it reads "Fool and knave, can't you leave the old reading alone and not alter it!"—"ἀμαθέστατε καὶ κακέ, ἄφες τὸν παλαιόν, μὴ μεταποίει". This obviously is an indication that scribal alteration of the text was a known problem, even then! It is also an indication that the scribe who made the note knew the codex had been altered! Additionally, there is another "umlaut" at this same verse but it occurs on the "wrong" side.[109] This is most likely because of the note on the opposite side. But if this is true, then at least some of the umlauts were placed on the manuscript at a later date. The logical conclusion is that at least two different persons understood that the manuscript was corrupted. In fact, it is believed that up to ten different scribes made corrections to this manuscript[110]. The Vatican kept tight control of this manuscript until the 1800s when scholars were finally permitted to study its contents. The Codex Vaticanus also includes the Apocrypha and is one of the main manuscripts of the Alexandrian family. It was given the greatest weight in the construction of the Critical Text which has become the basis for almost all succeeding English translations since that time. The existence of this manuscript would have been known by the King James translators and especially to Erasmus yet there is no indication that either desired to use it. Most likely, and judging

---

[106] "Notice also that instead of the letters "OUDEN," this manuscript has the two words "OUDE EN." Either one of the epsilons has been dropped (if P75 is the original reading) or it has been reduplicated (if P66 represents the original reading). The meaning is actually altered little, only making the expression more emphatic." - Timothy W. Seid, Ph.D., Prof. of New Testament Studies, Earlham School of Religion

[107] Grady, William; Final Authority; pg 28

[108] http://www-user.uni-bremen.de/~wie/Vaticanus/umlauts.html

[109] www.user.uni-bremen.de/~wie/Vaticanus/note1512.html

[110] It was corrected in the 8th, 10th, and 15th centuries (W. Eugene Scott, Codex Vaticanus, 1996).

from some of the comments concerning the Catholics in their letter to the readers, the Catholic church would not have cooperated with the translators anyway. But Erasmus could have used them if he desired. He was a well-known scholar and priest in the good graces of the Catholic Church.

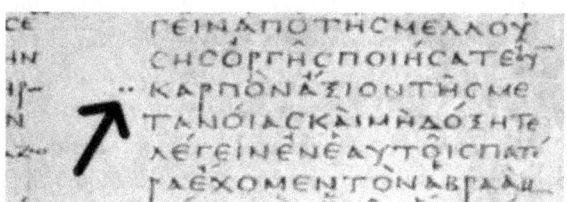

A typical example of umlauts

Lots of people are under the false impression that this manuscript was totally unknown until its use by Westcott and Hort in the late 1800s but this is not accurate. In actuality, Johann Bengel (AD 1742) felt that the document should be compared to others. But unfortunately, it was highly protected by the Vatican library and was virtually inaccessible during most of the 19th century. When the Vatican finally allowed scholars to examine it, Tischendorf released his edition in 1867. But before this time, Cardinal Angelo Mai, who was well-known for his publication of ancient texts, published a copy of the Codex Vaticanus in 1857 but it was not considered to be a very good edition. So the idea that it was an unknown manuscript is not really accurate. It would also be false to assume no one could get access to it. The Vatican had apparently granted access to numerous people, although it was definitely not free for all to see.

**Codex Sinaiticus** – It was written in the 4th century, in uncial letters. The common story is that the manuscript was discovered by Constantin Tischendorf in the monastery of Saint Catherine at Mount Sinai in 1844. He reported that he found the manuscripts in a basket of scraps that the monks were going to use to start fires with.

However, J. Silvester Davies in 1863 makes the observation, "a monk of Sinai who... stated that according to the librarian of the monastery the whole of Codex Sinaiticus had been in the library for many years and was marked in the ancient catalogues... Is it likely... that a manuscript known in the library catalogue would have been jettisoned in the rubbish basket?"[111] In addition, it should be noted that the codex is in rather remarkable condition to have been placed in a

---

[111] http://en.wikipedia.org/wiki/Codex_Sinaiticus, 15 October 2008

trash bin! In fact Tischendorf himself made statements that would appear to refute the claim:

*"On the afternoon of this day I was taking a walk with the steward of the convent in the neighbourhood, and as we returned, towards sunset, he begged me to take some refreshment with him in his cell. Scarcely had he entered the room, when, resuming our former subject of conversation, he said: "And I, too, have read a Septuagint"--i.e. a copy of the Greek translation made by the Seventy. And so saying, he took down from the corner of the room a bulky kind of volume, wrapped up in a red cloth, and laid it before me. I unrolled the cover, and discovered, to my great surprise, not only those very fragments which, fifteen years before, I had taken out of the basket, but also other parts of the Old Testament, the New Testament complete, and, in addition, the Epistle of Barnabas and a part of the Pastor of Hermas. Full of joy, which this time I had the self-command to conceal from the steward and the rest of the community, I asked, as if in a careless way, for permission to take the manuscript into my sleeping chamber to look over it more at leisure. There by myself I could give way to the transport of joy which I fat. I knew that I held in my hand the most precious Biblical treasure in existence--a document whose age and importance exceeded that of all the manuscripts which I had ever examined during twenty years' study of the subject. I cannot now, I confess, recall all the emotions which I felt in that exciting moment with such a diamond in my possession." (rosetta.reltech.org)*

As one of my former church members stated as we discussed this issue, "Monks don't wrap garbage in Red cloth Pastor. And if it was trash, why did Tischendorf feel the need to conceal from the steward and the rest of the community?" Point well made. The fact that it was found in a wastebasket to be burned may very well be an oft-repeated myth.

But these facts by no means validate the credibility of the codex for it is obvious that from the 4th to 12th century, at least 9 different scribes have made corrections to it making it the most corrected manuscript ever discovered. Tischendorf himself is said to have counted 14,800 corrections in what was then the Saint Petersburg portion alone!

Besides missing many words, phrases, and verses, it also contains variants heretofore unmatched by any other document. (In Matt 13:54 εις την πατριδα αυτου changed into εις την αντιπατριδα αυτου; Acts 8:5 εις την πολιν της Σαμαρειας replaced with εις την πολιν της Καισαριας.) It also contains the Epistle of Barnabas and the Shepherd of Hermas, both of which are not inspired and not considered scripture.

## IN DEFENSE OF THE TEXTUS RECEPTUS

This codex, along with Codex Vaticanus, is thought to be one of fifty copies of the Bible commissioned from Eusebius by Roman Emperor Constantine after his conversion to Christianity.[112] However, due to the incredible number of textual variants between the two, we would be forced to come to the conclusion that, if this theory is true, then Eusebius was a very sloppy scholar!

But there is one thing about the codex for which we can be thankful. There is a colophon[113] at the end of the manuscript that identified Origin's Hexapla as being the source of the Septuagint, which was also included in the Codex Siaiticus. This is very helpful because it helps us to solve an argument about the Septuagint and why its readings are so often found in the New Testament.

It is almost beyond belief that quite a few scholars hold the position that "Codex Sinaiticus is one of the most valuable manuscripts for establishing the original text"[114]

**Codex Alexandrinus** – (A.D. 450) This manuscript contains the majority of the Septuagint, a few books from the Apocrypha, 1st and 2nd Clement, and, except for certain portions that have been damaged, the entire New Testament. It is so named because it resided in Alexandria for some time before being sent to the British in the 17th century. Although it is commonly classified as "Alexandrian text type", the gospels are in agreement with the Byzantine texts. In fact, is one of the oldest extant manuscripts containing Byzantine readings.[115] It is considered by Alexandrian manuscript supporters to be third in importance only to Codex Vaticanus and Codex Sinaiticus.

**Codex Ephraemi** – (5th Century) This is often considered to be the last of the "four great uncials". It is so named because it is a codex of vellum which at one time contained the complete Old and New Testaments. However, the scriptures had been scratched away and replaced by the treatices of Ephraem the Syrian, thus forming a palimpsest.[116] Although this particular manuscript is

---

[112] I.M. Price, The Ancestry of Our English Bible an Account of Manuscripts, Texts and Versions of the Bible, Sunday School Times Co, 1923, p. 146 f.

[113] A colophon is a statement at the end of a book which gives information about its author, source, or printing.

[114] http://en.wikipedia.org/wiki/Codex_Sinaiticus, 15 October 2008

[115] Uncials 026, 032, 061, and 069 also contain Byzantine readings and are dated around 450 AD, the same time period as Codex Alexandrinus. Again, older is not better. Older is simply, older.

[116] A palimpsest is a page that has been written on, scraped off, and used again.

usually considered to be part of the Alexandrian family, the actual classification is much more complex than that. In the gospels, it is said to be "more Byzantine than Alexandrian."[117] Until the discovery of the Codex Sinaiticus, it was highly regarded as second in importance to the Codex Vaticanus (by Critical Text supporters).

**Other Alexandrian Manuscripts.** In addition to the more well known manuscripts mentioned above, there are numerous others such as Codex Guelferbytanus B (5th century – contains fragments of Luke and John; Codex Borgianus (5th century – contains fragments of Luke and John); Codex Freerianus (5th century – contains portions of the Pauline epistles except Romans and Hebrews); Codex Dublinensis (6th century contains fragments of Matthew); Codex Regius (8th century contains the Gospels[118]) Codex Washingtonianus (5th century - Luke 1:1–8:12[119]); Uncial 057 (4/5th century - Acts 3:5–6,10-12); Uncial 0220 ( 6th century – contains the Epistle to Romans); Minuscule 33 (9th century – contains all of the New Testament except Revelation); Minuscule 81 (1044 - Acts, Pauline Epistles); Minuscule 892 (9th century – Gospels)

## The Byzantine family

### History of the Textus Receptus

"Textus Receptus", which is Latin for "received text" is the name of the Greek text which is the basis for the original German Luther Bible, for the translation of the New Testament into English by William Tyndale, the King James Version, and for most other Reformation-era New Testament translations throughout Western and Central Europe.

It is the form found in the largest number of surviving manuscripts, especially since the utilization of minuscule (lower case) writing starting about the 9th century. The Institute for New Testament Textual research in Munster, Germany has collated many of the manuscripts containing the general epistles and

---

[117] www.skypoint.com/members/waltzmn/ManuscriptsUncials.html#uC, 24 January 2007

[118] Interestingly, this particular manuscript contains two endings to the gospel of Mark. It is also contains a large number of distinctly Byzantine readings throughout the Gospel of Matthew.

[119] Although classified by many as Alexandrian, this text is a mixture of Byzantine, Western, Caesarean, and Alexandrian readings making this a truly eclectic text. It also contains a very odd addition after Mark 16:14 which is found in no other manuscript.

## IN DEFENSE OF THE TEXTUS RECEPTUS

has found that 372 of the 522 manuscripts that they examined are distinctly Byzantine readings in 90% of the examined areas.

In actuality, the Textus Receptus is not a single edition. Around 30 editions of the Textus Receptus have been published and each is slightly different from the others. A few writers have concluded that the Textus Receptus is actually a sort of text-type of its own consisting of extremely similar but not identical manuscripts. Generally speaking, every copy of the Textus Receptus was either derived from, or revised from the Byzantine family of manuscripts.

Although it is not commonly known, and many of my KJV only brethren would not want to acknowledge it, the fact still remains that there are a few readings in the Textus Receptus that are not found in the Byzantine manuscripts. For example, Matthew 10:8 it has the reading νεκρους εγειρετε (raise the dead) which is omitted by the Byzantine text but is found in Aleph, B, C, D, and the Latin Vulgate. The Peshitta, which is generally acknowledged to be in agreement with the Byzantine manuscripts, also omits this phrase.

So why is it there? It is also found in Wycliffe's Bible (AD 1535), Tyndale's Bible (AD 1534), the Great Bible (AD 1540), Bishop's Bible (AD 1568), and the Geneva Bible (AD 1594). It was also in Erasmus Greek edition of AD 1519 and Stephanus' 1550 edition of the Greek Text. But again, why? Simply saying, "because it was right" just doesn't seem to be very satisfying to me.

Another passage is Acts 20:28 which, in the Textus Receptus reads "of God" but the Byzantine manuscripts say "of the Lord and God". We could look at the other varied translations and Greek texts to see where else this is found but what difference would it make? The fact remains, the Greek reading agrees with the Alexandrian manuscripts and are not found in the Byzantine manuscripts. Again, why? Simply saying, "because it was right" or "God providentially led them" does not solve the problem. We claim that the Byzantine manuscripts are the providentially preserved manuscripts and that the Alexandrian manuscripts are corrupt. And yet we have at least two readings (and there may be more that I am not aware of) in the Textus Receptus. It would not be academic honesty to ignore this.

Again, there are around 30 different variations of the Textus Receptus with the most common being the most recent work by Scrivener in 1894. There have been no revisions since that time, and Scrivener's 1894 is the edition that the majority of Textus Receptus supporters use. The following are the more well-known editions:

- The Erasmus editions of 1516, 1519, 1522, 1527 and 1535

## IN DEFENSE OF THE TEXTUS RECEPTUS

- The Stephanus editions of 1546, 1549, 1550 and 1551 (actually the man's name was Robert Estienne. He also was the one who put in the verse number divisions)

- Theodore Beza produced 10 more editions (In fact his edition of 1598 along with Stephanus 1550 and 1551 editions, were used as the Greek basis of the King James Version)[120]

- The Elzevir editions of 1624, 1633 and 1641.

According to the Trinitarian Bible Society, "There are approximately 190 differences between the Scrivener text and the Beza 1598. There are 283

---

[120] Beza is often accused of making emendations to the Greek text. But Beza's own notes make it clear that his justifications were based upon sound reasoning and often existing translations. One example is Rev 16:5 where "and shalt be" is emended. Existing Greek manuscripts read, "holy one" (και οσιος), "that holy one" (ο οσιος) or "and holy one" (και οσιος). Beza justified the change by saying, "The Vulgate, however, whether it is articulately correct or not, is not proper in making the change to "οσιος, Sanctus," since a section (of the text) has worn away the part after "και," which would be absolutely necessary in connecting "δικαιος" and "οσιος." But with John there remains a completeness where the name of Jehovah (the Lord) is used, just as we have said before, 1:4; he always uses the three closely together, therefore it is certainly "και ο εσομενος," for why would he pass over it in this place? And so without doubting the genuine writing in this ancient manuscript, I faithfully restored in the good book what was certainly there, "ο εσομενος." So why not truthfully, with good reason, write "ο ερχομενος" as before in four other places, namely 1:4 and 8; likewise in 4:3 and 11:17, because the point is the just Christ shall come away from there and bring them into being: in this way he will in fact appear sitting in judgment and exercising his just and eternal decrees." (Theodore Beza, Novum Sive Novum Foedus Iesu Christi, 1589). There is no Greek support for Beza's decision. However, this particular reading is found in an 8th century Latin commentary by Beatus of Liebana where he writes the phrase "qui fuisti et futures es".

The Received Bible Society, whose purpose is to maintain, translate, publish, and distribute Bibles translated from the Received Text explained it this way: "When examining the textual support for this verse, we found some interesting results - The 3rd word "ἐσόμενος" (future participle form of the verb ειμι "to be") did not appear in the TR editions of Erasmus, Stephens, or Elzevir. Further research into the matter indicates that this word appears only in Beza's edition (1598, 5th Ed., which probably is the Greek New Testament used by KJV translators). Of course, it also appears in Scrivener's reconstructed Greek New Testament containing the Greek text underlying the KJV.

Apparently, Beza drew from the logic that this particular statement should be consistent in every place. NA25 lists 10 emendations that were supposed to have been made by Beza. Yet NA27 actually retains 8 of the ten.(Recent developments in Textual criticism: New Testament, Other Early Christian Literature; edited by Wilhelmus Johannes Cornelis Weren, Dietrich-Alex Koch; pgs. 112-123) in the case of our example, Rev 16:5, it was not retained. We should add that of all the manuscripts which are now extant, this section of scripture only appears in four manuscripts.

## IN DEFENSE OF THE TEXTUS RECEPTUS

differences between the Scrivener text and the Stephanus 1550."[121] According to Kirk DiVietro, most of the differences between Stephanus and Scrivener is found in the titles of the books and the subscripts. (Cleaning Up Hazardous Materials, pg 19) With that being said, this is a far cry from the 6000 differences between the Critical Text and the Textus Receptus!

The term "Textus Receptus" is used to describe the printed Greek editions of the New Testament that follow the early prototype done by Desiderius Erasmus who lived from 1479 to 1536. Erasmus, who was a Roman Catholic scholar, had in mind to prepare a New Testament, which had the Greek in one column and his own Latin translation beside it in order to validate the new translational work found in his Latin version. He had been working on the project for several years.

At that time, the Complutensian Polyglot[122], a Greek New Testament, had already been printed but had not been published because it did not have the sanction of the Pope. In the meantime, word of the Complutensian polyglot reached Erasmus, who then hastily finished his own works and went quickly to print. Erasmus obtained an exclusive four-year publishing privilege from Emperor Maximilian and Pope Leo X in 1516. Work on the Complutensian Old Testament was completed in 1517 but because of Erasmus' exclusive rights, it could not be published until it was sanctioned by Pope Leo X in 1520.

It is not clear what Erasmus' motives were concerning his decision to finish and publish his work so quickly. Some believe he wanted to have the first Greek testament published. Others disagree citing the fact that Erasmus first consideration was not his Greek text but the corresponding Latin text. Even Erasmus himself seems to agree with this perception. Erasmus wrote,

*"My mind is so excited at the thought of emending Jerome's text, with notes, that I seem to myself inspired by some god. I have already almost finished emending him by collating a large number of ancient manuscripts, and this I am doing at enormous personal expense."*[123]

---

[121] http://www.tbsbibles.org/pdf_information/202-1.pdf

[122] The name given to the first printed polyglot of the scriptures which was accomplished by Cardinal Francisco Jiménez de Cisneros (1436-1517). It included the Greek New Testament, Septuagint, and the Targum Onkelos. 600 were printed of which only 123 are now extant.

[123] Epistle 273" in Collected *Works of Erasmus Vol. 2: Letters 142 to 297, 1501-1514* (tr. R.A.B. Mynors and D.F.S. Thomson; annotated Wallace K. Ferguson; Toronto: University of Toronto Press, 1976), 253.

## IN DEFENSE OF THE TEXTUS RECEPTUS

Whatever the reason, Erasmus holds the honor of having the first Greek New Testament published although the Complutensian Polyglot holds the honor of being the first in print.

In 1515 Erasmus traveled to Basel, Switzerland and started his work. He knew that there were Greek manuscripts in the Dominican Library at Basel so he did not take any manuscripts with him. He borrowed five manuscripts from the library at Basel and two others from Johannes Reuchlin[124]. It is quite possible, in fact probable, that he used others as well, although we have no record as such. But looking at some of his work, we could come to the conclusion that he had access to other manuscripts that helped to guide him in his word choices. The manuscripts that we know he used are as follows[125]:

| BOOK | MANUSCRIPT |
|---|---|
| Gospels | Minuscule 1$^{eap.}$ Minuscule 2$^{e.}$ Minuscule 817 |
| Acts - Jude | Minuscule 1$^{eap.}$ Minuscule 2$^{ap.}$ Minuscule 4$^{ap.}$ Minuscule 7 |
| Revelation | Minuscule1$^{rK}$ (Except the last six verses. See next table.); Manuscript 2049 |

It is important to note at this point that the manuscripts that we know Erasmus used came mostly from the 8$^{th}$ and 9$^{th}$ century. While some would claim that this was detrimental to getting the right readings, because after all, "older is better", yet I see this as a strength.

Apparently, Erasmus did not feel the need to go the route of the "older is better" argument. One may argue that there were relatively few older manuscripts available at that time. In fact, one author dogmatically stated that the older and better manuscripts were unknown to Erasmus (referring to the Codex Vaticanus and Codex Sinaiticus). However, this is not true, as even though the Codex Vaticanus had been discovered, yet he did not choose to use it. Being one of the Catholic Church's more prominent priests, if anyone could have gotten access to the manuscripts, it would no doubt have been him. Apparently, he thought that the manuscripts that he chose were the best manuscripts for the job!

---

[124] A German humanist as well as a Greek and Hebrew scholar who for much of his life was the leading authority in Greek and Hebrew teaching in Germany.

[125] W. W. Combs, *Erasmus and the Textus Receptus*, DBSJ 1 (Spring 1996), pg. 45.

## IN DEFENSE OF THE TEXTUS RECEPTUS

We need to realize that the manuscripts Erasmus used were the manuscripts which had been preserved and used by God's people. And this is a major point in the discussion of textual analysis. Erasmus was no dummy. He didn't just choose those particular manuscripts simply because they were easy to read. He chose them because he believed they were the best. We have already seen a statement concerning the fact that he personally collated a large number of ancient manuscripts at his own expense. We don't know how many manuscripts the "large number" was, but it is fair to say in doing so Erasmus certainly would have become familiar with what was good and what was not!

Erasmus was able to compare several manuscripts for every book of the New Testament except for the Book of Revelation. In this, he only had one source, Minuscule$1^{rK}$. However, as already noted in the chart above, this manuscript was missing the last six verses. It is now generally believed that he back-translated the passage in question from the Latin Vulgate. Critics point to Erasmus' use of the phrase "book of life" in Revelation 22:19 since that would be in agreement with the Latin Vulgate yet at odds with many of the existing Greek manuscripts which have "tree of life".

Much ado is made concerning the differences between the Textus Receptus, and consequently, the King James Version with the Critical Text concerning Revelation 22:19.

> ***Revelation 22:19*** *And if any man shall take away from the words of the book of this prophecy, God shall take away his part out of the <u>book of life</u>, and out of the holy city, and from the things which are written in this book.*

But if Erasmus back-translated from the Latin Vulgate for the last few verses of Revelation, he did a near miraculous job (some would say he was providentially guided) because two very important facts have come to light.

First of all, when a comparison is made between the Critical Text and the Textus Receptus, the type, number, and consistency of textual variants throughout the New Testament are fairly consistent. Erasmus' work in the last six verses falls well within the normal range. If Erasmus did indeed back-translate from Latin, we could reasonably expect this number of variants to be much higher.

Secondly, according to Dr. H. C. Hoskier, in his book, *Concerning the Text of the Apocalype*, it appears that Erasmus had Manuscript 2049, (which

**God's Preserved Word to Every Generation**

Hoskier called 141) which contained these verses.[126] Dr. Hoskier showed that the Greek manuscripts 2049 and 57 agree with the Latin in stating "book of life" as versus "tree of life" as found in many other manuscripts.[127]

There are other factors to consider. For example, the Old Bohairic Coptic version reads "book of life." Add to this the quotations in the writings of Ambrose (340-397 AD), Bachiarius (late fourth century), and Primasius in his commentary on Revelation in 552 AD. Some of this evidence predates the Latin Vulgate and illustrates that this reading did not originate there.

Another point of interest is the fact that there is very little Greek support for the passage in reference anyway. Take a look at the chart in Appendix A. None of the papyri contain this section. Only four uncials contain it (Sinaiticus, Alexandrinus, 046, and 051). However, there are numerous minuscules which contain these verses (94, 1611, 1854, 1859, 2042, and 2138). Naturally, this does not mean that the verses in question were never in any papyri. It only means that we haven't found any[128]. So basically, only 10 manuscripts out of over 6600 have this portion of scripture anyway!

Another possibility is that the whole allegation concerning Erasmus back-translating could be the result of a false understanding of his own words to Stunica in his "Apologia" In his Annotations to the Apocalypse. He wrote, "In Apocalypsi non suppetebat nobis nisi vnicum exemplar, sed vetustissimum, quod nobis exhibuit eximius ille litterarum heros Ioh. Reuchlinus." The phrase means, "For the Book of Revelation only [non ... nisi] one copy was immediately available to us, but that was a very ancient one, which John Reuchlin, that illustrious hero of the literary sciences provided for our perusal." This statement is thought by some to have been misunderstood later by Johann Albrecht Bengel, who was a German Lutheran Pietist. Bengel thought that Erasmus meant he only had one manuscript of Revelation. But what Bengel missed is the fact that Erasmus later makes it clear that he only had one manuscript because he was not

---

[126] H. C. Hoskier, *Concerning the Text of the Apocalypse*, vol. 2 (London: Bernard Quaritch, Ltd., 1929), 644.

[127] And here is something else to think about. The people who normally make the allegation that Erasmus back-translated from Latin are normally the same ones who have a low view of inspiration to begin with. Some of these same people would contend that we don't really have exactly what God gave while others would say that the exact wording is not so important. I think it is a bit hypocritical to lambast Erasmus for something that they would have done themselves!

[128] Nevertheless, evidence of the verse is found in other than the Latin Vulgate. They are also found in the Old Latin, Coptic, Syriac, Armenian, and Ethiopic translations as well.

*God's Preserved Word to Every Generation*

in Basel at that time. So it is possible, in fact, very likely that Erasmus later had access to other manuscripts.[129]

But even if Erasmus did back-translate, so what? Do we not have multiple revisions since his work? Have there not been 30 revisions of the Textus Receptus since that time by great men using existing Greek manuscripts? For the record, there currently exists Greek support for this section of scripture for every word except two – one conjunction and one particle.

With that being said, the biggest reason that the whole back-translation issue is so often spoken of is because there are those who would seek to use this to discredit the Textus Receptus, and consequently, the King James Version of the Bible. But in doing so, they assume that the reading from the Vulgate is inaccurate as well. And this is a bit ironic because so many scholars appeal to the Vulgate to support their position in one situation and yet vilify it usage when it comes to Erasmus!

With the subject of Erasmus being completed, we should add that, in reality, Erasmus did not construct the Textus Receptus at all. If anything, he laid a good foundation, collated a proto-Textus Receptus, and made monumental leaps in the area of textual analysis. But in actuality, he did not publish a "Textus Receptus". In fact, the term "Textus Receptus" was not even used until 1633 when the Elzivirs published their edition which contained in the preface, "textum…receptum". By that time, the King James version had already been in print for 22 years!

At least 30 editions of the Textus Receptus have been completed since Erasmus did his first edition in 1516. Each edition has been slightly different than the previous works. And for the most part, each edition built upon the previous works accomplished before them. The last revision to be made to what we now call the Textus Receptus was done by Scrivener in 1894. There hasn't been an edition of the Textus Receptus since that time.

## *Major Manuscripts of the Textus Receptus*

Before we discuss the major manuscripts of the Textus Receptus, we should first restate that there are over 5700 extant manuscripts, the majority of which agree with the Textus Receptus. The manuscripts that we are about to discuss are only a few of the more prevalent manuscripts.

---

[129] This theory is not mine but belongs to an internet author who goes by the name of "Brother Richard". He wrote a book called "The Great Bible Text Fraud" in which he spends a great deal of time in chapter 5 developing this theory.

## IN DEFENSE OF THE TEXTUS RECEPTUS

If we want to consider the major manuscripts that were used in the construction of the Textus Receptus, we first must consider the manuscripts that we know Erasmus used. Logically, these are the "major" manuscripts. However, since the percentage of accuracy in the Byzantine family is so high, it is really a moot point anyway. But for the record, and for the sake of consistency, the following is a more in-depth discussion of the manuscripts that Erasmus used:

| Manuscript | Content | Date |
|---|---|---|
| Minuscule $1^{eap}$ | Entire New Testament except for Revelation. It is said to be Caesarean in the gospels with the remainder being Byzantine. It contains a scholion questioning the authenticity of Mark 16:9-20. The Pericope Adulterae is placed after John 21:25. Erasmus obviously did not follow the criticism concerning Mark 16:9-20 nor did he place the Pericope Adulterae at the end. Actually Erasmus used this codex very little, because its text was different from the manuscripts that he was used to. He strongly felt that it had been altered from the Latin manuscripts, and had secondary value. | 12th century |
| Minuscule $1^r$ K | Contains the Book of Revelation with a commentary written by Andreas from Caesarea. The last six verses are lost (22:16-21). It is distinctively Byzantine. | 12th century |
| Minuscule $2^e$ | A Greek text of the Gospels and is distinctively Byzantine. | 12th century |
| Minuscule $2^{ap}$ | Contains a complete text of the Acts of the Apostles, General epistles, and Pauline epistles. Byzantine. | 12th century |
| Minuscule $4^{ap}$ | Contains a complete text of the Acts of the Apostles, Pauline epistles, and General epistles with the Pauline epistles preceding the General epistles. Byzantine. | 15th century |
| Minuscule 7 | Contains Acts and Epistles. Byzantine. | 12th century |
| Minuscule 817 | Gospels | 15th century |

*God's Preserved Word to Every Generation*

## IN DEFENSE OF THE TEXTUS RECEPTUS

## MANUSCRIPT SUPPORT FOR THE TEXTUS RECEPTUS

I have heard on many occasions that the Textus Receptus did not really exist until after the work of Erasmus. True. But in my opinion, this is nothing more than a straw man argument that doesn't take into account the facts. If the Textus Receptus is an edition of Byzantine manuscripts, then the Textus Receptus existed in that form. Academically, we can speak of the Byzantine family to describe the manuscripts and speak of the Textus Receptus to speak of an edition of the Byzantine family. But that is all academics. Practically, they are basically the same thing.

So even though it is often attested that the Textus Receptus did not exist until the 1500s, there is ample evidence that, although it had not been published in one version yet, those readings clearly existed! In fact, evidence for this text type can be found in various manuscripts, translations, and writings of the "church fathers" going back to the middle of the second century.

The name, "Textus Receptus" did not exist until 1633. An edition of the Greek text was published by the Elzivirs with a preface written by Daniel Heinsius. He included the Latin phrase "textum receptum" which means "the received text". Thus, the 1633 edition became known as the Textus Receptus and the name has carried on since that time.

Before this time, the Greek manuscripts were not given names, types, classifications, categories, etc. Those who were involved in using or translating the Greek texts simply viewed them as authoritative or non-authoritative, depending upon what they believed concerning each manuscript's accuracy. It has only been in the last 250 years that textual "families" have become recognized in the scholastic circles of textual criticism. Currently, there are numerous textual families into which scholars seek to place each manuscript. And to further confuse the issue, various scholars chose to rename the manuscripts or rename the families of manuscripts. Additionally, there is quite a bit of disagreement between textual critics concerning some of the manuscripts as to exactly which family they should be in!

We must remember that the Textus Receptus comes from the family which is normally called the "Byzantine" family. However, depending upon who did the classification, or whose books you read, the Byzantine family is

## IN DEFENSE OF THE TEXTUS RECEPTUS

sometimes called "Syrian", "Delta", "Kappa", "Koine", "K", "A", or "Alpha".[130] This makes everything so much easier to understand doesn't it?

Add to this the fact that the Textus Receptus is a printed volume. The Byzantine manuscripts which preceded them were hand-made copies. As is true with anything that is hand-made, they don't all agree with one another. It has been noted that the rate of agreement is over 99%, yet not 100%. Some believe this fact causes problems as we take into consideration the biblical principle of preservation. How could there NOT be 100% accuracy? Didn't God promise to preserve every word? But in reality, there is no difficulty at all. A simple illustration shows why:

| *Manuscript* | *Reading* |
|---|---|
| MS 1 | However, a simple illustration shows why this presents almost no problems at all: |
| MS 2 | However, a simple illustration shows why this presents almost **on** problems at all: |
| MS 3 | However, a simple illustration shows why this presents almost no problems at all: |
| MS 4 | However, a simple illustration shows **wiy** this presents almost no problems at all: |
| MS 5 | However, **an** simple illustration shows why this presents almost no problems at all: |

I realize that this is a very simplistic illustration. I know that in some cases, two readings have roughly equal manuscript support, or there is no majority reading at all. There are other types of variants[131] which could be added to the illustration but this should suffice to show how, in almost all cases, we know what the reading should be. Also remember that the illustration only uses six manuscripts whereas since the first published Greek text (Erasmus' text of 1516), many more have been added to this that only increases the certainty.

One of the arguments against the Textus Receptus is the fact that if we compare it to any Byzantine manuscript, we will find differences in the two texts.

---

[130] The Byzantine family is called "Syrian", or "Delta" by Westcott and Hort; Called "Kappa", "Koine" or "K" by Von Soden; Called "A" or "Alpha" by Kenyon and Lagrange.

[131] A variant is a difference in the manuscripts. This difference can be an added word, deleted word, misspelling, or when two words are transposed.

## IN DEFENSE OF THE TEXTUS RECEPTUS

The conclusion is then drawn that since there are differences, we cannot conclude that the Textus Receptus is God's preserved Word.

However, what is good for the goose is good for the gander! If we were to compare the Critical Text to any extant manuscript, whether Byzantine or otherwise, we would find variants in the readings. Can we now draw the conclusion that the Critical Text is not God's preserved Word?

Have we now imposed a standard that is neither logical nor biblical? For if we impose this "test" as an evidence of legitimacy we would have to come to the conclusion that there is no uncorrupted "Word of God". And since we know that this is contrary to the promises of the scriptures, we must categorically reject this line of reasoning.

It has been pointed out in the past that there are a few readings in the Textus Receptus where there is very little Greek support. And sometimes, this can cause a person to question the validity of the Textus Receptus. But let's consider two points on this topic.

First of all, if we were to apply the same criteria to the Critical text that we have applied to the Textus Receptus, we would find that there is a much larger number of readings which contain very little Greek evidence. We need to remember that the bulk of the differences between the Textus Receptus and the Critical Text are only found in the Codex Vaticanus, Codex Siniaticus and the Codex Alexandrinus.

Secondly, what we are really questioning when we ponder why we have so little manuscript support for any particular reading is whether it can be accepted if it is only supported by one manuscript. But the doctrine of preservation does not require that a reading exist in ample quantity. It merely requires that a reading exist.

As we consider manuscript support for the Textus Receptus, we will look at three basic types of support – Greek manuscripts, early translations, writings of the early Christians, and then support in some other "unusual" places. Some authors like to include another category for lectionaries but in fact, these are either Greek excerpts of the scriptures or excerpts from other translations. Thus, we can rightly include them in the aforementioned categories.

### Greek Manuscript Support

As we discuss manuscript support for the Textus Receptus, we should first consider Greek manuscript support. According to my research, there are 5369 manuscripts out of 5773 existing manuscripts that support the Textus

Receptus. The remaining manuscripts are either in support of the Critical Text, of a very mixed text, or else yet unclassified. However, to be fair, we should recognize that some of these "manuscripts" are very small, in poor condition, and almost unreadable. Very few of the Greek manuscripts contain the entire New Testament. Most contain various passages but all of these factors need to be taken into consideration as we look at Greek support for any passage of scripture. Other manuscripts have never really been examined for a variety of reasons and are cataloged without a great amount of examination. With that being said, the following is a chart showing the sheer volume of Greek textual support for the Textus Receptus:

|  | Total | Byz. | Byz. with Alex. reading | Byz. with Mixed Readings | Mixed | Alex. With Mixed Readings | Alex. with Byz. Readings | Alex. | Unclass. |
|---|---|---|---|---|---|---|---|---|---|
| Papyri | 127 | 2 | 0 | 0 | 11 | 1 | 2 | 86 | 25 |
| Uncial | 323 | 53 | 17 | 8 | 97 | 6 | 19 | 56 | 67 |
| Minuscule | 2911 | 2840 | 3 | 10 | 25 | 0 | 3 | 29 | 1 |
| Lectionary | 2412 | 2407 | 0 | 0 | 0 | 0 | 5 (?) * | 0 | 0 |
| Totals | 5773 | 5302 | 20 | 18 | 133 | 7 | 29 | 171 | 93 |

* Although the lectionaries are all classified as being Byzantine, several of the lectionaries, lectionary 0269 and 1602 for example, contain spurious Alexandrian readings. And we should expect this to be the case with at least a few of the lectionaries since at least four of them were located in Egypt. Lectionary 1575 was said by the Alands to be in remarkably good quality, which, from their perspective may have meant that it is heavily Alexandrian. Since it was part of a codex with Uncial 0129 it is most likely Alexandrian although this has not yet been verified.
* Admittedly, I was not able to verify the classifications of many of the minuscules and thus, the information related to the minuscules is reliant upon many different sources. But as much as possible, I have tried to verify the accuracy of the information reflected.

## *Lectionaries*

2412 of the existing manuscripts are classified as lectionaries. These are very important for several reasons. First of all, they tell us what text the churches were generally using and that is significant because that tells us which family of texts was "received". Although the lectionaries are all classified as being Byzantine, several of the lectionaries - lectionary 0269, 1602, and 147 for example - contain spurious Alexandrian readings. And we should expect this to be the case with at least a few of the lectionaries since at least four of them were located in Egypt. Lectionary 1575 was said by the Alands to be in remarkably good quality, which, from their perspective may have meant that it is heavily Alexandrian. Since it was part of a codex with Uncial 0129 it is most likely Alexandrian although this has not yet been verified.

With that being said, up until the 1800s, almost no one used anything but the Byzantine manuscripts anyway. Partly because they were unfamiliar with anything else, and partly because other manuscripts were not considered to be of any value anyway. In short, the believers weren't trying to "find the original readings". They were busy enough just trying to live by what they already had!

Churches would make lectionaries for reading during their worship services. These readings were arranged in a systematic fashion and are overwhelmingly in support of the Byzantine family of manuscripts. Other than the four previously mentioned lectionaries, apparently none of the churches used anything else.

## *Early Translations*

What would be the purpose of including translations in a discussion of Greek manuscript superiority? Well, a couple of things can be gleaned from them. First, early translations validate the existence of the family of Greek manuscripts from which it was taken. Second, a translation adds credibility to a particular family of manuscripts because it obviously shows favor of one Greek text over another. With that being said, it may be useful to know some basic information about a few of the ancient translations.

The **Greek Orthodox Bible**, which is said to have been in use since the $2^{nd}$ century up to modern times, is in agreement with the Textus Receptus over and against the Critical Text. That is not to say that the Greek Orthodox Church was fundamental in any way. Actually, they held to many false doctrines that we would not espouse. But the point is, as a Greek text in use, it shows the very early existence and use of the Byzantine family of manuscripts going back to the $2^{nd}$ century.

The **Old Syriac** which dates to around 150 to 160 AD exists in the form of two gospels today. However, in the course of time, Acts and the Pauline Epistles have been either lost or inadvertently destroyed. Nevertheless, scholars have been able to reconstruct the text from other existing writings. It is said to agree with the Byzantine manuscript but at the same time, it comes with its own set of problems. For example, the Pericope Adultura, 2nd Peter, 2nd and 3rd

John, Jude, and Revelation were totally missing until the sections were restored from other manuscripts. So any variant readings in these sections may not have been the result of the translators of the original work.

The first of the two existing works is called the **Curetonian Gospel** and it shares a 53% agreement with the Byzantine manuscripts. The date of the manuscript is a bit of an enigma however because those who hold to a Critical Text position usually date this at the 5th century. But those who support the Textus Receptus typically date it during the 2nd century. Others believe that the manuscript itself should be dated to the 5th century while the text can be traced back to the 2nd century. This manuscript is often designated as Syr$^c$.

The second manuscript is a palimpsest[132] discovered in St Catherine's Monastery (the same place that the Codex Sinaiticus was discovered), and is appropriately named the **Sinaitic Syriac**, and designated by Syr$^s$. It is representative of the Critical Text. Keep in mind that the original words were scraped off and written over with other material. Apparently, somebody thought it was not worth preserving!

A possible third Syriac version would be the **Diatesseron.** It is primarily a harmony of the gospels which were combined by Tatian into a single narrative between 150 and 160 AD. Tatian, was a student of Justin Martyr. Justin Martyr is known for often quoting the gospels in a harmonized form himself and some scholars believe he may have used a Greek harmony text.

It is possible that Tatian used this text, or at least the narrative sequence while constructing the Diatesseron. However, it is clear that when the Diatesseron quotes from the Old Testament (actually, the quotes of Christ from the Old Testament), it is in agreement with the Peshitta, which is in agreement with the Textus Receptus, rather than the Septuagint. This has led many to the logical conclusion that the Peshitta predates the Diatesseron, at least in the Old Testament. It is equally possible, however, that the Peshitta quotes from the Diatesseron, although this is highly unlikely. Interestingly, the Diatesseron was the standard gospel narrative used in Syrian liturgy for 200 years but now, no complete copy in Greek or Syriac is in existence. The reasons are quite simple.

In 423 A.D., Biship Theodoret of Cyrrhus suspected Tatian of heresy. He then collected every copy of the Diatessaron which he could find. He removed these from circulation and replaced them with the separate narratives of the

---

[132] A palimpsest is a page that has been written on, scraped off, and used again.

## IN DEFENSE OF THE TEXTUS RECEPTUS

gospels. In time, without extant copies to which to refer, the Diatesseron not only fell out of existence, but also developed a reputation of being heretical.

While it is true that the Diatesseron was a corrupted text[133] it still shows the existence of Textus Receptus readings in the second century. Interestingly, the Diatessaron contains numerous readings that are in the Textus Receptus but not in the Critical Text (Matt 1:25; Matt 6:13; Matt 22:30; Mark 6:20; Mark 7:16; Mark 9:49; Luke 4:4; John 3:13; John 5:3,4)

Scholars are divided on exactly what language the Diatesseron was written in. Some believe it to have been in Syriac, which would put it in the category of the Old Syriac versions. This is most likely the case since it was primarily used as a standard text in at least a portion of the Syrian churches.

On the other hand, it is just as likely that, even if it were first written in Syriac, it was probably translated into Greek. And it is believed that this would have happened very shortly after its original writing, and may have even been accomplished by Tatian himself.

The Syriac translations are of great interest and importance to textual critics. The reasons for such interest are both historical and analytical. One reason is because the Syrian language is relatively close in relationship to the Aramaic dialect that was spoken in the first century by Jesus and the apostles. But more importantly to our discussion, what can be said concerning the various Syriac versions? They attest to the early existence and use of the Byzantine manuscripts.

The **Peshitta** dates to around 150 to 170 AD. This version is very closely aligned with the Textus Receptus. So much so, that the date of its writing is often made a point of heated contention. Those who hold to a Critical Text position would much rather see a 5$^{th}$ century date because this would be chronologically after the Codex Vaticanus and Codex Sinaiticus. Since one of their main arguments is the idea that older manuscripts are better, they feel it necessary to offer a later date. However, the date of the Peshitta was rarely if ever called into question until modern scholarship came along. But nowadays it seems that scholars have forgotten that we have recorded history telling us that the Arminian Bible of 411 AD was translated from the Peshitta making a 5th century date for the. Peshitta very unlikely. With that being said, we should not assume that the Peshitta is purely Textus Receptus in its readings. It still reads "God" and not "Son" at John 1:18; lacks entirely John 7:53-8:11; Acts 8:37; I John 5:7 (and other

---

[133] It omits 56 verses of the canonical gospels and is said to have been 28% smaller than the four gospels.

passages found in the Textus Receptus); has a relative pronoun at I Timothy 3:16 rather that "God;" and also contains many other readings which favor the Critical Texts instead of the Byzantine Text or the Textus Receptus.

The history of the **Armenian Bible** is both intriguing and fascinating. It is said to be dated around 411 AD and there are still 1244 copies in existence. According to history, King Sapor became the ruler over Armenia in 378 AD and began to greatly persecute Christians. He also tried to cut all outside influence from the then Byzantine world. Hence, he closed all the schools, condemned any type of Greek scholarship or learning, and burned all the Greek books he could find. Naturally, this included Greek manuscripts of the Bible.

Many believers became convinced that if something were not done quickly, Christianity may be totally destroyed so several attempts were made to translate the scriptures into Armenian. Finally, in 397 AD, Mesrob Mashtots, who had a good knowledge of Syriac and Greek, took up the task to produce an Arminian Bible.

The first major obstacle for Mesrob and his team was a lack of a suitable alphabet to express the phonetic sounds of the Armenian language. And so the first task was to create a written language. By 406 AD, Mesrob had completed the alphabet by modifying the Greek and Pahlavi alphabet.

Unfortunately, Mesrob and his helpers were unable to find any Greek manuscripts in the country so they began their translation from the Peshitta. This initial work was published in 411 AD but was not considered to be as accurate as needed. Thus, two men were sent to Constantinople for Greek manuscripts. These manuscripts would have almost most certainly been of the Byzantine family because that was the major family of texts in use in Constantinople at that time. It is also believed that other copies were obtained from Alexandria, Egypt and those are believed to have been from Origen's Hexapla. After all was said and done, a revision of the original work was produced in 436 AD.

Again, many of those who support the superiority of the Textus Receptus would point out that there is a high percentage of agreement between the Armenian Bible and the Textus Receptus. But we can't have our cake and eat it too. The Armenian Bible does not contain 1 John 5:7, either. So what can we say? Only that this translation validates the early existence of the Byzantine family.

## IN DEFENSE OF THE TEXTUS RECEPTUS

The **Gothic Bible** was translated by Ulfilas[134] around 330 to 350 AD. This was the first major Germanic translation and even those in support of the Critical Text agree that it is obviously translated from the Textus Receptus family of manuscripts. But again, what does this prove? It proves that the Byzantine manuscripts were not only in existence at an early date, but also preferred!

Add to this numerous other early translations such as the Palestinian Syriac (450 AD), the Philoxenian Bible (508 AD), and others and we can state a pretty good case for the preferential use of the Byzantine manuscripts over the others. The Byzantine family not only existed but was also very much in use!

### *Early Christian Writings*

Another source of support for the Textus Receptus comes from early Christian writings. While it is true that many of the early Christians quoted both Critical Text readings and Textus Receptus readings, it serves to show that the Textus Receptus (in the form of the Byzantine manuscripts) was not only in existence but also widely used. We should be clear on the fact that these writers were not necessarily supporters of the Byzantine manuscripts. However, it can be easily shown that they used it.

We should also note that the writers come from a wide range of geographical locations. In other words, the Byzantine manuscripts were not, as some would claim, a "regional" text. In fact, contrary to the opinion of some scholars, the Byzantine manuscripts were used world-wide – even in areas where the majority of early manuscripts, such as the papyri, seemingly support the Critical Text. Textual critics have assigned names to the various families based upon geographic locations. Yet, this is not really possible and pretty misleading to say the least. It could be shown fairly easily that some of the writers, who were from "Alexandria" quoted from the Byzantine texts. And some of the writers from the area around "Antioch" quoted from Alexandrian texts.

But our purpose here is to show how various writers from geographically separated locations all used the Byzantine texts from where the Textus Receptus was constructed. Note the following:

### *Western Writers*

---

[134] Ulfilas, the great intellect that he was, actually devised an alphabet for the Gothic language using letters from both the Greek and Roman alphabets. His supreme purpose for doing so was that he wanted to put a Bible into the hands of the Goths. We do not know how much of this monumental task he completed but we do have large sections of the gospels as well as the epistles.

- **Irenaeus** (A.D. 180) – In his treatise, "Against Heresies, Book III", he quotes from Mark 1:1-2 which clearly agrees with the Byzantine manuscripts. He also quotes from John 1:18 and uses the phrase "only begotten Son" whereas the Critical text uses "only begotten God" instead. However, in Book IV, he also uses "only begotten God". So what can we make of this? Irenaeus, like so many others of our day, apparently used more than one text!

- **Tertullian** (A.D. 150-220) – In his book on baptism, Tertullian refers to John 5:3-4 in order to make his point on baptism. He specifically mentions the reference to an angel troubling the waters. Keep in mind that this is not included in the Critical Text. Thus, Tertullian must have been referring to the Byzantine manuscripts. In his book on Modesty he closely paraphrases Rev 22:14. As he does so, he mentions the tree of life, which is a Byzantine reading. The Critical Text reading is "book of life". Therefore, Tertullian must have used the Byzantine manuscripts.

- **Cyprian** (A.D. 200-258) – In his writings he quotes from 1 John 5:7, known as the Comma Johanneum. This was a full 150 years or more before the Codex Vaticanus and Codex Sinaiticus. See Appendix D for me information concerning Cyprian's quote.

### Alexandrian Writers

- **Clement** (A.D. 200) – Dean Burgon points out that Clement's quotations of scripture are usually western but he also quoted from John 17:24–26 which are clearly Byzantine

- **Origen** (A.D. 182-251) - It is often noted that Origen quoted quite often from the Alexandrian Text. However, he also quoted quite a lot, at least from the first few chapters of John, using the Byzantine Text. In seeking to discredit his quotes, a few Critical text supporters have alleged that Origen's work was revised by later scribes. But as Dean John Burgon points out,

*"The evidence of Papyrus Bodmer II, however, indicates that this is not an adequate explanation of the facts. Certainly it seems a very unsatisfactory way to account for the phenomena which appear in the first fourteen chapters of John. In these chapters, 5 out of 20 "distinctively" Byzantine readings which occur in Origen occur also in Papyrus Bodmer II. These five readings at least must have been Origen's readings, not those of scribes who copied Origen's works..." (The Last 12 Verses of Mark, Dean John W. Burgon, pg 58)*

### Antioch and Asia Minor

## IN DEFENSE OF THE TEXTUS RECEPTUS

**Chrysostom** (A.D. 345 – 407) – Is considered to be one of the earliest church writers to refer to the Byzantine Text.[135] But very obviously, looking back at the men we have just mentioned, he is not.

In the end, it has been said that Tertullian, Irenaeus, Hippolytus, Origen, and Clement have supplied for us over 30,147 scripture citations attesting to the early use of the Byzantine Text. The resulting evidence from the "church fathers" alone would lead us to believe that the Textus Receptus was not only in existence, but also was greatly used.

### Support in Unexpected Places

When we say. "Support in unexpected places" what we really mean is support in places where we are most often led to believe there is none. For instance, how often have we heard the critics of the Textus Receptus speak of the absence of Byzantine readings in the extant papyri? They trumpet this statement as if to say, "See, we told you that the Byzantine manuscripts were changed because there is no evidence that they even existed in the first 300 years!" But it may come as a surprise to some, but the fact remains that even in some of the papyri manuscripts, which are said to solely support the Critical Text, there are distinctively Byzantine readings. Note the chart below:

| Number | Approx. Date | Type |
|---|---|---|
| P11 | 600-700 AD | Alexandrian Text but also contains Byzantine readings |
| P42 | 600-800 AD | Alexandrian Text but also contains Byzantine readings |
| P90 | 100-200 AD | Many scholars like to place P90 in the Alexandrian family but it is as much in agreement with the Byzantine family as it is with the Alexandrian family. |

So even though the common argument about the papyri being totally in support of the Alexandrian Text is often put forth, a simple and realistic look at the truth shows that even among the papyri, support for the early existence of the Byzantine manuscripts can be found.

So what happens when we judiciously analyze the uncials as we have just done with the papyri? Well, first of all, textual critics that support the Critical

---

[135] Gordon D. Fee, "The Use of Greek Patristic Citations in New Testament Textual Criticism: The State of the Question," pp. 344-359 in Studies in the Theory and Method of New Testament Textual Criticism (ed. Eldon J. Epp and Gordon D. Fee; Studies & Documents 45; Grand Rapids: Eerdmans, 1993), 358.

## IN DEFENSE OF THE TEXTUS RECEPTUS

Text often point out that the Codex Sinaiticus, which is dated between 330 and 360 AD is very clearly Alexandrian Text. However, it is rare to find a scholar who will divulge ALL the information concerning this codex.

One fact that is so often unstated is that, although it is an Alexandrian Text manuscript, it contains quite a number of corrections made by later scribes, which brings a number of readings into agreement with the Byzantine manuscripts. In other words, the readings were initially in agreement with the Critical text but a scribe came along that "fixed" the reading. After the "fix" was made, the reading was then in agreement with the Textus Receptus.

So what are we to make of that? The implications are pretty obvious. Somebody who had the authority to correct this manuscript did not agree with the readings and took the opportunity to fix them. In fact, the text of the Codex Sinaiticus has been corrected thousands of times by as many as ten different scribes! One would think that it was almost a scribal training document, if such a thing ever existed!

Actually, there is quite a number of uncial manuscript evidences from before 450 AD, give or take a few years. When we take an objective look at the manuscripts, some more very interesting facts begin to emerge.

| No. | Approx Date | Type |
| --- | --- | --- |
| 01 | 350 AD | Alexandrian Text – although many corrections have been made which contain Byzantine readings. |
| 02 | 450 AD | Byzantine in the Gospels; Alexandrian Text in the rest books |
| 026 | 450 AD | Byzantine Text - Also contains Alexandrian Text readings. |
| 029 | 450 AD | Alexandrian Text - Contains a few Byzantine readings |
| 032 | 450 AD | Byzantine in Matthew and Luke 8 to the end. Alexandrian text in other areas. |
| 048 | 450 AD | Alexandrian Text - Contains a few Byzantine readings |
| 061 | 450 AD | Byzantine Text - Also contains Alexandrian Text readings. |
| 069 | 450 AD | Byzantine Text |
| 0113 | 450 AD | Alexandrian Text - Contains a few Byzantine readings |
| 0125 | 450 AD | Alexandrian Text - Contains a few Byzantine readings |
| 0139 | 450 AD | Alexandrian Text - Contains a few Byzantine readings |
| 0172 | 450 AD | Alexandrian Text - Contains a few Byzantine readings |
| 0173 | 450 AD | Alexandrian Text - Contains a few Byzantine readings |

*God's Preserved Word to Every Generation*

## IN DEFENSE OF THE TEXTUS RECEPTUS

| 0175 | 450 AD | Alexandrian Text - Contains a few Byzantine readings |
| 0201 | 450 AD | Alexandrian Text - Contains a few Byzantine readings |
| 0274 | 450 AD | Alexandrian Text - Contains a few Byzantine readings |

Once again, the results are pretty clear. There is substantial evidence in the early uncials to prove that the Byzantine readings were known and in use.

Take note of Uncial 02. It is better known as "Codex Alexandrinus". It is considered to be very important because along with Codex Sinaiticus and Codex Vaticanus, it is one of the earliest and most complete manuscripts of the Bible. Although it is commonly classified as being in agreement with the Critical Text, the gospels are mainly in agreement with the Textus Receptus. But the Critical text guys rarely mention that. In fact, of all the books I have read on the issue, I cannot remember reading this information in one book in support of the Critical text.

Also, take notice of Uncial 069. This one is interesting because it is Byzantine and dates to the same period as Codex Sinaiticus and Codex Vaticanus and yet very rarely is this manuscript mentioned. The text is clearly Byzantine and yet some would seek to totally ignore it. Others blow a smoke screen with the statement, "This text concurs with "Codex Alexandrinus" because they know that the Codex Alexandrinus has been officially classified as "Alexandrian". But what they don't normally tell you is that the only surviving portion of Uncial 069 is Mark 10:50,51 and Mark 11:11,12. But, as we have just pointed out, this portion of the Codex Alexandrinus is actually Byzantine!

Kurt Aland, founder of the Institute for New Testament textual Research, and supporter of the Critical Text, placed Uncial 069 in category III. What does that mean? It means that in Aland's opinion, the text was "eclectic", or as we would say, "mixed". But why? What could have been his motives seeing that the only surviving portion of the text is obviously Byzantine? I will leave it up to the reader to ponder.

So what is the point? Simply this. Very often the average believer will go to the bookstore and buy a book on the textual or translation issue and depending upon the author, he may not be given the full truth concerning the manuscripts. One writer may point out that the Codex Sinaiticus and the Codex Alexandrinus are very early uncials which support the Critical Text yet never mention that they are contain readings and full portions in support of the Textus Receptus. While on the other hand, another writer may tell you that the King James Version is exactly the same as the original languages when in fact, it is not.[136] Then another person will tell us that the King James Version is not a good translation because it uses the word "Easter" when it can be shown that it was a good choice. What we need is a little bit of intellectual honesty!

## CONFLICT IN THE FAMILY

Another often understated fact is the almost unbelievable margin of disagreements that exist in the family of manuscripts that constitute the basis of the Critical Text. Whereas the margin of disagreement in the Byzantine family is uncannily small – less than 1%, according to many textual critics. But shouldn't it be the other way around? After all the majority of the manuscripts are Byzantine and the more manuscripts you have, the more disagreements, you should find, right?

Well, that all depends how you count. You could count each difference as one. Or, if more than one manuscript have the same difference, then you could count each same difference as one. But in either case, the result is the same. The Byzantine family has way fewer textual variants than the Alexandrian manuscripts.

As we have already stated, there is less than a 1% margin of variants in over 4300 purely Byzantine manuscripts. One would have to believe it was some kind of supernatural thing to have such a minute margin of disagreement among so many witnesses over a span of 1200 years. And indeed it was a supernatural thing. And we call it "preservation"!

With all that being said, what are the details? What are the facts? Let's begin by taking a look at two of the oldest manuscripts in existence - the "Chester Beatty" and the "Bodmer" papyri. The Chester Beatty papyri dates from about A.D. 250 and is said to be in agreement with the Codex Sinaiticus. The Bodmer Papyri –dates between A.D. 175 and 225 and is said to be is agreement with the Codex Vaticanus.[137] Between the two manuscripts, they share about 78 verses in common with each other. The passages that they share in common are John 10:7-25; 10:30-11:10; 11:18-37; and 11:42-57. But incredibly, these two manuscripts

---

[136] Again, before anyone comes to the conclusion that I am criticizing the King James Version, take into account the information I share in this book on some of the differences and why they exist. Yes, there are differences. I will not close my eyes to obvious facts simply to appease others. However, I have not found any difference between the King James Version and the Textus Receptus which was of any consequence to my understanding of a passage. See the section on translations for clarification on these statements.

[137] Metzger; The Text of the New Testaments; pg 42

## IN DEFENSE OF THE TEXTUS RECEPTUS

disagree in over 70 places – and that is not including copyists' errors made during transmission!

The Byzantine manuscripts, from which the Textus Receptus was taken, have the least disagreements between the various manuscripts. The disagreements tend to be copyists' errors or such bizarre changes that it is readily apparent. When a comparison is made with the many other copies, it is extremely simple to identify the true reading of the text. One writer called this agreement "consistent harmony". And consistent harmony is an important witness no matter what the situation is.

### THE ROLE OF GEOGRAPHY IN TEXTUAL ANALYSIS

One of the aspects to textual analysis that is often overlooked is the aspect of geography. By this we are referring to where, geographically speaking, the different types of manuscripts are generally found. This is important because it gives us a good indication of which text types were in common use and which ones were not.

We have placed a lot of emphasis on the basis that the Textus Receptus is the superior text because it meets the criteria of inspiration and preservation. We have pointed out that historically, there was an extended period of time when the only texts in use were the Byzantine texts. We have also shown that the Alexandrian texts and the Byzantine Texts both existed from the very beginning.[138]

We then went on to disqualify the Alexandrian manuscripts, and consequently the Critical Text because it was not accepted and in common use by God's people from at least the 1400s until the 1880s. Our reasoning was that God promised to preserve his word to every generation and therefore the Alexandrian manuscripts do not meet the criteria.

But conceivably, someone could point back to the first 1400 years of Christianity and argue that Christians were indeed using the Alexandrian Text. Thus, if we take a look at the geographical locations where the various text types were found, we can get a better idea of how much "in use" each text type really was!

Let's remember that this whole discussion is about identifying which Greek manuscripts match the original manuscripts. So it stands to reasons that

---

[138] We have shown this by using the papyrus manuscript evidence as well as early writings of Christians from the first three centuries, including early translations.

we should first identify where the original manuscripts - penned by the hand of Peter, Paul, and John – where were they written from?

Let us take a look at this according to location:

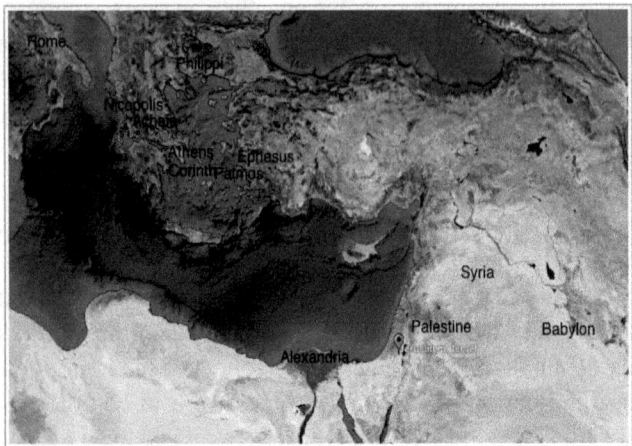

The following is a list of the places where it is commonly believed that the New Testament books were written:[139]

- Palestine – Matthew
- Rome – Mark(?), Acts, Galatians, Ephesians, Philippians, Colossians, 2nd Timothy, Philemon, Hebrews,
- Syria – (Mark?)
- Achaia – Luke
- Ephesus – John, 1st John, 2nd John, 3rd John
- Corinth – Romans
- Phillippi – 1st Corinthians, 2nd Corinthians, 1st Timothy,
- Athens – 1st Thessalonians, 2nd Thessalonians,
- Nicopolis – Titus
- Jerusalem – James, Jude(?)
- Babylon – 1st Peter, 2nd Peter
- Patmos - Revelation

If you take a look at the map, you will notice that none of the New Testament books were written in Egypt. It stands to reason that the most dependable copies, those closest to the original autographs, would be found in

---

[139] As you can see there are a couple books where there isn't a lot of certainty. The place of the authorship of Mark is debatable. The place where Jude was written is merely conjecture based upon the tone and content of the letter itself but no real evidence exists.

areas closest to where they books were first penned. Add to this the obvious fact that the Greek language was predominant in the Byzantine Empire making it possible for scribes to be a bit more skilled than the ones who lived in Egypt. It is a historical fact that by the time of Christ, the use of Greek in Egypt was already on the decline.

Yet at the same time, Byzantine manuscripts were also found in Egypt. So what does this tell us? It tells us that the text of choice was not limited to any one geographical location, no matter how small in number. On the other hand, we don't find any of the Alexandrian text type anywhere else but in Egypt. In other words, the Byzantine text had a worldwide distribution while the Alexandrian text did not.

It is at this point that more than a few authors would point of that Egypt is a type of the world and therefore whatever came from Egypt, in their thinking, is evil. But that is not the argument I am making here. Actually, if we really followed that line of thinking then we would have to reject all manuscripts for "the whole world lieth in wickedness"! Indeed, Egypt is a picture of the world! But that also means the world is as bad as Egypt. In fact, the type is never as perfect as the antitype. In this case, the world is the problem, not simply Egypt![140]

So we do not reject a manuscript simply because it is from Egypt. No, we reject it because it does not meet the criteria of preservation. It was not used worldwide. God's people did not receive it. That being said, I find it interesting that Origen, writing in the early 3rd century said,

*". . .differences among the manuscripts [of the Gospels] have become great, either through the negligence of some copyists or through the perverse audacity of others; they either neglect to check over what they have transcribed, or, in the process of checking, they lengthen or shorten, as they please." (Bruce Metzger, The Text of the New Testament: Its Transmission, Corruption, and Restoration, 3rd ed. (1991), pp. 151-152)*

Origen, being from Alexandria, would have no doubt been speaking of those manuscripts being circulated in his area.

So now we have come to another crucial question. Why would the believers in Egypt purposefully (in some cases) or even ignorantly (probably many unintentional variants) use or propagate corrupted texts?

---

[140] Also, Matt 2:14, 15 make it clear that Jesus fulfilled Bible prophecy when he went down to Egypt and then came back into Israel. The lesson we learn is that we must not push more meaning into a type than what is meant.

## IN DEFENSE OF THE TEXTUS RECEPTUS

I will answer that question with an example that best explains the reasons. For over 100 years the nation of South Korea had a mediocre, second-generation[141] translation of the Critical Text. Every pastor and missionary used it because there just simply was nothing else available. Many of these men, fine men, knew that the translation had issues but they had no other options at the time and so they used it. They used it in their churches. They used it in their homes. They reprinted it. They used it in their literature. Virtually no other Bible existed and so that is what they used.

Now, in relating this back to the first three centuries, we are talking about a time period in history when persecution was great. People died for the scriptures. Even in Egypt, which came under Roman rule in 30 BC, it was dangerous to be a believer. But the believers in Egypt often stood in open defiance of the Roman Empire and many of them paid the price. So before we begin to bash the Egyptian believers for using inferior manuscripts, maybe we should ask ourselves why.

The most likely answer is this. Whatever manuscripts they had to start with were obviously copies from outside of Egypt. That may have been the first step in the chain of manuscript corruption. Add to this the fact that the believers in Egypt were greatly influenced by the school of Alexandria, which subscribed to more of an allegorical interpretation of the scriptures and not so much of a literal interpretation. As copies were made of copies, it was not so important that every word be exactly preserved as long as the main idea remained in tact.[142] Obviously this was not always true, but for the most part, it was their philosophy.

To complicate matters, at least in the 1st century, the believers in Egypt were fervently trying to spread their faith just as the believers in the rest of the world were doing. But they did not have Paul traveling through their territory and then writing letters of follow-up to keep them straight. They obviously had to begin their labors with copies that were carried into Egypt from other areas. So these locally evangelistic believers used whatever copies they had to spread Christianity where they were. They recopied. They used it in their literature. It is unfortunate that they didn't really have the good stuff but they did what they could with what they had. So before we start painting all of the Egyptian believers as some kind of geographically isolated cult, let's remind ourselves of the

---

[141] A translation of a translation.

[142] Nothing saying but isn't that the same type of mentality that we find so prevalent in some circles when discussing the Textus Receptus and the Critical Text today? "As long as we can teach every doctrine from it, it is okay. As long as the variant doesn't affect the sense of the reading..." That all sounds nice but it conflicts with the doctrine of verbal inspiration and preservation.

limitations that they faced. Let's remind ourselves of the stories from history which show us a group of believers, misguided in some ways as they were, who still paid dearly for their faith. If they really hated Christianity as much as some say they did, then why would so many die for it?

Another way in which geography plays an important part in the preservation of one text over another is because of the climate. It has been pointed out that the papyri are all found in Egypt where the climate is more conducive to preserving that type of material. But in reality, only one manuscript of any type prior to the 5$^{th}$ century survived outside of Egypt (Uncial 0212).

Let's take a step back and argue from a different perspective. Based upon the evidence, could I not hypothesize that the only people who knew how to use plants to make paper were Egyptian? Sure, I could do that but we know that it is ludicrous to say such a thing. Just because we have only found papyri in Egypt does not mean the rest of the world did not know how to make papyri. So, would it not be a huge assumption to suggest that the rest of the world did not have the proper text type simply because the papyri were found in Egypt? Of course it is.

## HISTORY OF TEXT-TYPE CRITICISM

As we have already looked at some of the information concerning the history of textual criticism, some of this information is repeated. But for the sake of clarity of information, and understanding of how we got to the convoluted mess that we call "textual criticism" today, we need to take a deeper look at the history of textual criticism.

We noted earlier that Irenaeus and Origin, as early as the 2nd and 3rd century were already taking note that there were corruptions creeping into the manuscripts of their day. Augustine, in the 4th century, in examining a passage in Matthew, wrote concerning the differences in some of the manuscripts that he was aware of.

So again, we have to reiterate that textual analysis has been around since the very beginning. Keep in mind that the scribes who were charged with making copies of the manuscripts were also making choices concerning which manuscripts they would use. And this was happening on a very large scale for the first eight centuries.

No doubt there were already those who took an interest in the types of relationships between the various manuscripts very early on but as far as modern scholarship is concerned, Johann Albrecht Bengel seems to have been the first to suggest "companies, families, tribes, or nations". In 1725 he wrote an essay where he classified the manuscripts into two basic families – Asiatic (basically what we would refer to as "Byzantine), and African (all others). And that might not have been a bad way to look at it because the idea was basically along the lines of "good" and "bad".

But then Johann Salomo Semler and Johann Jakob Griesbach (1745 – 1812) took Bengel's system and "refined" it. When Griesbach was finished with his modifications, there were three text types (families) to contend with.

Griesbach divided the manuscripts into three families – Byzantine, Alexandrian, and Western. Griesbach sought to identify the family by geographical names based upon where the majority of that particular text-type was discovered.

Later, Westcott and Hort built upon this but the only real difference was how they viewed the Alexandrian text. They renamed the Byzantine text as "Syrian", retained the name "Western" but felt that the Alexandrian text should be further divided into two groups.

## IN DEFENSE OF THE TEXTUS RECEPTUS

The first group they called "Neutral" which contained what they believed to be the best witnesses because they were, in their minds, the closest to the original autographs. This group contained the Codex Sinaiticus and the Codex Vaticanus. Whenever these two manuscripts were in agreement, Westcott and Hort felt that they were very near the original readings.[143] The second group, Westcott and Hort called the "Alexandrian" text.

And it is at this point where it should be stressed that up to this point in history, almost all "textual critics" began with the belief that they had the true text and others were categorized based upon their agreement with the true text. But Westcott and Hort took a different and dangerous approach.

In their way of viewing the text types, they did not begin with a standard. They began examining the texts according to their own reason which led them to become the judges with the final say as to what should constitute the Word of God and what should not.

More lately, even many of those who hold to a critical text position have come to the understanding that much of Westcott and Hort's reasoning was faulty and yet the damage has been done!

Currently, a system outlined by Kurt and Barbara Aland, founders of the Institute for New Testament Textual Research, is the most commonly used method of viewing text types. They divided the texts into five categories: I – Alexandrian (which they also considered to be the closest to the original), II – Egyptian (which they still considered pretty good as long as it agreed with the Alexandrian!), III – Eclectic (a mixture of readings which disallow identifying the manuscript in any other category), IV – Western (actually very few manuscripts were placed in this category and it is a wonder why they didn't just lump this category in with category III), V – Byzantine (which the Alands believed to be the furthest from the original autographs).

The most recent attempt at categorizing text types was done by a German theologian named Hermann Von Soden in a book entitled *"Die Schriften des Neuen Testaments"*. Other than renaming the groups, it appears that the bulk of his work was focused on further categorizing the manuscripts in the Byzantine family.

---

[143] At this point, I feel it necessary to remind the reader that because of the promises of preservation, the original readings were never lost. In saying that we have something that is "very near" the original reading, we are really saying what we have is slightly different. This goes against all that the scriptures teach concerning verbal inspiration and preservation.

## IN DEFENSE OF THE TEXTUS RECEPTUS

Although Von Soden's works did receive a lot of attention, his categorizations never really caught on and the world of textual scholarship, for the most part, still uses Aland's system of categorizing the manuscripts. The biggest blow to Von Soden's approach is that the majority of supporters for the Critical text and the majority of supporters for the Textus Receptus viewed Von Soden's work as inaccurate and unacceptable.

## CONSIDERATION OF PREVAILING TEXTUAL CRITICISM

We know from examining the scriptures that much of what is say in the realm of modern textual criticism is false. In fact the Bible has much to say about our approach to God's word and how we ought to view it. As we look at the following teachings from scripture, we will also be comparing it to the usual approach taken by modern textual critics.

The first and most obvious truth is that **God has established his Word.** The scriptures abound with references which clearly show us this:

*1 Peter 1:10-12 Of which salvation the prophets have enquired and searched diligently, who prophesied of the grace that should come unto you: (11) Searching what, or what manner of **time the Spirit of Christ which was in them did signify**, when **it testified beforehand** the sufferings of Christ, and the glory that should follow. (12) Unto whom it was revealed, that not unto themselves, but unto us they did minister the things, which are now reported unto you by them that have preached the gospel unto you with the Holy Ghost sent down from heaven; which things the angels desire to look into.*

*2 Peter 1:16-21 For we have not followed cunningly devised fables, when we made known unto you the power and coming of our Lord Jesus Christ, but were eyewitnesses of his majesty. (17) For he received from God the Father honour and glory, when there came such a voice to him from the excellent glory, This is my beloved Son, in whom I am well pleased. (18) And this voice which came from heaven we heard, when we were with him in the holy mount. (19) **We have also a more sure word of prophecy;** whereunto ye do well that ye take heed, as unto a light that shineth in a dark place, until the day dawn, and the day star arise in your hearts: (20) Knowing this first, that **no prophecy of the scripture is of any private interpretation. (21) For the prophecy came not in old time by the will of man: but holy men of God spake as they were moved by the Holy Ghost.***

*John 6:63 It is the spirit that quickeneth; the flesh profiteth nothing**: the words that I speak unto you, they are spirit, and they are life.***

*Psalm 119:89 For ever, O LORD, **thy word is settled in heaven**.*

Knowing what the Bible teaches about itself is the foundation of our approach to the scriptures. Since God gave his Word, and established his Word, our approach must be one of faith. Yet most modern textual critics take a totally

**God's Preserved Word to Every Generation**

different approach. Their approach is very much a man-centered approach which was strongly promoted by Westcott and Hort.

In fact, according to their approach, man can improve upon the scriptures without any assistance from God's Spirit whatsoever.[144] This is a very major fallacy since the Bible teaches us that spiritual truth can only be understood when taught by the Holy Spirit.

> *1Corinthians 2:11-16 For what man knoweth the things of a man, save the spirit of man which is in him? even so the **things of God knoweth no man, but the Spirit of God**. (12) Now we have received, not the spirit of the world, **but the spirit which is of God; that we might know the things that are freely given to us of God.** (13) Which things also we speak, not in the words which man's wisdom teacheth, **but which the Holy Ghost teacheth; comparing spiritual things with spiritual.** (14) But the natural man receiveth not the things of the Spirit of God: for they are foolishness unto him: neither can he know them, because **they are spiritually discerned**. (15) But he that is spiritual judgeth all things, yet he himself is judged of no man. (16) For **who hath known the mind of the Lord, that he may instruct him**? But we have the mind of Christ.*

It is a very grave error to assume that the scriptures have somehow become corrupted or lost and this is only compounded when a man believes he can somehow improve upon perfection!

A second and equally important truth that we must remember is that God has promised, and performed, the preservation of His Word to every generation. In other words, from the time that the words were written, they have been preserved by God from corruption or extinction. Again, consider the following references:

> **Psalm 12:6-7** *The words of the LORD are pure words: as silver tried in a furnace of earth, purified seven times. (7) Thou shalt keep them, O LORD, thou shalt preserve them from this generation for ever.*

> **Psalm 33:11** *The counsel of the LORD standeth for ever, the thoughts of his heart to all generations.*

---

[144] *An Introduction to the Study of the New Testament*, 2nd Ed., A. H. McNeile, Oxford at the Clarendon Press, 1955. p. 426, 428 429, 430; see also *The New Testament in the Original Greek Text* revised by Brooke Foss Westcott, D. D., and Fenton John Anthony Hort, D.D. Cambridge and London 1881. Volume 2 Introduction. p. 32

## IN DEFENSE OF THE TEXTUS RECEPTUS

***Psalm 100:5** For the LORD is good; his mercy is everlasting; and his truth endureth to all generations.*

But as we have discussed earlier, the modern assumption is that the Byzantine manuscripts somehow were intentionally changed in the 3rd or 4th century by a guy named Lucian.[145] And since the Textus Receptus was derived from the Byzantine manuscripts, in their opinion, it too, is corrupted. Yet we know that for a period of 450 years or so, no other manuscripts were in use by God's people!

For the most part, modern textual criticism is based upon the "man-centered" approach of Westcott and Hort. Since the 1800's, the Greek text has been "corrected", "revised", and modified many times over.[146]

We could also point out that in reality, Westcott and Hort formed new principles of textual criticism and then used these principles to justify their major premise. Now, if that is not a case for circular reasoning, what is? In fact, it is often pointed out that Hort reasoned that the Codex Vaticanus and Codex Siniaticus, the main manuscripts in support of the Critical Text, had a "ring of genuiness" to them. Upon what did he base this opinion? And notice that we use the word, "opinion". This is clearly personal bias.

But again, we must emphasize that the private beliefs of Wescott and Hort are not really the issue here. But knowing what they believed concerning the scriptures in relation to inspiration and preservation helps us to understand why they took the approach that they took.

The end result of their lack of understanding of biblical preservation led them to a very "man-centered" approach in the area of textual criticism. And since they did not have a solid biblical foundation, they ended up adopting a corrupted text as their basis.

Even Eusebius, who, by the way, was no friend of the fundamental Bible believer, saw the problems related to corruptions in the Greek texts:

*"If anyone will take the trouble to collect their several copies and compare them, he will discover frequent divergencies; for example, Ascelepiades's copies do not agree with Theodotus's. A large number are obtainable, thanks to the emulous energy with which disciples copied the 'emendations' or rather perversions of the*

---

[145] *An Introduction to the Study of the New Testament*, 2nd Ed., A. H. McNeile, Oxford at the Clarendon Press, 1955. p. 133, 426, 428

[146] However, we should also note that more and more modern textual critics have come to understand that the Lucian theory is false. In fact, some critics are beginning to change the corrupted readings of the Critical text back to readings which agree with the Textus Receptus.

*text by their respective masters....it is possible to collate the ones which his disciples made first with those that have undergone further manipulation, and to find endless discrepancies." [Eusebius, The History of the Church from Christ to Constantine, Translated with an introduction by G. A. Williamson. Penguin Books Baltimore, Maryland 1965, p. 237]*

If we simply compare the Codex Vaticanus and the Codex Siniaticus, we find in the gospels alone, close to 1000 differences in their readings.[147] Yet for some reason, Westcott and Hort felt that these were to be accepted over the Byzantine manuscripts. Why? Because they felt that the Textus Receptus was "vile" or "villainous".[148]

But let's not lose sight of the fact that the big issue today has more to do with translations than it does with Greek texts. Normally, when the issue is discussed, statements concerning the inferiority of one translation or another is at the heart of the debate. But the reason why there are so many problems in the translations is because there are problems with the Greeks texts. If the Greek texts were never modified, then the question of "which Bible" would be based upon translational principles and not on textual analysis!

---

[147] *The Revision Revised,* John William Burgon B.D. Dean of Chichester. October 31, 1883. p. 318

[148] See the section of John Anthony Hort for further information on their views.

# IN DEFENSE OF THE TEXTUS RECEPTUS

## DEAN BURGON'S SEVEN TESTS OF TRUTH

Dean John William Burgon [149], Anglican "divine" (clergy whose theological writings are considered authoritative), who was Dean of Chichester Cathedral, proposed that there are seven tests of truth when seeking to determine the correct text. None of these points can be considered to stand alone as a definitive test in and of itself but need to be taken as a whole.

### AGE OF THE MANUSCRIPT

The "age of the manuscript" is just that. How old is the manuscript? Obviously, the older a manuscript is, the closer to the originals which were written by Peter, Paul, etc. Logically, this increases the probability that the manuscript will match the original autographa.

Although there is great disagreement concerning the age of manuscripts, nearly all scholars would agree that the age of a manuscript is important. Note the following quotations:

Stewart Custer, former teacher of Bible and Theology at Bob Jones University writes in *The Truth About the King James Version Controversy*:

*"The Alexandrian text is older and better attested than the others."*

He goes on to say,

*"The Byzantine text is later than the others and is a derived text." (p. 9)*

He continues,

*"Thus the earliest evidence for the Byzantine text is the middle of the fourth century two centuries later than the Alexandrian text." (p. 9)*

Keep in mind that Dr. Custer is fairly neutral in his support of texts, basically holding to the position that either text, whether the Textus Receptus or the Critical Text, is acceptable. He has no real bias toward one text or the other. Yet he

---

[149] James R. White makes a point in one of his books, The King James Controversy, pg 130, that Dean Burgon himself believed that the Textus Receptus was in need of revision. White knows that a great many Textus Receptus supporters use Dean Burgon's works extensively. His point is that those who hold to the Textus Receptus or King James Version position ought to follow Burgon in his desire for a revision of the Textus Receptus. But what did Burgon really say? He did not say any revision should be made from manuscripts outside of the Byzantine family. In fact, he made it clear that he considered Aleph, B, C, D and the Latin copies to be corrupt witnesses. Also keep in mind that Burgon said this in 1883 before Scrivener did his final work on the Textus Receptus in 1894.

assigns a later date to the Byzantine text even though there is evidence to the contrary.

D.A. Carson, research professor at Trinity Evangelical Divinity School, writes in *"The King James Version Debate: A Plea for Realism"*:

*"They [scholars] argued that the Byzantine textual tradition [which includes the TR] did not originate before the mid-fourth century, and that it was the result of a conflation of earlier texts." (The King James Version Debate, p.40)*

Conflation is the idea that two or more manuscripts were combined into one manuscript effectively eliminating any differences and also making various readings appear longer than originally meant. The Diatesseron would be a very good example of this type of corruption. But what is to say that a scribe had to make a text longer by combining two similar readings? Could we not also argue the possibility that a scribe chose to simplify a longer reading? The point is, in either case, we are arguing from mere conjecture.

D.A. Carson is a supporter of the critical text. He states that scholars agree that the Byzantine text is a mid-fourth century invention when in fact there is ample evidence that the Byzantine text existed as far back as the 2$^{nd}$ century:

| Number | Date | Type |
|---|---|---|
| P90 | 100-200 AD | Many scholars like to place P90 in the Alexandrian family but it is as much in agreement with the Byzantine family as it is with the Alexandrian family |
| 01 | 350 AD | Alexandrian Text – although many corrections have been made which contain Byzantine readings. |
| 02 | 450 AD | Byzantine in the Gospels; Critical Text in the rest books |
| 026 | 450 AD | Byzantine Text - Also contains Critical Text readings. |
| 032 | 450 AD | Byzantine in Matthew and Luke 8 to the end. Critical text - Western, Caesarean, and Alexandrian - in other areas. |
| 061 | 450 AD | Byzantine Text - Also contains Critical Text readings. |
| 069 | 450 AD | Byzantine Text |

Dr. Harry A. Sturz, Greek scholar and one of the translators of the New King James Version, in his book, *The Byzantine Text-Type and New Testament Textual Criticism*, gives the following information:

*"These 150 readings (Byzantine) are early. They go back to the second century, for they are supported by papyri which range from the third to the second century in date." (p. 62) "...it is startling from the standpoint of the Westcott - Hort theory*

*to find that the so-called 'Byzantine' readings not only existed early but were present in Egypt before the end of the second century." (Sturz, p. 62)*

Sturz later wrote:

*"Westcott and Hort, therefore, were mistaken in regard to their insistence that all the pre-Syrian [Westcott-Hort term for "pre-Byzantine"] evidence for readings was to be found in the Alexandrian, Neutral, and Western texts, i.e., that these three text-types and their chief witnesses reserved the complete second-century picture of the textual tradition on which the Syrian editor(s) built." (pp. 62-63)*

Dr. Sturz is a supporter of the Byzantine manuscripts. He makes no bones about pointing out that Westcott and Hort were wrong about their position concerning the age of the Byzantine Texts.

Dean Burgon surveyed early Christian writers as to the text they used and this is what he wrote:

*"The original predominance of the Traditional text is shown in the list given of the earliest Fathers. Their record proves that in their writings, and so in the church generally, corruption had made itself felt in the earliest times, but that the pure waters generally prevailed. The Tradition is also carried on through the majority of the Fathers who succeeded them. There is no break or interval: the witness is continuous. Again, not the slightest confirmation is given to Dr. Hort's notion that a revision or recension was definitely accomplished at Antioch in the middle of the fourth century." (The Traditional Text of the Holy Gospels, vol 1, p. 121)*

*"For the 76 Church Fathers examined, [Fathers that died before A.D. 400] there were 2,630 references to the Traditional Text and only 1,753 to the Neologian[150] text. The Traditional Text was definitely in existence well before A.D. 400. In other words, not only is the Traditional Text present in these church fathers' time, who lived and died prior to A.D. 400, the Traditional Text predominated over the Neologian 3 to 2."*

*"No one, I believe, has till now made a systematic examination of the quotations occurring in the writings of the Fathers who died before A.D. 400 and in public documents written prior to that date. . . . The testimony therefore of the Early Fathers is emphatically according to the issue of numbers in*

---

[150] Neologian is a person who brings in new interpretations to traditional theology. Burgon's reference to "neologian" was meant for Westcott and Hort.

*favor of the Traditional Text, being about 3:2. But it is also necessary to inform the readers of this treatise, that here quality confirms quantity. A list will now be given of thirty important passages in which evidence is borne on both sides, and it will be seen that 530 testimonies are given in favour of the Traditional readings as against 170 on the other side. In other words, the Traditional Text beats its opponent in a general proportion to 3 to 1." [Dean Burgon, The Traditional Text, pp. 94, 101-102]*

Dr. Burgon is obviously in support of the Byzantine manuscripts. And he definitively points out that BOTH texts existed in the writings of the early Christian writers.

Westcott and Hort, knowing that the age of the manuscript was important, spent a lot of time trying to prove that the Byzantine text did not precede the Alexandrian manuscripts. In fact, D.A. Carson references their attempts:

Westcott and Hort with their followers *"...argued that the Byzantine textual tradition (which includes the TR) did not originate before the mid-fourth century, and that it was the result of a conflation of earlier texts. This text was taken to Constantinople, where it became popular spreading throughout the Byzantine Empire." (D. A. Carson, The King James Version Debate, pp. 40-41)*

According to one writer, Westcott and Hort believed that the only reason why the Byzantine Text became predominant was because it was taken to Constantinople where it received ecclesiastical sanction.

So before we move on to Burgon's next test of truth, let's take another look at the "age of the manuscript" idea. Since it can be clearly shown that both the Alexandrian Texts and the Byzantine Texts co-existed all the way back to the beginning, the only thing that we can dogmatically say is that they both existed. We cannot know, based upon this test alone, that either one necessarily agrees with the original writings from the hands of Peter, Paul, etc.

In my opinion, this first test does absolutely nothing to help us determine the true text type at all. Even if we could show that one text was older than another, any attempt to use age as a "proof" of any kind is pure conjecture. We have, to my knowledge, absolutely no evidence, based upon age alone, to prove that either text type is the same as the autographa. This is something that we must conclude by faith as we look at history and how God preserved one text over and against the other.

## NUMBER OF EXISTING MANUSCRIPTS

## IN DEFENSE OF THE TEXTUS RECEPTUS

The idea here is that the more witnesses to a particular text type we have, the more likely it is that it is in agreement with the autographa. Dean Burgon wrote:

> *"'Number' is the most ordinary ingredient of weight, and indeed in matters of human testimony, is an element which even cannot be cast away. Ask one of Her Majesty's Judges if it be not so. Ten witnesses (suppose) are called in to give evidence: of whom one resolutely contradicts what is solemnly deposed to by the other nine. Which of the two parties do we suppose the Judge will be inclined to believe?"* [Dean Burgon, The Traditional Text, p. 43]

Obviously, in the foregoing set of circumstances, "Her Majesty's Judges" would believe the nine witnesses. We have, in our day, over 99% of the evidence of our manuscripts favoring the type of text that underlies our King James Version of the Bible. 5369 of these manuscripts are in support of the Textus Receptus, either in full or in part. Another 227 support the Critical Text either in full or in part. The remaining manuscripts (226 manuscripts) are either mixed texts or unclassified texts. So the score is 5369 manuscripts to 227 manuscripts.

So in a court of law, how would this work out? 5369 witnesses tell the same story. 227 tell a different story but even their stories widely disagree. If you were the judge and jury, which would you believe?

### VARIETY OF WITNESSES FROM DIFFERENT LOCATIONS

> *"Witnesses of different kinds; from different countries; speaking different tongues:--witnesses who can never have met and between whom it is incredible that there should exist collusion of any kind:--such witnesses deserve to be listened to most respectfully. Indeed, when witnesses of so varied a sort agree in large numbers, they must needs be accounted worthy of even implicit confidence."* [Dean Burgon, The Traditional Text, p. 50]

> *"It is precisely this consideration which constrains us to pay supreme attention to the combined testimony of the Uncials and of the whole body of the Cursive (miniscule) Copies. They are (a) dotted over at least 1000 years: (b) they evidently belong to so many divers countries,--Greece, Constantinople, Asia Minor, Palestine, Syria, Alexandria, and other parts of Africa, not to say Sicily, Southern Italy, Gaul, England, and Ireland: (c) they exhibit so many strange characteristics and peculiar sympathies: (d) they so clearly represent countless families of MSS., being in no single instance absolutely identical in their text, and certainly*

*not being copies of any other Codex in existence,--that their unanimous decision I hold to be an absolutely irrefragable evidence of the Truth." [Dean Burgon, The Traditional Text, p. 50-51]*

This is an incredibly powerful witness for the Byzantine text since we are talking about twelve or more countries, several parts of the world, all witnessing to this same family of texts with no sign of collusion or relationship.

Dean Burgon mentioned the uncials and minuscules but failed to mention that we now have Byzantine papyri in our possession as well. This is significant because the papyri originate from Egypt where was once believed that only the Alexandrian Text was in use. But we now know this to be untrue. So we could add Egypt as another location to Dean Burgon's list of nations.

## RESPECTABILITY OR WEIGHT AS A TEST OF TRUTH

*"In the first place, the witnesses in favor of any given reading should be respectable. 'Respectability' is of course a relative term; but its use and applicability in this department of Science will be generally understood and admitted by scholars, although they may not be altogether agreed as to the classification of their authorities." [Dean Burgon, The Traditional Text, p. 53]*

Going back to our courtroom illustration, a witness is considered more respectable based upon his agreement with other witnesses as well as the personal character of the witness himself. A doctor's testimony will always carry more weight than the testimony of a drug addicted felon. But then again, the druggie's testimony may carry more weight than the doctor's if his testimony is in agreement with several other testimonies while the doctor's testimony is not. So Dean Burgon is right. "Respectability" is definitely a relative term but the reasons why one witness may be weightier than another is not so difficult to see.

Can it be shown that the Byzantine text has respectability? Absolutely, since there is over a 99% agreement between the manuscripts of the Byzantine family, I would say that the witnesses have a great level of respectability.

And what about the Critical Text? Going back to our illustration, when one person's testimony is different than the majority of others, it cannot be considered as "respectable". With that being said, let's consider some facts that we have already learned about the Alexandrian manuscripts:

## IN DEFENSE OF THE TEXTUS RECEPTUS

- The Chester Beatty papyri which was once thought to be of the Caesarean[151] family but it is now generally considered to be an eclectic text. It is also said to be in agreement with the Codex Sinaiticus with frequent "independent" readings. In other words, they disagree frequently.
- The Bodmer papyri is said to be is agreement with the Codex Vaticanus, however it has been edited in several places[152]. Even in the texts itself, (P75, P66) there are differences.
- The Chester Beatty and Bodmer Papyri only share about 78 verses in common, but differ in over 70 places!
- Codex Vaticanus is an interesting manuscript in its own right. It contains mysterious double-dots (umlauts) in the column which seem to indicate places of textual uncertainty. These dots were discovered in 1995 by Philip Payne who concluded that they indicated a place where a textual variant was known to the writer. Almost all scholars agree with this conclusion.[153]
- Another interesting marginal note in the Codex Vaticanus is found next to Hebrews 1:3, where the note reads "Fool and knave, can't you leave the old reading alone and not alter it!"—"ἀμαθέστατε καὶ κακέ, ἄφες τὸν παλαιόν, μὴ μεταποίει". This obviously is an indication that scribal altering was a known problem, even then! Additionally, there is another "umlaut" at this same verse but it occurs on the "wrong" side. This is most likely because of the note on the opposite side. But if this is true, then at least some of the umlauts were placed on the manuscript at a later date. The logical conclusion is that at least two different persons understood that the manuscript was corrupted.
- The Codex Vaticanus disagrees with the Codex Sinaiticus in over 3,000 substantial places just in the Gospels alone.
- The Codex Sinaiticus has been corrected by at least 9 different scribes from the 4th to 12th century. That makes this manuscript the most corrected manuscript discovered. Tischendorf counted 14,800 corrections in what was

---

[151] As a text type, it is really hard to say what exactly this is since it has been described as "mildly paraphrastic" and 'falls between the Alexandrian and Western texts". No pure manuscript containing this text-type is in existence. It is so named because Origen used it while he was in Caeserea.

[152] http://www.earlham.edu/~seidti/iam/tc_pap75.html

[153] http://www-user.uni-bremen.de/~wie/Vaticanus/umlauts.html

## IN DEFENSE OF THE TEXTUS RECEPTUS

then the Saint Petersburg portion[154] alone! By one count, there have been more than 23,000 corrections total.
- Besides missing many words, phrases, and verses in the Codex Sinaiticus, it also contains variants heretofore unmatched by any other document.
- The Codex Alexandrinus is commonly classified as "Alexandrian text type", yet the Gospels are mainly in agreement with the Textus Receptus. In fact, it is one of the oldest extant manuscripts containing Textus Receptus readings.

So what conclusion can we come to concerning the Alexandrian manuscripts? Obviously, we cannot call these witnesses "respectable" by objective standards.

### CONTINUITY AS A TEST OF TRUTH

*When therefore a reading is observed to leave traces of its existence and of its use all down the ages, it comes with an authority of a peculiarly commanding nature. And on the contrary, when a chasm of greater or less breadth of years yawns in the vast mass of evidence which is ready for employment, or when a tradition is found to have died out, upon such a fact alone suspicion or grave doubt, or rejection must inevitably ensue." [Dean Burgon, The Traditional Text, p. 59]*

To put this in simpler terms, the fact that a manuscript has been in use throughout the generations lends great credibility to the authenticity of a manuscript. On the flip-side, if a manuscript has not been in use throughout the generations, this indicates that it was not considered to be authentic.

Again, as the following chart shows, the Byzantine manuscript can be shown to exist in every century from the 2nd century on:

| Number | Date | Type |
| --- | --- | --- |
| P90 | 100-200 AD | Many scholars like to place P90 in the Alexandrian family but it is as much in agreement with the Byzantine family as it is with the Alexandrian family. It also disagrees with both equally as often. |
| 01 | 350 AD | Alexandrian Text – although many corrections have been made which contain Byzantine readings. |
| 02 | 450 AD | Byzantine in the Gospels; Critical Text in the rest books |
| 026 | 450 AD | Byzantine Text - Also contains Critical Text readings. |
| 032 | | Byzantine in Matthew and Luke 8 to the end. Critical text - Western, Caesarean, and Alexandrian - in other areas. |

---

[154] Portions of six leaves which are currently kept at the National Library of Russia in Saint Petersburg.

## IN DEFENSE OF THE TEXTUS RECEPTUS

| Number | Date | Type |
|---|---|---|
| 069 | | Byzantine Text |
| Papyrus 084, P84 | 500 AD | |
| 08 | 550 AD | |
| 022 | | |
| 023 | | |
| 024 | | |
| 042 | | |
| 064 =074 =090 | | |
| 065 | | |
| 078 | | |
| 079 | | |
| 090 | | |
| 0104 | | |
| 0246 | | |
| 0253 | | |
| 0265 | | |
| 074=064 =090 | | |
| Papyrus 073, P73 | 600-700 AD | |
| 0303 | | |
| 097 | 650 AD | |
| 099 | | |
| 0103 | | |
| 0211 | | |
| 054 | 750 AD | |

# IN DEFENSE OF THE TEXTUS RECEPTUS

| Number | Date | Type |
|---|---|---|
| 0116 | | |
| 0134 | | |
| 07 | | |
| 011 | 800-1000 AD | |
| 036 | | |
| 014 | 800-900 AD | |
| 041 | | |
| 013 | 850 AD | |
| 017 | | |
| 018 | | |
| 020 | | |
| 031 | | |
| 039 | | |
| 049 | | |
| 053 | | |
| 0133 | | |
| 0135 | | |
| 0136=0137 | | |
| 0137 | | |
| 0151 | | |
| 0197 | | |
| 0248 | | |
| 0257 | | |
| 0272 | | |
| 0273 | | |
| 041 | 900-1000 AD | |

## IN DEFENSE OF THE TEXTUS RECEPTUS

| Number | Date | Type |
|---|---|---|
| 046 | 950 AD | |
| 052 | | |
| 056 | | |
| 0142 | | |
| Nearly all Minuscules | 1000-1500 AD | |

But what about the Critical text? Can it be shown that it was also in use throughout every generation? The following chart should illustrate this:

| Number | Date | Type |
|---|---|---|
| P4 | 100-200 AD | Alexandrian Text |
| P64 | | |
| P66 | | |
| P67 | | |
| P104 | | |
| P23 | 100-300 AD | |
| P75 | | |
| P77 | | |
| P103 | | |
| P46 | 175-225 AD | |
| P32 | 200 AD | |
| 0189 | | |
| P1 | 200-300 AD | |
| P5 | | |
| P15 | | |

*God's Preserved Word to Every Generation*

## IN DEFENSE OF THE TEXTUS RECEPTUS

| Number | Date | Type |
|---|---|---|
| P27 | | |
| P30 | | |
| PapyP39 | | |
| P40 | | |
| P47 | | |
| P48 | | |
| P49 | | |
| P53 | | |
| P65 | | |
| P70 | | |
| P91 | | |
| P101 | | |
| P107 | | |
| P108 | | |
| P111 | | |
| P13 | 200-400 AD | |
| P16 | | |
| P17 | | |
| P18 | | |
| P72 | | |
| P92 | | |
| P115 | | |
| 0212 | 250 AD | |
| P45 | | |
| P119 | | |
| P86 | 300 AD | |
| 0162 | | |

## IN DEFENSE OF THE TEXTUS RECEPTUS

| Number | Date | Type |
|---|---|---|
| 0220 | | |
| P125 | | |
| P2 | 300-400 AD | |
| P6 | | |
| P8 | | |
| P10 | | |
| P62 | | |
| P71 | | |
| P81 | | |
| P110 | | Alexandrian Text - with a few variant readings |
| P35 | | Alexandrian Text |
| P19 | 300-500 AD | |
| P21 | | |
| P50 | | |
| P57 | | |
| P82 | | |
| P85 | | |
| P122 | | |
| 01 | 350 AD | Alexandrian Text – although many corrections have been made which contain Byzantine readings. |
| 03 | | Alexandrian Text |
| 058 | | |
| 0192 | | |
| P120 | | |
| P123 | | |
| 057 | 400 AD | |
| 059 | | |
| 0181 | | |

*God's Preserved Word to Every Generation*

## IN DEFENSE OF THE TEXTUS RECEPTUS

| Number | Date | Type |
|---|---|---|
| P93 | 400-500 AD | |
| P14 | | |
| P54 | 400-600 AD | |
| P56 | | |
| P94 | | |
| P105 | | |
| 02 | 450 AD | Byzantine in the Gospels; Critical Text in the rest books |
| 016 | | Alexandrian Text - with a few variant readings |
| 029 =[0113= 0125=0139] | | Alexandrian Text - Contains a few Byzantine readings |
| 032 | | Byzantine in Matthew and Luke 8 to the end. Critical text - Western, Caesarean, and Alexandrian - in other areas. |
| 048 | | Alexandrian Text - Contains a few Byzantine readings |
| 061 | | Byzantine Text - Also contains Critical Text readings. |
| 068 | | Alexandrian Text |
| 077 | | Alexandrian Text |
| 0113 | | Alexandrian Text - Contains a few Byzantine readings |
| 0125 | | |
| 0139 | | |
| 0163 | | Alexandrian Text |
| 0172 | | Alexandrian Text - Contains a few Byzantine readings |
| 0173 | | |
| 0175 | | |
| 0201 | | |
| 0240 | | Alexandrian Text |
| 0244 | | |
| 0254 | | |

## IN DEFENSE OF THE TEXTUS RECEPTUS

| Number | Date | Type |
|---|---|---|
| 0274 | | Alexandrian Text - Contains a few Byzantine readings |
| P63 | 500 AD | Alexandrian Text |
| 071 | | Alexandrian Text - Contains a few Byzantine readings |
| 076 | | Alexandrian Text |
| 083=0112=0235 | | Alexandrian Text - Contains a few Byzantine readings |
| 088 | | Alexandrian Text |
| 0232 | | Alexandrian Text - Contains a few Byzantine readings |
| 0247 | | Alexandrian Text |
| 0270 | | |
| 0112=083=0235 | | Alexandrian Text - Contains a few Byzantine readings |
| P33 | 500-600 AD | Alexandrian Text |
| P36 | | |
| P58 | | |
| P76 | | |
| P96 | | Alexandrian Text - but has not yet been thoroughly examined. |
| P3 | 500-700 AD | Alexandrian Text |
| P43 | | |
| P44 | | |
| P55 | | |
| P97 | | Alexandrian Text - but has not yet been thoroughly examined. |
| 035 | 550 AD | Alexandrian Text |
| 040 | | Alexandrian Text - Contains a few Byzantine readings |
| 070 =0110 | | Alexandrian Text |
| 073=084 | | |
| 081 | | |

*God's Preserved Word to Every Generation*

## *IN DEFENSE OF THE TEXTUS RECEPTUS*

| Number | Date | Type |
|---|---|---|
| 082 | | |
| 086 | | |
| 089=092a | | |
| 091 | | |
| 094 | | |
| 0110 | | |
| 0124 | | |
| 0178 | | |
| 0179 | | |
| 0180 | | |
| 0184 | | |
| 0190 | | |
| 0191 | | |
| 0193 | | |
| 0202 | | |
| 0223 | | Alexandrian Text - with a few variant readings |
| 0225 | | |
| 0241 | | Alexandrian Text |
| 0245 | | |
| 0285 | | |
| 084=073 | | |
| 092a=089 | | |
| P124 | | |
| P26 | 600 AD | |
| 0164 | | |
| P11 | | Alexandrian Text - Contains a few Byzantine readings |

## IN DEFENSE OF THE TEXTUS RECEPTUS

| Number | Date | Type |
|---|---|---|
| P31 | 600-700 AD | Alexandrian Text |
| P34 | | |
| P59 | | |
| P60 | | |
| P79 | | |
| P74 | | |
| P68 | | |
| P42 | 600-800 AD | Alexandrian Text - Contains a few Byzantine readings |
| 098 | 650 AD | Alexandrian Text |
| 0102=0138 | | |
| 0138 | | |
| 0204 | | |
| P61 | 700 AD | |
| 0281 | | |
| 0293 | | |
| P41 | 700-800 AD | |
| 0101 | 750 AD | |
| 0205 | | |
| 0234 | | |
| 025 | 850 AD | Alexandrian Text - Except in Acts and Revelation where text is typical of the Byzantine type. |
| 0129=0203 | | Alexandrian Text |
| 0203 = 0129 | | |
| 0255 | | |
| 0271 | | |

## IN DEFENSE OF THE TEXTUS RECEPTUS

| Number | Date | Type |
|---|---|---|
| 0177 | 950 AD | Alexandrian Text - Contains a few Byzantine readings |
| 0243 | | |
| 436 | 1000-1100 AD | Alexandrian Text |
| 437 | | |
| 451 | | |
| 916 | 1100-1200 AD | |
| 1764 | | |
| 2814 | | |
| 383 | 1200-1300 AD | |
| 441 | | |
| 2002 | | |
| 1523 | 1200-1400 AD | |
| 452 | 1300-1400 AD | |
| 453 | | |
| 1769 | | |
| 1771 | | |
| 1772 | | |
| 2820 | | |

    A thinking man would notice right away that we have a stream of manuscripts running directly through the centuries all the way up to the 1400s. But does this validate their use? Does this lend itself to the thought that these manuscripts also fall under God's umbrella of preservation? Let's try to answer these questions.

    First of all, as to their use, we have to note that after the 900s the sheer volume of support for the Byzantine manuscripts is incredible. Noting that almost all of these manuscripts are minuscules, we need to reiterate that out of 2911 in existence, 2840 are purely Byzantine while a mere 31 are Alexandrian. There can be no doubt that the question of use is clearly answered by the quantity of Byzantine manuscripts that have been discovered.

## IN DEFENSE OF THE TEXTUS RECEPTUS

You might wonder why we do not say the same thing about the papyri in the first three centuries. You might ask, "Well, if the majority of manuscripts in the first three centuries were Alexandrian, doesn't that show that the Alexandrian manuscript was the text of choice in the beginning?" The reason we do not take the same approach with the papyri manuscripts is because they were all found in the same geographical location. The same cannot be said concerning the uncials or the minuscules. When we take into consideration that these were found virtually all over the known world, we come to the conclusion that the Alexandrian text, though it was in use for some time along with the Byzantine text, fell out of use between the 900s and the 1400s.

Add to this the obvious fact that there are 2412 lectionaries, almost all of which are Byzantine[155]. And since the lectionaries were constructed for reading in the churches, we have to admit that the manuscripts in use were the Byzantine manuscripts.

But we must also answer the question concerning God's preservation of the Alexandrian text. To this we simply reply that no matter how we look at it, from the 1400s until the late 1800s the Alexandrian manuscripts were not in use at all. In fact, we have no Greek manuscripts from this portion of history. The only Alexandrian manuscript that was known to be in existence was the Codex Vaticanus, which was neatly tucked away in the Vatican libraries away from the eyes of man. And scholars readily admit that this manuscript has been altered in many places to which one of the scribes even condemned himself!

Aside from this, there is evidence that this manuscript was known to both Erasmus when he did the first prototype of the Textus Receptus as well as known to the King James translators (at least 48 Greek and Hebrew linguists and scholars). Yet they rejected its use as being corrupted[156]. So it may have been in existence, but it certainly was NOT in use!

Again, we need to remember that during this time the Roman Catholic Church was very much in the forefront and would have naturally wanted to use their own manuscripts, hence the Codex Vaticanus, or at the very least, the Latin

---

[155] Although the lectionaries are all classified as being Byzantine, several of the lectionaries - lectionary 0269, 1602, and 147 for example - contain spurious Alexandrian readings. And we should expect this to be the case with at least a few of the lectionaries since at least four of them were located in Egypt. Lectionary 1575 was said by the Alands to be in remarkably good quality, which, from their perspective may have meant that it is heavily Alexandrian. Since it was part of a codex with Uncial 0129 it is most likely Alexandrian although this has not yet been verified.

[156] Which Version is The Bible?, Floyd Jones; Global Evangelism of Goodyear Arizona; p. 68

*God's Preserved Word to Every Generation*

## IN DEFENSE OF THE TEXTUS RECEPTUS

Vulgate. And history shows us that this is exactly what they did. The Latin Vulgate was their Bible of choice.

We must categorically reject the idea that this in any way meets the criteria of God's perfect preservation of every word! Bottom line? For over 400 years, the Alexandrian manuscripts, by all intents and purposes, did not exist. But let's not lose sight of what we are doing here. We are examining the continuity of the texts.

Dean Burgon points out that Erasmus had one set of manuscripts from Basel and Cardinal Ximenes had manuscripts from Spain and yet there is so little variation. His point is since their manuscripts come from the same family, they would naturally be so similar!

### CONTEXT AS A TEST OF TRUTH

> *"A word,--a phrase,--a clause,--or even a sentence or a paragraph,--must have some relation to the rest of the entire passage which precedes or comes after it. Therefore it will often be necessary, in order to reach all the evidence that bears upon a disputed question, to examine both the meaning and the language living on both sides of the point in dispute." [Dean Burgon, The Traditional Text, p. 61]*

This is an obvious and essential test of truth. This is the point that causes the rejection of scribal notes in the text. In most cases, they just don't fit the context. An example would best illustrate this:

> *"A word,--a phrase,--a clause,--or even a sentence or a paragraph,--must have some relation to the rest of the entire passage which precedes or comes after it. Therefore it will often be necessary, in order to reach all the evidence (**Evidence**, broadly construed, is anything presented in support of an assertion. This support may be strong or weak.) that bears upon a disputed question, to examine both the meaning and the language living on both sides of the point in dispute." [Dean Burgon, The Traditional Text, p. 61]*

In the above example, it is easy to see how the added phrase may be related and yet does not fit the context. When this happens, it is necessary to do a bit more research in order to validate the existence of the reading in question.

### INTERNAL EVIDENCE AS A TEST OF TRUTH

> *"Accordingly, the true reading of passages must be ascertained, with very slight exception indeed, from the preponderating weight of external*

*evidence, just according to its antiquity, to number, variety, relative value, continuousness, and with the help of the context. Internal considerations, unless in exceptional cases they are found in strong opposition to evident error, have only a subsidiary force."* [Dean Burgon, The Traditional Text, p. 67]

This test is pretty subjective, and yet, it is something that we will still invariably need to consider when looking at manuscript evidence.

Again, none of these truths can stand alone. And they do not offer for us a complete checklist of manuscript evaluation considerations. But these are very worthy observations and help to guide us into a better understanding of what manuscripts should be further considered.

## EARLY CORRUPTIONS OF THE NEW TESTAMENT

It has often been pointed out that the challenge between light and darkness began on the first day of creation. And that seems to be the prevailing theme throughout the scriptures and history. Any time we see truth manifest, it is also evident that error will be manifest to challenge the truth. The blessedness of our hope is that we know that darkness does not, and cannot, overpower the light.

But even as the New Testament itself was being written and distributed among God's saints, error began to creep in and challenge the truth. The scriptures themselves speak of this in numerous passages.

Sometimes this error came in by way of false teaching within the churches of the 1st century:

> **2 Corinthians 2:17** *For we are not as many, which corrupt the word of God: but as of sincerity, but as of God, in the sight of God speak we in Christ.*

In some cases, letters were written and passed off as authoritative when in reality they were forgeries:

> **2 Thessalonians 2:1-2** *Now we beseech you, brethren, by the coming of our Lord Jesus Christ, and by our gathering together unto him, (2) That ye be not soon shaken in mind, or be troubled, neither by spirit, nor by word, nor by letter as from us, as that the day of Christ is at hand.*

This was one reason why we read statements by Paul concerning how he had written or signed certain letters:

> **2 Thessalonians 3:17** *The salutation of Paul with mine own hand, <u>which is the token in every epistle</u>: so I write.*

> **Galatians 6:11** *Ye see how large a letter I have written unto you with mine own hand.*

> **Philemon 1:19** *I Paul have written it with mine own hand, I will repay it: albeit I do not say to thee how thou owest unto me even thine own self besides.*

## IN DEFENSE OF THE TEXTUS RECEPTUS

In fact, F.H.A. Scrivener wrote in his *Introduction to the New Testament* that "It is no less true to fact than paradoxical in sound, that the worst corruptions to which the New Testament has ever been subjected, originated within a hundred years after it was composed; that Irenaeus and the African Fathers and the whole Western, with a portion of the Syriac church used far inferior manuscripts to those employed by Stunica, or Erasmus, or Stephen, thirteen centuries after, when molding the Textus Receptus…"

Another scholar said that the majority of readings, whether corrupted or otherwise were created before AD 200. [157] And why? Because it would have been increasingly more difficult to propagate a false reading after so many of the believers had already seen the true readings. So what does that mean? Just what we have been observing all along – that any time the truth is manifest, error will also raise its ugly head.

So let's restate our goal here. We are seeking to show that the Textus Receptus is superior to the Critical Text. In doing so, we have considered a great deal of information concerning the Greek manuscripts. And we have come to the conclusion that a simple declaration concerning the age of a manuscript can only show that it existed but can never prove its validity.

If we are to prove that the Textus Receptus is superior to the Critical Text, we cannot do it based upon the age of manuscripts, nor can we make a dogmatic statement based upon the stream of existing manuscripts unless we consider other options.

But what about early translations of the Greek manuscripts? What can we find if we examine the New Testament translations of the Bible? Can we find legitimate representations of the Byzantine manuscripts? Sure we can. As we have already pointed out, there are quite a number of representatives to the Byzantine family. On the other hand, we can also find a few representatives of the Alexandrian family as well. For example, the earliest translation of the New Testament into an Egyptian Coptic version, the Sahidic of the late 2nd century, is a translation of the Alexandrian manuscript.

So what is the point of even concerning ourselves with the early translations? It is because they help us to see what existed and to what extent were they used. They also give us a good idea of who was using the translations as well. So as we take a deeper look at the early translations, we should also keep these things in mind.

---

[157] "The Origin of Text types" in *Early Christian Origins* by Earnest Colwell, 1961

## IN DEFENSE OF THE TEXTUS RECEPTUS

## EARLY TRANSLATIONS BASED ON INFERIOR TEXTS

We have already pointed out that translations of the Greek texts help us to determine the frequency of use, level of acceptance, and existence or certain readings or manuscript families. But now I would like to look at the translations from another angle. Let's consider their representation of the text types a little more closely.

You may recall that we have already considered several of the early translations as we looked at manuscript support for the Textus Receptus. At that time we only considered the fact that they proved the existence of the Byzantine manuscripts. But now, taking a broader look at the translations, we want to also consider who used them, and whether or not we should even cast any validity upon the translation.

Why would we even care to do that? Well, consider this. Would you want to put your faith in a text that was used exclusively by a cult? The New World Translation was done by a known cult, the Jehovah's Witnesses. Would we want to use the New World Translation as evidence that the Critical Text from which it was taken is now valid?

On the other hand, the Mormons, by and large, use the King James Version (when they actually use the Bible, that is!) So do we now reject the Textus Receptus because it was the basis of their Bible of choice?

There are several very well-known translations that were done early in church history which we should learn a few things about. In doing so, we will get a better understanding of why those translations were accomplished as well as gather some significant info about how those translations have impacted the issue of Bible translations today.

### *The Septuagint (LXX)*[158]

One early but inaccurate translation that we should discuss is the Septuagint (LXX). In reality, it is a translation of the Hebrew Old Testament. Yet we are placed in the position of having to deal with it here because there are so many quotations in the Greek New Testament which are said to be taken from the LXX.

The LXX takes its name from the story told in "The Letter of Aristeas" which claims that the LXX was translated under the direction of Ptolemy II

---

[158] See Appendix E for a fuller discussion of this translation

## IN DEFENSE OF THE TEXTUS RECEPTUS

Philadelphus of Egypt (reigned 285-246 B.C.), who wanted a version of the Jewish scriptures for the Alexandrian library. 70 (in some accounts, 72) scholars were commissioned to translate the Pentateuch, hence the name LXX.

The whole account is most certainly a legend for several reasons but at the same time we are fairly certain that some form of the Old Testament existed as a Greek translation during the first century. It has been said that the LXX was one of several Greek translations in circulation in the 1st century but in reality, we cannot be certain that whatever existed was actually the Septuagint. And it was most certainly not the same as the Septuagint that is in circulation today.

We know that some form of a Greek translation of the Old Testament existed in the first century based upon Greek manuscripts found in the Dead Sea caves but again, we have very little evidence to say much about it beyond this point.

Other early Greek translations of the Old Testament were the Works of Aquila of Sinope (128 AD), Theodotion (2nd century AD) and Symmachus (3rd century AD). Many modern scholars assume that the LXX was the only Greek translation of the Old Testament that was in existence during the time of Christ. However, this is simply not true. One of the manuscript discoveries made in the Dead Sea scrolls was a Greek translation of the Hebrew text. But this Greek translation did not match the LXX. Thus, it must have been a portion of a different Greek translation.

It doesn't take a lot of investigation to see that the LXX is not a very good work as translations go. And this makes some people uncomfortable because it is obvious that portions of the New Testament are in agreement with the LXX. They are uncomfortable because it looks like the New Testament writers used a bad translation. The next logical step would be something that I hear from time to time - "if Paul could use a bad translation, then why can't I?"

There are a few possible conclusions to this dilemma. First of all, the Holy Spirit wrote the New Testament and he can use whatever he wants. There are places where Paul quoted from heathen philosophers but that does not validate everything the philosophers said. We don't have a problem understanding how Paul, or Jude, could quote from uninspired sources, and yet this does not place a stamp of approval upon the totality of the sources that they used. But suddenly, when it come to the Bible text controversy, we get disquieted because we fear the conclusion some folks may come to.

But Jesus most certainly would not have used Greek in any form since he ministered in Israel; and we cannot state with any certainty that apostles did either.[159] But even if they did, their use would not give any credence to the entirety of the Greek translation anyway.

However, since Greek was the language of the known world at that time, if the apostles wanted to do any world-wide evangelism, then obviously, they would have had to use a Greek translation. Jesus would have ministered to Jews who would have known Hebrew or Aramaic. But what about Andrew who went to what we now call Russia? Or Nathaniel who went to India? And what about John who spent the last years of his life in Ephesus. Not to mention Paul! No doubt they used a Greek translation. I'm quite sure they didn't say, "Well, I'd like to show you the Bible but since this translation has so many problems, I wouldn't dare use it". They may not have <u>liked</u> the translation, but would have <u>used</u> it because there simply were no other options.

But there is another very plausible reason why the LXX contains passages the match the New Testament. The second possible solution is that the LXX has been revised since the completion of the New Testament in order to bring it into agreement with the New Testament texts. The idea that a revision of the LXX was accomplished is no longer a theory. It is pretty much an established fact.

The original LXX was supposed to have been done around 250 BC and supposedly, only the first five books were translated. If this is true in any sense of the word then the apocryphal books as well as everything else had to be added later.

There was some conjecture that the LXX was actually a <u>new</u> work completed by Origen around A.D. 240. This is not totally the case but it is probably true for material beginning with 1 Samuel to the end of Esther. According to conclusions based on a colophon found in the Codex Sinaiticus, it was corrected in the sixth or seventh century using Origen's Hexapla.[160]

It is also possible that the LXX was edited much earlier by a man named Lucian. According to Ira Maurice Price, author of "<u>The Ancestry of Our English Bible</u>", Lucian "worked with a Hebrew scholar in a revision of the Septuagint" (pg 222). But whether Origen did it, or Lucian did it, or someone else did it, the

---

[159] However, there were times when Jesus spoke with those who would most likely not have any knowledge of Aramaic, such as the Roman centurion in Matt 8 or even Pontius Pilate. So Jesus could have spoken Greek but would not have done so while preaching and teaching among the Jews.

[160] Metzger, Bruce M., (1992). The Text of the New Testament: Its Transmission, Corruption and Restoration, (3rd Ed.), Oxford: Oxford University Press, p. 46.

result is still the same. The point is, someone has obviously revised the LXX to read the same as the New Testament.

It is also pretty interesting that Augustine and Jerome, in letters that they wrote to one another spoke of the LXX as well. Jerome thought that the LXX carried great authority and wanted Augustine to clearly mark the differences between his Latin translation and the LXX. Augustine asked Jerome for his opinion concerning the differences between the Hebrew and the LXX. In Jerome's response, he mentions that the LXX was revised by Origen using portions of Theodotion's Greek translation.[161]

## *Origen's Hexapla*

Origen Adamantius lived from 185 to 254 AD. He is considered by many to be one of the most brilliant scholars and theologians of his time. At one point in his life, Eusebius reports that Origen had become the head of the Catechetical School of Alexandria. This particular school was known for its allegorical approach to scripture interpretation rather than literal interpretation of the Bible.

Origen is often quoted and is generally highly spoken of in many Christian circles today. But if Origen were living today, it is highly doubtful that many of our more conservative churches would have anything to do with him. You see, as brilliant as Origen was, he certainly had his theological hang-ups. He was an extreme ascetic who kept only one coat, no shoes, slept on the floor and castrated himself because of a misunderstanding of Matthew 19:12.

Some have even called him the "first Bible critic" because he removed "thou shalt love thy neighbor as thyself" from Matt 19:19. He believed, because the phrase is not found in the parallel passages, that it was inserted by a scribe. Of course, everyone agreed that he came to a wrong conclusion but the fact remains, he was practicing textual criticism. And what does that mean to us today? It means the early believers knew there was a need to examine the manuscripts because they knew that there were corrupted manuscripts in circulation.

But the biggest mark that Origen left on history was his six-columned Bible, called the Hexapla. The Hexapla (six-fold book) was an edition of the

---

[161] From the Letters of Augustine (No. 28, 71, 82) the Letters of Jerome (No. 112) in A Select Library of Nicene and Post-Nicene Fathers of the Christian Church, Translated into English with Prolegomena and Explanatory Notes under the Editorial Supervision of Henry Wace and Philip Schaff. (Oxford: Parker; New York: Christian Literature Co., 1890-1900)

Bible that had six different versions of the Old Testament side by side. It was about 7000 pages long and took 20 years to complete. And with all that, we only have a few small portions of it today. Most of what we know concerning the Hexapla comes from the writings of others. With that being said, we can make certain statements concerning his work but it is hard to draw any hard and fast conclusions because we just don't have enough evidence. But here is what we know.

The first column was the Hebrew text of the Old Testament, the second column was a transliteration of the Greek text by Secunda; the third, fourth and sixth columns were Greek translations by Aquila of Sinope, (128 AD), Symmachus the Ebionite (early 3rd century) and Theodotion (2nd century).

The fifth column was identified as the Septuagint (LXX) but some have made the claim that it may have been Origen's own translation. In light of the fact that we have no evidence, it is impossible to prove one way or the other but I personally have my doubts. Having been a translator myself, and having laid out my translation next to four others, I can say with absolute confidence that he would have put his own work in the last column. It is just so much easier to work with that way. But again, this is an opinion and not conclusive evidence.

But there is one more interesting thing about the fifth column. Not only did it contain the LXX, but it also contained markers showing places where Origen realized that the LXX did not agree with the Old Testament Hebrew text. If the LXX were a work of Origen, it seems odd that he would mark the differences and not simply change them. At any rate, Origen was practicing textual criticism at a basic level, and as a result, his work has had a tremendous effect on the history of textual criticism. We may believe whatever we want about why he did the work, or even how many changes he may or may not have made to the fifth column text, but we cannot deny the impact his work has had, both positive and negative.

### Constantine's 50 Bibles

In 331 AD the Emperor Constantine commissioned Eusebius to prepare fifty copies of the Bible for use in the churches of Constantinople. The only real historical proof of this event actually happening is a quote in Eusebius' own writings concerning Constantine's commission. (Eusebius, The Life of the Blessed Emperor Constantine, Bk 4, Ch 36 Constantine's letter of commission)

So who exactly was Eusebius? He was a student of Pamphilus who schooled Eusebius in the doctrines of Origen of Alexandria. He was also a close associate of Emperor Constantine as well as a fairly skilled church historian. In fact, his work, *Ecclesiastical History*, is considered a fairly reliable reference work on the history of early Christianity.

Yet with all of Eusebius' intellectual abilities, he, like Origen before him, still held to some pretty erroneous beliefs. In fact, he was in support of the teachings of Arius at the Council of Nicaea (A.D. 325) but later accepted the compromise teaching.[162]

Constantine is a pretty interesting case study himself. The emperors previous to him were very hostile toward Christianity. And up until 313 AD, a Christian's life was not only difficult but downright dangerous.

But in 313 AD, Constantine issued the Edict of Milan granting religious freedom for all. In 312 AD, After seeing a vision of a cross in the sky with the inscription, "In this sign conquer", before a crucial battle for the city of Rome, he put that sign on the shields of his soldiers and they marched off to win a very important victory. At that point, Constantine decided that the whole world should become Christians. He marched his soldiers through a river, called them baptized, and filled the churches with lost, paganistic converts.

Constantine's new policies put a lot of pagan priests out of work as well. They were not only jobless, but after the new edict, on the wrong side of the law. So according to some historians, a number of paganistic priests simply varnished their old teachings in Christian vocabulary and brought their heathenistic beliefs right in to the churches. So not only did Constantine inadvertently fill the churches with false believers, he also filled the churches with false teachers.

A lot of time has been spent in debate as to whether Constantine was really a believer and trying to help, or an evil villain trying to hurt the faith. But whatever, Constantine's motives were, the outcome was disastrous for the churches.

But that is not the end of his influence. According to Eusebius' writings, since Constantinople had a sudden growth of churches, there was also a sudden need for more Bibles. So in 331 AD, Constantine instructed Eusebius to make 50 copies of the scriptures for the churches to use. It has been said that Eusebius' Bibles were sadly inferior. If that is true then Constantine not only filled the churches with false believers and false teachers, he also filled the churches with inferior Bibles!

---

[162] Arianism is the theological teaching attributed to Arius (AD 250–336), a Christian leader in Alexandria, Egypt, asserting that the Son of God was subordinate to God the Father.

## IN DEFENSE OF THE TEXTUS RECEPTUS

The result of all this was that the true believers, rather than see their churches weakened, went underground. They had to draw away in order to maintain purity. Constantine wanted all the churches to be a part of the family and so he tried to persuade the dissenters to cooperate. But when that didn't work, Constantine used his power to persecute the Donatists, 4th century believers in North Africa, in A.D. 317 because they would not accept the doctrines and authority of the "catholic" church.

Fast forward 1500 years to the time of Constantin von Tischendorf. He discovered the Codex Sinaiticus in Saint Catherines Monastary, and after examination, Constantin von T. made the proclamation that the Codex Sinaiticus and Codex Vaticanus were two of Eusebius' Bibles.

But it is extremely hard to believe this since the two codices have so many differences between them. Not only are there many variant readings but the two manuscripts are laid out differently as well. Frederick Henry Ambrose Scrivener, the man who brought us Scrivener's 1894 revision of the Textus Receptus believed that Constantin von Tischendorf was wrong about his conclusions.

In retrospect, it may be that one of the codices is a copy of Eusebius' 50 Bibles, but not both. And if I had to choose, I would say that most likely, it was the Codex Vaticanus just based upon its layout and location. But again, we can never know for sure.

### Jerome's Latin Vulgate

Jerome's Latin Vulgate is another ancient translation which came from inferior sources. Jerome himself was a very educated man who rose to positions of prominence as secretary to Pope Damasus in 382 AD and was the "spiritual advisor" to a number of Roman ladies, including St. Paula, who paid for a monastery in Bethlehem where Jerome lived the last 34 years of his life.

Jerome greatly admired the teachings of Origen and even defended the false teaching of the perpetual virginity of Mary [163], clerical celibacy and monasticism. So theologically, Jerome had his issues too.

---

[163] Interestingly, the Post-Nicene Fathers, Second Series, Volume 6 mentions how a man named Helvidius accused Jerome of using corrupted manuscripts. Helvidius accused Jerome of holding to the false teaching of the perpetual virginity of Mary because Jerome believed that the scripture reading in the Byzantine manuscripts were corrupt. The passage in question was Luke 2:33 where Jerome preferred the Alexandrian reading, "His father and his mother" whereas the Byzantine

## IN DEFENSE OF THE TEXTUS RECEPTUS

In 382 AD, Pope Damasus commissioned Jerome to revise the Old Latin (Old Italic) of the Latin because there were so many other Latin translations in circulation. Jerome's work was based upon Origen's Hexapla for the Old Testament and revised the existing Latin translations to create the Latin Vulgate. His Vulgate was declared the official Bible of the Roman Catholic Church in 1546 at the Council of Trent.

Jerome's Latin Vulgate generally agrees with the Westcott and Hort Text. The instances where it disagrees with Westcott and Hort and is correct are places where Jerome stayed with the ancient readings of the Old Latin Vulgate.

So, by the year A.D. 400, the ancient inferior translations of scripture were already established and only waited to be rediscovered in modern times.

---

reading is "Joseph and his mother". So what can we infer from this? That even in the fourth century, there were those who believed the Alexandrian reading to be corrupt.

## THE REAL ISSUE

So now we have come to the end of our study and it is appropriate to ask ourselves what we have learned. We have seen how this issue has drawn people into 7 basic positions on the Greek texts. We have also done a fairly thorough study of inspiration, interpretation, preservation, and canonization.

We have discussed how the text is transmitted, including a lengthy section on how, once a text is transmitted, how is it to be translated. We have examined papyri, uncials, minuscule, lectionaries, English translations, and the historical and physical relationships between them. We have talked about schools of theology, climatology, and geography. We have applied logic, reason, and good, old-fashioned common sense to our understanding of very many passages of the Bible.

We have defined (or redefined) a lot of terms: Revelation is the revealing of God's truth which was previously unknown. Inspiration is the process of recording that truth. Preservation is the keeping of the truth which has been recorded. Transmission is the moving of God's truth from one manuscript to another. Translation is the moving of God's truth from one language to another.

Wow! We have certainly considered a lot of information as we sought to show how the Textus Receptus is God's preserved word. Then we added even more information in a discussion of the King James Version showing its superiority until finally, we have arrived at our destination both logically and biblically. The Textus Receptus is God's preserved word to every generation. In proving this we have appealed to facts from history and then applied them to the principles of God's Word in order to come to a balanced conclusion.

The real issue concerning the Bible is whether we are willing to begin from the position of faith in God's promises and then evaluate all the other information in the light of what God has said in his Word. But in doing so, we need to be extremely cautious not to impose our own definitions on God's promises. We must go no farther than the scriptures go and stop no sooner than the scriptures stop.

And what do we mean by this? Well, to use an example from our studies, if we believe that God promised to preserve his Word only through one translation or one manuscript, or even one family of manuscripts, we will no doubt find passages that do not fit our biblical framework. When this happens, we will become confused or obstinate as we seek to discern what went wrong.

But if we take God at his word and apply the simple principles of inspiration and preservation, it is easy to see how we can come to the conclusions that the Textus Receptus is God's preserved word. But we will never get there if we don't begin with a sound biblical framework and solid belief in God's promises.

I have been a layperson, a pastor, and a translator. As such, I have been able to take a step back and look at the whole Bible issue from three different perspectives. As the average layperson in the pew, I wanted to know that I had God's Word, that I could trust it, and that I could live my life by its direction. When my pastor held up his King James Version and said, "This is God's inspired word", I was glad! He wasn't trying to make any points about translations or textual criticism. He was simply saying, "We have God's Word. It is a special book. Trust it." I did not question him about translations or manuscripts. I didn't need to dig into history or theories concerning translation principles. I just needed to know and trust my Bible.

As a pastor, I spend a lot of time studying the scriptures at a deeper level than I will ever be able to present to a congregation. After all, how much use is it to tell them that "luo" means "to loose" when that is clearly stated in almost every usage? And after all I have done to encourage my folks by telling them that the scriptures are inspired and inerrant, why would I want to then send them into a spiritual tail-spin by introducing difficulties that they could not comprehend without some maturity and knowledge of the original languages? But at the same time, I must be careful not to use terms or to present application of a passage as if it were the interpretation. I must not present my thoughts as God's thoughts. I must learn to speak what the scriptures speak, make it clear when I am drawing out principles from a passage in order to promote a deeper walk, and then be silent when I cannot give a good biblically based reason for my opinions. But ANY false teaching, whether intentional or not, can have its repercussions.

Imagine a missionary on the field who cannot preach to his people because he does not have a good translation in their language and he has been taught that all other translations are "the Devil's brew". Should he do what he can to get a good translation in their language? Of course! But in the meantime, should he let the lost die and go to hell because he cannot use a bad translation? I say he should use the best available. Just like the believers of the first century, he does not have time to be a textual critic while souls are dying and going to hell.

Imagine a translator who is faced with the dilemma of having to translate into a language where the word "sheep" does not exist. What is he to do? Should he change the passage to make it more understandable? And what if he sees a difference between the King James Version and the Textus Receptus and it will affect his word choice in the target language? Will the work suddenly stop while he wrestles with which Bible, or which text, is the preserved scriptures?

## IN DEFENSE OF THE TEXTUS RECEPTUS

I am well aware that some of the things presented in this book will only be meaningful to the translator. I applaud you. No matter what decisions you make, you will be loved by some and hated by others. The best you can do is to do your best.

It seems to me that the majority of the division is caused by good men who sincerely desire to defend the truth, but at the same time, inadvertently teach things that are less than accurate themselves. The fact is, it is not really about translations or texts at all. God doesn't inspire translations or even texts. He inspired and preserves his truth, no matter what "container" it happens to be in. I choose to use a "container" that contains ONLY his truth and ALL of his truth. May the reader, prayerfully choose to do the same.

## APPENDIX A – TABLE OF MANUSCRIPTS

### *PAPYRI*

| Papyrus No. | Date (century) | Contents | Manuscript Type |
|---|---|---|---|
| Papyrus 1, P[1] | 3rd | Matt 1:1-9, 12 and 13, 14-20 | Alexandrian Text |
| Papyrus 2, P[2] | 4th | Portions of John (recto) portion of Luke 7:22-26,50 in Coptic (verso) | Alexandrian Text |
| Papyrus 3, P[3] | 6th-7th | Portions of Luke | Alexandrian Text |
| Papyrus 4, P[4] | Classed as a fragment of P[64] | Luke 1:58-59; 1:62-2:1, 6-7; 3:8-4:2, 29-32, 34-35; 5:3-8; 5:30-6:16 | Alexandrian Text - originally given a 3rd-century date by Charles Huleatt, the one who donated the Manuscript to Magdalen College, and then papyrologist A. S. Hunt studied the manuscript and dated it to the early 4th century. But in reaction to what he thought was far too late a dating for the manuscript, Colin Roberts published the manuscript and gave it a dating of ca. 200, which was confirmed by three other leading papyrologists: Harold Bell, T. C. Skeat and E. G. Turner, and this has been the general accepted date since then. (http://en.wikipedia.org/wiki/Magdalen_papyrus#Date) |
| Papyrus 5, P[5] | 3rd | John 1:23-31, 33-41; 16:14-30; 20:11-17, 20:19-25 | Alexandrian Text |
| Papyrus 6, P[6] | 4th | In Greek - John 10:1-2.4-7. 9-10; 11:1-8. 45-52. In Coptic - John 10:1-12.20; 13:1-2.11-12; Jas 1:13-5:20. | Alexandrian Text |
| Papyrus 7, P[7] | 3rd(?) 5th(?) | Portions of Luke 4 | Too small to classify |
| Papyrus 8, P[8] | 4th | Portions of Acts | Alexandrian Text |
| Papyrus 9, P[9] | 3rd | I John 4:11-12, 14-17 | Unintelligible – Carelessly written, unintelligible spellings, small fragment. |
| Papyrus 10, P[10] | 4th | John 1:1-7 | Alexandrian Text |

| Papyrus 11, p¹¹ | 7th | 1 Corinthians 1:17-22, 2:9-12, 2:14, 3:1-3, 3:5-6, 4:3-5:5, 5:7-8, 6:5-9, 6:11-18, 7:3-6, 7:10-14 | Alexandrian Text but also contains Byzantine readings |
|---|---|---|---|
| Papyrus 12, p¹² | 3rd | Hebrews 1:1. | Unascertainable - Only three lines are present. |
| Papyrus 13, p¹³ | 3rd-4th | Hebrews 2:14-18; 3:1-19; 4:1-16; 5:1-5; 10:8-22, 29-39; 11:1-13, 28-40; 12:1-17. | Alexandrian Text but also contains Byzantine readings |
| Papyrus 14, p¹⁴ | 5th ? | 1 Cor 1:25-27; 2:6-8; 3:8-10.20 | Alexandrian Text |
| Papyrus 15, p¹⁵ | 3rd | I Corinthians 7:18-40 and 7:40 - 8:1-4 | Alexandrian Text |
| Papyrus 16, p¹⁶ | 3r-4th | Philippians 3:9-17 and Philippians 4:2-8 | Alexandrian Text |
| Papyrus 17, p¹⁷ | 3rd-4th | Hebrews 9:12-19. | Alexandrian Text |
| Papyrus 18, p¹⁸ | 3rd-4th | Revelation 1:4-7. | Alexandrian Text |
| Papyrus 19, p¹⁹ | 4th-5th | Matt 10:32-11:5 | Alexandrian Text |
| Papyrus 20, p²⁰ | 3rd | James 2:19-3:2 and James 3:3-9 | Less than 4.5 cm wide at the widest point – difficult to classify though some have classified it as Alexandrian Text. |
| Papyrus 21, p²¹ | 4th-5th | Matt 12:24-26.32-33 | Alexandrian Text |
| Papyrus 22, p²² | 3rd | John 15:25-16:2 and John 16:21-32 | does not agree with any one group of the manuscripts |
| Papyrus 23, p²³ | 2nd-3rd | James 1:10-12 and James 1:15-18 | Alexandrian Text |
| Papyrus 24, p²⁴ | 3rd-4th | Portions of Rev. 5:5-8, 6:5-8 | With only 150 letters to examine, it is not possible ascertain text-type. |
| Papyrus 25, p²⁵ | Late 4th | Matt 18:32-34; 19:1-3.5-7.9-10 | Unclassified due to its Diatessaric nature |

## IN DEFENSE OF THE TEXTUS RECEPTUS

| | | | |
|---|---|---|---|
| Papyrus 26, p²⁶ | Late 5th early 6th | Romans 1:1-16 | Alexandrian Text |
| Papyrus 27, p²⁷ | 3rd | Romans 8:12-22, 24-27 (verso), 33-9:3, 5-9 (recto). | Alexandrian Text |
| Papyrus 28, p²⁸ | 3rd | John 6:8-12 (recto) and John 6:17-22 (verso). | Contains readings from several text types |
| Papyrus 29, p²⁹ | 3rd | Acts 26:7-8 (verso) and Acts 26:20 (recto). | Fragment too small to ascertain text type |
| Papyrus 30, p³⁰ | 3rd | I Thessalonians 4:12-13,16-17; 5:3, 8-10, 12-18, 25-28; II Thessalonians 1:1-2 | Alexandrian Text |
| Papyrus 31, p³¹ | 7th | Romans 12:3-8 | Alexandrian Text |
| Papyrus 32, p³² | 200 | Titus 1:11-15 and Titus 2:3-8 | Alexandrian Text |
| Papyrus 33, p³³ | 6th | Acts 7:6-10.13-18; 15:21-24.26-32. | Alexandrian Text |
| Papyrus 34, p³⁴ | 7th | 1 Cor 16:4-7.10; 2 Cor 5:18-21; 10:13-14; 11:2.4.6-7 | Alexandrian Text |
| Papyrus 35, p³⁵ | 4th (?) | Matt. 25:12-15.20-23 | Alexandrian Text |
| Papyrus 36, p³⁶ | 6th | John 3:14-18.31-32.34-35 | Alexandrian Text |
| Papyrus 37, p³⁷ | 3rd-4th | Matt 26:19-52. | Alexandrian Text (Western) |
| Papyrus 38, p³⁸ | 2nd-3rd | Acts 18:27 - 19:6, 12-16 | Alexandrian Text (Western) |
| Papyrus 39, p³⁹ | 3rd | John 8:14-22. | Alexandrian Text |
| Papyrus 40, p⁴⁰ | 3rd | Romans 1:24-27, 31-32; 2:1-3; 3:21-31; 4:1-8; 6:4-5,16; 9:16-17, 27. | Alexandrian Text |

**God's Preserved Word to Every Generation**

## IN DEFENSE OF THE TEXTUS RECEPTUS

| | | | |
|---|---|---|---|
| Papyrus 41, P[41] | 8th | In Greek - Acts 17:28-18:2.17-18.22-25.27; 19:1-4.6-8.13-16.18-19; 20:9-13.15-16.22-24.26-38; 21:3.4.26-27; 22:11-14.16-17.<br>In Coptic - Acts 17:30-18:2.25.27-28; 19:2-8.15.17-19; 20:11-16.24-28; 20:36-21:3; 22:12-14.16-17. | Alexandrian Text |
| Papyrus 42, P[42] | 7th-8th | Portions of Luke | Alexandrian Text with some Byzantine readings |
| Papyrus 43, P[43] | 6th-7th | Rev 2:12-13; 15:8-16:2 | Alexandrian Text |
| Papyrus 44, P[44] | 6th-7th | Matt. 17:1-3.6-7; 18:15-17.19; 25:8-10 John 9:3-4; 10:8-14; 12:16-18 | Alexandrian Text |
| Papyrus 45, P[45] | 2nd-3rd | Matt. 20:24-32, 21:13-19, 25:41-26:39; Mark 4:36-40, 5:15-26, 5:38-6:3, 6:16-25, 36-50, 7:3-15, 7:25-8:1, 8:10-26, 8:34-9:8, 9:18-31, 11:27-12:1, 12:5-8, 13-19, 24-28; Luke 6:31-41, 6:45-7:7, 9:26-41, 9:45-10:1, 10:6-22, 10:26-11:1, 11:6-25, 28-46, 11:50-12:12, 12:18-37, 12:42-13:1, 13:6-24, 13:29-14:10, 14:17-33; John 4:51, 54, 5:21, 24, 10:7-25, 10:31-11:10, 11:18-36, 43-57; Acts 4:27-36, 5:10-20, 30-39, 6:7-7:2, 7:10-21, 32-41, 7:52-8:1, 8:14-25, 8:34-9:6, 9:16-27, 9:35-10:2, 10:10-23, 31-41, 11:2-14, 11:24-12:5, 12:13-22, 13:6-16, 25-36, 13:46-14:3, 14:15-23, 15:2-7, 19-26, 15:38-16:4, 16:15-21, 16:32-40, 17:9-17. | Text varies in each book but basically Alexandrian Text |
| Papyrus 46, P[46] | 2nd-3rd | Romans 5:17-6:3, 6:5-14, 8:15-25, 27-35, 8:37-9:32, 10:1-11, 11, 24-33, 11:35-15:9, 15:11-end (with 16:25-27 following chapter 15!); 1 Cor. 1:1-9:2, 9:4-14:14, 14:16-15:15, 15:17-16:22; 2 Cor. 1:1-11:10, 12-21, 11:23-13:13; Gal. 1:1-8, 1:10-2:9, 2:12-21, 3:2-29, 4:2-18, 4:20-5:17, 5:20-6:8, 6:10-18; Eph. 1:1-2:7, 2:10-5:6, 5:8-6:6, 6:8-18, 20-24; Phil. 1:1, 1:5-15, 17-28, 1:30-2:12, 2:14-27, 2:29-3:8, 3:10-21, 4:2-12, 14-23; Col. | Alexandrian Text with readings in agreement with the Byzantine Text |

*God's Preserved Word to Every Generation*

## IN DEFENSE OF THE TEXTUS RECEPTUS

| | | | |
|---|---|---|---|
| | | 1:1-2, 5-13, 16-24, 1:27-2:19, 2:23-3:11, 3:13-24, 4:3-12, 16-18; 1 Thes. 1:1, 1:9-2:3, 5:5-9, 23-28; Heb. 1:1-9:16, 9:18-10:20, 10:22-30, 10:32-13:25 | |
| Papyrus 47, $P^{47}$ | 3rd | Revelation 9:10-17:2. | Alexandrian Text |
| Papyrus 48, $P^{48}$ | 3rd | Acts 23:11-17 (Verso), 23:24-29 (Recto). | Alexandrian Text |
| Papyrus 49, $P^{49}$ | 3rd | Ephesians 4:16-29; 4:31-5:13. | Alexandrian Text |
| Papyrus 50, $P^{50}$ | 4th-5th | Acts 8:26-32; 10:26-31 | Alexandrian Text |
| Papyrus 51, $P^{51}$ | c. 400 | Galatians 1:2-10, 13, 16-20 | Alexandrian Text with readings from Western text |
| Papyrus 52, $P^{52}$ | 2nd | Recto, John 18:31-33. Verso, John 18:37 and 38. | The writing is so small that it is impossible to determine the character of the text. |
| Papyrus 53, $P^{53}$ | 3rd | Matt 26:29-40. Acts 9:33-43; 10:1. | Alexandrian Text |
| Papyrus 54, $P^{54}$ | 5th-6th | James 2:16-18, 22, 24-25, 3:2-4. | Alexandrian Text |
| Papyrus 55, $P^{55}$ | 6th-7th | John 1:31-33.35-38 | Alexandrian Text |
| Papyrus 56, $P^{56}$ | 5th-6th | Acts 1:1.4-5.7.10-11 | Alexandrian Text |
| Papyrus 57, $P^{57}$ | 4th-5th | Acts 4:36-5:2-.8-10. | Alexandrian Text |
| Papyrus 58, $P^{58}$ | | | Classed as a fragment of $P^{33}$ |
| Papyrus 59, $P^{59}$ | 7th | John 1:26.28.48.51; 2:15-16; 11:40-52; 12:25.29.31.35; 17:24-26; 18:1-2.16-17.22; 21:7.12-13.15.17-20.23. | Alexandrian Text |
| Papyrus 60, $P^{60}$ | 7th | John 16:29-19:26 | Alexandrian Text |

## IN DEFENSE OF THE TEXTUS RECEPTUS

| | | | |
|---|---|---|---|
| Papyrus 61, p[61] | c. 700 | Ro 16:23-27; 1 Cor 1:1-2.4-6; 5:1-3.5-6.9-13; Philip 3:5-9.12-16; 1 Thess 1:2-3; Tit 3:1-5.8-11.14-15; Philem. 4-7 | Alexandrian Text |
| Papyrus 62, p[62] | 4th | Matt 11:25-30 | Alexandrian Text |
| Papyrus 63, p[63] | c. 500 | John are verses 3:14-18; 4:9-10 | Alexandrian Text |
| Papyrus 64, p[64] | 2nd | Matt 26:7-8, 10, 14-15, 22-23, 31-33. | Alexandrian - originally given a 3rd-century date by Charles Huleatt, the one who donated the Manuscript to Magdalen College, and then papyrologist A. S. Hunt studied the manuscript and dated it to the early 4th century. But in reaction to what he thought was far too late a dating for the manuscript, Colin Roberts published the manuscript and gave it a dating of ca. 200, which was confirmed by three other leading papyrologists: Harold Bell, T. C. Skeat and E. G. Turner,and this has been the general accepted date since then. (http://en.wikipedia.org/wiki/Magdalen_papyrus#Date) |
| Papyrus 65, p[65] | 3rd | I Thessalonians 1:3-2:1, 6-13. | Alexandrian Text - similarities between the script of P[65] and P[49]. may indicate that these are from the same codex. |
| Papyrus 66, p[66] | 2nd | John 1:1-6:11; 6:35-14:26, 29-30; 15:2-26; 16:2-4, 6-7; 16:10-20:20, 22-23; 20:25-21:9, 12, 17. | Alexandrian Text - does not include the pericope of the adulteress (7:53 - 8:11), |
| Papyrus 67, p[67] | Classed as a fragment of p[64] | Matt 3:9, 15; 5:20-22, 25-28 | Alexandrian Text |
| Papyrus 68, p[68] | 7th (?) | 1 Corinthians are verses 4:12-17; 4:19-5:3 | Alexandrian Text |
| Papyrus 69, p[69] | 3rd | Verso, Luke 22:58-61. Recto, Luke 22:41 and 45-48, 42-44 being omitted. | Alexandrian Text (Western) |
| Papyrus 70, P[70] | 3rd | Verso, Matt 11:26-27; Recto, Matt 12:4-5. Others are Matt 2:13-16 (verso), 2:22-3:1 (recto) and Matt 24:3-6 (verso) and Matt 24:12-15 (recto). | Alexandrian Text |

*God's Preserved Word to Every Generation*

| | | | |
|---|---|---|---|
| Papyrus 71, p⁷¹ | 4th | Matt 19:10-11.17-18 | Alexandrian Text |
| Papyrus 72, p⁷² | 3rd-4th | 1 Peter 1:1-25; 2:1-25; 3:1-22; 4:1-19; 5:1-14; 2 Peter 1:1-21; 2:1-22; 3:1-18; Jude 1-25. | Alexandrian Text |
| Papyrus 73, p⁷³ | 7th | Matt 25:43; 26:2-3 | Agrees with the Byzantine text |
| Papyrus 74, p⁷⁴ | 7th | Acts (1:2-5, 7-11, 13-15, 18-19, 22-25, 2:2-4, 2:6-3:26, 4:2-6, 8-27, 4:29-27:25, 27:27-28:31) and fragments of all seven Catholic Epistles (portions of 75 verses of James, 16 verses of 1 Peter, 4 of 2 Peter, 27 of 1 John, 4 of 2 John, 2 of 3 John, and 5 of Jude). | Often listed as "Byzantine" but in fact a mixture of Readings |
| Papyrus 75, p⁷⁵ | 2nd-3rd | Luke 3:18-22; 3:33 - 4:2; 4:34 - 5:10; 5:37 - 6:4; 6:10 - 7:32, 35-39, 41-43; 7:46 - 9:2; 9:4 - 17:15; 17:19 - 18:18; 22:4 - 24:53; John 1:1 - 11:45, 48-57; 12:3 - 13:1, 8-9; 14:8-29; 15:7-8. | Textual scholars have a high regard for P⁷⁵'s textual conformity to B. – Alexandrian Text |
| Papyrus 76, p⁷⁶ | 6th | Portions of John; Matt 4:9,12. | Alexandrian Text |
| Papyrus 77, p⁷⁷ | 2nd-3rd | Verso, Matt 23:30-34. Recto, Matt 23:35-39. | This part of Matthew is not represented on papyrus. It comes closest to Codex Sinaiticus – Thus is mainly Alexandrian Text |
| Papyrus 78, p⁷⁸ | 3rd-4th | Portions of Jude 4-5, 7-8 | An eccentric text: two unique and three rare readings in four verses, all in disagreement other witnesses |
| Papyrus 79, p⁷⁹ | 7th | Heb 10:10-12,28-30 | Alexandrian Text |
| Papyrus 80, p⁸⁰ | 3rd | John 3:34 (with *hermeneia*) | Too fragmentary to determine. |
| Papyrus 81, p⁸¹ | 4th | 1 Peter 2:20-3:1,4-12 | Alexandrian Text |
| Papyrus 82, p⁸² | 4th-5th | Luke 7:32-34,37-38 | Alexandrian Text |

| | | | |
|---|---|---|---|
| Papyrus 83, p83 | 6th | Matt 20:23-25,30-31; 23:39-24:1,6 | Considered to be a "mixed" text although it has yet to be thoroughly examined. |
| Papyrus 84, p84 | 6th | Mark 2:2-5,8-9; 6:30-31,33-34,36-37,39-41; John 5:5; 17:3,7-8 | Mostly Byzantine |
| Papyrus 85, p85 | 4th-5th | Revelation 9:19-10:2,5-9 | Alexandrian Text |
| Papyrus 86, p86 | c. 300 | Matt 5:13-16, 22-25. | Mostly Alexandrian Text. |
| Papyrus 87, p87 | 3rd | Philemon 13-15, 24-25. | Alexandrian Text (placed in Category 3 by Aland which also means it has a more eclectic nature). |
| Papyrus 88, p88 | 4th | Mark 2:1-26 | Alexandrian Text (placed in Category 3 by Aland which also means it has a more eclectic nature). |
| Papyrus 89, p89 | 4th | Hebrews 6:7-9,15-17 | Too small to classify |
| Papyrus 90, p90 | 2nd | Recto, John 18:36 - 19:1. Verso, John 19:2-7. | Many scholars like to place P90 in the Alexandrian family but it is as much in agreement with the Byzantine family as it is with the Alexandrian family |
| Papyrus 91, p91 | 3rd | Acts 2:30-37, 46-47; 3:1-2. | Alexandrian Text |
| Papyrus 92, p92 | 3rd-4th | Ephesians 1:11-13, 19-21. II Thessalonians 1:4-5, 11-12. | Alexandrian Text |
| Papyrus 93, p93 | 5th | John 13:15-17 | Thought to be Alexandrian Text but has not yet been thoroughly examined. |
| Papyrus 94, p94 | 5th-6th | Romans 6:10-13, 19-22 | Thought to be Alexandrian Text but has not yet been thoroughly examined. |
| Papyrus 95, p95 | 3rd | John 5:26-29, 36-38. | Too fragmentary to determine the character of text. |
| Papyrus 96, p96 | 6th | diglot papyrus manuscript - Matt 3:10-12 (Coptic, Greek lost), 3:13-15 (Greek, Coptic lost) | Thought to be Alexandrian Text but has not yet been thoroughly examined. |
| Papyrus 97, p97 | 6th-7th | Luke 14:7-14 | Thought to be Alexandrian Text but has not yet been thoroughly examined. |

## IN DEFENSE OF THE TEXTUS RECEPTUS

| | | | |
|---|---|---|---|
| Papyrus 98, $P^{98}$ | 2nd | Revelation 1:13-2:1. | Unclassified |
| Papyrus 99, $P^{99}$ | c. 400 | Considered by many to be a glossary with single words and phrases from: Rom 1:1; 2 Cor 1:3-6, 1:6-17, 1:20-24, 2:1-9, 2:9-5:13, 5:13-6:3, 6:3-8:13, 8:14-22, 9:2-11:8, 11:9-23, 11:26-13:11;Gal 1:4-11, 1:18-6:15,1:14-2:4, 2:4-3:19,3:19-4:9;Eph 1:4-2:21,1:22(?),3:8-6:24 | Unclassified |
| Papyrus 100, $P^{100}$ | 3rd-4th | Verso, James 4:9 - 5:1. Recto, James 3:13 - 4:4. | Thought to be Alexandrian Text but has not yet been thoroughly examined. |
| Papyrus 101, $P^{101}$ | 3rd | Verso, Matt 3:10-12. Recto, Matt 3:16 - 4:3. | Alexandrian Text |
| Papyrus 102, $P^{102}$ | 3rd-4th | Recto, Matt 4:11-12. Verso, Matt 4:22-23. | Too small to determine |
| Papyrus 103, $P^{103}$ | 2nd-3rd | Recto, Matt 13:55-56. Verso, Matt 14:3-5. | Alexandrian Text |
| Papyrus 104, $P^{104}$ | 2nd | Recto, Matt 21:34-37. Verso, Matt 21:45 | Alexandrian Text |
| Papyrus 105, $P^{105}$ | 5th-6th | Matt 27:62-64; 28:2-5 | Alexandrian Text |
| Papyrus 106, $P^{106}$ | 3rd | Verso, John 1:29-35. Recto, John 1:40-46. | Condition too poor to ascertain type. |
| Papyrus 107, $P^{107}$ | 3rd | Verso, John 17:1-2. Recto, John 17:11. | Alexandrian Text |
| Papyrus 108, $P^{108}$ | 3rd | Verso, John 17:23-24. Recto, John 18:1-5. | Alexandrian Text |
| Papyrus 109, $P^{109}$ | 3rd | Verso, John 21:18-20. Recto, John 21:23-25. | Too small to classify |
| Papyrus 110, $P^{110}$ | 4th | Matt 10:13-15; 10:25-27 | Alexandrian Text with numerous spurious readings in Matt 10:14 not in agreement with any existing manuscripts. |

*God's Preserved Word to Every Generation*

## IN DEFENSE OF THE TEXTUS RECEPTUS

| | | | |
|---|---|---|---|
| Papyrus 111, $p^{111}$ | 3rd | Luke 17:11-13; 22-23. | Alexandrian Text |
| Papyrus 112, $p^{112}$ | 5th | Acts 26:31-32; 27:6-7 | Too small to classify |
| Papyrus 113, $p^{113}$ | 3rd | Romans 2:12-13, 29. | Too small to classify |
| Papyrus 114, $p^{114}$ | 3rd | Hebrews 1:7-12. | Too small to determine which family but is most likely Alexandrian Text. |
| Papyrus 115, $p^{115}$ | 3rd-4th | Revelation 2:1-3,13-15,27-29; 3:10-12; 5:8-9; 6:5-6; 8:3-8,11-13; 9:1-5,7-16,18-21; 10:1-4,8-11; 11:1-5,8-15,18-19; 12:1-5,8-10,12-17; 13:1-3,6-16,18; 14:1-3,5-7,10-11,14-15,18-20;15:1,4-7. | Alexandrian Text. |
| Papyrus 116, $p^{116}$ | 6th | Hebrews 2:9-11; 3:3-6 | Too small to determine text type. |
| Papyrus 117, $p^{117}$ | 4th-5th | 2 Corinthians 7:6-8,9-11 | Unclassified |
| Papyrus 118, $p^{118}$ | 3rd | Romans 15,26–27.32–33; 16, 1.4–7.11–12. | Too small to determine text type. |

## UNCIALS

| Uncial No. | Name | Date (century) | Contents | Manuscript Type |
|---|---|---|---|---|
| 01 | Sinaiticus | 350 | The entire New Testament portion, plus part of the Old Testament, the Apocrypha, as well as non-Biblical books (Barnabas and the Shepherd of Hermas) | Alexandrian Text – although many corrections have been made which contain Byzantine readings. |
| 02 | Alexandrinus | 450 | Septuagint (LXX), including 3 and 4 Maccabees, Psalm 151, the 14 Odes, and the Epistle to Marcellinus; The entire New Testament including 1 and 2 Clement. | Byzantine in the Gospels; Alexandrian Text in the rest of the books |

| | | | | |
|---|---|---|---|---|
| 03 | Vaticanus | 350 | The complete Septuagint (LXX) minus Genesis 1:1 - 46:28a, Psalm 105:27 — 137:6 (filled in during the 15th century by another scribe) 2 Kings 2:5-7, 10-13 are also lost due to a tear in one of the pages; The New Testament lack 1 and 2 Timothy, Titus, Philemon and Revelation. | Alexandrian Text – It is believed to be the "standard" for the Alexandrian Text. |
| 04 | Ephraemi | 450 | Matt 1:1-2; 5:15-7:5; 17:26-18:28; 22:21-23:17; 24:10-45; 25:30-26:22; 27:11-46; 28:15-fin.; Mark: 1:1-17; 6:32-8:5; 12:30-13:19; Luke: 1:1-2; 2:5-42; 3:21-4:25; 6:4-36; 7:17-8:28; 12:4-19:42; 20:28-21:20; 22:19-23:25; 24:7-45; John: 1:1-3; 1:41-3:33; 5:17-6:38; 7:3-8:34; 9:11-11:7; 11:47-13:7; 14:8-16:21; 18:36-20:25; Acts 1:1-2; 4:3-5:34; 6:8; 10:43-13:1; 16:37-20:10; 21:31-22:20; 3:18-24:15; 26:19-27:16; 28:5-fin.; Rom 1:1-3; 2:5-3:21; 9:6-10:15; 11:31-13:10; 1st Cor 1:1-2; 7:18-9:6; 13:8-15:40; 2nd Cor 1:1-2; 10:8-fin. Gal 1:1-20; Eph 1:1-2:18; 4:17-fin.; Phil 1:1-22; 3:5-fin. Col 1:1-2;1st Thess: 1:1; 2:9-fin.; 1st Tim 1:1-3:9; 5:20-fin.;2nd Tim 1:1-2; Tit 1:1-2;Philemon 1-2 Heb 1:1-2:4; 7:26-9:15; 10:24-12:15;James 1:1-2; 44:2-fin.; 1st Peter 1:1-2; 4:5-fin.; 2nd Peter 1:1; 1st John 1:1-2; 4:3-fin.; 3rd John: 1-2; Jude: 1-2; Rev 1:1-2; 3:20-5:14; 7:14-17; 8:5-9:16; 10:10-11:3; 16:13-18:2; 19:5-fin | A mixed text containing Byzantine and Alexandrian Text readings. |
| 05 | Bezae (Codex D) | 450 | Most of the four Gospels and Acts, with a small portion of 3rd John. | The Greek text is unique with many readings not found in any other MSS. It looks more like a paraphrase than a copy of the scriptures. |
| 06 | Claromontanus | 550 | Greek/Latin diglot of the Pauline Epistles including Hebrews | Western text |
| 07 | Codex Basilens is A. N. III. 12 | 750-800 | Four Gospels but missing lacks Luke 3:4-15, 24:47-end. Luke 1:69-2:4, 12:58-13:12, 15:8-20 was written at a later date. | Byzantine |

## IN DEFENSE OF THE TEXTUS RECEPTUS

| | | | | |
|---|---|---|---|---|
| 08 | Laudianus | 550 | Greek/Latin diglot - Almost the complete Acts but lacking from 26:29 to 28:26. | Generally Byzantine with a few Western and Alexandrian Text readings. |
| 09 | Boreelianus | 850 | Contains Matt. 9:1- John 21:25. Lacks Matt. 12:1-44, 13:55-14:9, 15:20-31, 20:18-21:5, Mark 1:43-2:8, 2:23-3:5, 11:6-26, 14:54-15:5, 15:39-16:19, John 3:5-14, 4:23-38, 5:18-38, 6:39-63, 7:28-8:10, 10:32-11:3, 12:14-25, 13:34-end. | Byzantine with a few variant readings |
| 010 | Codex Augiensis | 850-900 | Diglot of Latin and Greek - lacks Romans 1:1-3:19, 1 Cor. 3:8-16, 6:7-14, Col. 2:1-8, Philem. 21-25, Hebrews | Generally considered to be Western text type. |
| 011 | Manuscript $G^e$ | $9^{th}$ - $10^{th}$ Century | Gospels, lacks Matt. 1:1-6:6; 7:25-8:9, 8:23-9:2, 28:18-Mark 1:13, Mark 14:19-25, Luke 1:1-13, 5:4-7:3, 8:46-9:5, 12:27-41, 24:41-end, John 18:5-19, 19:4-27 | Byzantine |
| 012 | Codex Boernerianus | $9^{th}$ Century | Greek/Latin Interlinear – Contians Pauline epistles minus Rom 1:1-4, 2:17-24, 1 Cor. 3:8-16, 6:7-14, Col. 2:1-8, Philem. 21-25, Hebrews | Generally considered to be Western text type. |
| 013 | Seidelianus II | 850 | The four Gospels minus Matt. 1:1-15:30, 25:33-26:3, Mark 1:32-2:4, 15:44-16:14, Luke 5:18-32, 6:8-22, 10:2-19, John 9:30-10:25, 18:2-18, 20:12-25 | Byzantine |
| 014 | Mutinensis | $9^{th}$ Century | Acts of the Apostles minus Acts 1:1-5:28, 9:39-10:19, 13:36-14:3, 27:4-28:31 | Byzantine |
| 015 | Coislinianus | 550 | Presumably, it originally contained all the Paulines writings but now only the following passages survive: contain 1 Cor. 10:22-29, 11:9-16; 2 Cor. 4:2-7, 10:5-11:8, 11:12-12:4; Gal. 1:1-10, 2:9-17, 4:30-5:5; Col. 1:26-2:8, 2:20-3:11; 1 Thes. 2:9-13, 4:5-11; 1 Tim. 1:7-2:13, 3:7-13, 6:9-13; 2 Tim. 2:1-9; Tit 1:1-3, 1:15-2:5, 3:13-15; Heb 1:3-8, 2:11-16, 3:13-18, 4:12-15, 10:1-7, 10:32-38, 12:10-15, 13:24-25. | This MSS has been classified as either largely Alexandrian Text with a large number of Byzantine readings – or – largely Byzantine with a large number of Alexandrian Text readings. |

*God's Preserved Word to Every Generation*

| | | | | |
|---|---|---|---|---|
| 016 | Freerianus | 450 | 1 Cor. 10:29, 11:9-10, 18-19, 26-27, 12:3-4, 27-28, 14:12-13, 22, 32-33, 15:3, 15, 27-28, 38-39, 59-50, 16:1-2, 12-13; 2 Cor. 1:1, 9, 16-17, 2:3-4, 14, 3:6-7, 16-17, 4:6-7, 16-17, 5:8-10, 17-18, 6:6-8, 16-18, 7:7-8, 13-14, 8:6-7, 14-17, 8:24-9:1, 9:7-8, 9:15-10:1, 10:8-10, 10:17-11:2, 11:9-10, 20-21, 28-29, 12:6-7, 14-15, 13:1-2, 10-11; Gal. 1:1-3, 11-13, 1:22-2:1, 2:8-9, 16-17, 3:6-8, 16-17, 24-28, 4:8-10, 20-23; Eph. 2:15-18, 3:6-8, 18-20, 4:9-11, 17-19, 28-30, 5:6-11, 20-24, 5:32-6:1, 6:10-12, 19-21; Phil. 1:1-4, 11-13, 20-23, 2:1-3, 12-14, 25-27, 3:4-6, 14-17, 4:3-6, 13-15; Col. 1:1-4, 10-12, 20-22, 27-29, 2:7-9, 16-19, 3:5-8, 15-17, 3:25-4:2, 4:11-13; 1 Thes. 1:1-2, 9-10, 2:7-9, 14-16, 3:2-5, 11-13, 4:7-10, 4:16-5:1, 5:9-12, 23-27; 2 Thes. 1:1-3, 10-11, 2:5-8, 14-17, 3:8-10; 1 Tim. 1:1-3, 10-13, 1:19-2:1, 2:9-13, 3:7-9, 4:1-3, 10-13, 5:5-9, 16-19, 6:1-2, 9-11, 17-19; 2 Tim. 1:1-3, 10-12, 2:2-5, 14-16, 22-24, 3:6-8, 3:16-4:1, 4:8-10, 18-20; Tit. 1:1-3, 10-11, 2:4-6, 14-15, 3:8-9; Philem. 1-3, 14-16; Heb. 1:1-3, 9-12, 2:4-7, 12-14, 3:4-6, 14-16, 4:3-6, 12-14, 5:5-7, 6:1-3, 10-13, 6:20-7:2, 7:7-11, 18-20, 7:27-8:1, 8:7-9, 9:1-4, 9-11, 16-19, 25-27, 10:5-8, 16-18, 26-29, 35-38, 11:6-7, 12-15, 22-24, 31-33, 11:38-12:1, 12:7-9, 16-18, 25-27, 13:7-9, 16-18, 23-25. | The majority of the reading agree with the Alexandrian Text with one reading in agreement with the Byzantine Text. Numerous other readings do not agree with either text. |
| 017 | Cyprius | 850 | Complete Gospels | Byzantine |
| 018 | Mosquensis | 850 | Acts, Pauline Epistles minus Rom 10:18—1 Cor 6:13; 1 Cor 8:8-11 | Byzantine |
| 019 | Regius | 750 | Gospels minus Matt. 4:22-5:14, 28:17-end, Mark 10:16-30, 15:2-20, John 21:15-end | Said to be Alexandrian yet also contains a large number of Byzantine readings(Most of Matthew). |
| 020 | Angelicus | 850 | Contains Acts and Pauline Epistles minus Acts 1:1-8:10 and Heb 13:10-end | Byzantine. |

## IN DEFENSE OF THE TEXTUS RECEPTUS

| | | | | |
|---|---|---|---|---|
| 021 | Campianus | 850 | Complete gospels | Byzantine with a number of Alexandrian Text readings. |
| 022 | Petropolitanus Purpureus | 550 | Matt 1:1-24, 2:7-20, 3:4-6:24, 7:15-8:1, 8:24-31, 10:28-11:3, 12:40-13:4, 13:33-41, 14:6-22, 15:14-31, 16:7-18:5, 18:26-19:6, 19:13-20:6, 21:19-26:57, 26:65-27:26, 26:34-end; Mark 1:1-5:20. 7:4-20, 8:32-9:1, 10:43-11:7, 12:19-24:25, 15:23-33, 15:42-16:20; Luke 1:1-2:23, 4:3-19, 4:26-35, 4:42-5:12, 5:33-9:7, 9:21-28, 9:36-58, 10:4-12, 10:35-11:14, 11:23-12:12, 12:21-29, 18:32-19:17, 20:30-21:22, 22:49-57, 23:41-24:13, 24:21-39, 24:49-end; John 1:1-21, 1:39-2:6, 3:30-4:5, 5:3-10, 5:19-26, 6:49-57, 9:33-14:2, 14:11-15:14, 15:22-16:15, 20:23-25, 20:28-30, 21:20-end. | Byzantine |
| 023 | Sinopensis | 550 | Matt 7:7-22; 11:5-12; 13:7-47; 13:54-14:4.13-20; 15:11-16:18; 17:2-24; 18:4-30; 19:3-10.17-25; 20:9-21:5; 21:12-22:7.15-14; 22:32-23:35; 24:3-12. | Byzantine Text – although a few scholars believe it better represents the Caesarean text. |
| 024 | Guelferbytanus A | 550 | Matthew 1:11-21; 3:13-4:19; 10:7-19; 10:42-11:11; 13:40-50; 14:15-15:3.29-39;Mark 1:2-11; 3:5-17; 14:13-24.48-61; 15:12-37;Luke 1:1-13; 2:9-20; 6:21-42; 7:32-8:2; 8:31-50; 9:26-36; 10:36-11:4; 12:34-45; 14:14-25; 15:13-16:22; 18:13-39; 20:21-21:3; 22:3-16; 23:20-33; 23:45-24:1; 24:14-37; John 1:29-40; 2:13-25; 21:1-11 | Byzantine Text type - According to Scrivener's count the codex agrees with A and B united 50 times, sides with B against A 29 times, accords with A against B in 102 places. |
| 025 | Porphyrianus | 850 | Palimpsest - Acts, General Epistles, Pauline Epistles, and Revelation minus Acts 1:1-2:13; Romans 2:16-3:4; 8:32-9:10; 11:23-12:1; 1 Cor. 7:15-17; 12:23-13:5; 14:23-39; 2 Cor. 2:13-16; Col. 3:16-4:8; 1 Thes. 3:5-4:17; 1 John 3:20-5:1; Jude 4-15; Rev. 16:12-17:1; 19:21-20:9; 22:6-end.. | Alexandrian Text except in Acts and Revelation where text is typical of the Byzantine type. |

| | | | | |
|---|---|---|---|---|
| 026 | Guelferbytanus B | 450 | Luke 4:34-5:4, 6:10-26, 12:6-43, 15:14-31, 17:34-18:15, 18:34-19:11, 19:47-20:17, 20:34-21:8, 22:27-46,23:30-49; John 12:3-20, 14:3-22. | Byzantine but also contains Alexandrian Text readings. |
| 027 (R) | Nitriensis | 550 | Luke 1:1-13, 1:69-2:4, 2:16-27, 4:38-5:5, 5:25-6:8, 6:18-36, 6:39, 6:49-7:22, 7:44, 7:46, 7:47, 7:50, 8:1-3, 8:5-15, 8:25-9:1, 9:12-43, 10:3-16, 11:5-27, 12:4-15, 12:40-52, 13:26-14:1, 14:12-15:1, 15:13-16:16, 17:21-18:10, 18:22-20:20, 20:33-47, 21:12-22:6, 22:8-15, 22:42-56, 22:71-23:11, 23:38-51. | Byzantine with mixed readings in Luke 20 |
| 028 | Codex Guelpherbytanus | 949 | Gospels | Typically Byzantine but contains marks at Luke 22:43.44, John 5:4, and Pericope Adultera (John 7:53-8:11) which would seem to indicate that the scribe was not in total agreement with their inclusion. |
| 029 = [0113=0125=0139 | Borgianus | 450 | Contains fragments of the gospels of Luke and John, in Greek and Sahidic (Sahidic on the verso), with the Greek containing Luke 6:18-26, 18:2-9, 10-16, 18:32-19:8, 21:33-22:3, 22:20-23:20, 24:25-27, 29-31; John 1:24-32, 3:10-17, 4:52-5:7, 6:28-67, 7:6-8:31 | Mainly in agreement with the Alexandrian Text but a few believe it also contains a few Byzantine readings as well. |
| 030 | Nanianus | 9th to 10th century | Gospels | Byzantine with a few Alexandrian Text readings |
| 031 | Mosqnsis II | 850 | Gospels minus Matthew 5:44-6:12, 9:18-10:1, 22:44-23:35, John 21:10-end | Byzantine |
| 032 | Washingtonianus | 450 | Originally contained the four complete gospels but now is missing Mark 15:13-38, John 14:27-16:7. John 1:1-5:11 were replaced by a later scribe most likely to replace this lost section. | Byzantine in Matthew and Luke 8 to the end. Alexandrian Text - Western, Caesarean, and Alexandrian - in other areas. |
| 033 | Codex Monacensis | 950 | Contains the Gospels although parts of Matthew is at the end of John (probably a binding error) | Byzantine with a few readings in agreement with the Alexandrian Text. |

| | | | | |
|---|---|---|---|---|
| 034 | Macedoniensis | 850 | Contains the Gospel with Matthew 1:1-9:11; 10:35-11:4; Luke 1:26-36; 15:25-16:5; 23:22-34; John 20:27-21:17 missing and Matt 16:2, 3 and John 7:53-8:11 purposefully omitted. | Other than the obvious omissions which would agree more with the Alexandrian Text, the remainder is pure Byzantine. |
| 035 | Dublinensis | 550 | Matt. 1:17-2:6, 2:13-20, 4:4-13, 5:45-6:15, 7:16-8:6, 10:40-11:18, 12:43-13:11, 13:57-14:19, 15:13-23, 17:9-17, 17:26-18:6, 19:4-12, 21-28, 20:7-21:8, 21:23-30, 22:16-25, 22:37-23:3, 23:15-23, 24:15-25, 25:1-11, 26:21-29, 62-71 | Alexandrian Text in close agreement to the Codex Sinaiticus. |
| 036 | Codex Tischendorfianus IV | 9th to 10th century | The Gospels with lucana at Matt 5:31-6:16, 6:30-7:26, 8:27-9:6, 21:19-22:25; Mark 3:34-6:21 | Byzantine |
| 037 | Sangallensis | 850 | Gospels with a lucana at John 19:17-35. Mark 7:16 and 11:26, John 7:53-8:11 are omitted. | Byzantine in Matthew, Luke and John with Mark being Alexandrian Text. Many other variants exist as well. |
| 038 | Codex Koridethi | 850 | Contains the Gospels with gaps in the text of Matthew 1:1-9, 1:21-4:4, and 4:17-5:4 are missing. | Considered Byzantine by many but also contains large sections which are more in agreement with the Alexandrian Text. |
| 039 | Tischendorfianus III | 850 | Contains Matthew and Mark written in minuscule with Luke and John written in uncial. Interesting notes at the end of each. | Byzantine |
| 040 | Zacythius | 550 | Originally contained the entire Gospel of Luke with a catena. However the surviving portions only contain Luke 1:1-9, 19-23, 27-28, 30-32, 36-60, 1:77-2:19, 2:21-22, 2:33-3, 3:5-8, 11-20, 4:1-2, 6-20, 32-43, 5:17-36, 6:21-7:6, 7:11-37, 39-47, 8:4-21, 25-35, 43-50, 9:1-28, 32-33, 35, 9:41-10:18, 10:21-40, 11:1-4, 24-33 | Alexandrian Text with a few Byzantine readings. |
| 041 | Codex Petropolitanus | 900s | Contains almost all of Gospels; There are lacunae for Matt 3:12-4:17; 19:12-20:2; Luke 1:76-2:18; John 6:15-35; 8:6-39; 9:21-10:3. | Byzantine |

## IN DEFENSE OF THE TEXTUS RECEPTUS

| | | | | |
|---|---|---|---|---|
| | | | According to Scrivener, John 21:22-25 was written by a different person. | |
| 042 | Rossanensis | 550 | Matthew, Mark with 16:14-20 missing. Also contains a letter written by Eusebius called the epistle to Carpian. | Byzantine |
| 043 | Beratinus | 550 | Matthew, Mark but missing Matthew 1:1-6:3, 7:26-8:7, 18:23-19:3, and Mark 14:62-end | Byzantine with a few spurious readings which agree with the western and Alexandrian Text. |
| 044 | Codex Athous Lavrensis | 900 | Said to have originally contained the entire New Testament except for Revelation. However, it is now missing Matthew, Mark 1:1 – 9:5 and Heb 8:11-9:19 | A mix of text types with a few unique readings which do not identify with any textual family per se. |
| 045 | Codex Athous Dionysiou | 850 | Gospels | Byzantine with a few reading in agreement with the Alexandrian Text. |
| 046 | Vaticanus 2066 | 950 | Contains Revelation and various other non-biblical writings | Byzantine |
| 047 | | 750 | Contains the Gospels with some lacuna Matthew 2:15-3:12; 28:10-20; Mark 5:40-6:18; 8:35-9:19; John 2:17-42; 14:7-15:1; 18:34-21:25. | Byzantine with obvious influence from the Alexandrian Text. |
| 048 | Vaticanus 2061 | 450 | Acts 26:6-27:4, 28:3-31; James 4:14-5:20; 1 Pet. 1:1-12; 2 Pet. 2:4-8, 2:13-3:15; 1 John 4:6-5:13, 5:17-18, 5:21; 2 John; 3 John; Romans 13:4-15:9; 1 Cor. 2:1-3:11, 3:22, 4:4-6, 5:5-11, 6:3-11, 12:23-15:17, 15:20-27; 2 Cor. 4:7-6:8, 8:9-18, 8:21-10:6; Eph. 5:8-end; Phil. 1:8-23, 2:1-4, 2:6-8; Col. 1:2-2:8, 2:11-14, 22-23, 3:7-8, 3:12-4:18; 1 Th. 1:1, 5-6, 1 Tim. 5:6-6:17, 6:20-21, 2 Tim. 1:4-6, 1:8, 2:2-25; Titus 3:13-end; Philemon; Heb. 11:32-13:4. | Mostly in agreement with the Alexandrian Text with some readings in agreement with the Byzantine Text. |
| 049 | | 850 | Contains Acts, General Epistles, Pauline Epistles with lucana in the Pauline epistles. (it contains only Romans; 1 Cor 1:1-5:8; 13:8- | Byzantine |

| | | | 16:24; 2 Cor 1:1-11:23; Eph 4:20-6:20 | |
|---|---|---|---|---|
| 050 | | 850 | Gospel of John | Very Mixed text types – said to be in concurrence with P75. If this is so, it would be more Alexandrian Text than anything else. |
| 051 | Ath. Pantokratoros | 950 | Revelation minus Rev 1:1-11:14, 13:2-3, 22:8-14 | Mixed text |
| 052 | Ath. Panteleimonos | 950 | Contains Revelation 7:16-8:12 | Byzantine |
| 053 | | 850 | Contains Luke 1:1-2:40 | Byzantine |
| 054 | Codex Barberini | 750 | Contains John 16:3-19:41 | Byzantine |
| 055 | | 1050 | Gospels | Although it have never been categorized, the text is distinctively Byzantine. |
| 056 | | 950 | Acts, Pauline epistles | Byzantine |
| 057 | | 400 | Acts 3:5-6,10-12 | Alexandrian Text |
| 058 | | 350 | Matt 18:18-19.22-23.25-26.28-29 | Alexandrian Text with mixed readings |
| 059 | | 400 | Mark 15:29-38 | Alexandrian Text with mixed readings |
| 060 | | 550 | John 14:14-17.19-21.23-24.26-28 | Considered to be an eclectic text with a variety of mixed readings. |
| 061 | | 450 | 1 Timothy 3:15-16; 4:1-3; 6:2-8 | Byzantine with Critical Text reading in verse 16. |
| 062 | | 450 | Galatians 4:15-5:14 | Considered to be an eclectic text with a variety of mixed readings. |
| 063=0117 | | 850 | Luke 16:19-18:14; 18:36-19:44; 20:19-23; 20:36-21:20; 22:6-30; 22:53-24:20.41-fin.; John 1:1-3:34; 4:45-6:29 | Byzantine with an errant reading in John 1:28. |
| 064 =074 =090 | | 550 | codex 064 - Matt 27:7-30; codex 074 - Mt 25; 26; 28 codex 090 - Mt 26:59-70; 27:44-56; Mk 1:34-2:12 | Byzantine |
| 065 | | 550 | John 11:50-12:9, 15:12-16:2, 19:11-24 | Byzantine |
| 066 | | 550 | Acts 28:8-17 | Alexandrian Text (Western) |

## IN DEFENSE OF THE TEXTUS RECEPTUS

| | | | |
|---|---|---|---|
| 067 | 550 | Matthew 14:13-16.19-23; 24:37-25:1.32-45; 26:31-45; Mark 9:14-22; 14:58-70 | Mixed text with strong Byzantine presence. |
| 068 | 450 | John 13:16-17.19-20.23-24.26-27; 16:7-9.12-13.15-16.18-19 | Alexandrian Text |
| 069 | 450 | Mark 10:50.51; 11:11.12 | Byzantine |
| 070 =0110 =0124= 0178=0 179 =0180= 0190=0 191 =0193= 0194=0 202 | 550 | 070 (13 folios) – Luke 9:9-17; 10:40-11:6; 12:15-13:32; John 5:31-42; 8:33-42; 12:27-36<br>0110 (1 folio) – John 8:13-22<br>0124 + 0194 (22 folios) – Luke 3:19-30;10:21-30; 11:24-42; 22:54-65; 23:4-24:26;John 5:22-31; 8:42-9:39;11:48-56; 12:46-13:4<br>0178(1 folio) – Luke 16:4-12<br>0179 (1 folio) – Luke 21:30-22:2<br>0180 (1 folio) – John 7:3-12<br>0190 (1 folio) – Luke 10:30-39<br>0191 (1 folio) – Luke 12:5-14<br>0193 (1 folio) – John 3:23-32<br>0202 (2 folios) – Luke 8:13-19; 8:55-9:9 | Alexandrian Text |
| 071 | c. 500 | Matt 1:21-24; 1:25-2:2 | Alexandrian Text with one reading in Matt 1:24 agreeing with the Byzantine Text. |
| 072 | 500 | Mark 2:23-3:5 | Mixed text – More Alexandrian Text than anything else. |
| 073=084 | 550 | 073 - Matt 14:28-31<br>074 – Matt 14:19-27; 15:2-8 | Alexandrian Text |
| 075 | 950 | Romans; 1 Corinthians 1:1-15:28; Hebrews 11:38-13:25 | Byzantine with a few Alexandrian readings |
| 076 | 500 | Acts 2:11-22 | Alexandrian Text |
| 077 | 450 | Acts 13:18-29 | Alexandrian Text |
| 078 | 550 | Matthew 17:22-18:3.11-19; 19:5-14; Luke 18:14-25; John 4:52-5:8; 20:17-26 | Byzantine |
| 079 | 550 | Luke 7:39-49; 24:10-19 | Byzantine |
| 080 | 550 | Mark 9:14-18.20-22; 10:23-24.29 | Too fragmentary to accurately classify. |
| 081 | 550 | 2 Cor 1:20-2:12 | Alexandrian Text |
| 082 | 550 | Ephesians 4:2-18 | Alexandrian Text |

*God's Preserved Word to Every Generation*

| | | | |
|---|---|---|---|
| 083=0112=0235 | 500 | John 1:25-41; 2:9-4:14,34-49<br>0112 - Mark 14:29-45; 15:27-16:8<br>0235 - Mark 13:12-14.16-19.21-24.26-28 | Classified as Alexandrian Text but contains several Byzantine readings (Mark 15:28, John 1:28; |
| 085 | 550 | Matt 20:3-32; 22:3-16 | Considered to be "Alexandrian" but is actually a mixed text to include numerous Byzantine readings. |
| 086 | 550 | John 1:23-26; 3:5-4:23-35.45-49 | Alexandrian Text |
| 087=092b | 550 | 087 - Matthew 1:23-2:2; 19:3-8; 21:19-24; John 18:29-35<br>092b - Mark 12:32-37 | Alexandrian Text |
| 088 | 500 | 1 Cor 15:53-16:9, Tit 1:1-13 | Alexandrian Text |
| 089=092a | 550 | Matt 26:2-19 | Alexandrian Text |
| 090 | 550 | Matt 26, 27; Mark 1-2 † | Byzantine |
| 091 | 550 | John 6:13-14.22-24 | Alexandrian Text |
| 093 | 550 | Acts 24:22-25:5; 1 Pet 2:22-24; 3:1,3-7 | Byzantine in Acts<br>Alexandrian Text in 1 Peter |
| 094 | 550 | Matt 24:9-21 | Alexandrian Text |
| 095=0123 | 750 | 095 - Acts 2:45-3:8<br>0123 - parts of Acts 2:22-28 | Very small mss making it very difficult to classify but it appears to be very similar to the Alexandrian Text. |
| 096 | 650 | Acts 2:6-17; 26:7-18 | Mixed text of Byzantine and Alexandrian Text readings |
| 097 | 650 | Acts 13:39-46 | Byzantine |
| 098 | 650 | 2 Cor 11:9-19 | Alexandrian Text |
| 099 | 650 | Mark 16:6-18 | Byzantine Text |
| 0100=0195 | 650 | John 20:26-27.30-31 | Unclassified |
| 0101 | 750 | John 1:29-32 | Alexandrian Text |
| 0102=0138 | 650 | Luke 3:23-4:43; 21:4-18<br>0138 contains Matt 21:24-24:15 | Alexandrian Text |
| 0103 | 650 | Mark 13:34-14:25 | Byzantine |
| 0104 | 550 | Matthew 23:7-22; Mark 1:27-41; 13:12-14:3 | Byzantine |
| 0105 | 950 | John 6:71-7:46 | Byzantine with some mixed readings. |

| | | | | |
|---|---|---|---|---|
| 0106=0119 | | 650 | Matthew 12:17-19.23-25; 13:32; 13:36-15:26 | Mixed text |
| 0107 | | 650 | Matthew 22:16-23:14; Mark 4:24-35; 5:14-23 | Mixed |
| 0108 | | 650 | Luke 11:37-41.42-45 | Mixed |
| 0109 | | 650 | John 16:30-17:9; 18:31-40 | Mixed text |
| 0110 | | 550 | 070 (13 folios) – Luke 9:9-17; 10:40-11:6; 12:15-13:32; John 5:31-42; 8:33-42; 12:27-36<br>0110 (1 folio) – John 8:13-22<br>0124 + 0194 (22 folios) – Luke 3:19-30;10:21-30; 11:24-42; 22:54-65; 23:4-24:26;John 5:22-31; 8:42-9:39;11:48-56; 12:46-13:4<br>0178(1 folio) – Luke 16:4-12<br>0179 (1 folio) – Luke 21:30-22:2<br>0180 (1 folio) – John 7:3-12<br>0190 (1 folio) – Luke 10:30-39<br>0191 (1 folio) – Luke 12:5-14<br>0193 (1 folio) – John 3:23-32<br>0202 (2 folios) – Luke 8:13-19; 8:55-9:9 | Alexandrian Text |
| 0111 | | 650 | 2 Thess 1:1-2:2 | Mixed Text |
| 0113 | Borgianus | 450 | Contains fragments of the gospels of Luke and John, in Greek and Sahidic (Sahidic on the verso), with the Greek containing Luke 6:18-26, 18:2-9, 10-16, 18:32-19:8, 21:33-22:3, 22:20-23:20, 24:25-27, 29-31; John 1:24-32, 3:10-17, 4:52-5:7, 6:28-67, 7:6-8:31 | Mainly in agreement with the Alexandrian Text but a few believe it also contains a few Byzantine readings as well. |
| 0114 | | 750 | John, 20:4-6,8-10 | Mixed Text |
| 0115 | | 900 | Luke 9:35-47; 10:12-22 | Mixed Text |
| 0116 | | 750 | Matthew 19:14-28; 20:23-21:2; 26:52-27:1; Mark 13:21-14:67; Luke 3:1-4:20 | Byzantine |
| 0117 | | 850 | Luke 16 — John 6 | Byzantine with an errant reading in John 1:28. |
| 0118 | | 750 | Matthew 11:27-28 | Too small to classify. |
| 0119 | | 650 | Matthew 12:17-19.23-25; 13:32; 13:36-15:26 | Mixed text |

| | | | | |
|---|---|---|---|---|
| 0120 | | Scrivener – 4th century Aland – 9th century | Acts 16:30-17:17; 17:27-29,31-34; 18:8-26 | Mixed text |
| 0121a | | 950 | 1 Cor. 15:42-end, 2 Cor. 1:1-15, 10:13-12:5 | Mixed text types |
| 0121b + 0243 | Codex Ruber | 950 | 1 Cor. 13:4-end and all of 2 Cor.; Heb. 1:2-4:3, 12:20-end. | Mixed text types |
| 0122 | | 950 | Gal. 5:12-6:4, Heb. 5:8-6:10 | Byzantine with independent readings in a few places |
| 0123 | | 750 | 095 - Acts 2:45-3:8 0123 - parts of Acts 2:22-28 | Very small mss making it very difficult to classify but it appears to be very similar to the Alexandrian Text. |
| 0124 | | 550 | 070 (13 folios) – Luke 9:9-17; 10:40-11:6; 12:15-13:32; John 5:31-42; 8:33-42; 12:27-36 0110 (1 folio) – John 8:13-22 0124 + 0194 (22 folios) – Luke 3:19-30;10:21-30; 11:24-42; 22:54-65; 23:4-24:26;John 5:22-31; 8:42-9:39;11:48-56; 12:46-13:4 0178(1 folio) – Luke 16:4-12 0179 (1 folio) – Luke 21:30-22:2 0180 (1 folio) – John 7:3-12 0190 (1 folio) – Luke 10:30-39 0191 (1 folio) – Luke 12:5-14 0193 (1 folio) – John 3:23-32 0202 (2 folios) – Luke 8:13-19; 8:55-9:9 | Alexandrian Text |
| 0125 | Borgianus | 450 | Contains fragments of the gospels of Luke and John, in Greek and Sahidic (Sahidic on the verso), with the Greek containing Luke 6:18-26, 18:2-9, 10-16, 18:32-19:8, 21:33-22:3, 22:20-23:20, 24:25-27, 29-31; John 1:24-32, 3:10-17, 4:52-5:7, 6:28-67, 7:6-8:31 | Mainly in agreement with the Alexandrian Text but a few believe it also contains a few Byzantine readings as well. |
| 0126 | | 750 | Mark 5:34-6:2 | Mixed Text |
| 0127 | | 750 | John 2:2-11 | Mixed Text |
| 0128 | | 850 | Matthew 25:32-37.40-42.44-45 | Mixed Text |

## IN DEFENSE OF THE TEXTUS RECEPTUS

| | | | | |
|---|---|---|---|---|
| 0129=0203 | | 850 | 1 Peter | Alexandrian Text |
| 0130 | Codex Sangallensis 18 | 850 | Mark 1:31-2:16; Luke 1:20-31.64-79; 2:24-48 | Mixed Text but with a strong element of Byzantine influence |
| 0131 | | 850 | Mark 7:3-4.6-8.30-8:16; 9:2.7-9 | Mixed Text |
| 0132 | | 850 | Mark 5:16-40 | Mixed Text but strongly Byzantine |
| 0133 | | 850 | Matthew 1:1-14; 5:3-19; 23:9-25:30; 25:43-26:26; 26:50-27:16; Mark 1:1-43; 2:21-5:1; 5:29-6:22; 10:51-11:13 | Byzantine |
| 0134 | | 750 | Mark 3:15-32; 5:16-31 | Byzantine |
| 0135 | | 850 | Matthew 25:35-26:2; 27:3-17; Mark 1:12-24; 2:26-3:10; Luke 1:24-37; 1:68-2:4; 4:28-40; 6:22-35; 8:22-30; 9:42-53; 17:2-14; 18:7-9.13-19; 22:11-25.52-66; 23:35-49(?); 24:32-46 | Byzantine |
| 0136=0137 | | 850 | Matthew 14:6-13; 25:9-16; 25:41-26:1 | Byzantine |
| 0137 | | 850 | Matthew 13:46-52 | Byzantine |
| 0138 | | 650 | Matthew 21:24-24:15 | Alexandrian Text |
| 0139 | Borgianus | 450 | Contains fragments of the gospels of Luke and John, in Greek and Sahidic (Sahidic on the verso), with the Greek containing Luke 6:18-26, 18:2-9, 10-16, 18:32-19:8, 21:33-22:3, 22:20-23:20, 24:25-27, 29-31; John 1:24-32, 3:10-17, 4:52-5:7, 6:28-67, 7:6-8:31 | Mainly in agreement with the Alexandrian Text but a few believe it also contains a few Byzantine readings as well. |
| 0140 | | 950 | Acts 5:34-38 | Mixed Text |
| 0141 | | 950 | John | Mixed Text with strong Byzantine influence |
| 0142 | | 950 | Contains most of the NT except the gospels and Revelation. | Byzantine |
| 0143 | | 750 | Mark 8:17-18,27-28 | Mixed Text |
| 0144 | | 650 | Mark 6:47-7:14 | Previously stored at Qubbat al-Khazna in Damascus. Location currently unknown. Ms lost. |

*God's Preserved Word to Every Generation*

| | | | | |
|---|---|---|---|---|
| 0145 | | 650 | John 6:26-31 | Previously stored at Qubbat al-Khazna in Damascus. Location currently unknown. Ms lost. |
| 0146 | | 750 | Mark 10:37-45 | Previously stored at Qubbat al-Khazna in Damascus. Location currently unknown. Ms lost. |
| 0147 | | 550 | Luke 6:23-35 | Previously stored at Qubbat al-Khazna in Damascus. Location currently unknown. Ms lost. |
| 0148 | | 750 | Matt 28:5-19 | Mixed Text |
| 0149=0187 | | 550 | Mark 6:30-41 | Mixed Text |
| 0150 | | 850 | Pauline epistles | mostly Byzantine with some Alexandrian readings |
| 0151 | | 850 | Pauline epistles | Byzantine |
| 0152 | Talisman Ms | | Very small fragment of Matthew | |
| 0153 | Ostracon (pottery) | | 2 Cor 4:7; 2 Timothy 2:20 | Too small to classify |
| 0154 | | 850 | Mark 10:35-46; 11:17-28 | Previously stored at Qubbat al-Khazna in Damascus. Location currently unknown. Ms lost. |
| 0155 | | 850 | Luke 3:1-2,5,7-11; 6:24-31 | Previously stored at Qubbat al-Khazna in Damascus. Location currently unknown. Ms lost. |
| 0156 | | 550 | 2 Peter 3:2-10 | Previously stored at Qubbat al-Khazna in Damascus. Location currently unknown. Ms lost. |
| 0157 | | 700 | 1 John 2:7-13 | Previously stored at Qubbat al-Khazna in Damascus. Location currently unknown. Ms lost. |
| 0158 | | 500 | Galatians 1 | Previously stored at Qubbat al-Khazna in Damascus. Location currently unknown. Ms lost. |
| 0159 | | 550 | Ephesians 4-5 | Previously stored at Qubbat al-Khazna in Damascus. Location currently unknown. Ms lost. |
| 0160 | | 400 | Matthew 26:25-26,34-36 | Mixed Text |
| 0161 | | 750 | Matthew 22:7-46 | Mixed Text but strongly Byzantine |
| 0162 | | 300 | John 2:11-22 | Alexandrian Text |
| 0163 | | 450 | Revelation 16:17-20 | Alexandrian Text |

## IN DEFENSE OF THE TEXTUS RECEPTUS

| | | | | |
|---|---|---|---|---|
| 0164 | | 600 | Matthew 13:20-21 | Alexandrian Text |
| 0165 | | 450 | Acts 3:24-4:13,17-20 | Mixed Text |
| 0166 | | 450 | Acts 28:30-31 (recto); James 1:11(verso) | Mixed Text |
| 0167 | | 650 | Mark 4:24-29,37-41; 6:9-11,13-14,37-39,41,45 | Mixed Text |
| 0168 | | 750 | Gospels | Unknown. Ms lost. |
| 0169 | | 350 | Revelation 3:19-4:3 | Mixed Text |
| 0170 | | 500 | Matthew 6:5-6,8-10,13-15,17 | Mixed Text |
| 0171 | | 300 | Matthew10:17-23,25-32; Luke 22:44-50,52-56,61,63-64 | Mixed Text |
| 0172 | | 450 | Romans 1:27-30,32-2:2 | Alexandrian Text with some byzantine readings |
| 0173 | | 450 | James 1:25-27 | Alexandrian Text with some Byzantine readings |
| 0174 | | 450 | Galatians 2:5-6 | Too small to classify |
| 0175 | | 450 | Acts 6:7-15 | Alexandrian Text with some Byzantine readings |
| 0176 | | 400 | Galatians 3:16-25 | Mixed |
| 0177 | | 950 | Luke 1:73-2:7 | Alexandrian Text with some Byzantine readings |
| 0178 | | 550 | 070 (13 folios) – Luke 9:9-17; 10:40-11:6; 12:15-13:32; John 5:31-42; 8:33-42; 12:27-36<br>0110 (1 folio) – John 8:13-22<br>0124 + 0194 (22 folios) – Luke 3:19-30;10:21-30; 11:24-42; 22:54-65; 23:4-24:26;John 5:22-31; 8:42-9:39;11:48-56; 12:46-13:4<br>0178(1 folio) – Luke 16:4-12<br>0179 (1 folio) – Luke 21:30-22:2<br>0180 (1 folio) – John 7:3-12<br>0190 (1 folio) – Luke 10:30-39<br>0191 (1 folio) – Luke 12:5-14<br>0193 (1 folio) – John 3:23-32<br>0202 (2 folios) – Luke 8:13-19; 8:55-9:9 | Alexandrian Text |
| 0179 | See 070 | 550 | 070 (13 folios) – Luke 9:9-17; 10:40-11:6; 12:15-13:32; | Alexandrian Text |

*God's Preserved Word to Every Generation*

|  |  |  | John 5:31-42; 8:33-42; 12:27-36<br>0110 (1 folio) – John 8:13-22<br>0124 + 0194 (22 folios) – Luke 3:19-30;10:21-30; 11:24-42; 22:54-65; 23:4-24:26;John 5:22-31; 8:42-9:39;11:48-56; 12:46-13:4<br>0178(1 folio) – Luke 16:4-12<br>0179 (1 folio) – Luke 21:30-22:2<br>0180 (1 folio) – John 7:3-12<br>0190 (1 folio) – Luke 10:30-39<br>0191 (1 folio) – Luke 12:5-14<br>0193 (1 folio) – John 3:23-32<br>0202 (2 folios) – Luke 8:13-19; 8:55-9:9 |  |
|---|---|---|---|---|
| 0180 | See 070 | 550 | 070 (13 folios) – Luke 9:9-17; 10:40-11:6; 12:15-13:32; John 5:31-42; 8:33-42; 12:27-36<br>0110 (1 folio) – John 8:13-22<br>0124 + 0194 (22 folios) – Luke 3:19-30;10:21-30; 11:24-42; 22:54-65; 23:4-24:26;John 5:22-31; 8:42-9:39;11:48-56; 12:46-13:4<br>0178(1 folio) – Luke 16:4-12<br>0179 (1 folio) – Luke 21:30-22:2<br>0180 (1 folio) – John 7:3-12<br>0190 (1 folio) – Luke 10:30-39<br>0191 (1 folio) – Luke 12:5-14<br>0193 (1 folio) – John 3:23-32<br>0202 (2 folios) – Luke 8:13-19; 8:55-9:9 | Alexandrian Text |
| 0181 |  | 400 | Luke 9:59-10:14 | Alexandrian Text |
| 0182 |  | 450 | Luke 19:18-20,22-24 | Mixed |
| 0183 |  | 600s | 1 Thess 3:6-9; 4:1-5 | Mixed |
| 0184 |  | 550 | Mark 15:36-37,40-41 | Alexandrian Text |
| 0185 |  | 350 | 1 Cor 3:6-9; 4:1-5 | Very fragmentary but said to be Alexandrian Text. |
| 0186 |  | 500 | 2 Cor 4:5-8.10.13 | Mixed text |
| 0187=0149 |  | 550 | Mark 6:30-41 | Mixed Text |
| 0188 |  | 350 | Mark 11:11-17 | Mixed text |
| 0189 |  | 200 | Acts 5:3-21 | Alexandrian Text |

| | | | | |
|---|---|---|---|---|
| 0190 | See 070 | 550 | 070 (13 folios) – Luke 9:9-17; 10:40-11:6; 12:15-13:32; John 5:31-42; 8:33-42; 12:27-36<br>0110 (1 folio) – John 8:13-22<br>0124 + 0194 (22 folios) – Luke 3:19-30;10:21-30; 11:24-42; 22:54-65; 23:4-24:26;John 5:22-31; 8:42-9:39;11:48-56; 12:46-13:4<br>0178(1 folio) – Luke 16:4-12<br>0179 (1 folio) – Luke 21:30-22:2<br>0180 (1 folio) – John 7:3-12<br>0190 (1 folio) – Luke 10:30-39<br>0191 (1 folio) – Luke 12:5-14<br>0193 (1 folio) – John 3:23-32<br>0202 (2 folios) – Luke 8:13-19; 8:55-9:9 | Alexandrian Text |
| 0191 | See 070 | 550 | 070 (13 folios) – Luke 9:9-17; 10:40-11:6; 12:15-13:32; John 5:31-42; 8:33-42; 12:27-36<br>0110 (1 folio) – John 8:13-22<br>0124 + 0194 (22 folios) – Luke 3:19-30;10:21-30; 11:24-42; 22:54-65; 23:4-24:26;John 5:22-31; 8:42-9:39;11:48-56; 12:46-13:4<br>0178(1 folio) – Luke 16:4-12<br>0179 (1 folio) – Luke 21:30-22:2<br>0180 (1 folio) – John 7:3-12<br>0190 (1 folio) – Luke 10:30-39<br>0191 (1 folio) – Luke 12:5-14<br>0193 (1 folio) – John 3:23-32<br>0202 (2 folios) – Luke 8:13-19; 8:55-9:9 | Alexandrian Text |
| 0192 | ℓ *1604* | 350 | | |
| 0193 | See 070 | 550 | 070 (13 folios) – Luke 9:9-17; 10:40-11:6; 12:15-13:32; John 5:31-42; 8:33-42; 12:27-36<br>0110 (1 folio) – John 8:13-22<br>0124 + 0194 (22 folios) – Luke 3:19-30;10:21-30; 11:24-42; 22:54-65; 23:4-24:26;John 5:22-31; 8:42-9:39;11:48-56; 12:46-13:4<br>0178(1 folio) – Luke 16:4-12<br>0179 (1 folio) – Luke 21:30-22:2<br>0180 (1 folio) – John 7:3-12 | Alexandrian Text |

| | | | | |
|---|---|---|---|---|
| | | | 0190 (1 folio) – Luke 10:30-39<br>0191 (1 folio) – Luke 12:5-14<br>0193 (1 folio) – John 3:23-32<br>0202 (2 folios) – Luke 8:13-19; 8:55-9:9 | |
| 0194 | | 550 | 070 (13 folios) – Luke 9:9-17; 10:40-11:6; 12:15-13:32; John 5:31-42; 8:33-42; 12:27-36<br>0110 (1 folio) – John 8:13-22<br>0124 + 0194 (22 folios) – Luke 3:19-30;10:21-30; 11:24-42; 22:54-65; 23:4-24:26;John 5:22-31; 8:42-9:39;11:48-56; 12:46-13:4<br>0178(1 folio) – Luke 16:4-12<br>0179 (1 folio) – Luke 21:30-22:2<br>0180 (1 folio) – John 7:3-12<br>0190 (1 folio) – Luke 10:30-39<br>0191 (1 folio) – Luke 12:5-14<br>0193 (1 folio) – John 3:23-32<br>0202 (2 folios) – Luke 8:13-19; 8:55-9:9 | Alexandrian Text |
| 0195 =<br>0100 | | 650 | John 20:26-27.30-31 | Unclassified |
| 0196 | | 850 | Matthew 5:1-11; Luke 24:26-33 | Unclassified |
| 0197 | | 850 | Matthew 20:22-23,25-27; 22:30-32,34-37 | Byzantine |
| 0198 | | 550 | Colossians 3:15-16,20-21 | Mixed text |
| 0199 | | 600 | 1 Corinthians 11:17-19,22-24 | Mixed |
| 0200 | | 650 | Matthew 11:20-21 | Mixed |
| 0201 | | 450 | 1 Cor 12:2-3,6-13; 14:20-29 | Mostly Alexandrian Text with some Byzantine readings. |
| 0202 | See 070 | 550 | 070 (13 folios) – Luke 9:9-17; 10:40-11:6; 12:15-13:32; John 5:31-42; 8:33-42; 12:27-36<br>0110 (1 folio) – John 8:13-22<br>0124 + 0194 (22 folios) – Luke 3:19-30;10:21-30; 11:24-42; 22:54-65; 23:4-24:26;John 5:22-31; 8:42-9:39;11:48-56; 12:46-13:4<br>0178(1 folio) – Luke 16:4-12<br>0179 (1 folio) – Luke 21:30-22:2 | Alexandrian Text |

## IN DEFENSE OF THE TEXTUS RECEPTUS

| | | | | |
|---|---|---|---|---|
| | | | 0180 (1 folio) – John 7:3-12
0190 (1 folio) – Luke 10:30-39
0191 (1 folio) – Luke 12:5-14
0193 (1 folio) – John 3:23-32
0202 (2 folios) – Luke 8:13-19; 8:55-9:9 | |
| 0203 =
0129 | | 850 | a small part of the Pauline epistles | Alexandrian Text |
| 0204 | | 650 | Matt 24:39-42,44-48 | Alexandrian Text |
| 0205 | | 750 | Titus 2:15b-3:7 in Greek but from Titus 2:11 through Philemon written in Coptic | Alexandrian Text |
| 0206 | | 350 | 1 Peter 5:5-13 | Mixed Text |
| 0207 | | 350 | Revelation 9:2-15 | Mixed Text |
| 0208 | | 550 | Colossians 1:29-2:10,13-14; 1 Thessalonians 2:4-7,12-17 | Mixed Text |
| 0209 | | 650 | Romans 14:9-23; 16:25-27; 15:1-2; 2 Corinthians 1:1-15; 4:4-13; 6:11-7:2; 9:2-10:17; 2 Peter 1:1-2:3 | Mixed but with a strong Byzantine influence |
| 0210 | | 650 | John 5:44; 6:1-2,41-42 | Mixed text |
| 0211 | | 650 | Complete text of all four Gospels | Byzantine |
| 0212 | | 250 | Considered to be a fragment of Tatian's Diatessaron containing Matthew 27:56-57; Mark 15:40,42; Luke 23:49,50,51; John 19:38 | The text type is not really identifiable because of its diatessoric nature. However, it substantially agrees with the Alexandrian Text. |
| 0213 | | 500 | Mark 3:2-3,5 | Mixed text |
| 0214 | | 400 | Mark 8:33-37 | Mixed Text |
| 0215 | | 500 | Mark 15:20-21,26-27 | Mixed Text |
| 0216 | | 450 | John 8:51-53; 9:5-8 | Mixed text |
| 0217 | | 450 | John 11:57-12:7 | Mixed Text |
| 0218 | | 450 | John 12:2-6,9-11,14-16 | Mixed text |
| 0219 | | 400 | Romans 2:21-23; 3:8-9,23-25,27-30 | Mixed text |
| 0220 | Wyman Fragment | 300 | Romans 4:23-5:3; 5:8-13 | Alexandrian Text |
| 0221 | | 350 | Romans 5:16-17,19,21-6:3 | Mixed Text |

| | | | | |
|---|---|---|---|---|
| 0222 | | 350 | 1 Cor 9:5-7,10,12-13 | Mixed text |
| 0223 | | 550 | 2 Cor 1:17-2:2 | Alexandrian Text with alien readings. |
| 0224 | | 500 | 2 Corinthians 4:5,12,13 | Mixed Text |
| 0225 | | 550 | 2 Cor 5:1-2,8-9,14-16,19-6:1,3-5; 8:16-24 | Alexandrian Text with alien readings |
| 0226 | | 450 | 1 Thess 4:16-5:5 | Mixed text |
| 0227 | | 450 | Hebrews 11:18-19:29 | Mixed text |
| 0228 | | 350 | Hebrews 12:19-21,23-25 | Mixed Text |
| 0229 | | 750 | Rev 18:16-17; 19:4-6 | Mixed Text |
| 0230 | | 350 | Ephesians 6:11-12 | Currently uncategorized but some believe that it It has some kind of relationship to **06** making it "Western Text". So we can safely assume it is Alexandrian Text. |
| 0231 | | 350 | Matt 26:75-27:1,3-4 | Mixed Text |
| 0232 | | 500 | 2 John 1-5, 6-9 | Alexandrian Text with Byzantine influence |
| 0233 | | 750 | The Gospels | Mixed text but has a strong Byzantine overtone. |
| 0234 | | 750 | Matthew 28:11-15; John 1:4-8,20-24 | Alexandrian Text |
| 0236 | | 450 | Acts 3:12-13,15-16 | Mixed Text |
| 0237 | | 550 | Matt 15:12-15,17-19 | Mixed Text |
| 0238 | | 750 | John 7:10-12 | Mixed Text |
| 0239 | | 650 | Luke 2:27-30,34 | Mixed Text |
| 0240 | | 450 | Tit 1:4-8 | Alexandrian Text |
| 0241 | | 550 | 1 Tim 3:16-4:3,8-11 | Alexandrian Text |
| 0242 | | 350 | Matthew 8:25-9:2; 13:32-38,40-46 | Mixed Text |
| 0243 | Codex Ruber | 950 | 1 Cor. 13:4-end and all of 2 Cor.; Heb. 1:2-4:3, 12:20-end. | Mixed text types |
| 0244 | | 450 | Acts 11:29-12:5 | Alexandrian Text |
| 0245 | | 550 | 1 John 3:23-4:1,3-6 | Alexandrian Text |
| 0246 | | 550 | James 1:12-14,19-21 | Byzantine Text |
| 0247 | | 500 | 1 Peter 5:13-14 - 2 Peter 1:5-8,14-16; 2:1 | Alexandrian Text |

## IN DEFENSE OF THE TEXTUS RECEPTUS

| | | | | |
|---|---|---|---|---|
| 0248 | | 850 | Matthew 1; 12-14; 19-21 | Byzantine Text |
| 0249 | | 950 | Matthew 25:1-9 | Mixed text with strong Byzantine overtone |
| 0250 | Climaci Rescriptus | 750 | Gospels | Byzantine with some mixed readings |
| 0251 | | 550 | 3 John 12-15; Jude 3-5 | Mixed |
| 0252 | Pap. Barcinonensis | 450 | Hebrews 6:2-4,6-7 | Mixed |
| 0253 | | 550 | Luke 10:19-22 | Byzantine |
| 0254 | | 450 | Galatians 5:13-17 | Alexandrian Text |
| 0255 | | 850 | Matthew 26:2-9; 27:9-16 | Alexandrian Text |
| 0256 | | 750 | John 6:32-33,35-37 | Mixed |
| 0257 | | 850 | Matt 5:17-29; 8:4-19; 12:4-13:41; 13:55-14:15; 25:28-16:19; 21:20-43; 22:13-24:24; 25:6-36; 26:24-39; Mark 6:22-36; 7:15-37; 8:33-11:22; 14:21-16:12 | Byzantine |
| 0258 | | 500 | John 10:25-26 | Uncategorized; current location unknown. |
| 0259 | | 650 | 1 Tim 1:4-5.6-7 | Mixed |
| 0260 | | 550 | John 1:30-32 | Mixed |
| 0261 | | 450 | Gal 1:9-12,19-22; 4:25-31 | Mixed |
| 0262 | | 650 | 1 Tim 1:15-16 | Mixed |
| 0263 | | 550 | Mark 5:26-27,31 | Unclassified |
| 0264 | | 450 | John 8:19-20,23-24 | Unclassified |
| 0265 | | 550 | Luke 7:20-21,34-35 | Byzantine |
| 0266 | | 550 | Luke 20:19-25,30-39 | Mixed |
| 0267 | Pap. Barcinonensis 16 | 450 | Luke 8:25-27 | Unclassified |
| 0268 | | 650 | John 1:30-33 | Mixed |
| 0269 | | 850 | Mark 6:14-20 | Byzantine with alien readings |
| 0270 | | 500 | 1 Corinthians 15:10-15,19-25 | Alexandrian Text |
| 0271 | | 850 | Matthew 12:27-39 | Alexandrian Text |

*God's Preserved Word to Every Generation*

| | | | |
|---|---|---|---|
| 0272 | 850 | Luke 16:21-17:3; 19-35; 19:15-31 | Byzantine |
| 0273 | 850 | John 2:7-3:5; 4:23-37; 5:35-6:2 | Byzantine |
| 0274 | 450 | Mark 6:56-7:4.6-9.13-17.19-23.29-29.34-35; 8:3-4.8-11; 9:20-22.26-41; 9:43-10:1.17-22 | Alexandrian Text but agrees with the Byzantine Text in 6 places. |
| 0275 | 650 | Matthew 5:25-26,29-30 | Alexandrian Text with variant readings. |
| 0276 | 750 | Mark 14:65-67,68-71; 14:72-15:2,4-7 | Unclassified |
| 0277 | 700 | Matthew 14:22,28-29 | Unclassified |
| 0278 | 850 | Pauline epistles | Unclassified |
| 0279 | 800 | Luke 8:32-44; 22:3.15-16 | Unclassified |
| 0280 | 750 | Hebrews 9:14-18 | Unclassified |
| 0281 | 700 | Matt 6-27 | Alexandrian Text |
| 0282 | 550 | Phil 2:24-27; 3:6-8 | Unclassified |
| 0283 | 850 | Mark 2:21-3:18; 5:9-13.31-36; 6:9-13.39-40; 9:20-24.44-47; 14:54-62; 15:6-15 | Unclassified |
| 0284 | 750 | Matt 26:75-27:7; 27:9-11.13-17; 28:15-18.20 | Unclassified |
| 0285 | 550 | Romans 5:12.14; 8:37-9:5; 13:1-4; 13:11-14:3; 1 Corinthians 4:2-7; 12:16.18.21-30; 14:26-33; Ephesians 3:13-20; 5:28-6:1; 1 Timothy 1:1-7; Hebrews 8:9-9:1; 9:25-10:2; 11:3-7; 12:22-13:25; 1 Peter 3:17-4:1. | Alexandrian Text |
| 0286 | 550 | Matt 16:13-19; John 10:12-16 | Unclassified |
| 0287 | 550 | Matthew 1-8; 21; 22,1-3; Mark 16,19; Luke 1-12; John 2; 10; 12; 13; 17; 20; 21 | Unclassified |
| 0288 | 550 | Luke 5:33-34.36-37; 5:39-6:1.3-4 | Unclassified |
| 0289 | 700 | Romans 8:19-21.32-35; 1 Corinthians 2:11-4:12; 13:13-14:1.3-11.13-19 | Unclassified |
| 0290 | 850 | John 18:4-20:2 | Unclassified |

## IN DEFENSE OF THE TEXTUS RECEPTUS

| | | | |
|---|---|---|---|
| 0291 | 700 | Luke 8:45-9:2 | Unclassified |
| 0292 | 550 | Mark 6:55-7:5 | Unclassified |
| 0293 | 700 | Matt 26:4-7,10-12 | Alexandrian Text |
| 0294 | 700 | Acts 14:27-15:10 | Unclassified |
| 0295 | 850 AD | 2 Corinthians 12:14-13:1 | Unclassified |
| 0296 | 550 AD | 1 John 5:3-13; 2 Corinthians 7:3-4.9 | Unclassified |
| 0297 | 850 | Matt 1:1-14; 5:3-19 | Unclassified |
| 0298 | 700-900 AD | Matt 26:24-29 | Unclassified |
| 0299 | 1000 AD | John 20:1-7 | Mixed |
| 0300 | 600 AD | Matt 20:2-17 | Unclassified |
| 0301 | 400-500 AD | John 17:1-4 | Unclassified |
| 0302 | 550 AD | John 10:29-30 | Unclassified |
| 0303 | 600-700 AD | Luke 13:17-29 | Byzantine |
| 0304 | 850 AD | Acts 6:5-7:13 | Unclassified |
| 0305 | ? | Matt 20:22-23.30-31 | Unclassified |
| 0306 | 850 | John 9:22-10:3.5-8.10-12; 11:6-37.39-41 | Unclassified |
| 0307 | 800-900 AD | Matthew 11:21-12:4; Mark 11:29-12:21; Luke 9:39-10:5; 22:18-47 | Unclassified |
| 0308 | 350 AD | Rev 11:15-16; 11:17-18 | Too small to classify |
| 0309 | 550 AD | John 20:22-24.28-30 | Unclassified |
| 0310 | 950 AD | Tit 2:15-3:6; 3:6-7 | Unclassified |
| 0311 | 700-900 AD | Rom 8:1-13 | Unclassified |
| 0312 | 200-400 AD | Luke 5:23-24.30-31; 7:9.17-18 | Unclassified |
| 0313 | 400-500 AD | Mark 4:9.15 | Unclassified |
| 0314 | 550 AD | John 5:43 | Unclassified |
| 0315 | 400 AD | Mark 2:9.21.25; 3:1-2 | Unclassified |

*God's Preserved Word to Every Generation*

| 0316 | | 650 AD | Jude 18-25 | Unclassified |
| 0317 | | 600-700 AD | Mark 14:52-53.61-62 | Unclassified |
| 0319 | Sangermanensis | 900 | Pauline Epistles | Mixed |
| 0318 | | 650 | Mark 9:2-14:32 | Unclassified |

## IN DEFENSE OF THE TEXTUS RECEPTUS

## APPENDIX B - THE MEANING OF "WORD OF GOD"

One of the main problems in fundamental circles is an incorrect assumption of what exactly the phrase "word of God" means. Let me illustrate. I once had a discussion with a young man about whether or not the King James Version was inspired. I said it was not. He accused me of saying that the King James Version was not the Word of God.

That young man did not have a clear understanding of what the phrase "Word of God" means. Even the King James Version translators spoke of the other English translations as being God's word even though the other translations may not have been as good as they should have been. In their way of thinking, the king's message, even translated poorly, was still the king's message, howbeit could have been better expressed[164].

Note the following outline of quotations from the scriptures and the circumstances around which the phrase "word of God" were made:

### "Word of God" Used In a General Sense Referring to God's Message

> ***1 Samuel 9:27*** *And as they were going down to the end of the city, Samuel said to Saul, Bid the servant pass on before us, (and he passed on,) but stand thou still a while, that I may shew thee the word of God.*

The phrase "word of God" refers to God's message which was about to be verbally delivered to Saul. It is not so much what is written, though this obviously happened at a later date, but what God wanted Saul to know. The message itself is given in 1 Sa 10:1-8. Interestingly, every bit of the message was for Saul personally. Naturally, as God's Word, we may make application from what God said, but by all laws of scripture interpretation, it was for Saul. Therefore, the phrase, "word of God" simply meant "God's message" which was

---

[164] "Now to the latter we answer; that we do not deny, nay we affirm and avow, that the very meanest translation of the Bible in English, set forth by men of our profession, (for we have seen none of theirs of the whole Bible as yet) containeth the word of God, nay, is the word of God. As the King's speech, which he uttereth in Parliament, being translated into French, Dutch, Italian, and Latin, is still the King's speech, though it be not interpreted by every Translator with the like grace, nor peradventure so fitly for phrase, nor so expressly for sense, everywhere. " (THE TRANSLATORS TO THE READER, Preface to the King James Version 1611)

for that time only.[165] This same usage of "word of God" is found in other passages as well. (1 Ki 12:22, 1 Chron 17:3; Luke 3:2; Luke 5:1; Heb 11:3; 2 Pet 3:5[166])

In other places, the phrase "word of God" can very literally mean what has already been written. One example of this is in Acts 4:31:

> "And when they had prayed, the place was shaken where they were assembled together; and they were all filled with the Holy Ghost, and they spake the word of God with boldness"

Also, in Col 1:25:

> "Whereof I am made a minister, according to the dispensation of God which is given to me for you, to fulfil the word of God;"

The implication is that Paul was called of God to apply God's revelation concerning his apostleship in preaching the Gospel. This can have a dual application in that it obviously refers to God's personal instruction by revelation to him concerning his calling as well as the possibility that he was bound to obey scriptures in fulfilling that calling.

### "Word of God" Used In Reference to the Written Words of the Bible

> ***Proverbs 30:5*** *Every word of God is pure: he is a shield unto them that put their trust in him.*

This verse obviously applies to everything God has either spoken or what have been written. As such, it would only extend to a translation if that translation were "pure". In other words, it must be exactly what God delivered. If there are any differences whatsoever, then that portion of the translation which is not in agreement with the Greek text cannot be said to be pure. Thus, that same portion of the translation which differs from the Greek text cannot be referred to as the Word of God.

---

[165] On this point, I tread very lightly because I know some would misconstrue my statement. For the record, I believe that every part of God's Word is applicable to every living person in every age. However, a simple reading of the passage makes it clear that the interpretation was local. As a preacher of the Gospel, I am well aware that we can make application from the truths found in any passage of the Bible but let's not confuse interpretation with application. Interpretation is the primary meaning of a passage while application is how we may appropriate the truth by way of example or analogy.

[166] Although this passage also has a future prophetic aspect as well.

## IN DEFENSE OF THE TEXTUS RECEPTUS

The "purity" of the scripture is a natural outcome of the process of inspiration. Since the words of scripture are given by a pure and holy God, and since the very words of the scriptures were guided by the Holy Spirit so that the writers penned exactly what God wanted, then the scriptures are pure. Thus, we can not separate "purity" from the doctrine of inspiration.

If we were to assume that the human writers could somehow insert their own words or thoughts as they penned the scriptures, then we must conclude that we have NEVER had the pure Word of God. But since we believe that the scriptures are God's very words, word for word, we know that we DO have the pure Word of God. Notice that Jesus spoke of how it is possible to "make the word of God of none effect". But making the word of God of none effect does not mean it did not exist. Only that their traditions hindered the effect of the word of God in the lives of others.

> **Mark 7:13** *Making the word of God of none effect through your tradition, which ye have delivered: and many such like things do ye.*

This was Christ's charge against the religious crowd of his day who, because of religious tradition, had set aside the Old Testament commands. He was specifically referring to the Hebrew scriptures. The Jewish leaders would not have used a translation as there was no need to do so.

In this case, "word of God" would certainly apply to the recorded words of the Old Testament in a corporate sense. A corporate use of the term is often found in the Bible (Acts 18:11; Acts 19:20; Rom 9:6; Rom 10:17; 1 Cor 14:36; 2 Cor 2:17; 2 Cor 4:2; Eph 6:17; 1 Tim 4:5; 2 Tim 2:9; Tit 2:5; Heb 4:2,12; Heb 6:5; Heb 13:7; 1 Pet 1:23; 1 John 2:14; Rev 1:2, 9; Rev 6:9; Rev 20:4)

> **Luke 4:4** *And Jesus answered him, saying, It is written, That man shall not live by bread alone, but by every word of God.*

This verse is actually a quote from Deut 8:3. ". . .man doth not live by bread only, but by every *word* that proceedeth out of the mouth of the LORD doth man live."[167] The quote in Deuteronomy, in its context, is a statement to the Jews of how God taught them to rely on God's provisions and promises, and not on

---

[167] Interestingly, much ado is made over the use of italicized words in the King James Version yet Jesus uses the Greek word "ρηματι" (rhemati- from rhema) whereas the Old Testament Hebrew word "כל" (kole) simply means "whatsoever". This is just one indication that the King James translators knew what they were doing. They were not adding to the scriptures, as some like to assert. They were simply placing in the English language what was necessary for the full meaning to be seen. One the other hand, some teach that the italicized words are inspired based upon this verse. But the reality is that a noun is needed after "every" and "word" is the obvious inference.

their own circumstances. Jesus was simply applying this truth to his present situation.

Consider Luke 8:11 where Jesus makes another general reference to the word of God:

> ***Luke 8:11*** *Now the parable is this: The seed is the word of God.*

This is Jesus' interpretation of a parable where he refers to the "seed" which is sown as the "word of God". He is obviously referring to the gospel message since the thrust of the parable is about the reception and fruitfulness of different soils, or persons, as they receive the seed. This application of the term is also found several times in the Bible. (Luke 8:21; Luke 11:28; Acts 8:14; Acts 11:1; Acts 13:5; Acts 13:7; Acts 13:44; Acts 13:46; Acts 17:13; 1 Thess 2:13)

Again, these verses are not necessarily limited to the Gospel message as we are quite sure that a few of these passages refer to preaching or teaching of other subjects. The point being made here is that the use of the phrase "word of God" is steadily applied to the Gospel proper (i.e., the death, burial, and resurrection of Jesus Christ).

> ***John 10:35*** *If he called them gods, unto whom the word of God came, and the scripture cannot be broken;*

This is one of the more powerful verses of scripture concerning itself. First, it is a clear statement concerning the absolute sovereignty of God in that if He said it in His word, it WILL happen, no matter what. Secondly, it is also a promise of God's perfect preservation. But also, it defines "word of God" as "scripture" by using the two terms synonymously.

### "Word of God" Used in Reference to Preaching or Evangelism

> ***Acts 6:2*** *Then the twelve called the multitude of the disciples unto them, and said, It is not reason that we should leave the word of God, and serve tables.*

In a few cases, the term is used in a very broad and generalized sense. In some cases it applies not so much to the scriptures themselves but to the ministry thereof. Although it may be argued that the apostles were referring to their need for time in the scriptures, and this certainly could be true, there are also several other passages (Acts 6:7; Acts 12:24) where the term is obviously referring to the ministry of preaching or evangelism with the Word of God.

### "Word of God" is used as the Personal Name of Christ Himself

## IN DEFENSE OF THE TEXTUS RECEPTUS

***Revelation 19:13*** *And he was clothed with a vesture dipped in blood: and his name is called The Word of God.*

Although we believe that in order for a written document to be called "scripture" it must have been given by inspiration, we must be careful not to make the two terms synonymous since even in biblical usage, "the word of God" does not always apply to what was directly given by God and written down as scripture.

Obviously, in this case, the Bible is not referring to a written document at all. It is referring to Jesus Christ. This is also true in John 1:1,14.

Again, we must be careful in how we equate the term "word of God" with the term "scripture". Scripture is given by inspiration. But when we speak of the use of the "Word of God" we must ensure that contextually, it is referring to what has been written as versus some other application of the term.

In conclusion, any part of any translation, rightly translated, and in full agreement with the Greek or Hebrew text, can be called scripture. We would state with the translators, the message of God to man, though it may not be perfectly translated, and may not share the same beauty or accuracy that we would find in the King James. Version, may be referred to as the Word of God, though it may not be accurate in all places.

I have heard a preacher say, "If your have your King James Bible tonight, turn to John 1:9. If you have any other translation, throw it on the floor and we will sweep it up with the rest of the trash at the end of the church service." Can you imagine a newly-saved person hearing something like this? He may not be carrying the best translation but "trash"? Pretty harsh.

Any correctly translated passage of scripture, in any translation, can be referred to as the inspired Word of God, if it is in agreement with the Textus Receptus. That being said, we also realize that many verses in the Critical text are exactly the same as in the Textus Receptus. Those places where the Critical text does not match the Textus Receptus, we conclude that the passage is inferior. There are quite a number of verses that read exactly the same in translations other than the King James Version. Should we condemn a verse simply because it is in an inferior translation taken from an inferior Greek text? The issue is whether or not a verse is correct.

# IN DEFENSE OF THE TEXTUS RECEPTUS

## APPENDIX C – THE MAJORITY TEXT

The Majority text is a new text which is often called either the "Hodges-Farstad text" or sometimes "Robinson-Pierpont" Text. Although these are two separate works, they are often lumped together because of the methods and philosophy in their creation.

It has often been pointed out that there are a great many similarities between the Textus Receptus and the Majority text. There is good reason for this. Since the majority of the extant manuscripts are Byzantine, it stands to reason that the Majority text will be heavily Byzantine in its text as well. And since the Textus Receptus was constructed from Byzantine manuscripts as well, the Majority text and the Byzantine manuscripts would naturally be very similar. Yes they are similar but there are still over 1000 differences![168]

In the construction of the Majority text, each Greek manuscript is considered as one witness to the readings that it contains. In this way, each variant is given equal weight with all the other variants in a passage. Basically, the variant with the most witnesses is considered the correct reading.

Initially, this sounds like a pretty good method but there are problems with this that we need to take into account. The first problem is really simple logic. The majority is not always right. And the only valid way to know if the majority IS right is if there is an established standard to measure the majority with. In the case of the Textus Receptus, the Byzantine family of manuscripts are the standard. It has been the family of manuscripts used and preserved since the beginning. With the majority text, there is no standard. It is more of a popularity contest. The variant with the most votes wins. Let's not forget that there was a time when the majority of the scientists believed that the world was flat. Even today, the majority of scientists believe in evolution. So simply being in the majority does not make someone right, does it?

Another problem is that although the Majority text is supposed to be a text constructed from all the extant manuscripts, in practice, this is just not possible. To begin with, a healthy number of the manuscripts have never really been studied or collated to determine the common readings on a verse-by-verse

---

[168] Dr. Daniel Wallace, professor of New Testament Studies at Dallas Theological Seminary, gave an exact count of 1838 differences but since the Majority text has been revised since then, this number may no longer be accurate.

level. According to some scholars, less than 80% of the Byzantine manuscripts were even considered in the construction of this text.

A third major problem with the Majority text is that the editors made the conscious choice to ignore the witness of ancient versions, the writings of early Christians, or lectionaries. And that is crucial in helping us determine what text type was truly in use in the early centuries. Notice this statement by the editors:

*The present edition does not cite the testimony [1] of the ancient versions or [2] church fathers. [3] Nor are the lectionary texts considered. This Is not because such sources have no value for textual criticism. Rather; it is due to the specific aims of this edition, in which the primary goal has been the presentation of the Majority Text as this appears in the regular manuscript tradition (The Greek New Testament According to the Majority Text, edited by Zane Hodges, published by Nelson, 1982, p. xviii).*

A fourth problem, and perhaps the most crucial, is that the approach taken toward to manuscripts is not really one of faith at all. The editors of the Majority text readily admit that they do not believe they have the right text. They are trying to recover the original readings, just as Westcott and Hort were, the exception being that they do not limit themselves to the Alexandrian family alone. The Majority Text is viewed as a fluid text that has the ability to change based upon new evidence. Again, this sounds logical until we consider what it really means to the doctrine of preservation.

If we say that we are seeking to recover the true readings, we are, in practicality, also saying that we do not believe we have the true readings yet and we must find them. This is admitted by the editors of the Hodges and Farstad text:

*"The editors do not imagine that the text of this edition represents In all particulars the exact form of the orlginals. Desirable as such a text certainly is, much further work must be done before it can be produced. It should therefore be kept in mind that the present work, The Greek New Testament According to the Majority Text, Is both preliminary and provisional. It represents a first step in the direction of recognizing the value and authority of the great mass of surviving Greek documents. The use made of those documents In this edition must be subjected to scrutiny and evaluation by competent scholars. Such scrutiny, If properly carried out, can result in further progress toward a Greek New Testament which most accurately reflects the inspired autographs." (Introduction," page x, The Greek New Testament According to the Majority Text, Zane C. Hodges/Authur Farstad, Thomas Nelson Publishers, 1982).*

## IN DEFENSE OF THE TEXTUS RECEPTUS

Below is a list of some of the major differences between the Textus Receptus and the Majority text. I would like to emphasize that these are not all the differences but a list of those differences which change the meaning of the passage in some way. There are hundreds more differences, which, if we believe in verbal-plenary inspiration (and we do!) give us plenty of reasons to make a choice between the two texts.

**Matthew 3:11** - Majority text omits "and [with] fire" after "Holy Ghost". This is a significant change because the statement "and with fire" was a reference to judgement. Without this phrase, the verse is limited to teaching only about Pentecost and misses the context of the next verse.

**Matthew 5:47** - Majority text changes "brethren" to "friends". The meaning of the text is not really affected as far as the main teaching is concerned but there is a difference between a friend and a brother.

**Matthew 6:18** - Majority text omits "openly" after "reward thee". Meaning is not affected much except that were do not get to know how we will be rewarded.

**Matthew 8:15** Majority text changes "unto them" to "unto him". Clear change to the meaning of the text.

**Mat 10:8** - Majority text omits "raise the dead" after "cleanse the lepers". Overall meaning not greatly affected except that the disciples are now under no obligation to raise the dead.

**Mat 12:35** - Majority text omits "of the heart" after "good treasure". This appears to be an attempt to make the parallelism of the verse more obvious.

**Mat 21:7** - Majority text changes "they set him" to "he sat". Did they set Jesus down or did he set himself? The point is, his disciples did it. He did not do this of himself.

**Mat 23:25** - Majority text changes "excess" to "unrighteousness". This is a big change. The Greek word is only used twice and in the second case (1 Cor 7:5) it would make restraining oneself during fasting an unrighteousness act.

**Mat 27:35** - The Majority Text omits the following words: "that might be fulfilled which was spoken by the prophet, They parted my garments among them, and upon my vesture did they cast lots."

**Mark 15:3** - The Majority Text omits "but he answered nothing." The fact that Jesus did not answer is a fulfillment of prophecy and important to the story.

## IN DEFENSE OF THE TEXTUS RECEPTUS

**Luke 2:22** - Majority text changes "her purification" to "their purification". This is actually a Byzantine variant. But the correct reading is clearly "her" seeing that the law did not require Joseph to observe any time of purification. However, the mother is in accordance with Lev 12:3,4

**Luke 14:5** - Majority text changes "an ass" to "a son". This is another example where the meaning is not affected but even the context itself should have made it clear that "an ass" would be the correct parallel to "an ox". Jesus had just used the ox and ass together in Luke 13:15 dealing with the same problem.

**Luke 17:36** - The Majority Text omits "Two men shall be in the field; the one shall betaken, and the other left."

**John 1:28** - Majority text changes "Bethabara" to "Bethany". Bethabara is undoubtedly the correct reading. Please refer to the section on scribal errors for a fuller explanation.

**Acts 8:37** - The Majority Text omits "And Philip said, If thou believest with all thine heart, thou mayest. And he answered and said, I believe that Jesus Christ is the Son of God". In this case, the Majority text comes into agreement with the Critical text. This is unfortunate since it can be clearly shown that the reading is authentic. See Appendix D for fuller discussion.

**Acts 9:5** - The Majority Text omits "[it is] hard for thee to kick against the pricks" at end of the verse.

**Acts 9:6** - The Majority Text omits "And he trembling and astonished said, Lord, what wilt thou have me to do? And the Lord [said] unto him" at beginning of verse. Acts 9:5,6 both agree with the Critical text which is proof that the editors were less than academically honest in calling their text "Byzantine", which is an assertion that is made.

**Acts 13:23** - Majority text changes "a Saviour, Jesus" to "salvation". Although this is certainly true. The point is that their salvation was Jesus. Incidentally, this is the only place in Paul's sermon where Jesus is specifically named. We understand that Paul is referring to Jesus from the things that he says in his sermon. But Paul's audience may not have.

**Acts 15:34** - The Majority Text omits "Notwithstanding it pleased Silas to abide there still". Yet another place where the Majority text agrees with the Alexandrian manuscripts although the passage was included by Stephanus and Beza based upon Greek manuscript support that they had at their disposal.

**2 Cor 7:12** - Majority text changes "our care for you" to "your care for us". Majority text agrees with the Alexandrian text against the Byzantine texts.

*God's Preserved Word to Every Generation*

This is one place where the differences very clearly DO make a difference in the meaning.

**1 John 2:23** - The Majority Text omits "[but] he that acknowledgeth the Son hath the Father also" after "hath not the Father". There is no legitimate reason for the omission since the reading clearly Exists in A, B, C, P, Y, 5, 33, 206, 223, 323, 614, 623, 630, 1243, 1505, 1611, 1739, 1799, 2138, 2412, and 2495. It is generally believed that the reason the passage was put in italics is because the King James Version translators had secondary evidence that the reading was authentic but did not have any Greek support at the time. Since then, ample Greek evidence has been discovered.

**1 John 5:7, 8** - The Majority Text omits "in heaven, the Father, the Word, and the Holy Ghost: and these three are one" at end of verse 7 and omits "And there are three that bear witness in earth" at beginning of verse 8. See appendix D for proof of the authenticity of this passage.

**Rev 20:2** - The Majority texts adds "which deceiveth the whole world" after "Satan". The Critical text crowd often accuses the Byzantine manuscript of being corrupted by "conflation". but could this not be an example of "conflation" in the Majority text as well as the Critical Text?

**Rev 20:12** - The Majority text changes "before God" to "before the throne". Theologically, this is true. But what does the text say? And is "what does the text say" a good argument when the whole point is "what is the text SUPPOSED to say?"

Having said all this, there is still another important point to ponder. If the Majority text is the pure text, then we have only had the pure text since the 1980s. What does this say about the doctrine of preservation? The Majority text contains readings that are found in only a handful of manuscript support over and against a wealth of support for the Textus Receptus readings. Again, if we feel we have to recover a lost reading, then what we are really saying is that we don't believe God could preserve his words. Personally, I can't agree with that.

# IN DEFENSE OF THE TEXTUS RECEPTUS

## APPENDIX D – OFTEN DISPUTED READINGS

In my studies on the textual issue, I have continuously come across a small handful of references which are put forth as "questionable" or "not authentic". To which I would reply, "I am not in the habit of questioning God's Word and I would not want to be the one to claim something was not authentic when it was."

Initially, I was simply going to ignore the allegations made against the following passages. However, they came up so often that I came to the conclusion that they should be addressed for the sake of those who may not have the time or references to research it for themselves. The sad thing about all of this is that most of this information is readily available in libraries or on the internet. The truth is not hidden. It may have been obscured but those who really desire to know it can find it.

There is not time or space to deal with every disputed passage. That would take the writing of another complete book. I have chosen the most often referenced passages with a couple of objectives in mind.

First, the reason these are the most referenced passages is because, in the minds of the Bible critics, they are the most doubtful and the hardest to defend. We shall see that they are not hard to defend. And if our critics were to be totally honest, they have probably come across the same information I am about to share but DISMISSED it because it didn't fit their theology.

Second, I want to give the reader a quick reference of information so that when he reads a footnote in his Bible that says, "this passage is missing in many manuscripts; the Syriac, Arabic, and Coptic versions; and is regarded as spurious by Dr. Big-shot and his sidekick, Tobias", the reader can reference the truth. Or when he reads, "This passage is not found in the oldest and most reliable (best) manuscripts" he may understand that they really mean, "this passage is not found in the Codex Vaticanus or Codex Sinaiticus which, in my OPINION, are better than the Textus Receptus"

Now, if it sounds like I am a bit upset about all of this, I am. For the life of me, I cannot understand why anyone would want to tear down the only thing that can change a man or his eternal destination. Why would anyone want to cast doubt, unreasonable doubt, on God's Word? What makes a man think he is smart enough to find something that 2000 years and countless millions of others have not found? How dare we criticize God's eternal Word?

But enough preaching! Let's take a look at the passages:

## IN DEFENSE OF THE TEXTUS RECEPTUS

### MARK 16:9-20

One of the sharpest differences between the Byzantine manuscripts and the Alexandrian manuscripts are the last twelve verses of the Gospel of Mark. And for those who seriously try to study Mark 16, he will read in the commentaries:

*"This, to the conclusion of the Gospel, is wanting in the famous Codex Vaticanus, and has anciently been wanting in many others." (Adam Clarke's Commentary on the Bible)*

*"This has been greatly doubted for the following reasons: (1.) They are not found in the two oldest and best manuscripts of the New Testament (the Sinaitic and the Vatican); but in one of them (the Vatican) there is a column left blank after Mar 16:8, and the words: 'According to Mark,' while in every other instance the next book begins on the next column. In some other manuscripts it is indicated that the passage is doubtful. (2.) In the times of Jerome (d. 419), according to the testimony of some Church Fathers, the passage was wanting in most copies. (3.) The section contains no less than twenty words and expressions not found elsewhere in Mark's Gospel, and has a compendious and supplementary character." (A Popular Commentary on the New Testament)*

*"The passage from verse 9 to the end is not found in the two most ancient manuscripts, the Sinaitic and Vatican, and others have it with partial omissions and variations. But it is quoted by Irenaeus and Hippolytus in the second or third century." (Scofield Reference Notes, 1917 Edition)*

Their point is that since the passage is not found in their pet manuscript, the Alexandrian manuscripts, then the passage must be wrong because they will never entertain the possibility that their Critical text is wrong! Unfortunately for them, but fortunately for us, there is a wealth of information that proves the passage is genuine.

But to be totally academically honest. There is more than just two endings to the book of Mark. So now for a bit more information:

**There is the ending which ends at v. 8**. This particular ending is the one used in the critical text. I understand that the longer passage is often placed in brackets depending upon who's copy you happen to purchase. But there is usually a footnote explaining that the bracketed text is not in the "older and better manuscripts". But to be academically accurate, we should at least acknowledge that there is compelling evidence of the longer endings existence even before the highly revered codices.

*God's Preserved Word to Every Generation*

## IN DEFENSE OF THE TEXTUS RECEPTUS

The reality is that in all of the Greek manuscripts that SHOULD have this passage, only three do not - the Codex Vaticanus, Codex Sinaiticus, and minuscule 304. It is not surprising that it would be missing in the two mentioned codices. But again, those who tell us that the passage is missing in "the oldest and most reliable manuscripts" are usually not academically honest enough to tell us the full truth. The full truth is that one of their Alexandrian codices, Codex Regius, contains BOTH endings to Mark. Codex Alexandrinus, classified as Alexandrian, is actually Byzantine in the Gospels. This includes the long ending of Mark 16:9-20. But for some reason, the Critical text crowd rarely ever divulges this information.

I find it almost incomprehensible that a gospel (good news) would end with , "for they were afraid." The statement practically begs for more.

***There is the shorter ending that is added on to that.*** I have found some references made to this ending by various writers in the field of Textual criticism but none who believe that it is original. Many of them base their decision on the vocabulary used in this ending - stylistically unlike the rest of the gospel. One expression, "the sacred and imperishable proclamation of eternal salvation," also attests to a later date and is not something that Mark would have written in the 1st century.

I am sure that someone out there will stake a claim to originality of this ending but for the most part, the general consensus is that it is spurious.

***There is the longer ending known as vv. 9-16.*** This is the ending supported by the Text Receptus and based on Byzantine manuscript evidence. There are plenty of quotations from this section by early writers as well - From the 2nd century, Papius, Justin Martyr, Irenaeus, Tertullian. From the 3rd Century – Hippolytus, Vincentius at the seventh counsel of Carthage. From the 4th Century – Eusebius, Macarius Magnes, Aphraates, Didymus, Chrysostom, Jerome, Augustine. Although some of these men also quoted from sources other than the Byzantine Texts, the fact that they quoted from a passage found only in the Byzantine text shows that not only were the manuscripts in existence, they were also in frequent use.

And of course, we also have the testimony of the Latin Vulgate. Even scholars who may disagree with the longer ending still purport that it can be dated to at least the 2nd century (For instance, James Kelhoffer believes it was added to finish off the apparent abrupt ending at verse8.).

Aland himself, though he did not support the longer ending stated that it is found in 99% of the Greek manuscripts (although it is probably more like 95%)

***There is the longer ending with the Freer Logion appended to it.*** This fourth ending is pretty much ignored by the majority of textual critics because it is clearly not written by the author. It is only found in the Codex Washintonius. Although classified by many as Alexandrian, this text is a mixture of Byzantine, Western, Caesarean, and Alexandrian readings making this a truly eclectic text.

*God's Preserved Word to Every Generation*

# IN DEFENSE OF THE TEXTUS RECEPTUS

Keep in mind that the Codex Vaticanus and Codex Sinaiticus were 4th century manuscripts. So we have to show that the passage existed, and was in use before the 4th century. And indeed we can. But let's add some more fuel to the fire. By showing that the passage was in use in the first four centuries, we are also showing that the Byzantine manuscripts were in use. And this blows a serious hole in the false theory that the Byzantine manuscripts were a later text. It also shows that the so-called "Lucian Recension" is false.

The following early church writers quoted or referred to the passage which clearly shows the existence of the Byzantine manuscripts in the first four centuries:

- **2nd Century:**
    - Papius
    - Justin Martyr made a very strong allusion to Mark 16:19 in his First Apology, chapter 45
    - Irenaeus, who lived from 130 to 202, and was a disciple of Polycarp, who was the disciple of John the apostle, quoted from Mark 16:19 and says very clearly that it was "towards the conclusion" of Mark's gospel:

*"Also, towards the conclusion of his Gospel, Mark says: 'So then, after the Lord Jesus had spoken to them, He was received up into heaven, and sitteth on the right hand of God." (Against Heresies III:10:6)*

    - Tatian, the collator of the Diatesseron included the whole section
    - Also translated into the Old Latin and Syriac Versians

- **3rd Century**
    - Hippolytus
    - Vincentius at the seventh counsel of Carthage
    - Also translated into the Coptic and Sahidic versions

- **4th Century:**
    - Eusebius
    - Macarius Magnes
    - Aphraates
    - Didymus

## IN DEFENSE OF THE TEXTUS RECEPTUS

- Chrysostom
- Jerome
- Augustine

As to Greek manuscript support, it is found in full or in part in over 600 manuscripts. The ending of Mark 16:8 seems very abrupt, and some writers state that it is too abrupt to be a proper ending in Greek. It is so abrupt that some of the people who reject this section still believe there must be another ending which has been lost in antiquity.

The reality is that in all of the Greek manuscripts that SHOULD have this passage, only three do not - the Codex Vaticanus, Codex Sinaiticus, and minuscule 304[169]. It is not surprising that it would be missing in the two mentioned codices. But again, those who tell us that the passage is missing in "the oldest and most reliable manuscripts" are usually not academically honest enough to tell us the full truth. The full truth is that one of their Alexandrian codices, Codex Regius, contains BOTH endings to Mark[170]. And Codex Regius was written in 750 AD!

It seems that I am not the only one to notice the lack of factual information either! Notice this quote from the Expositor's Bible Commentary:

*"From the ninth verse to the end of St. Mark's account it is curiously difficult to decide on the true reading. And it must be said that the note in the Revised Version, however accurate, does not succeed in giving any notion of the strength of the case in favor of the remainder of the Gospel. It tells us that the two oldest manuscripts omit them, but we do not read that in one of these a space is left for the insertion of something, known by the scribe to be wanting there. Nor does it mention the twelve manuscripts of almost equal antiquity in which they are contained, nor the early date at which they were quoted." (From the Mark 16:1-18 verse comments in Expositor's Bible Commentary)*

As we have noted before, Codex Alexandrinus, classified as Alexandrian, is Byzantine in the Gospels. This includes the long ending of. Mark 16:9-20. But for some reason, the Critical text crowd never divulges this information. . .

---

[169] Interestingly, this particular minuscule is classified as Byzantine in every other respect.

[170] Why would a manuscript have both endings? Because the scribe knew that the ending was in dispute but did not want to be the one to sit in judgement over God's Word.

## IN DEFENSE OF THE TEXTUS RECEPTUS

All of the Greek support, along with the early church writers should be enough to show the genuineness of the passage.

### I JOHN 5:7-8 - COMMA JOHANNEUM

It is hard to say which passage is more controversial. Is it Mark 16:9-20 or 1 John 5:7-8? I became aware that there were some pretty big differences years ago when, as a young preacher, I brought forth a message on eternal security from 1 John chapter 5. The title was, "The Witnesses and the Record Agree". After I preached, a man in our church who did not use the King James Version politely informed me that the three that bear record in heaven weren't actually a part of the Bible.

I was shocked. How was it possible? The context seemed to demand it. The approach of the writer seemed to demand it. Even the parallel of three on earth seemed to demand it. No clearer statement on the trinity exists in all of the Word of God. But this dear brother says it should not be in the Bible. So I started to do a little digging and what did I find? More academic dishonesty. Now, you can believe what you want to believe but if you are going to try and sway someone else, you should at least present all the info. So what is all the info?

According to the Bible, the passage should read:

*"For there are three that bear record [in heaven, the Father, the Word, and the Holy Spirit: and these three are one. And there are three that bear witness on earth,] the Spirit, and the water, and the blood; and these three agree in one."*

I have placed a portion in brackets to denote the contested portion. So, if we were to remove the disputed portion, the passage would read:

*"For there are three that bear record, the Spirit, and the water, and the blood; and these three agree in one."*

So what do the critics say?

*"It is missing in all the earlier Greek manuscripts, for it is found in no Greek manuscript written before the 16th century. Indeed, it is found in only two Greek manuscripts of any age . . . It is missing in the earliest versions, and, indeed, in a large part of the versions of the New Testament which have been made in all former times. It is never quoted by the Greek fathers in their controversies on the doctrine of the Trinity - a passage which would be so much in point, and which could not have failed to be quoted if it were genuine; and it is not referred to by the Latin fathers until the time of Vigilius, at the end of the 5th century. (Barnes' New Testament Notes)*

## IN DEFENSE OF THE TEXTUS RECEPTUS

*"We dismiss, without any misgiving, the clause respecting the heavenly Trinity from 1Jn 5:7. The sentence is irrelevant to this context, and foreign to the apostle's mode of conception." (The Biblical Illustrator)*

*"The words are not found in any Greek. MS. before the sixteenth century. They were first seen in the margin of some Latin copies. Thence they have crept into the text." (The Companion Bible, E.W. Bullinger)*

*"The words occur first towards the end of the fifth century in Latin, and are found in no other language until the fourteenth century." (Cambridge Bible)*

*"But it is likely this verse is not genuine. It is wanting in every MS. of this epistle written before the invention of printing, one excepted, the Codex Montfortii, in Trinity College, Dublin: the others which omit this verse amount to one hundred and twelve." (Adam Clarke's Commentary on the Bible)*

And that pretty much sums it up. To take the above quotes and summarize them quickly, they are all basically saying, "We have no proof". Then comes the long and drawn out explanation why an argument from silence is justified.

But the fact is, they are wrong about the silence. There really is evidence. For instance, we have a quote from Cyprian, who lived from 200 to 258 AD:

*"The Lord says, 'I and the father are one,' and again it is written of the Father, and of the Son, and of the Holy Spirit, 'and these three are one.'" (The Treatises of Cyprian I:1:6)*

Cyprian was quoting from John 10:30 in the first portion. There is no disputing that. But he goes on to say "again it is written". He is not talking about what might have been written in some other book because he is appealing to the scriptures as his authority as he defends the doctrine of the trinity. And he uses the same two verses that I would probably use in doing so. The second passage, "these three are one" can be found in no other passage of the scriptures but 1 John 5:7. He does not say, "these three agree as one". No, that would be verse 8. But he says, "these three are one".

So what are we to make of this? The answer is simple. Regardless of the allegations that this passage is "never quoted by the Greek fathers in their controversies on the doctrine of the Trinity", it most clearly was. I don't know who was the first scholar to make the allegation without checking the facts but he was wrong. And a whole lot of people have been repeating that same wrong information since then.

D.A. Carson himself points out in *The King James Version Debate*, page 29, that if an early writer quotes a passage found in a 10th century text then that gives more credibility to the passage than a manuscript whose readings cannot be traced further back than the fourth century. Now, D.A. Carson supports the Critical text. But he is right about that.

Beside all this, there is also the following supporting manuscript evidence – G. Ravianus, Dubliniensis, 61, 88 mg, 429 mg, 918, 636 mg, 629, 634 mg, Omega 110[171], 60, 173, 221, and 2318.

But what about the allegations? The critics like to point out that the passage is not found in the ancient Syriac version but the Syriac version is not really a good translation to build a case on anyway since it has been mostly restored from quotes or references made in other sources. So any problems in the Old Syriac may have come as the result of the restoration work and not of the original translation itself. John Gill writes:

*". . . as to the Syriac version, which is the most ancient, and of the greatest consequence, it is but a version, and a defective one. The history of the adulterous woman in the eighth of John, the second epistle of Peter, the second and third epistles of John, the epistle of Jude, and the book of the Revelations, were formerly wanting in it, till restored from Bishop Usher's copy by De Dieu and Dr. Pocock, and who also, from an eastern copy, has supplied this version with this text. " (From the 1 John 5:7 verse comments in John Gill's Exposition of the Bible)*

1 John 5:7 is also found in a few early Latin translations as well as Jerome's Latin Vulgate, who also made a note lamenting the fact that other translators had omitted it. So what does this tell us? It tells us that the text existed as a part of the scriptures as far back as the Latin translations are concerned. Let's remember that in 382 AD, Pope Damasus commissioned Jerome to revise the Old Latin (Old Italic) because there were so many other Latin translations in circulation. Jerome's work was based upon Origen's Hexapla for the Old Testament and revised the existing Latin translations to create the Latin Vulgate. Among other things, this shows us that 1 John. 5:7 was believed to be a part of the text as far back as 382 AD.

To be honest, at least historically speaking, 1 John 5:7 was never really a controversial text until Erasmus left it out of his first edition in AD 1516. He

---

[171] Listed as confirmed by Dr. D.A. Waite. I have not been able to verify this since I cannot find this manuscript. Dr. Waite cites evidence of some twenty manuscripts containing it (those confirmed are 61, 88mg, 629, 634mg, 636mg, omega 110, 429mg, 221, and 2318) along with two lectionaries (60, 173) and four citations by the Church Fathers (namely, Tertullian, Cyprian, Augustine, and Jerome).

claimed that he could find no Greek support for it. Later, he was provided with a Greek manuscript with the passage and so he included it in his next edition. Nowadays, it is not uncommon to read after someone who tries to cast suspicion on the validity of the manuscript provided to Erasmus. But apparently, it was good enough to convince Erasmus, who was considered one of the best intellects of his day.

John Gill, goes on to state:

*"it is cited by Athanasius about the year 350; and before him by Cyprian, in the middle, of the "third" century, about the year 250; and is referred to by Tertullian about, the year 200; and which was within a "hundred" years, or little more, of the writing of the epistle" (From the 1 John 5:7 verse comments in John Gill's Exposition of the Bible)*

From a purely logical perspective we can ask ourselves a few questions. What is gained by the inclusion of this passage? What is lost by the inclusion of this passage? What is gained by the exclusion of this passage? What is lost by the exclusion of this passage?

As to its inclusion, the teaching of that particular section, being the eternal security of the believer, is made fuller and clearer. Add to this a very direct statement, in fact the only complete statement, concerning the trinity. On the other hand, nothing is lost. If we take away 1 John 5:7, we remove the only clear teaching of the trinity. It is true that other passages can be used to support the trinity, but this is the ONLY passage that is clearly trinitarian.

Only about 500 manuscripts actually include the chapter 1 John 5. Contrary to popular belief, 10 of these manuscripts contain the passage. Metzger lists 8. Since then two more have been discovered (manuscripts #634 and Omega 110). Daniel Wallace mentions that it has also been added to the column of #117.

But the point is, these are Byzantine manuscripts.

As to its exclusion, the passage would still teach eternal security. But understanding that the complete Godhead is now in heaven giving witness of eternal life through the Son could not be learned from this passage. And the fact that both heaven and earth have a witness to this truth is very reassuring. But this depth of assurance is lost when this passage is excluded. Add to this the fact that we lose the only complete statement of the trinity made in the scriptures. So we have some Greek support, the writings of early church leaders, and common sense.

**REV 22:14 – BOOK OF LIFE**

## IN DEFENSE OF THE TEXTUS RECEPTUS

We have already dealt with the allegations made against Erasmus that he back-translated this portion from the Latin Vulgate, and therefore, inadvertently inserted "book of life" into the Greek text when, according to the critics, it should read "tree of life". Refer to the section on Erasmus' work on page 100.

But the fact remains, even if Erasmus back-translated it from the Latin Vulgate, we still need to explain why it was in the Vulgate to begin with. I remind you that Erasmus main objective was his Latin revision more so than his new Greek edition. He constructed the Greek text to support his work in Latin. So surely he would have been familiar enough with the Greek and Latin manuscripts to know which phrase to use!

To say that there is no Greek support is not correct. It is more correct to say that there is very little Greek support for the passage in reference, no matter which reading you prefer. Only 10 manuscripts out of over 6600 have this portion of scripture anyway. But there are other factors to consider.

The phrase "book of life" is found in some early translations as well. This verse is found in the Old Latin, Coptic, Syriac, Armenian, and Ethiopic translations which show it existed as far back as the 2nd century. Add to this the quotations in the writings of Ambrose (340-397 AD), Bachiarius (late fourth century), and Primasius in his commentary on Revelation in 552 AD. Some of this evidence predates the Latin Vulgate and illustrates that this reading did not originate there.

As we stated in the section on Erasmus, there currently exists Greek support for this section of scripture for every word except two – one conjunction and one particle.

### ACTS 8:37

A person who uses the New International Version wrote in to the internet to ask the question, "During bible study I noticed that Acts 8:37 was missing from my bible. Verse 36 goes straight onto verse 38. Some cursory Google searches show that this happens in the NIV but not the KJV. Is there some controversy with the verse? A translation error? Hidden conspiracy? Are there other verses of the Bible like this? What is the story here?"

Another person wrote in to a Bible study web site to ask, "Why is Acts 8:37 missing from some versions of the Bible?...Is it because it conflicts with the holy trinity?"

One person with whom I had a lengthy discussion informed me that he believed Acts 8:37 was in our Bibles because of influence from the Western manuscripts. Now, I don't have time or space to go into a lengthy discussion of the Western family of manuscripts but just know this. They are so bad that nobody uses them!

So what is the impact of this matter? It has an impact on how clearly we can teach the importance of baptism for believers only.

There are numerous places where we can show that baptism is for believers but none so clearly as here in Acts 8:37. The question is asked, "What doth hinder me to be baptized" in Acts 8:36. And then the answer of Philip is given, "If thou believest with all thine heart, thou mayest" in Acts 8:37. It doesn't get any clearer than that. You must believe before you can be baptized.

But sadly, Philip's answer is missing from the ASV, CEB, CSB, ESV, the ISV, MSG, NET, the RV, and numerous others.

Then, there are numerous more modern translations with footnotes that cast doubt on the validity of Acts 8:37.

So in many of the modern translations, according to Acts chapter 8, the only prerequisite to baptism is the existence of water. How sad.

What's the proof for this verse? After having done a lot of digging around the various authorities, this is what I have found:

According to Ellicott's Commentary, "It existed in the time of Irenæus, who quotes it (3:12), but is wanting in all the best MSS., including the Sinaitic, and many versions". Now, a point about Irenaeus. First of all, we are looking at a date around 180 AD. So this proves that the reading existed in 180 AD. Secondly, Irenaeus quoted the Byzantine manuscripts A LOT. (Can't quantify this but I know it to be true.) So MAYBE it is not as "Western" as some folks may think. Thirdly, Irenaeus was known to defend Byzantine readings over Alexandrian readings so it seems to me that he may have preferred the Byzantine manuscripts.

The earliest existing manuscript to include the verse is Codex Laudianus from the 6th century (Byzantine with Western Readings). Papyrus 37 and Papyrus 38 both date to the 200-300s and both are distinctively Western. Yet neither of them contain Acts 8:37 simply because that portion of the scriptures is not in the manuscript at all. So there is literally no GREEK evidence until the 600s. So what are we saying? Acts 8:37 does not belong in the Bible? And if it doesn't, Do we believe that God has allowed this to creep into the text as a corruption?

We also find that Cyprian luted the passage in one of his works in the 200s and Augustine quotes it again in one of his sermons in the late 300s.

## IN DEFENSE OF THE TEXTUS RECEPTUS

The Latin Vulgate generally agrees with the Alexandrian Manuscripts except in some places where Jerome kept the Old Latin readings (based primarily on Byzantine manuscripts) Since Acts 8:37 is NOT in the Alexandrian manuscripts, we must assume Jerome took this from the Old Latin manuscripts which were translated from Byzantine manuscripts. And if Acts 8:37 was in the Old Latin manuscripts (l, m, e, r, ar, ph, gig) then it must have existed by the 600s.

The verse is also found in some of the ancient Arabic Versions, according to commentator John Gill. So obviously the reading is older than 600 AD. My conclusion on Acts 8:37 is that the only reason it is in dispute is because it is NOT in the Alexandrian texts but IS in the TR.

The passage is also found in a few lectionaries, which were basically portions of scripture used in public worship services for public reading. So what does this tell us? It tells us that Christian have always accepted this verse as authentic. So why are some people questioning it now? Good question! I have a feeling the answer has nothing to do with faith.

Admittedly, we would not want to use an ancient translation, or really, any other ancient external evidence, to show "word-for-word" evidence. I'm not saying it can't be done, but it would be difficult. But it can be used to show the existence of a reading in a particular period of time.

One Bible student finally quit running around the bushes and spoke directly. He said this, "I reject Acts 8:37 as an authentic verse, not because I'm on the Alexandrian Team, and you're on the Textus Receptus Team, but rather because I'm not convinced that it was in the Bible originally".

So what is he really saying? He is saying, "I believe that God was not powerful enough to keep his promises of preservation and therefore corruption has crept in to the text. Now I have no idea whether I should believe the bible or not."

He went on to say, "The problem I have with the TR position is that a TR advocate first determines that the TR is correct, and then goes looking for the evidence to substantiate it. I think that's backwards. Consequently, any evidence becomes "good enough evidence" to substantiate the TR's reading".

But honestly, is this not what EVERYONE does? I have learned that the world is round. I KNOW the world is round. If a flat-earther shows me "evidence" to the contrary, I KNOW the evidence is somehow being misinterpreted. I may not be able to discern WHY the evidence is wrong, but I KNOW it is wrong.

## IN DEFENSE OF THE TEXTUS RECEPTUS

Many are convinced that the Critical Text is the best text. I will never be able to prove them wrong. Many believe the Textus Receptus is the best text. You will never be able to prove us wrong.

Those who say that no major doctrine is affected are either sadly misinformed, ignorant, or just flat out lying. The great doctrines of the Bible ARE affected. The doctrines are either denied, twisted or weakened. And we need to understand that this is what is happening in so many of the modern Bible translations. Those who use them find that in some cases, doctrine is twisted. In other cases, doctrine is weakened. But those of us who stand by the King James Bible don't have these problems, do we!

## HEBREWS 8:9

Now here is an interesting verse! But before we discuss this at length, we need some background information.

Hebrews 8:9 states:

***Hebrews 8:9*** *Not according to the covenant that I made with their fathers in the day when I took them by the hand to lead them out of the land of Egypt; because they continued not in my covenant, and I regarded them not, saith the Lord.*

This is a quote from Jeremiah:

***Jeremiah 31:32*** *Not according to the covenant that I made with their fathers in the day that I took them by the hand to bring them out of the land of Egypt; which my covenant they brake, although I was an husband unto them, saith the LORD:*

But then again, its not really a quote from the Hebrew. It is actually a quote from a Greek translation which appears to read exactly as the Septuagint does today. Thus, it may even be a quote from the Septuagint itself. And then, to add to the quagmire, we then translate from the Hebrew in the Old Testament and the Greek in the New Testament in English!

So it looks like the writer of the book of Hebrews didn't have a problem using a translation that is quite obviously different from the Hebrew. And what are we to make of this? Some say this is proof that the use of poor translations is somehow justifiable.

The Hebrew word in Jeremiah 31:32 is clearly, "ba'alti. "Ba'al" means "to marry". "Ti" is a common Hebrew suffix which conjugates a verb into the first person singular, past tense. In other words, the verse very clearly says "I was an husband".

*God's Preserved Word to Every Generation*

But the writer of Hebrews wrote, "I regarded them not" which is exactly what it says in the Greek. Now, there is quite a difference between "I was an husband" and "I regarded them not". The rational person would want to know why there is such a difference.

The answer is that the writer of Hebrews was quoting from a Greek mistranslation of the Book of Jeremiah. Many believe it to have been the Septuagint but it could very well have been a different Greek translation. At any rate, the Greek translation is flat-out wrong. This is quite undeniable.

So what do we have here? A New Testament writer who quotes from a bad translation. And we can't say he didn't know what he was doing becuase this particular writer had an extensive knowledge of the Old Testament, as the book of Hebrews illustrates.

So why would he quote from something that is obviously different?

Notice that I said, "different", and not, "wrong". I am choosing my words carefully because something „wrong" teaches something not true. In this case, both readings are doctrinally correct. But they are certainly not the same.

Having said all that, let me make some observations before I get to the real issue.

First of all, the overall teaching of Jeremiah's statements have been conveyed by the writer of Hebrews. But the sense of the quote is found in the earlier portion of the verse. The writer of Hebrews is using a Greek translation from the 1st century because this is what many of the non-hebrew speaking Jews of his day, living outside of Israel, would have readily understood and used. It would have been familiar to them. His emphasis is not on the latter portion of the verse but on the sense of the first portion oft he verse.

Secondly, in the margin of the book of Hebrews, this statement is rendered interrogatively, "should I have continued an husband unto them?" as an alternate translation. Keep in mind that the basic root Hebrew word is "ba'al" which has also been translated in the KJV as, "marry" (Exo 21:3, Deu 22:22, etc); or, "have dominion over" (1 Chron 4:22; Isa 26:13). The sense is obvious. "Why should I have a relationship with those who have disobeyed me?" or "Why should I regard them?" So the sense of the statement is not really lost. However, I readily admit that this would be a VERY dynamic approach from the translators of the Greek translation from which the writer of Hebrews quoted.

Thirdly, John Gill writes,

> *"Others, observing the great difference there is between the Hebrew text, and the apostle's version, have supposed a different Hebrew copy*

*from the present, used by the Septuagint, or the apostle, in which, instead of* בעלתי, *it was read either* בחלתי, *or* געלתי; *but there is no need of such a supposition, since Dr. Pocock has shown, that* בעל, *in the Arabic language, signifies to loath and abhor, and so to disregard; and Kimchi relates it as a rule laid down by his father, that wherever this word is used in construction with* ב, *it is to be taken in an ill part, and signifies the same as áçiúé, "I have loathed"; in which sense that word is used in Zechariah 11:8 and so here, I have loathed them, I abhorred* **them, I rejected them, I took no care of them, disregarded them, left their house desolate, and suffered wrath to come upon them to the uttermost."**

**By this logic, the Septuagint (or whatever Greek translation it may have been at the time) got it right.**

Dr. White has stated that there is a variant of „ga'al" in the Hebrew manuscripts. After diligently serching for this, I could not find it. If there is such a variant, I would love to see it. He, or whatever his source is, believes this to be true based upon the mistranslation from the Septuagint. There is no real credence for the change in the Septuagint. As far as I could discover, there is not one Hebrew manuscript with "ga'al" (despise). It is possible that the translators of the Septuagint believed that the letter "ain" in "ba'alti" should be changed to "chet", based on Hebrew spelling rules, and so the word should read "bachalti". This is the correct Hebrew form for "I have despised them". But then we have only shifted the problem from a quote in Hebrews of a mistranslation to a mistranslation in the KJV.

But what ist he real issue here? The question on our mind is whether or not it ia allowable for a New Testament writer to quote from a mistranslation of the Old Testament and it still be "inspired" or "preserved". The answer is yes. Consider that there are New Testament quotations from even baser sources than the Septuagint, such as Paul's quotes from stoic philosophers and Jude's quote from the Book of Enoch which is not even canonical. Bottom line: The Holy Spirit can use whatever he wants.

There are actually quite a number of extra biblical sources referred to in the Bible: the book of Jasher, the Book of the Wars of the Lord, the Book of Shemmaiah, Records of Samuel the Seer (1 Chron 29:29), etc. What was recorded in those books is not inspired or else those books would not have been lost. But apparently, God doesn't have any problems with using the words of those sources, which have been learned and embedded in the minds of the man, as God delivers that truth to man. God uses the man to record his words. That is the essence of inspiration.

Apparently the writer of Hebrews, who I believe was Paul, thought that the Greek translation contained truth, and led by the Spirit of God, he had no issues writing it down in the book of Hebrews.

Paul seems to have a knack for using writings that his audience would be familiar with. In Athens (Acts 17) he quotes from philosophers; In 1 Cor 15:33 Paul quotes from Menander, a well-known Greek Dramatist. And now, here in Hebrews 8:9, he is using the Septuagint (or some other first century Greek translation) because his audience would have been familiar with it.

If we believe that the words of the Scripture are guided by God, and we do, then whatever difference we find between the Old Testament Hebrew and the New Testament Greek, is of God's design.

And this is conjecture on my part, but in the few places where I have studied out those differences, I have found them to teach even more detail concerning their subject. In this case, we see that God was Israel's husband but they had so disobeyed Him that God was at the point of totally disregarding that relationship. This is in accordance with Jer 3:8 where God says he would divorce Israel as a lesson to Judah.

Yes, it is a mistake in the translation of the Septuagint, but God has the liberty to use it as long as it is theologically accurate. And that's why we KJV guys don't really have a big problem with it. Obviously, Paul would have known of the difference. But maybe he used it anyway because God moved him to do so. That's what inspiration is all about.

### 1 PETER 2:2

My church has a wonderful service every Friday that is completely different from anything I have seen in any other church. The men of the church, who actively memorize scripture, sit around a large table and quote Bible verses to one another. Then we discuss what those verses mean. In doing so, several things come to light.

First of all, it becomes very clear what the spiritual depth of each man really is. Secondly, it becomes very clear what translation each person uses in their private life. And then thirdly, any differences between the translations become glaringly obvious.

During one such service, one of the men was quoting from a translation that our church does not use or promote. We only allow the use of the King James

## IN DEFENSE OF THE TEXTUS RECEPTUS

Version in all preaching and teaching. So when this man began to quote from another translation, we all began looking for the differences.

This is not the first time that this man, or others like him, have quoted from other translations. And usually, the readings between the translations are fairly similar. But there are times when there are radical differences. In this case, the difference was not just radical, but I believe it is also heretical.

Take a look at the differences between the translations of 1st Peter 2:2. I have listed the Greek manuscripts first for those who can read Greek:

- **(Westcott and Hort 1881)** ὡς ἀρτιγέννητα βρέφη τὸ λογικὸν ἄδολον γάλα ἐπιποθήσατε, ἵνα ἐν αὐτῷ αὐξηθῆτε **εἰς σωτηρίαν,**

- **(Westcott and Hort / [NA27 variants])** ὡς ἀρτιγέννητα βρέφη τὸ λογικὸν ἄδολον γάλα ἐπιποθήσατε, ἵνα ἐν αὐτῷ αὐξηθῆτε **εἰς σωτηρίαν,**

- **(RP Byzantine Majority Text 2005)** ὡς ἀρτιγέννητα βρέφη, τὸ λογικὸν ἄδολον γάλα ἐπιποθήσατε, ἵνα ἐν αὐτῷ αὐξηθῆτε, **[omit εἰς σωτηρίαν]**

- **(Scrivener's Textus Receptus 1894)** ὡς ἀρτιγέννητα βρέφη, τὸ λογικὸν ἄδολον γάλα ἐπιποθήσατε, ἵνα ἐν αὐτῷ αὐξηθῆτε, **[omit εἰς σωτηρίαν]**

As you can see, The Byzantine Majority Text and the Textus Receptus both omit **εἰς σωτηρίαν.**

For those who do not read or speak Greek, these two words are typically translated in English as "unto salvation" or something similar.

Now, take a look at this partial comparison of the English translations:

- *(American Standard Version) as newborn babes, long for the spiritual milk which is without guile, that ye may grow thereby unto salvation;*

- *(Bible in Basic English) Be full of desire for the true milk of the word, as babies at their mothers' breasts, so that you may go on to salvation;*

- *(Contemporary English Version) Be like newborn babies who are thirsty for the pure spiritual milk that will help you grow and be saved.*

- *(English Standard Version) Like newborn infants, long for the pure spiritual milk, that by it you may grow up into salvation—*

- *(Revised Version) as newborn babes, long for the spiritual milk which is without guile, that ye may grow thereby unto salvation;*

- *(New International Version) Like newborn babies, crave pure spiritual milk, so that by it you may grow up in your salvation,*

*God's Preserved Word to Every Generation*

## IN DEFENSE OF THE TEXTUS RECEPTUS

- *(New American Standard) like newborn babies, long for the <u>pure milk of the word</u>, so that by it you may grow <u>in respect to salvation</u>*

- *(King James Version) As newborn babes, desire the <u>sincere milk of the word</u>, that ye may grow thereby: <u>[omit "unto salvation"]</u>*

As you can see, there are really two separate areas in the verse which we need to consider separately. The first area has to do with HOW the Greek is translated. In this case, there is no difference in the way the various Greek texts read. Yet the English translations are significantly different. This is a translational issue.

The second area which has been underlined has to do with the Greek texts themselves. In this case, we are looking at a textual difference. To add to the problem, this textual difference is translated in numerous ways in the modern English translations.

With this as our basis, and understanding why these differences exist, let's examine both aspects - The Translational Issue, and The Textual Issue.

### The Translational Issue

Just for clarity's sake, let's take another look at the Greek texts:

- **(Westcott and Hort 1881)** ὡς ἀρτιγέννητα βρέφη τὸ **λογικὸν** ἄδολον γάλα ἐπιποθήσατε, ἵνα ἐν αὐτῷ αὐξηθῆτε εἰς σωτηρίαν,

- **(Westcott and Hort / [NA27 variants])** ὡς ἀρτιγέννητα βρέφη τὸ **λογικὸν** ἄδολον γάλα ἐπιποθήσατε, ἵνα ἐν αὐτῷ αὐξηθῆτε εἰς σωτηρίαν,

- **(RP Byzantine Majority Text 2005)** ὡς ἀρτιγέννητα βρέφη, τὸ **λογικὸν** ἄδολον γάλα ἐπιποθήσατε, ἵνα ἐν αὐτῷ αὐξηθῆτε, [omit εἰς σωτηρίαν]

- **(Scrivener's Textus Receptus 1894)** ὡς ἀρτιγέννητα βρέφη, τὸ **λογικὸν** ἄδολον γάλα ἐπιποθήσατε, ἵνα ἐν αὐτῷ αὐξηθῆτε, [omit εἰς σωτηρίαν]

For those who do not read Greek, the highlighted word in the texts is the word "logikon". But if you remember, the various translations have rendered this word quite differently:

- *[American Standard Version (ASV), Revised Version (RV)] ... spiritual milk which is without guile,*

- *[Bible in Basic English (BBE)]...true milk of the word,*

- *[Contemporary English Version (CEV), English Standard Version (ESV), New International Version (NIV)]... pure spiritual milk*

## IN DEFENSE OF THE TEXTUS RECEPTUS

- *[New American Standard (NASB)]... pure milk of the word,*
- *[King James Version (KJV)] ... sincere milk of the word,*

Notice the variations! To begin with we have four different descriptions of the milk. We have spiritual milk, true milk, pure milk, and sincere milk. And I suppose these are all similar in meaning. And they are all the translator's choice for the Greek word "ἄδολος" (adolos).

Now, adolos is a construction of "a", meaning "not", and "dolos" which is found 12 times in the Bible and is translated as:

- guile (7 times) - Joh 1:47, 2Co 12:16, 1Th 2:3, 1Pe 2:1, 1Pe 2:22, 1Pe 3:10, Rev 14:5
- deceit (2 times) - Mar 7:22, Rom 1:29
- subtlety (2 times) - Mat 26:4, Act 13:10
- craft (1 time) - Mar 14:1

So the idea of "adolos" is that it is something without guile or deceit, something that is not subtil or crafty. With this in mind, either "true", "pure", "sincere", or "without guile" would be acceptable translations.

Take note of the fact that "dolos", the opposite of "adolos" is used in 1 Peter 2:1. In this case, it is translated as "guile". According to the thesaurus, "sincerity" and "truth" are acceptable antonyms for "guile". With this in mind, the BBE and the KJV are the best expressions, contextually speaking.

Five of the above mentioned translations, the ASV, RV, CEV, ESV, and NIV, add the word "spiritual". Three of the above mentioned translations say "of the word". While we can see the relationship between the two phrases, they are obviously different. The word may be spiritual but on the other hand, a man can be spiritual too. So these two translations cannot both be accurate.

Both renderings are a translation of the Greek word "λογικός" (logikos). This is where we get the English word "logic". It is the idea of being reasonable. In fact, the word is only used in two places in the New Testament - here and in Romans 12:1 where it is actually translated as "reasonable". Obviously, there is a difference between "reasonable" and "the word" so how did the translators get there from here? The answer is simple. Context.

At the end of 1st Peter chapter 1, Peter has drawn attention to the word of God:

## IN DEFENSE OF THE TEXTUS RECEPTUS

*1 Peter 1:23-25 Being born again, not of corruptible seed, but of incorruptible, by the word of God, which liveth and abideth for ever. 24 For all flesh is as grass, and all the glory of man as the flower of grass. The grass withereth, and the flower thereof falleth away: 25 But the word of the Lord endureth for ever. And this is the word which by the gospel is preached unto you.*

So even though numerous translations have used "spiritual" to translated the Greek, the phrase, "of the word" is the better rendering, in light of the context. And this is not a far stretch at all for the basic root of the word "logikos" is the word "logos". "Logos" is a Greek word that typically expresses something that is spoken. It is used over 325 times in the New Testament and is always rendered in the KJV as something that is spoken. Thus, when considering the context of 1 Peter 2:2, "of the word" seems most logical.

But what about using the English word "spiritual" to represent "logikos"? Again, words are defined by the their context and in this case, Peter uses the word "spiritual", or, "pneumatikos" (πνευματικός) in verse 5. And there is no argument about the meaning of this word. It is translated as "spiritual" in over 25 places. So it stands to reason that if Peter meant to say "spiritual" in such a close context, that he would have used the same word.

Another point that should be made is the difference in the way Peter used "logikos" as versus his usage of the word "pneumatikos". Symantically speaking, "logikos" is used in a concrete sense whereas "pneumatikos" is being used in more of a metaphorical sense (Christians are not stones in a house in the literal sense).

So even in usage, it stands to reason that if Peter meant to say "spiritual" in verse 2, and meant it to be a metaphorical adjective to "milk", he would have used "pneumatikos" instead of "logikos".

Typically, Peter's use of vocabulary is that he uses the same words, or their cognates, in the same fashion throughout his writings. And as we have already seen, "logikos" is from the word "logos". So how does Peter use the word logos? Does he use it metaphorically or in a more concrete and literal sense?

As the verses below will attest, every use of the word "logos", to include all of the biblical Greek cognates, are used in a very concrete and literal manner.

*1 Peter 1:23 Being born again, not of corruptible seed, but of incorruptible, by the <u>word</u> of God, which liveth and abideth for ever.*

## IN DEFENSE OF THE TEXTUS RECEPTUS

*1 Peter 2:8 And a stone of stumbling, and a rock of offence, even to them which stumble at the <u>word</u>, being disobedient: whereunto also they were appointed.*

*1 Peter 3:1 Likewise, ye wives, be in subjection to your own husbands; that, if any obey not the <u>word</u>, they also may without the word be won by the conversation of the wives;*

*1 Peter 3:15 But sanctify the Lord God in your hearts: and be ready always to give an answer to every man that asketh you a <u>reason</u> of the hope that is in you with meekness and fear:*

*1 Peter 4:5 Who shall give <u>account</u> to him that is ready to judge the quick and the dead.*

*2 Peter 1:19 We have also a more sure <u>word</u> of prophecy; whereunto ye do well that ye take heed, as unto a light that shineth in a dark place, until the day dawn, and the day star arise in your hearts:*

*2 Peter 2:3 And through covetousness shall they with feigned <u>words</u> make merchandise of you: whose judgment now of a long time lingereth not, and their damnation slumbereth not.*

*2 Peter 3:5 For this they willingly are ignorant of, that by the <u>word</u> of God the heavens were of old, and the earth standing out of the water and in the water:*

*2 Peter 3:7 But the heavens and the earth, which are now, by the same <u>word</u> are kept in store, reserved unto fire against the day of judgment and perdition of ungodly men.*

As is very clear from the above passages, not once can it be shown where Peter ever used any form of "logos", which naturally includes "logikos", in a metaphorical sense.

It has also been pointed out that the construction of the Greek lends itself to the translation "milk of the word". We might expect " τὸ ἄδολον γάλα λογικόν " which literally means "the pure milk *which is* reasonable " if we wanted to say "spiritual milk". Instead we find "τὸ λογικὸν ἄδολον γάλα " which would tend to show that Peter was referring back to a known topic. In this case, the topic would be "the word" from 1 Peter 1:23.

The Jamieson, Fausset and Brown Commentary has this to say:

*"Not as Alford, "spiritual," nor "reasonable," as English Version in Rom 12:1. The Greek "logos" in Scripture is not used of the reason, or mind, but of the WORD; the preceding context requires that "the word" should be meant here;*

**God's Preserved Word to Every Generation**

*the adjective "logikos" follows the meaning of the noun logos, "word." Jas 1:21, "Lay apart all filthiness ... and receive with meekness the engrafted WORD," is exactly parallel, and confirms English Version here."*

Of course, other sources stating the same position could be sited, but for the brevity of this article we should move on to the next point.

## The Textual Issue

In my mind this is the bigger problem of the two issues. This issue, the textual issue, has a doctrinal impact on two levels. First, there are the subjects of inspiration and preservation in relation to the Greek text. And then, secondly, there is the issue of false teaching.

But before we get into all of that, let's get the facts straight. As in the introduction above, there is a very important variant reading at the end of the verse. The Westcott/Hort texts (which includes the Nestle Alands Text) contains "εἰς σωτηρίαν" (eis sōtērian) which is accurately translated as "into salvation". However, the Textus Receptus (and Byzantine Majority Text) omit this reading altogether. So the big question is whether Peter wrote these words or not.

Before we go any further, let's review some information we need to keep in mind. The difference in Greek words in a manuscript is commonly referred to as a "variant" reading. There are numerous kinds of variant readings such as missing words, added words, differences in spelling, differences in word order, and so on. And variants can be translatable, or in the case of spelling, sometimes NOT translatable. In fact, it has been estimated that over 70% of all variants are spelling differences and NOT translatable.

There are times, however, when a variant can change the meaning of sentence. One good example would be 1 John 1:4 where the variant reading in Greek changes the meaning from "that **your** joy may be full.(KJV)" to "that **our** joy may be full.(ASV)" In this case, the change does not appear to be a big theological impact yet it obviously changes the meaning of the verse.

But in the case of 1 Peter 2:2, the variant has a direct doctrinal impact. We would have to completely ignore the facts to say otherwise.

Bruce Metzger made a statement which has been put forth again by Bart Ehrman concerning the variant reading of the New Testament manuscripts. They basically say, "Essential Christian beliefs are not affected by textual variants in the manuscript tradition of the New Testament." Who are they fooling?

One of the most obvious examples is 1 John 5:7 as expressed in the Textus Receptus. This verse is the only full statement of the trinity in the whole

## IN DEFENSE OF THE TEXTUS RECEPTUS

New Testament. But it is not found in the Critical Text. I would say that the trinity is a major Bible doctrine!

But I don't think that even men like Bruce Metzger and Bart Erhman really believe what they taught because they seemed to have spent an awful lot of time and energy trying to be scholarly in the area of textual criticism!

Our first approach to any and every subject in life should be a biblical approach. And in this case, a biblical approach is crucial because the variant reading implies that if we desire spiritual milk we will grow into salvation. Obviously, this is a works-based salvation idea which is completely contrary to other passages in the Bible that speak of how we are saved. It is always by grace. it is always through faith. It is never by any work which we do - including drinking up the sincere milk of the word, as many of the modern English translations of 1 Peter 2:2 assert. That would be like saying, "If you want to be saved someday, then study your Bible more."

So is there any proof that Peter wrote this or not? Well first of all, we need to remember that we don't possess the original manuscript that Peter wrote. What we have are copies. Keep in mind that many of the manuscripts are damaged or incomplete and do not contain the passage at all. So we are confined to examining what we have to see which manuscripts testify to the authenticity of the variant, and which do not.

So when we begin to examine the manuscripts, we find that "εἰς σωτηρίαν" (eis sōtērian) can be traced as far back as the third century with its inclusion in Papyrus 72 and Uncial 01 (Codex Sinaiticus). On the other hand, Papyrus 125, which also dates to the 3rd century does not include the reading.

The reading itself is isolated to manuscripts that are in general agreement with the Critical Text. As such, it does not have a continuous stream of usage throughout the generations. And since God has promised to preserve his word to every generation (Psalm 12:6-7; 1 Peter 1:23; Psalm 105:8; Psa 100:5, etc.) we know that the reading does not bear the stamp of preservation, and thus, is not genuine. To put it more plainly, it is not a part of God's inspired words and should not be in our Bibles.

But the second issue with this reading is that it actually supports a heretical teaching. Those who argue for its inclusion appeal to various interpretations of the phrase in order to put a spin on it that sounds more doctrinally accurate. But I think the words speak for themselves.

Take another look at "εἰς σωτηρίαν" (eis sōtērian). "Eis" is a Greek word which, according to the Strong's Concordance:

**God's Preserved Word to Every Generation**

## IN DEFENSE OF THE TEXTUS RECEPTUS

*"A primary preposition; to or into (indicating the point reached or entered), of place, time, or (figuratively) purpose (result, etc.); also in adverbial phrases.. . . .Often used in composition with the same general import, but only with verbs (etc.) expressing motion (literallyor figuratively." (Strong's Number G1519)*

So "eis" indicates the point reached. It indicates motion. And as it is used in 1 Peter 2:2, there really is no other acceptable way to translated "eis sōtērian" except to say "grow into/unto/to salvation". And since we know the Bible teaches salvation by grace, then we cannot grow into salvation by feasting on the sincere milk of the word.

There have been attempts to lessen the impact of this problem by changing the way it is translated. Both the Holman Christian Standard Bible and the New American Standard Bible have said "so that you may grow by it for your salvation" (HCSB) or "by it you may grow in respect to salvation"(NASB). Nevertheless, one would have to be less than literal in their translation of the Greek "eis sōtērian". Again, the phrase must be translated as "grow into/unto/to salvation" if we want to translate it literally.

But nobody grows into salvation. A person is immediately saved as soon as they ask Christ to save them. Salvation is not a process. Salvation is a one-time event which is binding and sure forever. And that may be why some of the modern English translations has taken the same approach that the translators of the HCSB and the NASB did.

So what is the final conclusion? It is not possible that "εἰς σωτηρίαν" (eis sōtērian) could be a legitimate reading because it does not bear the stamp of preservation, having fallen out of use for hundreds of years (along with all the other Alexandrian manuscripts). It is not possible that it is written from the hand of Peter because it introduces a false teaching that neither God nor Peter would have allowed. And no amount of textual gymnastics can clear up these issues.

### JOHN 7:53 - JOHN 8:11 - PERICOPE ADULTERAE

Another passage that is often doubted as to its validity is the story of Jesus and the woman caught in adultery. This passage is also known as the Pericope Adulterae. According to a number of so-called experts, this story should not be in the inspired scriptures. Their reasons are:

- "Most of the ancient authorities omit John 7:53 – 8:11. Those which contain it vary much from each other." (ASV marginal note)
- Some of the manuscripts which contain this passage place it in varying places in the text.

## IN DEFENSE OF THE TEXTUS RECEPTUS

- Some state that the story breaks the flow of the narrative from John 7:52 to John 8:11.
- There are 14 different distinct Greek words that John never uses anywhere else in the Gospel.

Sounds like a pretty open and shut case right? Except it is not that simple. The sheer volume of manuscripts that include the passage is a very strong argument for its inclusion.

It is true that some of the earlier manuscripts do not contain this passage. But which manuscripts? And why? It would be very helpful to consider the details in this discussion.

The first extant manuscript to contain the passage is Codex Bezae which is dated to roughly 450 AD and is a very mixed text with quite a number of variants. We are not using this manuscript to validate the existence of the Pericope Adulterae but rather, to identify a beginning point.

So what do we find when we look at all the existing manuscripts before Codex Bezae in 450 AD which could possibly contain this passage? We would need to consider all the manuscripts that are dated before 500 AD AND contain this section of John. There are over 150 manuscripts that are dated before 500 AD but only a small percentage of these actually contain John chapters 7 and 8, where the Pericope Adulterae would appear. Note the following:

- P66 - Alexandrian Text - does not include the Pericope Adulterae.
- P75 - Textual scholars have a high regard for P75's textual conformity to Codex Vaticanus. It lacks the Pericope Adulterae. – Alexandrian Text
- Uncial 01 (Codex Sinaiticus) - Alexandrian Text, although many corrections have been made which contain Byzantine readings. It does not contain the Pericope Adulterae.
- Uncial 02 (Codex Alexandrinus) Byzantine in the Gospels; Alexandrian Text in the rest of the books. However, there is no way of really proving it wasn't in the manuscript initially since the passage would have appeared on two leaves that have been lost.
- Uncial 03 (Codex Vaticanus) - Alexandrian Text – It is believed to be the "standard" for the Alexandrian Text. It does not contain the Pericope Adulterae.
- Uncial 04 (Codex Ephraemi Rescriptus)- A mixed text containing Byzantine and Alexandrian Text readings. This is one of the four supposed great codices (according to the scholars). It does not contain the Pericope Adulterae but interestingly enough, it DOES contain the long ending of Mark. Yet the scholars who lean upon this manuscript as an authority do not use it to argue

*God's Preserved Word to Every Generation*

for the inclusion of the Mark passage. It seems that it is okay to take away from the scriptures as long as we don't defend them! You can't have your cake and eat it too.

- Uncial 032 (Codex Washingtonianus) - Originally contained the four complete gospels but now is missing Mark 15:13-38, John 14:27-16:7. John 1:1-5:11 were most likely replaced by a later scribe - Byzantine in Matthew and Luke 8 to the end - Western, Caesarean, and Alexandrian in other areas. The passage in John where the Pericope Adulterae would have been written is Alexandrian. And the Pericope is not there.
- Uncial 029 = 0139 – Mainly in agreement with the Alexandrian Text but a few believe it also contains a few Byzantine readings as well. The passage in question would have been in a section of the manuscript which was translated into Sahidic. It does not contain the Pericope Adulterae.

The average Bible student is told to believe the lie that there is very little evidence for the inclusion of the Pericope Adulterae but how true is that? Absolutely untrue. Consider the following defense made by Burgon in "Causes of Corruption":

- Ambrose at Milan (374) quotes it at least nine times; as well as Augustine in North Africa (396) about twice as often.
- It is quoted by Pacian, in the north of Spain (370)
- by Faustus the African (400)
- by Rufinus of Aquilea (400)
- by Chrysologus at Ravenna (433)
- by Sedulius a Scot (434)
- It is referred to by Victorius or Victorinus (475)
- by Vigilius of Tapsus (484) in North Africa
- by Gelasius, bishop of Rome (492)
- by Cassiodorus in Southern Italy
- by Gregory the Great

And that's not all. Other than Dean Burgon's information, there are citings that he did not mention, such as:

- Quoted in the Didascalia Apostolorum (around 230 AD)
- Mentioned in the Apostolic Constitutions (380AD)
- Quoted by Jerome (385 AD)
- Quoted by Augustine (420 AD)

## IN DEFENSE OF THE TEXTUS RECEPTUS

Now, take note that a good portion of the people on these lists were quoting from the passage well before the scribe wrote it down in Codex Bezae which is dated to roughly 450 AD.

Since this is true, somebody has to explain how these men quoted a passage that supposedly did not exist!

In short, of the five oldest uncials, only one of them even contains the disputed passage. Two are damaged, having lost the leaves which may have contained the passage. Only two of the uncials can truly be described as categorically NOT containing the passage.

So it is pretty clear why the passage is not in the "older and most reliable manuscripts" (I speak in sarcasm. This is the line that the Critical text crowd consistently uses). The manuscripts are all Alexandrian in the portions where the Pericope Adultera would have been written. In my opinion, the reason that the Critical Text crowd denies the authority of the passage is because, if the passage is received as authentic, then their darling manuscripts must be inferior.

Let me just point out one more thing that we should think long and hard about. If the Pericope Adulterae was in the manuscripts of the Byzantine family, and the Alexandrian family had fallen out of use, we have either accept it as authentic or come to the conclusion that for hundreds of years, we had no pure word of God because it was corrupted. Like I said, we can't have our cake and eat it too.

## APPENDIX E – THE SEPTUAGINT

The Septuagint, also referred to as the LXX, is the oldest Greek translation of the Old Testament. It is said to have been translated by 70 (or possibly 72) Jewish scholars who were living in Alexandria, Egypt. The city itself was founded in 332 BC and at that time, Alexander the Great granted the Jewish people citizenship. Based upon this fact alone, we know that there had to be a very strong Jewish presence in the city.

There are a couple of theories as to why the Greek translation was accomplished. One idea is that the Jews of Egypt had begun to forget Hebrew and spoke Greek instead. Therefore, they needed a Greek translation. This is very possible and even the New Testament speaks of "Grecians" who were basically hellenized Jews.

A second theory is based on a story found in a letter called, *The Letter of Aristeas*. The letter claims that Demetrius Phalereus, who ran the royal library in Alexandria, asked the king to get a copy of the Jewish law for the library. The King, Philadelphus sent some representatives to the high priest Eleazar in Jerusalem, and requested help. In turn, the high priest sent 72 elders to Egypt with a copy of the Hebrew law written on rolls of skins in golden letters. According to the legend, the 72 translators were separated into 72 different rooms on the island of Pharos where they each did a complete translation of the entire Old Testament in 72 days. When they were finished, supposedly, every one of the translations were the same. The same basic account is repeated in the writings of Aristobulus, Philo, and Josephus.

But, other than the letter itself, there really is no proof that the story is factual. Others have simply repeated what someone else said about it as if it were fact, when in fact, it is more legend than anything else.[172] As a translator, I am inclined to believe it is simply impossible. It would take longer than 72 days just to accomplish the Torah, much less the rest of the Old Testament. Additionally, for 72 people to have all done the exact same translation would definitely require an act of God. And if it was an act of God, then why is the LXX so obviously different from the Hebrew text in so many places? Couldn't God make up his mind? Sorry but I just don't buy it!

---

[172] I ask the reader to call to mind what was said earlier about a position that I called, "the parrot position". This is where a person repeats what he has been taught but has never really sought to validate the teachings for himself.

## IN DEFENSE OF THE TEXTUS RECEPTUS

It is no secret that the LXX has certain translational problems. And if we are aware of it in our day, I am quite sure that those who knew both Greek and Hebrew of the first century could see the mistakes too. And that may be one reason why, in time, other Greek translations were accomplished.

For instance, a proselyte to Judaism named Aquila completed a translation of the Old Testament into Greek about the year A.D. 128. Other translations were made by Theodotion of Ephesus and a certain Symmachus, called an Ebionite, also in the second century A.D.

The Septuagint departs from the Masoretic text frequently. By one count, there are over 190 differences between the LXX and the Masoretic text. One writer states:

*"The book of Jeremiah is noteworthy in that the present Hebrew text differs substantially from the Greek version (the Septuagint) in both content and order. Thus the Septuagint omits several passages (e.g., 33.14-26) and combines the oracles against foreign nations into a single section following 25.14, though in a different order. In addition, there are many smaller differences from verse to verse. Remarkably, among the portions of the text of Jeremiah in Hebrew that are found among the Dead Sea Scrolls are not only those that reflect the standard Hebrew text but also those that reflect the text tradition represented by the Septuagint. It is likely, then, that these two text traditions represent the contrasting editorial work on the book of Jeremiah that took place in Egypt (the Septuagint tradition) and in Palestine or Babylon (the traditional Hebrew text)." (Introduction to the book of Jeremiah, The New Oxford Annotated Bible, page 960.)*

Another issue between the LXX and the Masoretic text is the canon of scripture. The LXX includes 1 Esdras; Tobit; Judith; 1-3 Maccabees; the Wisdom of Solomon; the Wisdom of Sirach (Ecclesiasticus); Baruch; the Epistle of Jeremiah; The Song of the Three Children; Daniel and Susanna; Daniel, Bel and the Dragon; Additions to the Book of Esther; Psalm 151; and the Prayer of Manasseh.

But one thing is certain. There are numerous places where the currently used LXX and the New Testament agree quite well. Note the following passages:

- "Their throat is an open sepulcher" - Ps. 5:9 quoted in Rom. 3:13

- "Out of the mouth of babes" – Ps. 8:2 quoted in Matt. 21:16

- "What is man, that thou art mindful of him?" - Ps. 8:4-6 quoted in Heb. 2:6-8

- "Whose mouth is full of cursing and bitterness" - Ps. 10:7 quoted in Rom. 3:14

## IN DEFENSE OF THE TEXTUS RECEPTUS

- "They are together become unprofitable" - Ps. 14:1-3 quoted in Rom. 3:10-12
- "Thou wilt not leave my soul unto Hades" - Ps. 16:8-11 quoted in Acts 2:25-28
- "Their sound went out into all the earth" - Ps. 19:4 quoted in Rom. 10:18
- "I will declare thy name unto my brethren" - Ps. 22:22 quoted in Heb. 2:12
- "Sacrifice and offering thou wouldest not" - Ps. 40:6-8 quoted in Heb. 10:5-6
- "That thou mightest be justified in thy words" - Ps. 51:4 quoted in Rom. 3:4
- "They are together become unprofitable" - Ps. 53:1-3 quoted in Rom 3:10-12
- "Let their table be made a snare" – Ps. 69:22-23 quoted in Rom. 11:9-10
- "He gave them bread out of heaven to eat" - Ps. 78:24 quoted in John 6:31
- "Today, if ye shall hear his voice" - Ps. 95:7-8 quoted in Heb. 3:15 and 4:7
- "And they all shall wax old as doth a garment" - Ps. 102:25-27 quoted in Heb. 1:10-12
- "I believed, and therefore did I speak" - Ps. 116:10 quoted in 2 Cor. 4:13
- "The Lord is my helper" - Ps. 118:6 quoted in Heb. 13:6
- "The poison of asps in under their lips" - Ps. 140:3 quoted in Rom. 3:13
- "For whom the Lord loveth he chasteneth" - Pr. 3:11-12 quoted in Heb. 12:5-6
- "God resisteth the proud, but giveth grace to the humble" - Pr. 3:34 quoted in James 4:6 and 1 Pet. 5:5
- "And if the righteous is scarcely saved, where shall the ungodly and sinner appear" - Pr. 11:31 quoted in 1 Pet. 4:18
- "If thine enemy hunger, feed him" - Pr. 25:21-22 quoted in Rom. 12:20
- "Except the Lord of Sabaoth had left us a seed, we should have been as Sodom" – Is. 1:9 quoted in Rom. 9:29
- "By hearing ye shall hear, and in no wise understand" – Is. 6:9-10 quoted in Matt. 13:14-15 and Mark 4:12

We can't honestly deny that they are in agreement, but the real question is "why"? Since there are obviously similarities, we have to find an explanation. A flat denial simply will not work.

So what we are dealing with here is really a three-part issue. First, did the LXX exist in the first century so that the Christians would use it? And after reading how the LXX came into being, you can understand why there are quite a few very intelligent people who actually have good reasons for questioning its existence during the time of Christ.

Second, if it did, was it revised at a later date in order to bring it into agreement with the New Testament passages? And since we are dealing with so little solid evidence, this can prove to be a bit difficult, however, not impossible.

And then thirdly, since we know that the LXX is different from the Masoretic text we should discuss whether or not it can even be considered worthy of the title "scripture" at all.

In order to prove it was revised, we have to find a copy of it from the first century and compare it to what is currently in use. And this is currently impossible since the oldest classified manuscripts of the LXX which are large enough to verify only date to the 3rd century. The oldest manuscripts of the LXX include 2nd century BC fragments of Leviticus and Deuteronomy and first century BC fragments of the Pentateuch and the Minor Prophets but these fragments are too small to actually prove they are actually LXX. They may as well be a different Greek translation with similar readings in the portions that the manuscripts contain.

As you can see, we have our work cut out for us. Find a substantially sized 1st century manuscript and then compare it to a modern document to see if it has been changed. Not an easy task, to say the least!

The manuscript evidence is spotty at best. There just simply isn't enough to state a dogmatic case one way or the other. On the one hand, we have a letter that is most certainly a legend and not true. Then we have several other authors who repeat this legend which is most certainly not true.

There is one manuscript called the Ryland's Papyrus 458 which has been dated to the 2nd century BC but it is practically impossible to use in proving our case one way or the other. Actually, 458 is 8 small pieces of papyrus written on front and back. Three of the pieces are so small that there is room for only one or two Greek letters at all. About the only thing it can prove is that a Greek translation of Deuteronomy existed and that in this place, it appear to be LXX. But I have to say that the sample size that we have to work with is incredibly small and not very conclusive. Two different translations often have a large percentage of similarity. Even the Textus Receptus and the Critical Text have a large percentage of similarity!

And then there are the discoveries in the Qumran caves.

Cave 7 contained several very small Greek fragments which included portions of Exodus 28:7 and from the apocryphal Letter of Jeremiah 43-44. Some of the fragments are so small that it is difficult to accurately identify them and it is practically impossible to compare them the LXX to see if there are any revisions.

But Cave 4 contains much longer Greek "fragments." These include a collection of small fragments from Lev. 1-11-6:5 (pap4QLXXLeviticus(b) = 4q120), fragments from Numbers 3:40 - 4:16 (4QLXXNumbers = 4Q121), and a fragment from Dt. 11:4 (4QLXXDeuteronomy=4Q122). In determining whether the first century LXX matches what we have today, these are of little help.

But we also have a 26-line manuscript of Lev. 26:2-16 (4qlxxLeviticus(a) = 4Q119), which dates from the first century BC and is paraphrased in 2 Cor 6:16. You may recall that Lev 26:2-16 contains a list of promises that God makes to the Jews conditional on their obedience to his commands. One part of this passage, Lev 26:12, is repeated numerous times in the Old Testament (Jer 31:33; Jer 32:38; Eze 37:26, Eze 37:27). Most likely, all refer back to Lev 26:12. And Paul must have been referring to them in 2 Cor 6:16-18 through 7:1, as he says in 7:1, " Having therefore these promises. . ."

The words of Paul in 2 Cor 6:16 is in agreement with 4Q119. And this is significant because we know that the Qumran community was destroyed in the latter part of the first century. What was found in the cave is the same as the LXX of today. And the New Testament quotation of Paul is the same as well. But what does this really mean? The only thing we can state with any surety is that Paul quoted the Old Testament. His words match the modern LXX which, in this one verse, matches an existing Greek translation from the first century.

So it appears very likely that Paul was quoting from the LXX. Or was he? As I said earlier, the sample size that we have to work with is incredibly small and not very conclusive. Two different translations often have a large percentage of similarity. So all that we can dogmatically state is that Paul quoted something in Greek that matched a Greek translation of the 1st century which reads exactly like the LXX in this particular place.

I understand that there are a few people who do not believe that what was found in the caves at Qumran was actually the LXX but was in fact a different translation.[173] In some cases, the manuscripts are too small to classify. But a number of others are quite sizable and easily verifiable with the LXX and there doesn't seem to be any difference to speak of. But once again, none of the

---

[173] This is at least partly true because the scroll known as pap7QLXXExod—a Greek text from Cave 7—is more closely aligned to the Masoretic text than it is to the Modern Greek Septuagint.

fragments give us a very substantial sample size. So the best we can say is that it MAY be LXX. But we certainly can't prove it.

Others believe it is entirely possible that Origen edited the LXX and changed it to match what was already written in the New Testament manuscripts. But in order to be sure of this, and in the interest of academic honesty, we should at least consider the counter-argument.

The counter-argument is based upon our assumptions of how a man would have acted in light of what he believed. Origen was an allegorist and as such, it stands to reason that he would not be so concerned with a word-for-word rendition of the scriptures. So why would Origen go through all the trouble of trying to fix the LXX? That is a good question. But we know that he DID make changes in the manuscripts because he marked many of the places he changed. He also marked any differences between the LXX and the Masoretic text. He would then correct the Greek text using one of the others in order to bring it into agreement with the Masoretic text.

I have personally come to the conclusion that those who ministered outside of Israel probably used a Greek translation which in many cases agreed with the LXX. Yes, it was an inferior translation. But seeing that they were ministering to people who could not read Hebrew, what else could they have done? I also believe that if they had something better, they would have used it. But apparently, they did not.

Another question that is sometimes raised is whether a translation can legitimately be considered to be "scripture" at all. But a simple examination of the use of the word "scripture" in the New Testament clearly shows that a translation can be referred to as scripture. Take for instance the passage in Luke 4:17-21.

> ***Luke 4:17-21*** *And there was delivered unto him the book of the prophet Esaias. And when he had opened the book, he found the place where it was written, (18) The Spirit of the Lord is upon me, because he hath anointed me to preach the gospel to the poor; he hath sent me to heal the brokenhearted, to preach deliverance to the captives, and recovering of sight to the blind, to set at liberty them that are bruised, (19) To preach the acceptable year of the Lord. (20) And he closed the book, and he gave it again to the minister, and sat down. And the eyes of all them that were in the synagogue were fastened on him. (21) And he began to say unto them, This day is this scripture fulfilled in your ears.*

## IN DEFENSE OF THE TEXTUS RECEPTUS

In the passage, Jesus had gone into the synagogue in his hometown Nazareth and had taken the book of Isaiah to read. He read a passage from Isaiah 61 and then closed the book and sat down. The quote in Luke 4:18-19 departs from the Masoretic Text as translated by the KJV in Isaiah 61:1-2. However, there is a missing phrase found in Luke which is not in the LXX. "To set at liberty them that are bruised".

So what do we make of this? Well, first of all, Jesus did not quote from the LXX. Secondly, Luke did not record from the LXX. And thirdly, those who say that this passage in Luke matches the LXX did not read far enough.

Keep in mind that the passage was recorded by Luke around 65-70 AD some 35 years or more after the earthly ministry of Christ and because he was writing to a man named Theophilus, who was most likely a Gentile, he probably used a Greek translation (which was not the LXX). But lets not lose sight of the original point. What Luke wrote does not match the Masoretic text. So the question is, can we call it scripture? Well, Luke did.

But in reality, what is the difference? Luke, writing under the inspiration of the Holy Spirit, believed it was scripture and he used it. So lets not make the assumption that a translation must be perfect to be called "scripture".

Another passage is in Acts chapter 8, where Philip meets the Ethiopian eunuch in the wilderness as he is reading from the scroll of Isaiah. The eunuch is actually reading from Isaiah chapter 53. Now, it is possible that he read Hebrew. But it is most likely that the eunuch read in Greek, especially since he was not from Israel. He would have known Greek but probably would not have been at least somewhat familiar with Hebrew. But notice what the passage says:

> ***Acts 8:32-35*** *The place of the <u>scripture</u> which he read was this, He was led as a sheep to the slaughter; and like a lamb dumb before his shearer, so opened he not his mouth: (33) In his humiliation his judgment was taken away: and who shall declare his generation? for his life is taken from the earth. (34) And the eunuch answered Philip, and said, I pray thee, of whom speaketh the prophet this? of himself, or of some other man? (35) Then Philip opened his mouth, and began at the same <u>scripture</u>, and preached unto him Jesus.*

The passage that the Eunuch read matches the Septuagint. Again, we must come to the conclusion that a translation can rightly be called "scripture".

We can also find several instances in the writings of Paul where the New Testament matches the Septuagint and yet Paul refers to the passage he used as "scripture". Note the following:

## IN DEFENSE OF THE TEXTUS RECEPTUS

***Romans 9:17*** *For the scripture saith unto Pharaoh, Even for this same purpose have I raised thee up, that I might shew my power in thee, and that my name might be declared throughout all the earth.*

***Romans 10:11*** *For the scripture saith, Whosoever believeth on him shall not be ashamed.*

But having looked at several historical sources, we can be relatively sure that these passages were revised through history and have good reason to read the same. On this point, I encourage the reader to review the section on the legitimacy of a translation.

We have already come to the conclusion that insofar as a translation is a faithful and accurate reflection of what God gave in the preserved Greek and Hebrew manuscripts, it can be called "scripture". We do not deny the reality that there are some translations that are so bad we would hesitate to say anything positive about them. On the other hand, there are other translations, though we would not use them, which contain the scriptures.

To again quote the translators:

*"Now to the later we answere; that wee doe not deny, nay wee affirme and avow, that **the very meanest translation** of the Bible in English, set foorth by men of our profession (for wee have seene none of theirs of the whole Bible as yet) **containeth the word of God, nay, is the word of God**. As the Kings Speech which hee uttered in Parliament, being translated into French, Dutch, Italian and Latine, is still the Kings Speech, though it be not interpreted by every Translator with the like grace, nor peradventure so fitly for phrase, nor so expresly for sence, every where."*

For the record, I do not agree with false notion that "the apostles used a faulty translation so why do we care so much about it". Just as the translators pointed out, their desire was to make of many good translations a better one which was even more trustworthy.

The King James translators in their second preface called, Translators to the Readers, wrote the following:

*"Truly, good Christian Reader, we never thought from the beginning, that we should need to make a new Translation, nor yet to make of a bad one a good one...but to make a good one better, or <u>out of many good ones, one principal good one</u>..."*

But don't come away from this statement thinking that the translators merely mixed and matched what was already done in earlier works. They certainly consulted the original languages as they so stated:

*God's Preserved Word to Every Generation*

## IN DEFENSE OF THE TEXTUS RECEPTUS

*"Neither did we think much to consult the Translators or Commentators, Chaldee, Hebrew, Syrian, Greek or Latin, no nor the Spanish, French, Italian, or Dutch; neither did we disdain to revise that which we had done, and to bring back to the anvil that which we had hammered: but having and using as great helps as were needful, and fearing no reproach for slowness, nor coveting praise for expedition, we have at length, through the good hand of the Lord upon us, brought the work to that pass that you see."*

So how does this all relate to the issue of Greek texts, LXXs, and modern translations? The point is, the translators did not settle to keep something that they knew to be inferior simply because it had a few good passages in it. They desired to produce, using everything available, a translation that was more trustworthy than anything the English world had ever seen before.

And to use the obviously flawed translation of the LXX as a justification for whatever fits your fancy, is not only faulty logic, but also, foolish.

## APPENDIX F - KJV RULES FOR TRANSLATION[174]

The King was for appointing fifty-four learned men to this great and good work; but the number actually employed upon it, in the first instance, was forty-seven. Order was also taken, that the bishops, in their several dioceses, should find what men of learning there were, who might be able to assist; and the bishops were to write to them, earnestly charging them, at the king's desire, to send in their suggestions and critical observations, that so, as his Majesty remarks, "our said intended translation may have the help and furtherance of all our principal learned men within this our kingdom."

Seventeen of the translators were to work at Westminster, fifteen at Cambridge, and as many at Oxford. Those who met at each place were divided into two companies; so that there were, in all, six distinct companies of translators. They received a set of rules for their direction.

1. The first instructed them to make the "Bishop's Bible," so called, the basis of their work, altering it no further than fidelity to the originals required...

2. The second rule requires that the mode then used of spelling the proper names should be retained as far as might be.

3. The third rule requires "the old ecclesiastical words to be kept," such as "church" instead of "congregation."

4. The fourth rule prescribes, that where a word has different meanings, that is to be preferred which has the general sanction of the most ancient Fathers, regard being had to "the propriety of the place, and the analogy of faith."

5. The fifth rule directs that the divisions into chapters be altered as little as may be.

6. The sixth rule, agreeably to Dr. Reynolds's wise suggestion at Hampton Court, prohibits all notes or comments, thus obliging the translators to make their version intelligible without those dangerous helps.

7. The seventh rule provides for marginal references to parallel or explanatory passages.

---

[174] Source Unknown

8. The eighth rule enjoins that each man in each company shall separately examine the same chapter or chapters, and put the translation into the best shape he can. The whole company must then come together, and compare what they have done, and agree on what shall stand. Thus in each company, according to the number of members, there would be from seven to ten distinct and carefully labored revisions, the whole to be compared, and digested into one copy of the portion of the Bible assigned to each particular company.

9. The ninth rule directs that as fast as any company shall, in this manner, complete any one of the sacred books, it is to be sent to each of the other companies, to be critically reviewed by them all.

10. The tenth rule prescribes, that if any company, upon reviewing a book so sent to them, find any thing doubtful or unsatisfactory, they are to note the places, and their reasons for objecting thereto, and send it back to the company from whence it came. If that company should not concur in the suggestions thus made, the matter was to be finally arranged at a general meeting of the chief persons of all the companies at the end of the work. Thus every part of the Bible would be fully considered, first, separately, by each member of the company to which it was originally assigned; secondly, by that whole company in concert; thirdly, by the other five companies severally; and fourthly, by the general committee of revision. By this judicious plan, each part must have been closely scrutinized at least fourteen times.

11. The eleventh rule provides that in case of any special difficulty or obscurity, letters shall be issued by authority to any learned man in the land, calling for his judgment thereon.

12. The twelfth rule requires every bishop to notify the clergy of his diocese as to the work in hand, and to "move and charge as many as, being skilful in the tongues, have taken pains in that kind, to send his particular observations" to some one of the companies.

13. The thirteenth rule appoints the directors of the different companies.

14. The fourteenth rule names five other translations to be used, "when they agree better with the text than the Bishop's Bible." These are Tyndale's; Matthew's, which is by Tyndale and John Rogers; Coverdale's; Whitchurch's, which is "Cranmer's," or the "Great Bible," and was printed by Whitchurch; and the Geneva Bible. The object of this regulation was to avoid, as far as possible, the suspicious stamp of novelty. To the careful observance of these injunctions, which, with the exception of the first five, are highly

judicious, is to be ascribed much of the excellence of the completed translation.

To these rules, Which were delivered to the Translators, there appears to have been added another, providing that, besides the directors of the six companies, "three or four of the most ancient and grave divines in either of the Universities, not employed in translating be designated by the Vice-Chancellors and Heads of Colleges, to be overseers of the Translation, as well Hebrew as Greek, for the better observation of the fourth rule."

The learned Selden says, that when the Translators met to compare what they had done, each of them held in his hand a Bible in some language. If any thing struck any one as requiring alteration, he spoke; otherwise the reading went on. The final revision was made, not by six men, as the tenth of the above rules would seem to indicate, but by twelve. At least, such was the statement made in the Synod of Dort in--1618, by Dr. Samuel Weird, who was one of the most active of the Translators. It seems to have been carried through the press by Dr. Miles Smith and Bishop Bilson, aided perhaps by Archbishop Bancroft and other prelates. All the expense of making and printing the translation was defrayed by Robert Barker, "Printer to the King's most excellent Maiestie." The copyright thus cost him three thousand five hundred pounds; and his heirs and assigns retained their privilege down to the year 1709.

# APPENDIX G – TERMS AND DEFINITIONS

| | |
|---|---|
| **Agnostic** | A person or position that states that the existence of God cannot truly be known. |
| **Agreement (textual)** | Textual agreement is when two manuscripts contain readings which are the same. |
| **Alexandrian Text** | The name of a family of texts. It is called "Alexandrian" because the majority of the manuscripts are associated with, or in agreement with manuscripts originating from around Alexandria, Egypt. It is a small group of discordant manuscripts which underlies the critical Text. In this book, references to the "Critical Text" is a reference to that which was constructed from the Alexandrian Texts after 1881. |
| **Apograph** | Refers to an exact copy of the original manuscript, or, autograph. |
| **Apologetics** | Biblically speaking, this refers to the written or oral defense or the Bible or its teachings. |
| **Aramaic** | A Semitic language used from around the 6th century BC to around the 7th century AD. It was the major language spoken in Israel during the life of Christ. |
| **Atheism, Atheist** | A position that sates that there is no God. |
| **Authenticity** | This refers to the credibility of a document as being from the source it claims to be from. |
| **Autograph** | This refers to the actual manuscript penned by the original writers. It is sometimes used to refer to the copies (apograph) but should not be used in this way. |
| **Byzantine** | The name of a family of texts. It is called "Byzantine" because the majority of the manuscripts are associated with, or in agreement with manuscripts originating in the Byzantine Empire. |
| **Canon** | The collection of 66 books now found in the Bible. |
| **Canonization** | The process by which the books of the bible were recognized as inspired and accepted for use. |
| **Codex** | Manuscripts which are bound in book form as versus a scroll form. It is usually made from animal skin but can be made from papyrus. Codices are normally named after the place where they were found. So the Codex Sinaiticus is a book from Mt Sinai (Actually St. Catherine's monastery) and Codex Vaticanus is a book from the Vatican. |
| **Corrupt, Corruption** | Any change, deletion, or addition to the biblical text (whether intentional or unintentional). |
| **Critical Text** | The name of the Greek manuscript composed from the Alexandrian family of manuscripts. It was done in 1881 by a committee of men of |

## IN DEFENSE OF THE TEXTUS RECEPTUS

| | |
|---|---|
| | whom Westcott and Hort are the most well known and most influential. |
| **Derivative Inspiration** | The concept that a copy or translation "derives" its inspired properties from the original autographs. NOTE: Since inspiration is not an ongoing process, nor a quality, "derivative inspiration" is not possible. |
| **Disagreement (manuscript)** | Textual disagreement is when two manuscripts contain readings which are not the same. |
| **Double-Inspiration** | Simply, the position that states that the KJV translators were supernaturally empowered to the extent that the translation itself now become the standard as versus the Texts Receipts and Masoretic Text |
| **Dynamic Equivalency** | A method of translation which is more concerned with capturing the perceived meaning of a text as versus a literal word for word rendering of the source text. |
| **Eclectic, Eclecticism** | A concept that does not hold rigidly to a single text or textual family, but instead draws upon multiple manuscripts, families, and sometimes, even extra-biblical sources in order to reconstruct a reading or text. |
| **Error (doctrinal)** | A doctrinal error is a doctrinal position which does not agree with the teachings of scripture but does not impact one's salvation. Example: mode of baptism, church polity. |
| **Error (translational)** | A variant from the source document to the target document, whether intentional or unintentional. |
| **Formal-Equivalency** | A method of translation which is more concerned with a word for word rendering of the source text as versus seeking to explain any perceived meaning. |
| **Fundamental, Fundamentalism** | In relation to biblical doctrine, it refers to a person or position who takes the Bible literally and seriously. |
| **Harmonize, Harmonization** | An attempt to make similar passages or readings match in every phrase. |
| **Heresy** | Any teaching which is contrary to the doctrine of salvation. EXAMPLE: Baptismal regeneration. |
| **Higher Criticism** | An examination of the books of the Bible in order to determine their authenticity and value. |
| **Illumination** | The act of the Holy Spirit in enabling a person to understand the scriptures. |
| **Incorruptible** | Not susceptible to corruption. |
| **Inerrancy** | Incapable of being wrong; free from any statements of error |
| **Infallible** | Incapable of making mistakes in its guidance or precepts |

*God's Preserved Word to Every Generation*

## IN DEFENSE OF THE TEXTUS RECEPTUS

| | |
|---|---|
| **Inspiration** | A process by which God breathed out his very words through holy men in order that his very words could be recorded. |
| **Interpret, Interpretation** | The act of explaining what something means in a way that is easily understood. Sometimes we speak of a translation as interpreted from a source document but in reality, that would be transmission. A translator moves the very words from one language to another whereas and interpreter seeks to explain what he believes the source meant to communicate. |
| **Lectionary** | A passage of scripture meant to be read in a public format, usually in a worship service. There are currently 2412 lectionaries and nearly all are Byzantine texts clearly showing that the Byzantine family was the preferred text. |
| **Lower Criticism** | The act of examining a passage to determine what the correct reading should be. |
| **Majuscule** | Greek manuscripts which were written in capital letters. Also referred to as uncials. |
| **Manuscript** | In relation to the Bible text, it refers to any Greek or Hebrew document which contains portions of the Bible. |
| **Minuscule** | Greek manuscripts which have lower case Greek letters, spaces, and punctuation. The paper is vellum. There are 2911 minuscules - 2853 support the Byzantine Text in full or in part. 31 support the Alexandrian Text in full or in part. 26 either mixed or unclassified. |
| **Papyrus** | Greek manuscripts, written in capital letters with no punctuation and no spaces between words. The "paper" was made from the papyrus plant and is not very durable. All are found in Egypt where the climate is dry enough to preserve the manuscripts. There are 127 papyri - 2 support the Byzantine Text in full or in part. 89 support the Alexandrian Text in full or in part. 36 either mixed or unclassified. |
| **Preservation** | The acts of God to ensure that what He gave by inspiration would never be lost, changed, or destroyed. |
| **Reading** | In regards to the scriptures, "reading" refers to a word or phrase in an extant manuscript. |
| **Revelation** | The act of God whereby He gives man a message of His truth. 2. May also refer to the last book of the New Testament. |
| **Revision** | The process of checking and correcting an existing translation. EXAMPLE: The King James Version has been edited to correct mistakes in print or updates in spelling but the meaning of words or text has never been corrected to produce a new revision. |
| **Scribal Error** | Any mistake made by a copyist in transmitting the words of one manuscript to another manuscript. |
| **Scripture(s)** | The writings of the Bible |

## IN DEFENSE OF THE TEXTUS RECEPTUS

| | |
|---|---|
| **Text Type** | A group of manuscripts that have a high level of agreement are classified into one family. This "family" is called a "text-type". The Byzantine family is often referred to as the Byzantine text-type. |
| **Textus Receptus** | This is a Greek Text which is composed from the Byzantine family of manuscripts. The first "Textus Receptus" was put together by Erasmus in AD 1516 with the last revision done by Scrivener in the 1894. In this book, when referring to manuscripts before Erasmus did his work, we use the term "Byzantine" but we use the term "Textus Receptus" for Greek texts after Erasmus' work. |
| **Translation** | the act of transferring the words and meaning of one language into another language. |
| **Transmission** | Sometimes the word is used (incorrectly) in the act of recording the word of one language into another but this is actually translation. Transmission correctly refers to the propagating of a text from one generation to the next. |
| **Uncial** | Greek manuscripts, written in capital letters with no punctuation and no spaces between words. The "paper" is vellum (animal skin) and is much more durable. There are 323 uncials - 78 support the Byzantine Text in full or in part. 81 support the Alexandrian Text in full or in part. 164 either mixed or unclassified. |
| **Variant** | A reading in one manuscript that differs from the reading other manuscripts. |
| **Vellum** | A parchment made from the skin of an animal. |
| **Verbal-Plenary Inspiration** | The position which states that each individual word in the Bible is God-breathed and that every part of the bible is equally God-breathed with every other part of the Bible. |
| **Version** | A form of something (in this case the Bible) that differs in certain aspects from other forms of the same work. |

*God's Preserved Word to Every Generation*

# INDEX OF WORDS AND PHRASES

## 6

666, 111

## A

Abbot, George, 193
Academic Dishonesty, 29, 136, 336
Academic Honesty, 133, 148, 202, 328, 335, 366
Accuracy of Translation, 24, 25, 28, 29, 30, 31, 79, 80, 115, 117, 119, 124, 138, 143, 148, 167, 168, 182, 209, 211, 212, 215, 323
Adam, 41, 50, 70, 141, 331, 337
Advanced Revelation, 24, 27, 157
Age of Manuscripts, 21, 132, 241, 266
Aland, Kurt and Barbara, 11, 130, 167, 169, 172, 190, 225, 234, 235, 287, 303
Aleph, 168, 201, 241
Alexandria, 111, 165, 184, 199, 219, 220, 230, 231, 246, 271, 273, 361, 375
Alexandrian Text, 10, 11, 22, 23, 73, 84, 86, 87, 88, 89, 90, 91, 93, 94, 95, 96, 97, 125, 129, 131, 132, 133, 134, 159, 161, 163, 164, 165, 168, 169, 170, 171, 172, 182, 183, 184, 185, 187, 191, 194, 196, 199, 200, 201, 202, 214, 215, 221, 223, 224, 225, 226, 227, 229, 233, 234, 241, 242, 243, 244, 245, 247, 248, 249, 250, 253, 255, 256, 257, 258, 259, 260, 261, 262, 263, 267, 268, 275, 279, 280, 281, 282, 283, 284, 285, 286, 287, 288, 289, 290, 291, 292, 293, 294, 295, 296, 297, 298, 299, 300, 301, 302, 303, 304, 305, 306, 307, 308, 309, 310, 311, 312, 313, 314, 315, 316, 325, 328, 331, 335, 375, 376, 377, 378
Allegorical View, 176, 184, 231, 271
Alliteration, 146
Ambrose, 207, 274, 341
**American King James Version**, 138, 143
American Standard Version, 50, 154, 157
Andrews, Roger, 192
Antecedent, 66, 67
Antioch, 131, 180, 188, 189, 221, 222, 244
Antiochan, 170
Aphraates, 93, 334
Apocrypha, 103, 114, 196, 199, 290
Apograph, 45, 375
Aquila of Sinope, 268, 272
Arianism, 112, 273
Aristeas, Letter of, 268, 361
Aristotle, 87
Arius, 273
Ark, 103
Armenian Bible, 94, 131, 135, 219
Ascension, 75
Athanasius, 103, 109, 339
Augustine, 93, 165, 166, 233, 270, 271, 334
Augustus, Caesar, 116
Autographa, 241, 245
Autographs, 14, 21, 44, 45, 52, 53, 82, 83, 84, 85, 86, 119, 170, 187, 229, 234, 235, 326, 376

## B

Bachiarius, 207, 341
Bede, The Venerable, 135
Bengel, J.A., 167, 196, 208, 233
Bethabara, 127, 128, 327
Bethany, 127, 327
Beza, 88, 168, 169, 202, 203, 328
Bible in Basic English, 151
Bishops, 99, 140
**Bodmer Papyri**, 194, 226, 248
Browning, Oscar, 174
Burgon, Dean John William, 192, 221, 222, 239, 241, 243, 244, 245, 246, 247, 249, 263, 264
Byzantine Family, 17, 22, 23, 29, 39, 84, 89, 95, 96, 125, 129, 131, 134, 159, 163, 169, 171, 172, 183, 184, 187, 191, 200,

201, 209, 211, 212, 215, 216, 219, 220, 223, 226, 235, 241, 242, 247, 250, 266, 287, 324, 377, 378
Byzantine Text, 10, 73, 89, 91, 92, 93, 131, 132, 136, 163, 164, 171, 183, 185, 186, 194, 201, 229, 234, 241, 242, 244, 246, 247, 262, 286, 378

## C

Caesarean, 170, 171, 183, 194, 200, 209, 242, 248, 250, 256, 294, 296
Canon, 47, 48, 102, 103, 105, 106, 108, 109, 111, 112, 113, 114, 115, 116, 117, 118, 162, 362
Canonicity, 104, 113, 114, 117
Canonization, 72, 102, 104, 114, 116, 276
Carson, D.A., 242, 244, 245, 338
Catholic, 88, 95, 96, 131, 134, 135, 136, 196, 203, 205, 263, 275, 286
Catholicism, 95, 112, 177
Chester Beatty Papyri, 167, 194, 195, 226, 248
Chrysostom, 93, 127, 222, 334
Circulation, 107, 109, 115, 116, 130, 134, 217, 268, 271, 275, 339
Circumstantial Evidence, 92
Clement, 93, 110, 111, 160, 187, 199, 221, 222, 290
Codex, 88, 89, 95, 123, 163, 168, 195, 197, 198, 199, 209, 215, 223, 262, 285, 294, 299
Codex Alexandrinus, 126, 160, 168, 171, 199, 207, 213, 224, 225, 249, 290, 335
Codex Bezae, 168
Codex Borgianus, 200
Codex D, 168
Codex Dublinensis, 200
Codex Ephraemi, 168, 199
Codex Freerianus, 200
Codex Guelferbytanus B, 200
Codex Regius, 200, 335
Codex Sinaiticus, 22, 90, 91, 126, 164, 168, 197, 199, 200, 205, 217, 218, 221, 223, 224, 225, 226, 234, 248, 249, 270, 274, 286, 296, 330, 333, 334, 376

Codex Vaticanus, 17, 22, 88, 90, 91, 96, 131, 135, 160, 164, 168, 169, 195, 196, 198, 199, 200, 205, 213, 218, 221, 224, 225, 226, 234, 238, 239, 248, 262, 263, 274, 330, 331, 333, 334, 376
Codex Washingtonianus, 200
Collating, 169, 204
Colophon, 199, 270
Comba, Emilio, 135
Combs, W.W., 205
Complutensian Polyglot, 204
Conflation, 128, 129, 188, 242, 245, 329
Conjectural Emendations, 16
Constantine, 123, 130, 131, 169, 198, 239, 272, 273, 274
Constantinople, 125, 131, 134, 219, 245, 246, 272, 274
Copies, 14, 19, 22, 45, 47, 52, 53, 54, 82, 83, 107, 111, 119, 120, 121, 123, 127, 129, 130, 131, 132, 133, 135, 146, 149, 162, 163, 170, 179, 181, 182, 183, 185, 186, 187, 198, 212, 217, 219, 227, 229, 231, 233, 239, 241, 246, 272, 274, 331, 337, 375
Copyist Errors, 124
Copy-text Editing, 16, 17
Corruption, 61, 62, 69, 70, 71, 75, 76, 77, 81, 83, 136, 160, 190, 231, 238, 242, 243, 377
Coverdale Bible, 140, 373
Creation, 41, 42, 176, 265, 324
Critical Apparatus, 166
Critical Text, 10, 17, 19, 20, 21, 23, 24, 27, 32, 73, 74, 75, 76, 80, 81, 86, 87, 88, 93, 94, 100, 125, 128, 131, 133, 135, 136, 138, 140, 151, 152, 159, 160, 164, 165, 171, 172, 175, 181, 182, 183, 184, 185, 186, 187, 191, 194, 196, 200, 203, 206, 213, 214, 216, 217, 218, 220, 221, 222, 223, 225, 226, 227, 230, 231, 235, 238, 242, 243, 246, 247, 250, 253, 256, 266, 267, 299, 323, 328, 329, 331, 335, 338, 365, 375, 376
Curetonian Gospel, 216
Custer, Stewart, 241, 242
Cyprian, 93, 187, 221, 337, 339

## D

Dalrymple, David, 118
Damasus, 275, 339
Darby Translation, 151
Darwin, E.A., 173
Davies, J.S., 197
Dead Sea Scrolls, 161, 269
Derivative Inspiration, 52, 53, 102, 376
Diatesseron, 23, 217, 218, 242, 334
Dictation, Dictation Theory, 39, 40, 41
Didache, 103, 109
Didymus, 93, 334
Diglot, 95
Dillingham, Francis, 192
Diocletian, 131
DiVietro, K., 203
Donatists, 274
Dynamic Translation, 99, 117, 144, 145, 146, 157

## E

Ebonics Bible, 153
Eclecticism, 16
Egypt, 95, 111, 123, 131, 162, 163, 165, 168, 170, 171, 180, 184, 187, 194, 215, 219, 229, 230, 231, 232, 243, 247, 262, 268, 273, 361, 362, 375, 377
Elzever, 169
English Revised Version, 151
English Standard Version, 148, 150, 152, 157
Enoch, Book of, 105, 194
Ephraemi Rescriptus, 168
Erasmus, 10, 17, 29, 88, 89, 137, 172, 173, 196, 201, 202, 203, 204, 205, 206, 207, 208, 209, 211, 213, 262, 263, 266, 339, 340, 341, 378
Estienne, Robert, 166, 202
Eusebius, 93, 108, 135, 189, 198, 239, 271, 272, 273, 274, 297, 334
Eve, 43, 69, 70, 71

## F

Fee, Gordon, 222
Formal Equivalency, 140, 144
Formal-Equivalent, 45, 145, 154
Formal-Literal Translation, 62
Fundamental, Fundamentalism, 12, 13, 77, 179, 216, 239, 318
Fundamentalist, 20

## G

Gallic Bible, 94
Geneva, 99, 140, 201, 373
Genizah, 82
Good News Bible, 152
Gospel of Marcion, 71
Gothic Bible, 94, 130, 134, 220
Graphe, 48, 49
Great Bible, 140, 201, 208, 373
Greek Orthodox Bible, 23, 94, 216
Greek Orthodox Church, 94, 216
Gregory, C.R., 167
Griesbach, J.J., 233
Gutenburg, Johannes, 134

## H

Harcourt, William, 174
Harding, John, 193
Harrison, Thomas, 192
Heinsius, Daniel, 211
Hermas, Shepherd of, 103, 197, 198, 290
Herodotus, 86
Hexapla, Origin's, 199, 219, 270, 271, 272, 275, 339
Higher Criticism, 17, 18, 72
Hills, Edward, 132, 136, 137, 178
Hippo, Council of, 112
Hippolytus, 93, 187, 222, 331, 334
Hodges, Zane, 3, 324, 325, 326
Hodges-Farstad Text, 324
Holy Spirit, 37, 41, 45, 52, 55, 105, 117, 180, 237, 269, 320, 336, 337, 368, 377
Homer, 87, 195
Homoeoteluton, 125
Hort, F.J.A., 16, 17, 21, 38, 73, 164, 172, 175, 176, 177, 178, 179, 180, 181, 182, 183, 185, 186, 187, 188, 189, 190, 191,

192, 194, 196, 212, 234, 237, 238, 239, 243, 244, 245, 275, 325, 376
Hoskier, H.C., 206, 207
Hypothesis, 17

## I

Ignatius, 109, 110
Iliad, 87
Incorruptible, 44
Independent Baptist, 12
Inerrant, 38, 44, 277
Infallible, 44
Inspiration, 12, 14, 15, 17, 19, 21, 25, 27, 28, 29, 30, 31, 32, 33, 35, 36, 37, 38, 39, 41, 42, 43, 44, 45, 46, 47, 49, 50, 51, 52, 53, 54, 55, 56, 57, 58, 61, 62, 67, 72, 74, 77, 78, 79, 81, 83, 85, 86, 88, 100, 101, 104, 105, 106, 114, 115, 134, 145, 150, 160, 175, 178, 181, 207, 227, 231, 234, 239, 276, 277, 320, 322, 326, 368, 376, 377, 378, 379
Interpretation, 50, 56, 62, 72, 121, 146, 176, 184, 231, 236, 271, 276, 277, 318, 319, 321, 394
Irenaeus, 70, 93, 110, 111, 165, 187, 221, 222, 233, 266, 331, 333
Italics, 154, 155, 156, 157, 158, 321

## J

Jackson, Henry, 174
Jasher, Book of, 105, 113
Jerome, 93, 166, 204, 270, 271, 275, 331, 334, 339
Jimenez, 88
Jiménez, 88, 204
Jordan, 127, 128
Judith, 160, 362
Justin Martyr, 93, 111, 217, 333
Juxtaposition, 159

## K

Kai, 26
Kanon, 102, 103
**King James 2000 Version**, 138, 141

King James Version, 9, 12, 14, 15, 21, 24, 25, 26, 27, 28, 29, 30, 32, 33, 44, 45, 46, 53, 60, 62, 63, 64, 74, 79, 80, 81, 94, 97, 98, 100, 132, 136, 137, 138, 139, 140, 141, 142, 143, 145, 148, 150, 152, 153, 154, 157, 158, 166, 169, 175, 176, 177, 190, 191, 192, 193, 194, 200, 202, 206, 208, 225, 241, 242, 243, 245, 246, 267, 276, 277, 278, 318, 321, 323, 328, 336, 338, 378
**KJ3**, 138, 141, 142
Koine Greek, 80, 81
Kurios, 25, 97, 98

## L

Laodicea, Council of, 107, 112
Laodiceans, Epistle of, 107
Latin Vulgate, 87, 96, 131, 134, 136, 201, 206, 207, 263, 275, 339, 340, 341
Lectionaries, 94, 95, 96, 162, 165, 167, 168, 186, 214, 215, 262, 276, 325, 377
Lectionary, 94, 95, 168, 215, 262, 325
Leo X, 204
Liberty, 53, 367, 368
Lightfoot, J.B., 191
Lively, Edward, 192
Lollard, 136
Lower Criticism, 17, 18
Lucian, 180, 185, 188, 189, 238, 270, 333
Lucian Recension, 180, 185, 188, 333

## M

Macarius Magnes, 93, 334
Maccabees, 160, 290, 362
Madaba Map, 128
Mai, Angelo, 196
Majority Text, 143, 324, 325, 326, 327, 328, 329
Manuscript 2049, 205, 206
Marcellinus, Epistle to, 160, 290
Marcion, 70, 71, 112, 116, 129, 165
Mashtots, Mesrob, 219
Materials, 122, 123
Matthews, 99
Maurice, Fredrick, 173, 189, 270

Maximilian, Emperor, 204
McDowell, Joshua, 38, 39, 40
mechanical. *See* Dictation, Dictation Theory
Mechanical. *See* Dictation, Dictation Theory, *See* Dictation, Dictation Theory, *See* Dictation, Dictation Theory
Metzger, Bruce, 125, 165, 194, 226, 230, 270
Milan, Edict of, 109, 273
Miniscules, 123
Minuscule 33, 200
Minuscule 81, 200
Missionaries, 24, 28, 131, 143
Missionary, 24, 130, 135, 230, 278, 393
Missions, 24, 28
Mixed Text, 11, 214, 290, 301
Modern King James, 138, 139
Muratori, L.A., 109
Muratorian Fragment, 109

## N

NA28, 21, 75
Nazareth, 367
Neshamah, 50
Neutral Text, 183, 191, 234, 243
New American Standard, 94, 148, 158
New American Standard Bible, 148, 152
New International Version, 148, 152, 157
New King James Version, 138, 142, 158
New World Translation, 21, 71, 267
Nicaea, Council of, 112, 273

## O

Old Bohairic Coptic Version, 207
Old Syriac, 23, 94, 216, 218, 338
Ophelimos, 50
Origen, 93, 127, 165, 187, 219, 221, 222, 230, 248, 270, 271, 272, 273, 275, 339, 366
Origin, 17, 43, 51, 115, 135, 150, 171, 181, 186

## P

P90, 22, 84, 91, 163, 182, 187, 223, 242, 250, 287
Palestinian Syriac, 94, 131, 220
Palimpsest, 199, 217
Paper, 52, 122, 123, 162, 164, 232, 377, 378
Papias, 109, 110
Papius, 93, 333
Papyri, 22, 82, 123, 160, 162, 163, 167, 184, 185, 187, 194, 195, 207, 220, 222, 223, 226, 231, 232, 243, 247, 248, 261, 262, 276, 378
Papyrus, 84, 123, 160, 162, 163, 167, 227, 279, 285, 286, 288, 365, 375, 377
Papyrus 090, 91
Papyrus 90 (P90), 163, 187, 287
Parchment, 167
Parrot Position, 34, 361
Pasa, 47
Paul, 41, 45, 47, 48, 50, 55, 56, 57, 61, 68, 69, 71, 72, 83, 85, 105, 106, 107, 108, 113, 117, 119, 120, 129, 149, 228, 231, 241, 245, 265, 266, 269, 319, 328, 366, 369
Peshitta, 23, 94, 201, 217, 218, 219
Peter, 33, 48, 51, 61, 72, 106, 107, 109, 110, 111, 113, 117, 119, 158, 159, 216, 228, 229, 241, 245, 286, 290, 301, 304, 306, 311, 313, 315, 338
Philoxenian Bible, 94, 131, 135, 220
Pickering, Wilbur, 72, 127, 131
Plato, 86
Pliny, 86
Pneustos, 49
Pnuo, 49
Polycarp, 70, 109, 110, 333
preservation, 12, 14, 15, 16, 17, 19, 21, 22, 30, 31, 32, 33, 35, 38, 39, 45, 47, 48, 53, 54, 57, 58, 60, 61, 62, 64, 65, 67, 68, 72, 73, 74, 77, 78, 79, 81, 83, 85, 86, 88, 97, 101, 104, 106, 119, 120, 121, 129, 132, 134, 136, 137, 145, 150, 161, 175, 178, 180, 181, 185, 186, 187, 191, 212, 213, 226, 227, 230, 231, 234, 237, 239, 261, 262, 263, 276, 277, 322, 325, 329
Price, I.M., 174, 189, 198, 270

Pronouns, 65, 66, 67
Pseudo-Barnabas, 109, 110
Pseudopigrapha, 117
Purvey, John, 136

## Q

Qaneh, 102, 103
Qumran, 365, 366

## R

Rainolds, John, 193
Readability, 138, 142
Reuchlin, John, 204, 207
Revelation, 38, 40, 41, 42, 43, 44, 68, 99, 319
Revised Standard Version, 158
Revision, 14, 29, 140, 141, 177, 189, 191, 192, 209, 219, 241, 243, 270, 274, 340, 372, 373, 378
Robinson-Pierpont Text, 324
Romaunt Version, 135
Rome, 70, 110, 169, 228, 273
Ruckman, Peter, 33
Russell, Bertrand, 174

## S

Saint Catherine Monastery, 197
Sapor, 219
Satan, 43, 49, 56, 69, 70, 71, 329
Saville, Henry, 193
Schaff, Philip, 166, 271
Scrivener, F.H.A., 29, 167, 169, 192, 202, 203, 209, 241, 266, 274, 294, 297, 303, 378
Secunda, 272
Sedwick, Henry, 173
Semler, J.S., 233
Septuagint, 189, 197, 199, 204, 217, 268, 270, 272, 290, 361, 362, 366, 368, 369
Sidgwick, Henry, 174
Sirach, Wisdom of, 160, 362
Smith, Miles, 193, 373
Sophocles, 87
Source Criticism. *See* Higher Criticism

Sovereignty, 68, 321
Spencer, John, 193
Stemmatology, 16
Stephanus, 88, 137, 166, 169, 201, 202, 203, 328
Street Bible, 153
Strouse, Thomas, 66
Stunica, 207, 266
Sturz, Harry A., 243
Sudan, 123
Symmachus, 268, 272, 362
Synonyms, 15, 66, 67, 98, 159, 176
Syrian, 170, 191, 199, 212, 217, 218, 234, 243, 370

## T

Tatian, 217, 218, 311, 334
Tepl Bible, 135, 136
Tertullian, 93, 187, 221, 222, 339
Text Types, 84, 171, 183, 191, 227, 233, 234, 235, 267, 281, 297, 298, 303, 313
Textual Analysis, 17, 36, 72, 77, 96, 165, 166, 175, 194, 205, 208, 227, 233, 240
Textual Criticism, 15, 16, 17, 19, 58, 72, 73, 75, 171, 172, 178, 180, 181, 193, 211, 233, 236, 238, 239, 271, 272, 277, 325
Textus Receptus, 2, 10, 19, 20, 21, 23, 24, 25, 29, 30, 32, 46, 53, 59, 63, 72, 73, 74, 76, 77, 80, 81, 85, 86, 89, 90, 92, 93, 94, 96, 97, 98, 125, 129, 130, 135, 138, 140, 142, 143, 144, 151, 152, 159, 160, 163, 164, 165, 168, 169, 171, 172, 175, 177, 178, 179, 181, 182, 183, 187, 188, 192, 194, 200, 201, 202, 203, 205, 206, 208, 209, 211, 212, 213, 214, 216, 217, 218, 219, 220, 221, 222, 223, 225, 226, 227, 231, 235, 238, 239, 242, 246, 249, 262, 266, 267, 274, 276, 277, 278, 323, 324, 326, 329, 330, 365, 378
Textus Receptus Only, 21
Theodoret, 217
Theodotion, 268, 271, 272, 362
Theophilus, 115, 368
Theopneustos, 49
Theos, 49, 98, 99
Thessalonica, 68

Timothy, 14, 44, 46, 47, 49, 79, 110, 111, 125, 149, 155, 158, 195, 218, 228, 229, 290, 299, 306, 315
Tischendorf, Constantine, 169, 196, 197, 198, 249, 274
Tobit, 160, 362
Translation, 10, 12, 14, 15, 21, 23, 24, 27, 28, 29, 30, 31, 33, 45, 46, 50, 52, 53, 54, 60, 62, 63, 64, 79, 80, 81, 88, 94, 97, 98, 99, 100, 109, 111, 130, 134, 135, 136, 137, 138, 139, 140, 141, 142, 143, 144, 145, 146, 147, 148, 149, 150, 151, 153, 154, 157, 158, 162, 166, 176, 177, 189, 190, 192, 193, 194, 197, 200, 203, 208, 216, 219, 220, 225, 226, 230, 239, 267, 268, 269, 270, 271, 272, 275, 277, 278, 318, 319, 320, 322, 323, 338, 361, 362, 364, 365, 366, 367, 368, 369, 370, 371, 372, 373, 376, 377, 378, 394
Translators, 15, 24, 25, 26, 44, 45, 46, 50, 62, 63, 64, 88, 97, 99, 100, 134, 139, 140, 144, 146, 148, 151, 152, 154, 156, 157, 169, 174, 175, 192, 196, 203, 216, 243, 262, 318, 321, 322, 328, 339, 361, 369, 370, 371, 372, 376, 394
Translators to the Reader, 46, 318
Transliteration, 133, 272
Transmission, 15, 45, 59, 119, 120, 121, 129, 130, 136, 186, 227, 377
Tregelles, 169
Trench, R.C., 174
Triglot, 95
Trinitarian Bible Society, 203
Tyndale, William, 64, 99, 139, 140, 200, 201, 373

## U

umlaut, 195, 196, 248
Uncial 0220, 200
Uncial 057, 200
Uncials, 123, 128, 132, 133, 161, 162, 163, 164, 167, 168, 184, 199, 207, 223, 224, 225, 247, 262, 276, 377, 378
**Updated King James Version**, 138

## V

Valentinus, 165
Variants, 16, 17, 20, 75, 77, 84, 88, 91, 121, 125, 128, 159, 165, 166, 167, 169, 190, 195, 198, 206, 212, 213, 216, 226, 230, 231, 248, 249, 255, 256, 259, 274, 291, 296, 315, 324, 327, 376
Vellum, 123, 163, 164, 199, 377, 378
Verbal-Plenary Inspiration, 32, 53, 55, 58, 145, 326
Vincentius, 93, 334
Von Soden, Hermann, 212, 235

## W

Waldenses, 135
Waldensian Bible, 94
Westcott, B.F., 16, 17, 21, 38, 73, 164, 172, 173, 174, 175, 176, 177, 178, 179, 180, 181, 182, 183, 185, 186, 187, 188, 189, 190, 191, 192, 194, 196, 212, 234, 237, 238, 239, 243, 244, 245, 275, 325, 376
Western, 73, 84, 131, 132, 135, 137, 170, 171, 183, 191, 200, 221, 233, 234, 242, 243, 248, 250, 256, 266, 282, 284, 285, 291, 292, 296, 299, 312
Western Text, 73, 191, 284, 291, 292
Wettstein, J.J., 167
White, James R., 241
Whitehead, N., 174
Wilberforce, Samuel, 192
Williams, Rowland, 178
Word of God, 9, 13, 20, 27, 30, 33, 34, 38, 39, 41, 44, 45, 46, 58, 60, 67, 69, 70, 78, 81, 96, 99, 111, 114, 115, 126, 147, 148, 150, 153, 162, 179, 213, 234, 318, 319, 320, 322, 323, 336
Writers, 9, 12, 18, 39, 40, 41, 45, 47, 48, 49, 50, 51, 52, 53, 54, 55, 82, 93, 109, 110, 112, 115, 117, 136, 143, 150, 166, 179, 187, 188, 201, 220, 221, 222, 243, 244, 269, 320, 333, 334, 335, 375
Wycliffe, 99, 136, 201

## Y

Young's Literal Translation, 138, 140

## BIBLIOGRAPHY

1. Allen, Ward S., (1970) *Translating for King James*, Allen Lane: Penguin Press
2. Beacham, Roy E., and Bauder, Kevin T., eds., (2001), *One Bible Only?*, Grand Rapids: Kregel Publications
3. Brandenburg, Kent, (2003), *Thou Shalt Keep Them*, El Sobante, CA: Pillar and Ground Publishing
4. Brown Driver and Briggs, (1994), *Hebrew and English Lexicon,* Peabody, MS: Hendrickson Publishing
5. Bruce, FF. (1978), *History of the Bible in English. 3rd.* New York, NY: Oxford University Press
6. Burgon, Dean John William, (1883), *The Revision Revised,* Paradise, PA: Conservative Classics
7. Carson, D.A. (1978), *The King James Version Debate: A Plea for Realism.* Grand Rapids, MI: Baker Book House
8. Carter, Mickey P., (1993), *Things that are Different are not the Same,* Haines City, FL: Landmark Baptist Press
9. Cloud, David W.,(1993), *The Way of Life Encyclopedia of the Bible and Christianity,* Oak Harbor, WA: Way of Life Literature
10. Custer, Stewart, (1981), *The Truth About the King James Controversy*, Greenville, SC: Bob Jones University Press
11. Davey, Ciril, (1963), *Makers of the English Bible*, Londen: The Trinity Press
12. Epp, Eldon J.; Fee, Gordon D. (1993). *Studies in the Theory and Method of New Testament Textual Criticism.* Wm. B. Eerdmans Publishing.
13. Fuller, David Otis, (1972) *Which Bible?*, Grand Rapids: Grand Rapids International Publications
14. Geisler, Norman L., and Nix, William E.,(1986), *A General Introduction to the Bible,* Chicago: Moody Press
15. Gipp, Samuel C., (1989), *The Answer Book,* Shelbyville, TN: Bible and Literature Missionary Foundation
16. Grady, William P., (1993), *Final Authority,* Schererville, IN: Grady Publications
17. Green, Jay P., (1976) *The Interlinear Greek-English New Testament*, Lafayette,

IN: Associated Publishers & Authors, Inc

18. Green, Jay P., (1990) *Unholy Hands on the Bible,* Lafayette, Indiana: Sovereign Grace Trust Fund

19. Hayford, Jack W., (1995) *Hayford's Bible Handbook [computer file], electronic ed., Logos Library System*, Nashville, TN: Thomas Nelson

20. Hills, Edward F., (1984), *The King James Version Defended.* Des Moines, Iowa: Christian Research Press

21. Hoskier, H.C., (1929), Concerning the Text of the Apocalypse, London: Bernard Quarich Ltd.

22. Lindsell, Harold, (1976), *The Battle for the Bible, Grand Rapids, MI: Zondervan Publishing House*

23. Marshall, Alfred, (1973), Interlinear Greek-English New Testament, Grand Rapids, MI: Zondervan Publishing House

24. Martin, Walter R., (1997) *The Kingdom of the Cults, gen. ed. Hank Hanegraaff,* Minneapolis, MN: Bethany House Publishers

25. McDowell, Josh, (1999), Evidence that Demands a Verdict: Historical Evidences for the Christian Faith, Nashville, TN: Thomas Nelson Publishers

26. Metzger, Bruce M., (2005), *The Text of the New Testament*, New York: Oxford University Press. 4th edition

27. Miller, H.S., (1960), *General Biblical Introduction: From God to Us*, Houghten, NY: The Word Bearer Press

28. Moorman, Jack, (1999), *Forever Settled*, Collingwood, NJ: The Dean Burgon Society Press

29. Moorman, Jack, (2005), *Early Manuscripts, Church Fathers, and the Authorized Version*, Collingwood, NJ: The Bible For Today Press

30. Morris, Henry M. Ph.D., (1996), Should Creationists Abandon The King James Version?. *Acts & Facts.* 25

31. Moulton, William F.,(1911), The History of the English Bible, London: Charles H. Kelly. 5th edition

32. Nida, Eugene A., (1961), *Bible Translating: An Analysis of Principles and Procedures, with Special Reference to Aboriginal Languages, Revised Edition*, NY: United Bible Societies

33. Ouellette, R.B., (2008), *A More Sure Word,* Lancaster, CA: Striving Together

Publications

34. Pickering, Wilber N., (1980), *The Identity of the New Testament Text,* Nashville: Thomas Nelson Inc.

35. Price, James D., (2006). *King James Onlyism: A New Sect.* James D. Price Publisher

36. Ray, Jasper J., (1970), *God Wrote Only One Bible.* Junction City, Oregon: Eye Opener Publishers

37. Riplinger, Gail A., (2004) In Awe of They Word: Understanding the King James Bible, Its Mystery & History Letter by Letter, Authorized Version Publications

38. Riplinger, Gail A., (1993), *New Age Bible Versions* (Munroe Falls, Ohio: AV Publications

39. Ruckman, Peter S., (1976), *The Christian's Handbook of Manuscript Evidence,* Palatka, FL: Pensacola Bible Press

40. Scrivener, Frederick H.A., (1999), Scrivener's Annotated Greek New Testament, Collingwood, NJ: Dean Burgon Society Press

41. Shanks, Hershel, (1992), *The Dead Sea Scrolls After 40 Years,* Washington DC: Biblical Archeology Society

42. Sorenson, David, (2001), *Touch Not The Unclean Thing,* Duluth, Mn.: Northstar Baptist Ministries

43. Stauffer, Douglas, (2001), *One Book Stands Alone,* Hillbrook AL: McCowen Mills Publishers

44. Streeter, Lloyd L., (2001), *Seventy-Five Problems With Central Baptist's Book, The Bible Version Debate,* LaSalle, Illinois: First Baptist Church of LaSalle

45. Stringer, Phil, (2000), *Ready Answers,* Fort Pierce, FL: Faith Baptist Church Publications

46. Stringer, Phil, (1999), *The History of the English Bible,* Fort Pierce, FL: Faith Baptist Church Publications

47. Stringer, Phil, (2000), *The Means of Inspiration,* Fort Pierce, FL: Faith Baptist Church Publications

48. Stringer, Phil, (2000), *The Real Story of King James,* Fort Pierce, FL: Faith Baptist Church Publications

49. Strong, James, (2015), *A Comprehensive Strong Dictionary of the Bible*, Bestbooks

50. Strouse, Thomas M., (2001) *From The Mind of God?*, Pensacola, Florida: Pensacola Seminary

51. Thiede Garten Peter & D'Ancona, Matthew, (1996), *The Jesus Papyrus*, New York, NY: Random House Inc.

52. Waite, D.A., (1992), Defending the King James Bible: A Four-fold Superiority. Collingswood, NJ: Bible For Today Press

53. White, James A., (1995), *The King James Only Controversy: Can You Trust the Modern Translations?*, Minneapolis, MN: Bethany House Publishers

54. Williams, James B., (1999), *From the Mind of God to the Mind of Man*, Greenville,SC: Ambassador-Emerald International

## About the Author

Dr. Jim Taylor has been a missionary with Armed Forces Baptist Missions since 1991. God has given him a special burden for both the Korean people and the US military personnel who are stationed at Kunsan AB, South Korea.

Dr. Taylor accepted Christ on February 27$^{th}$, 1984 while stationed in Korea as a member of the United States Air Force. This was a very important time in his life because he not only accepted Christ but also married the sweetest young lady in the world just two weeks earlier.

For the next 16 years, Dr. Taylor and his wife, Suk would follow Uncle Sam's orders from Korea to Langley AFB, Virginia and then back to Korea again. In all, Dr. Taylor spent close to 13 years of his Air Force career at Kunsan AB, Korea. During all that time, he and his family stayed very active in their church, Haven Baptist Church serving as Sunday school teacher, treasurer, assistant pastor, and even interim-pastored for three years while still active duty in the Air Force!

Dr. Taylor retired from the Air Force in July 2000 and has been "full-time" in the ministry since then. During his time in the Air Force, he was able to complete his Doctorates in Religious Education and was awarded his degree in 2001.

Dr. Taylor served as assistant pastor for 16 years before leaving to start Victory Baptist Church in 2003. In 2012 the two churches merged making Dr. Taylor the pastor of the Haven Baptist Church, where he has served as pastor until the present.

Noticing an extreme lack of Christian education in Korea, Dr. Taylor and his wife, Suk, have planted a Christian foreign school for western children, a Christian language institute for Koreans, and a Bible college for training men and women for the ministry.

Dr. Taylor has also been involved in translating the Bible in the Korean language as well as lecturing and assisting translators in other parts of the world. As a result, he has developed a great deal of insight into the area of Greek manuscripts, translation, and proper application of biblical interpretation.

The Taylors are sent from Victory Baptist Church in Hampton, Virginia.

www.ingramcontent.com/pod-product-compliance
Lightning Source LLC
Chambersburg PA
CBHW070719160426
43192CB00009B/1244